# DEAD ZONE

# DEAD ZONE

## Where the Wild Things Were

PHILIP LYMBERY

BLOOMSBURY

LONDON · OXFORD · NEW YORK · NEW DELHI · SYDNEY

Bloomsbury Publishing
An imprint of Bloomsbury Publishing Plc

50 Bedford Square
London
WC1B 3DP
UK

1385 Broadway
New York
NY 10018
USA

www.bloomsbury.com

First published in Great Britain 2017

British Library Cataloguing-in-Publication Data
A catalogue record for this book is available from the British Library.

Library of Congress Cataloguing-in-Publication data has been applied for.

ISBN:   TPB:  978-1-4088-6826-3
EPUB:  978-1-4088-6827-0

2  4  6  8  10  9  7  5  3  1

Typeset by Newgen Knowledge Works (P) Ltd., Chennai, India
Printed and bound in Great Britain by CPI Group (UK) Ltd, Croydon CR0 4YY

To my parents, Reverend Peter and Evelyn Lymbery, with heartfelt gratitude

# Contents

# Acknowledgements

First and foremost I owe a huge debt of thanks to Isabel Oakeshott for editing the manuscript and for being my literary inspiration. I have learned so much from you and am hugely grateful for how you helped shape my writing style, as well as your pin-sharp eye for improving the text.

I am indebted to Jacky Turner for the many hours of painstaking research that form the backbone of this book. I couldn't have done it without you and offer my sincere gratitude.

Thank you to Tina Clark, my long-suffering assistant, for all the hard work that went into making the field trips come together and for endlessly reading over my words, making right those important details.

To Carol McKenna for huge support throughout what turned into a mammoth project.

To Katie Milward, my cameraperson on the various adventures to Brazil, Sumatra and the USA, and to everyone who came out on the road with me: Leah Garcés, Federica di Leonardo, Dendy Montgomery, Krzysztof Mularczyk, Annamaria Pisapia and Louise van der Merwe.

To Andrew Wasley and Luke Starr at Ecostorm for putting together field trips, arranging interviews and additional research, as well as Jim Wickens, whose early ideas gave me the confidence to make this book happen.

To my commissioning editors at Bloomsbury: Michael Fishwick, Nick Humphrey and Bill Swainson, to my copy editor, Steve Cox, and to my literary agent, Robin Jones, for support and encouragement.

Huge appreciation to all the trustees of Compassion in World Farming for their sponsorship and support for the book, and for having the vision to see so clearly the connections between factory farming and damage to wildlife and human society too: Teddy Bourne, Jeremy Hayward, Valerie James, Mahi Klosterhalfen, Rosemary Marshall, Sarah Petrini, Reverend Professor Michael Reiss, Michel Vandenbosch and Sir David Madden. To Sir David, particular thanks for being my literary mentor and sounding board.

Grateful thanks to all who commented on drafts and provided such helpful feedback – Carolina Galvani, Graham Harvey, John Meadley, René Olivieri, David Ramsden (Barn Owl Trust), Graham Roberts (Hampshire and Isle of Wight Wildlife Trust), Richard Brooks, Joyce D'Silva, Tracey Jones, Daphne Rieder, Peter Stevenson and Angela Wright.

To Joanna Blythman, Charlie Clutterbuck, Tim Lang, Debbie Tann at the Hampshire and Isle of Wight Wildlife Trust and Duncan Williamson at WWF UK for conversations that shaped ideas.

Finally, huge thanks to my wonderful wife, Helen, for believing in me and for unstinting support – this book truly would not have been possible without it.

# Preface

September in the South Pacific and a life-or-death competition is about to get under way. Nervous youths wait for the cue to throw themselves headlong into the ocean off Easter Island. In the next few moments, they will risk drowning, being eaten by sharks or falling to their deaths in a ritual that every year claims young lives.[1] Before them are small, near-inaccessible islets teeming with seabirds returning to nest. Somewhere on those rocky outcrops, more than a mile across treacherous seas, lies the prize.

A crowd gathers on the headland, and in a flash the young men are off, slipping down a hazardous cliff-face before plunging into foaming water in the ultimate struggle for supremacy. Clutching simple rafts made from reeds, they battle through the surf until, gasping for breath, they reach the islets. They clamber up slippery rocks, distant cheers from the crowd drowned out by screeching seabirds.[2]

It may take days to find what they are looking for, the first sooty tern egg of the year, and the search is only half the battle: the potential winner is not the young man who first captures an egg, but the one who is first to return it safely to shore.

A sudden cry goes up: a potential victor has emerged. Tucking the egg into his headband, the triumphant youth slips back into the sea, swimming carefully this time to avoid dislodging his precious cargo. Back at last on terra firma, he faces the final stretch of his gruelling ordeal – a perilous climb up a thousand-foot cliff. After a desperate ascent, clinging to anything that comes to hand, he races up the slope to the grassy plateau where his sponsor awaits. He has made it.[3]

On this isolated island around 1760, winning the egg race would bring great kudos to the youth and his sponsoring chief. The egg was regarded by Easter Island's inhabitants as a powerful symbol of the renewal of fertility when fresh food became available once more.[4]

For the coming months, the winning chief would be treated like a deity, his every need tended by a servant. Following ancient tradition, he would stop cutting his hair or nails, which grew to an extraordinary length. He became the representative on Earth of Makemake, the creator god of fertility.[5] When he died, he would be buried on a platform and a stone figure put up in his memory to stand alongside those of his predecessors.[6]

These striking stone statues with their elongated facial features have since become recognised throughout the world as the symbol of the civilisation that was Easter Island's. One of the remotest places on Earth, its rise and fall is one of the most fascinating stories in human history, and a vivid illustration of what happens when delicate ecosystems are upset by deforestation and rapacious farming.

The monuments took great strength and skill to create, the tallest standing as high as 30 ft and weighing 82 tons.[7] Made from volcanic rock, they were probably heaved on rollers or dragged from the quarries by large teams of people. That the ancient islanders had the energy, ability and resources to create something so impressive suggests that they were relatively sophisticated people, and yet they exploited their natural environment so recklessly that after a while it could no longer support them and led to decline. Their fate gives an ominous glimpse of what might happen to us.

The island lies some 2,500 miles off the coast of Chile, and its nearest neighbour, Pitcairn, is some 1,300 miles away. The first settlers were probably Polynesian navigators who made the voyage by around AD 1200 in nothing more capacious than an ocean-going canoe. For these adventurers, it must have been the ultimate journey of discovery: a one-way trip with no way of knowing what lay ahead.[8]

Many centuries before satellite navigation systems, they would have sailed for weeks before zeroing in on this isolated rocky triangle measuring 14 miles long by 7 miles wide.[9] They were probably guided ashore by the island's teeming seabird colonies. Long before seeing land, they would have noticed a gradual increase in seabird numbers at sea, and so homed in on a previously undiscovered island.[10]

These early settlers were part of an extraordinary culture that flourished for centuries before going bust. They ate plenty of fish, which they caught using canoes made from hollowed-out tree trunks, and this seems to have worked well. As the population grew, however, so they felled the forests that once covered the island to make way for fields. They grew crops to boost their diet, but when the last of the trees disappeared, so too did their means of fishing.[11] They were left marooned and impoverished.

Nonetheless the population continued to grow, until it outstripped the land's capacity to provide enough food. War broke out between rival clans. By 1774, when Captain Cook arrived, the islanders were poverty-stricken, at each other's throats, and down to a fraction of their peak number. They may well have asked if the gods had betrayed them or whether they had betrayed themselves.[12]

Other ancient civilisations, among them the Maya of Central America and the Greenland Norse, have undergone a similar rise and fall. Often their troubles were triggered by the heedless destruction of resources on which their societies depended.[13] Now we may face something similar. As global population pressure stretches the world's natural resources, the parallels are unnerving.

Life on Earth has thrived for billions of years. Wonderfully diverse civilisations have evolved, powered by an abundance of natural riches. The world is now home to more than 7 billion people and a multitude of different plants and animals, all with their part to play in the complex web of life.

In the blink of an evolutionary eye, one particular species has gone from newcomer to the dominant force shaping the planet: us. We stand at an almighty crossroads, during a unique period of history. Some scientists consider our era so significant (for a host of wrong reasons) that they believe it merits a special geological classification. They have dubbed this period the 'Anthropocene', to denote a new age in which we have inflicted wholesale and irreversible changes to the planet. But it is not too late to prevent more destruction.

If we simply carry on as before, scientists warn of a mass extinction, perhaps the biggest since an asteroid wiped out the dinosaurs. Species are already disappearing at a rate 1,000 times higher than previously expected.

While certain creatures are vanishing for ever, others that might appear more robust are also dwindling fast. In the last forty years, the total number of mammals, birds, reptiles, amphibians and fish has halved.[14] That's a terrifying statistic.

And the primary reason for all this destruction? Global demand for food. About two-thirds of the overall loss of wildlife is driven by food production.[15]

Planet-wide, the way we feed ourselves has become a dominant activity, affecting wildlife and the natural ecosystems that our existence depends on. Nearly half the world's usable land surface[16] and most human water use is devoted to agriculture.

Industrial agriculture – factory farming – is the most damaging.

Some 70 billion farm animals are reared for food every year, two-thirds of them on factory farms where they chomp their way through food that could otherwise feed billions of hungry people. Indeed, the biggest single area of food waste today comes not from what we discard in the dustbin but from feeding human-edible crops to industrially reared animals. Together they emit more greenhouse gases than all of the world's planes, trains and cars combined. Yet the global livestock population is expected to near enough double by 2050, further stepping up the pressure on a natural world in steep decline.

As agriculture expands at the expense of dwindling forests, wildlife gets squeezed out of the picture. This happens even more so when farming and nature part company.

Over the last half-century, this new and damaging form of agriculture has developed that involves applying industrial methods and concepts to the countryside. Food production has become just another industry, churning out raw materials in a way that is commonly presented as efficient but is in fact grossly wasteful.

Consciously or not, industrial farming has changed the way we think about food production. The system has switched from focusing on feeding people to producing more, regardless of whether consumed or not. More than half of all the world's food now either rots, is dumped in landfill, or feeds imprisoned animals.

The history of farming's industrial revolution spans much of the last century.

First came the capacity to turn atmospheric nitrogen into ammonia in the early 1900s, for explosives and artificial fertiliser. Then came the wartime development of nerve gases, put to use in agriculture as pesticide after the Second World War. Former US munitions factories were redeployed to turn ammonia into fertiliser instead of bombs.

Corn production went into overdrive due to US support for hard-pressed farmers, starting with the Great Depression in the 1930s. Subsidised cereals became so cheap and plentiful that they were seen as little more than animal feed. Cowboys roaming the Great Plains started to become a thing of the past, replaced by corn-fed cattle in 'feedlots' – a word we will have to come back to. Pastures were put to the plough for more animal feed.

Inevitably, US-style industrial farming soon made its way to Europe, perhaps with the aid of Marshall Plan money, and began to supplant traditional methods. Aimed at rebuilding war-torn Europe, the massive US aid package helped Europeans first to buy food from the US, and then to buy the means for growing food. As well as removing trade barriers and modernising industries, it provided the perfect conduit for the transatlantic spread of intensive farming techniques. Many of the countries that received most support became Europe's most intensive farmers, including the UK, Netherlands, France, Italy and Germany. Meat became cheap, but at what cost?

Whole landscapes were swept away by monocultures – carpets of uniform crops, sometimes stretching as far as the eye could see. Birds, bees and butterflies, along with the insects and plants that they feed on, went into decline. Chemical fertilisers and pesticide sprays replaced time-honoured natural ways of keeping soil fertile and problem bugs of all sorts at bay. Laying hens ended up in battery cages, pigs in narrow crates or barren, crowded pens, while chickens were selectively bred and reared to grow so fast that their legs could barely support their outsize bodies.

A competition started for food between people and animals. Where once land served for grazing and foraging – converting things people can't eat, like grass, into meat, milk and eggs – now it was turned over to crop production to feed incarcerated animals.

The food system became hijacked by the animal-feed industry. Growing animal feed became a massive operation in its own right. Today, one-third or more of the entire global cereal harvest, and nearly all of the world's soya, is devoted to feeding industrially reared animals – food enough for more than 4 billion extra people.

Yet today we still hear talk of a looming global food crisis and the need to almost double food production by mid-century. The fact that there's already enough food for everybody – and plenty more – is routinely ignored.

Rather than a shortage of food, it's what we do with it that now counts. And not just in developing countries. Even in a rich country like Britain, there are signs that the old way of thinking is running out of steam. Food has never been so cheap, yet the use of food banks – emergency food parcels – is rising. So too is the paradoxical scourge of malnourished obesity, a condition suffered when people eat too much of the wrong thing. Access to sufficient food of sufficient quality is the real issue, not the amount of dubious-quality food we can produce. Yet still policymakers pursue the expansion of industrial farming, seemingly at any cost.

The planet is now at a dangerous tipping point where approaching half the world's meat now comes from industrial rather than mixed farms.[17]

For the last twenty-five years, I have seen the effects of industrial farming first-hand. It was a chance meeting with a former dairy farmer that changed my life.

Peter Roberts was founder of the organisation I now run: Compassion in World Farming, the world's leading farm animal welfare charity.

Before then, he and his wife Anna milked cows and kept chickens on his mixed farm in Hampshire. During the 1960s he watched the rise of factory farming and didn't like what he saw. Factory farms started springing up where hens, pigs and veal calves spent their whole lives in cages or narrow crates. He became disturbed by what he saw as the pervading notion that animals were biological machines to be churned out as quickly as possible, just another product on an assembly line.

Peter became a leading voice calling for animals to be treated with compassion and respect. He believed farm animals should at least be given lives worth living before they died.

In 1990 I became so moved by what he was doing that I upped sticks from my life as a packaging designer in Bedfordshire to work with him in a small office in Petersfield, Hampshire. Before long I was travelling around the country, then abroad, meeting politicians, journalists, business people and celebrities about the way we rear animals for food. I also started to see industrial farming for myself.

During my first weeks, I suggested that Peter should write a book. Looking back, he probably thought I was trying to butter him up. He replied with nothing more than a wry smile. Twenty-five years later, the book was finally written – by me. I called it *Farmageddon: The true cost of cheap meat*, and wrote it with the then *Sunday Times* journalist Isabel Oakeshott. During the course of our research we travelled to remote parts of China, USA, Mexico, Argentina and Peru, to examine the worst – and best – ways of producing dairy products and meat.

I came home armed with fresh insights. I started to see what was happening to farmland birds, bees and butterflies, as well as to all sorts of creatures you don't associate with farming at all: penguins, polar bears, elephants, jaguars, orang-utans, rhinos. Their fate is intimately connected to industrial agriculture.

These insights are the ingredients for *Dead Zone*.

I have always been passionate about wildlife. I was a schoolboy conservationist and ended up a professional tour leader for a while. I would take people around the world seeing amazing creatures in places like the USA, Morocco, the Seychelles, the Pyrenees, the Gibraltar Strait, Turkey and Costa Rica.

I now live in a country village in the South Downs of England among farming neighbours. I spend a lot of time walking the fields and forests with my wife Helen and rescue dog Duke. Ours is a village surrounded by mixed farms and islands of rising chalk. A land of hedges and hilltops, pasture and the odd pond.

It is here that I started my journey for this second book. My travels took me crossing continents – Europe, the Americas, Asia and beyond – on a journey more urgent than the last. I wanted to find solutions to the ever-pressing problems closing in on the countryside. I searched for ways not just to reconcile traditionally competing demands of wildlife and food production, but to bring them together. For this is where I believe the future lies. Food and nature can and should go together. And when they do, food tastes better.

From my farming neighbours to lost tribes, from the ashes of forests to pioneering projects to put things back, I discovered stories that can help empower all of us to make a difference three times a day through our food choices. We are perhaps the last generation that can change things without having to look back on a world where the wild things were ...

Ultimately, *Dead Zone* asks the question: What kind of legacy do we want to leave for our children?

While visiting Easter Island, the naturalist and broadcaster Sir David Attenborough said: 'The future of life on Earth depends on our ability to take action. Many individuals are doing what they can.' Standing amongst the ancient statues, he concluded: 'Real success can only come if there is a change in our societies, in our economics, and in our politics.'[18]

This book explores what needs to change and why it matters to us all.

I

# Elephant

### WHAT'S THE BEEF WITH PALM?

'We are really scared for our children,' a villager told me. 'What if they are playing while we're away? Who will help them?' There had been a raid last night and the community was out in force. Police were already on site. Feelings were running high.

We were in northern Sumatra, in a place called Bangkeh. I shook hands with some locals, who seemed pleased to see us. The presence of a foreign film crew was a chance to tell their story, and they were eager for the outside world to know what they were going through.

A man in ceremonial dress stood stern-faced while excited children skittered around. Some of the adults simply looked shell-shocked.

At the crime scene, there was much finger-pointing and chatter about the assailant's entry and exit. Evidence of last night's assault lay broken and splintered on the floor. On the edge of the forest, the side of a simple wooden house had been ripped off. The room, festooned with laundry, was now open to the elements. There was something rather pitiful about the bedraggled clothes. Drying them was now the least of the inhabitants' problems. After a smash-and-grab raid, the assailant had fled back into the forest, leaving frightened villagers fearing his return.

Perhaps attracted by the smell of cooking, he had come in search of rice, renowned for its quality in the region. Though he left in a hurry, he had taken some persuading to go. Police had been forced to send him packing with gunfire. But that wasn't the end of the matter.

'He'll be back every three months,' sighed the village leader, Sarifuddw Aji.

So who was the shadowy figure with a taste for good rice? The clue lies in Sumatra's rich forests, home to an extraordinary array of exotic animals, among them tigers, rhinoceros, orang-utans and sunbears. The forests are also home to the critically endangered Sumatran elephant – and it was one of their number who was responsible for the village raid.

It was no isolated incident. Twenty or so elephants are thought to live in the area. With their forest home shrinking fast, they visit more often now, and are getting harder to scare off. 'This is the last piece of unspoiled jungle in the country,' Aji told me. 'We never went into the jungle but because it's a good place, the elephants are regrouping here.'

The community is frightened and frustrated. Locals don't want to harm the elephants, but if the government doesn't act, they feel they may have no choice. 'We love the animals,' Aji told me. 'The last thing we want to do is hurt them. But if the government doesn't help, we'll have to take to jungle rule.'

So how did it come to this, and what is the link between the elephants' plight and the demand for cheap meat in richer countries?

### IN A MESS WITH THE MAHOUTS

First light at the jungle camp of a Sumatran elephant patrol. I had come to see how the Sumatrans are using a small company of elephants that have been tamed and trained to help prevent their wild counterparts coming into conflict with people.

I peered out of my shack, a simple wooden shed where I'd spent a rough night, to catch a glimpse of the darkened forest. The trees made silhouettes against the dawn sky; the sound of wildlife was everywhere.

I was feeling dishevelled from long days on the road and hot restless nights. The airline had managed to lose my luggage, I had little more than the clothes I was wearing, and these were now blood-stained from leech bites. Judging by my stubbly chin, I also badly needed a shave. I didn't have a mirror, but I guessed that it was not a good look.

All the same, it was a thrill to be in Sumatra, the western teardrop island of Indonesia. The country has one of the most biologically and culturally rich landscapes in the world. Its rainforests contain a tenth of the world's known plants, 12 per cent of its mammals and 17 per cent of its birds[1] – an irresistible draw for a wildlife enthusiast like me.

Bleary-eyed, I stumbled out, to a chorus of birdsong. Thrilled by the sound, I scoured the trees for signs of warblers and the like – might I tick some new species off my bird-watching list? – but for all their clamour, they were too well camouflaged: I couldn't see a single bird. I was reminded of just how frustrating it can be trying to see wildlife in a rainforest. You can hear things everywhere, but seeing them is another matter.

Keen for a wash, I clambered down to a nearby river where I'd been told tigers come to drink. I looked around nervously, but couldn't see anything lurking. Crouching in a quiet shallow of the river, I was washing away the rough night when a flicker of movement caught my eye: rocks downriver burst into life in a flurry of exquisite little birds. They looked like wagtails. Resplendent with spots of black and white, I identified them as lesser forktails, a species I'd never seen before. I was delighted!

The roar of the river drowned out their sound, and pretty much everything else besides. Had a tiger been crouching in the forest, I would never have heard.

By the time I returned to camp, the elephant drivers, known as mahouts, had made breakfast. We gobbled down pancakes and coffee, to a soundtrack of gibbons. I couldn't see them (they were hidden by the dense foliage) but I could hear them calling and crashing about. They made a heck of a racket.

After we'd eaten, it was time to set off with the elephant patrol. In days gone by, when the operation was well funded, the elephants would have been kept closer to the mahouts in the forest next to the camp. Now there's no money to buy them food, so they are kept miles away in the thick of the jungle, where their meals are free.

Getting there meant a 3-mile hike through thick swampy vegetation. As we got ready to head off, the mahouts appeared, wearing rubber boots. That was when I discovered that my walking shoes, little better than trainers, weren't going to be much use. Within a few minutes, I was in a real mess. It amused the mahouts, but without the luxury of a change of clothes, I felt my heart sink a little more with every squelchy step.

Every now and then, I'd discover another leech stuck to an arm or a leg, or even worse, under my clothes – wriggly sluglike things that drew more blood than you'd believe. I looked as if I'd been to war.

We heard the first elephant before we saw her: a swoosh, swoosh, swooshing sound as she swatted at flies with a branch. She was chained. Instinctively I winced: there was something horribly discordant about seeing such a magnificent creature tethered in this wonderful wild place. The mahouts let her go, and she dutifully reeled in her own chain, leaving it in a neat pile.

There were four elephants, the gentlest of giants, with huge brown eyes and bristly eyelashes. On command, each elephant in turn would crouch down and allow their mahout to climb on their backs just behind floppy ears. Then, with a crack of undergrowth, they were off. It was an awe-inspiring sight, this line of one of the biggest living land creatures on Earth, trunks swishing, occasionally reaching for the animal in front. I was amazed at how quickly they blended into the forest. Around them flew butterflies as big as bats. I followed as best I could on foot.

They watched their step, carrying their riders with the care of a mother and child. It was touching to see – but these are no teddy bears. As if to remind me of the wild within, a big male beside me let out the most ear-splitting trumpet blast, making the ground around me shake.

Sumatran elephants are one of three subspecies of Asian elephant – the others are the Indian and Sri Lankan – smaller than their African cousins, with more compact ears that they keep flapping to cool themselves. Standing up to 9 feet tall and weighing 5 tons, they feed on a variety of plants, and drop seeds wherever they go, contributing to a healthy forest ecosystem.[2]

All the Sumatran elephants on the patrol are former raiders themselves, captured and trained to help keep their wild brethren where they belong in the forest. The idea is that they police the border between villages, cultivated land and jungle. Where they come across wild herds straying too close to the edge, they push the animals back into uncontested territory using fireworks and the like.

The mahouts treated the animals gently, and with respect.

Yet I had been dismayed by what I'd heard about the way elephants are trained for the tourist trade; how, whether born in captivity or captured from the wild, their mind, body and spirit are broken to tame them.[3]

As one environmental activist told me: 'It ain't pretty.' Although I didn't know how these elephants had been trained, and hoped it was gentle, I felt uncomfortable about taking up an invitation from the mahouts to ride, even though clambering through the undergrowth was filthy and uncomfortable.

With every passing day, the patrols are more necessary. Pressure is growing on what's left of Sumatra's rich jungle heritage, and the conflict between elephants and people is escalating.

Northern Sumatra, in particular the province of Aceh and a vast area of tropical rainforest known as the 'Leuser ecosystem', is one of the most important remaining wilderness areas in Southeast Asia. Covering over 2.6 million hectares, the Leuser ecosystem, which stretches from the coast of the Indian Ocean to the Malacca Strait, encompasses two huge mountain ranges, two volcanoes and nine major river systems. It is the last place on Earth where it is possible to see Sumatran elephants, tigers, rhinoceros and orang-utans in one area.[4] Parts are still relatively untouched – primarily because they are very inaccessible – but swathes of the richest areas, where the remaining wild elephants live, are under serious threat.

The rate of deforestation in Sumatra is staggering. Since the turn of the century, 1.2 million hectares of lowland forest cover and 1.5 million hectares of wetland forest have been lost.[5] Half a century ago, more than four-fifths of Indonesia was covered with tropical forests. Now with one of the highest rates of deforestation in the world, less than half of the country's original forests remain.[6]

For Sumatra's elephants, orang-utans and tigers, this is bad news: their homeland is literally disappearing under their feet. More than a third of the jungle habitat of the critically endangered Sumatran elephant has gone within just a single elephant generation. As a result, over the last twenty-five years, entire populations of elephants have disappeared.[7]

Though they face their own threats, African elephants are doing fine by comparison. Half a million of these magnificent beasts still exist in the wild, whereas official estimates suggest the critically endangered Sumatran elephant is down to its last 2,500.[8]

It is by far the most endangered elephant in the world, but its plight is little known. In Africa, ivory hunters are the big enemy. In Sumatra, poaching is not unknown, but the real enemy is something far less sinister-sounding: palm plantations.

Dominated by multinational networks based in Asia, Europe and North America, the global palm trade is worth some $42 billion a year.[9] On the face of it, it's an innocuous-sounding business. From the air, the plantations look like giant green carpets. Hard to imagine, then, that these luscious-looking canopies, reminiscent of holiday pictures, could be a source of so much harm.

Sadly, the truth is that they are no better than any other monoculture: plantations made up of mile upon mile of a single species of tree, supported by the usual barrage of herbicides and pesticides, creating a barren landscape. A single hectare of Sumatran rainforest (an area equivalent to roughly two football pitches) can hold more species of tree than there are native tree species in the whole of the UK.[10] By contrast, palm plantations are just that – palm, and more palm. Once the forest is gone, it's gone.

Over the last twenty years, deforestation has been driven chiefly by the expansion of palm-oil plantations.[11] It's in demand from the food industry as a cooking oil and in products such as margarine and ice cream. With a long shelf life, it is extraordinarily versatile. According to WWF, it can be found in about half of all packaged products sold in supermarkets.[12] Production has more than doubled since the year 2000, with most of the global supply coming from Indonesia and Malaysia. Since the end of the 1990s, the area under palm monocultures in Indonesia has increased up to fourfold.[13]

None of this is any secret. Indeed, in 2004, an industry group called the Roundtable on Sustainable Palm Oil (RSPO) was formed to work with the palm-oil industry to address concerns about the devastating environmental impact of felling trees to make way for the plantations.[14]

What is less well known is that palm products are being widely used to feed factory-farmed animals. The oil is derived from the reddish pulp of the fruit, but there's more to palm than the oil. Dig deeper into the fruit and you come across the edible seed or kernel. The industry renders these nuts down into kernel oil and palm-kernel meal or 'cake'. This palm-kernel meal is then transported as a protein source to the feed troughs of industrially reared animals all over the world, but especially in Europe. According to Malaysian researchers, it can be used to feed all manner of livestock including cattle, sheep, goats, pigs, poultry and even farmed fish.[15]

World production of palm-kernel meal more than doubled to 6.9 million tonnes a year in the decade to 2011.[16] The European Union (EU) is the biggest importer, accounting for around half the world's production in 2012. By country, the biggest users of palm-kernel meal are the Netherlands, New Zealand, South Korea, Germany, the UK and China. And it's not only palm kernel ending up in livestock feed troughs. According to UK government figures, some 150,000 tonnes of crude palm oil and its derivative (known as palm fatty acids distillate)[17] was also reported as having been used for animal feed in 2009.[18] Most palm feed goes to cattle. Under normal practice, up to a fifth of their rations can come from kernel. Up to a tenth of fodder for sheep can come from kernel; while the figure for calves, lambs and finishing pigs is up to 5 per cent.[19]

What I've found is that few people realise that palm kernel is being used for animal feed, and often those that do, don't like it. One environmental activist now working in Sumatra told me how he stopped working on dairy farms in his native New Zealand when he realised that palm kernel was going into the cows' feed hoppers. The South Pacific island nation that prides itself on its green image has become a top buyer of palm kernel. It's seen as a 'life-saver' by some dairy farmers, helping to feed their cows when grass is sparse. Yet the increasing spotlight from environmentalists has begun to unsettle some in the industry,[20] so much so that the major multinational dairy company in New Zealand, Fonterra, has been trying to persuade farmers to cut back on using palm kernel for fear of consumer backlash.[21]

But few shoppers realise that the milk, beef and bacon they buy may be coming from palm-fed animals, let alone contributing to the demise of iconic wildlife in the world's remaining jungles.

In Sumatra, the result of this booming industry is to force elephants to venture where no safety-loving wild elephant would roam: the forest edge. Unfortunately, they like the same flat lowland terrain as people.

In the competition between the two species, the elephants always lose one way or another – sometimes to poachers, for whom rogue animals attracting local media coverage mean easy pickings.

With luck, when wild elephants venture to the outskirts they will meet a patrol like the one I went to see, and will be pushed back into the jungle. The patrols – Conservation Response Units (CRU), to give them their official label – are the brainchild of Dr Wahdi Azmi, programme director for the Climate Change Initiative based at the University of Aceh. It's a system that works because elephants are quite predictable in their movements, tending to migrate along the bottom of river valleys. By patrolling those routes that border communities, the CRUs can head off conflict.

Sumatra's last remaining elephants are now scattered in isolated patches across an island twice as big as the UK. Simple conservation measures protecting piecemeal bits of habitat fall well short of what is needed. More than four-fifths of the remaining elephants now live outside designated conservation areas. 'If we are working to conserve the elephant using the old paradigm – that to conserve our species we just need to protect or maintain the conservation area – then you will lose over eighty per cent of them,' Azmi said.

The problem is heightened by the fact that conservation and forestry are matters for central government in Jakarta, yet most of the elephants live in areas under local government control. Conflicts with human communities are a growing problem. 'Some plantations are being allocated by government in the good habitat for elephants,' Azmi said.

His vision was that CRU teams would patrol elephant-migration corridors to head off conflict with human communities. Established when the global spotlight was on Indonesia following the 2004 tsunami, the CRU was originally a proud force: uniformed, trained and well equipped. Staff carried out education initiatives and even helped to capture illegal loggers. As the media spotlight waned, so too did much of the international money for conservation. The glory days are now long gone.

'It's not like the first year where we had enough money,' said head mahout Zainal Abidin of the Mane CRU. 'In the past, we could do a patrol for two nights – we had money to do that. Not any more. Now, we just take care of the elephants. Anything else is a bonus.'

Today elephant patrols rely on handouts from local government. Their work is limited to stepping in when they hear about trouble, rather than stopping trouble before it starts. The once proud sign to the entrance of the camp is so sun-bleached it's barely readable. It is nowhere near enough.


BEAR GRYLLS, EAT YOUR HEART OUT

A few days before I was due to leave for Sumatra, the Indonesian government suddenly announced new visa restrictions for journalists and representatives of international organisations, amid fears that some could be acting as spies. They declared that people undertaking the sort of trip we planned needed written permission, which would not be granted until details of the assignment were submitted to the National Intelligence Agency.

The process looked likely to take weeks, and we didn't have time, so it was either a case of cancelling the trip, or pressing on. Thankfully, the new rule was junked within days following an outcry about press freedom,[22] but the debacle showed how sensitive the government of Indonesia has become. It was the first sign that this would not be an easy trip.

After the fiasco with my luggage, things went from bad to worse. Long treks through muddy swamps took their toll. At night, we were either roughing it in the jungle or dossing down in cheap insect-ridden hotel rooms. Getting from A to B involved bumping along potholed roads that barely warranted the name. To top it all, something had marred the planning on the ground: our translator barely spoke English and our guide didn't know our itinerary.

After two days of madness, I could take no more. I made some urgent calls to HQ, impressing on colleagues the desperation of our situation, and somehow or other a fixer for the TV celebrity Bear Grylls was enlisted and flown in from Jakarta.

A former Reuters journalist who now makes wildlife documentaries, 37-year-old Dendy Montgomery was field producer and assistant director to Grylls during the filming of *Man versus Wild* in Sumatra. He was just what we needed. For the rest of the trip he regaled us with anecdotes about the TV action man and their adventures together.

Born in Banda Aceh, Dendy lost fifty family members during the tragic 2004 tsunami. He told me about the terrible moment when the tsunami struck the northern province, leading to the death or disappearance of 170,000 Indonesians.[23] Houses were collapsing around him from the initial earthquake as people fled the huge wave that was about to engulf the community. Dendy sped off with his wife in their jeep, stopping briefly to pick up passengers. As the wall of water closed in, he saw a blind woman and hauled her into the car. What he didn't know was that at around the same time, his mother had fled her home. He found her by pure chance. He told us that had he not stopped for the blind woman, he would probably never have seen his mother again.

The tsunami disaster helped precipitate the peace agreement between the government of Indonesia and the Free Aceh Movement (GAM – Gerakan Aceh Merdeka). Ironically, this paved the way for opening up the region's forests. During the 1970s, by agreement with Indonesia's central government, American oil and gas companies began exploiting Aceh's natural resources. Feeling that they weren't getting their fair share of the profits, Acehnese radicals started calling for independence. For years, much of Aceh remained untouched as a bitter civil war halted any kind of significant crop or road expansion. Whilst the ceasefire since 2004 has been a cause of celebration, it has also brought an influx of palm-oil companies into the last great forest habitat of the Sumatran elephant.

As a conflict reporter covering the civil war, Dendy was familiar with the story of Aceh's forests. He had watched the rise of the palm industry and knew where to go. So together we travelled across the northern province of Aceh, thought to be the place where Islam was first introduced to Indonesia. Pretty faces smiled from headdresses. Some of the women we saw were wearing fancy shoes, but otherwise they were cloaked in traditional Islamic clothing. There seemed to be no such restrictions for the men, who wore what they pleased.

We stopped for lunch on the main road heading east. Scooters rattled by. In the days that followed, the drone of these bikes seemed to follow us everywhere, no matter how remote the place.

In the open-fronted café, we were served bowls piled high with different types of fish and meat. Vegetables were noticeable by their absence.

'Have what you want, we only pay for what you touch,' we were told.

'OK, but how will they know which ones we've touched?' I asked.

'Oh, they'll know . . .' came the reply.

It seemed that the whole menu was now piled up in bowls in front of us, and yet still more came. A woman covered head to toe put yet more dishes on the table. Her otherwise expressionless face responded to a smile. 'Thank you,' I said. She smiled back for a moment and was gone.

With a long journey still ahead of us, we ate as much as we could manage and headed off along a busy street. A goat walked past a row of clothes shops, a precursor of things to come on the treacherous road we were about to take. Goats, chickens and even groups of cattle sauntered onto the highway, oblivious to the traffic, frequently forcing our driver to swerve and jam on the brakes. Then there were the other cars, overtaking wildly regardless of anyone or anything else on the road. I found myself both passenger and participant in a series of hair-raising near-misses. Nobody else seemed to flinch. I asked myself whether navigating this constant chaos makes for better drivers. Judging by our man's ability to duck disaster, I guessed it did.

Street traders hawked gasoline in plastic bottles to keep the hordes of scooters whining by. Three scooters headed our way too, each with a dead wild boar across the pannier, bound most likely for the Chinese and non-Muslim restaurant market. A fourth scooter zipped past with a dog peering out of the basket, presumably used for hunting – though he may have ended up in the pot himself. In North Sumatra the Christian population eat both wild boar and dogs, washed down with palm wine. 'There's a code in local restaurants,' Dendy told me. 'B1 is for dog, B2 is for pig. Dog meat is harder to find but B2, pigmeat, is everywhere.'

We drove through palm country for a solid four hours, along roadsides lined with little else but green palm canopies. 'Palm, palm, palm all the way,' Dendy sighed. Bright yellow palm-oil tankers were everywhere, along with container trucks piled high with knobbly palm fruits. I casually counted more than thirty trucks.

Bumping along a dirt track, we passed small communities huddled among the never-ending palm trees. Chickens, ducks and cattle wandered freely among homes and open-fronted cafés. At least the farm animals here were okay, I thought – they were certainly free-range. A scooter passed with its rider carrying a blade on the end of a long pole: the tool used for harvesting the fruit that causes so much fuss.

Amid warnings of hostage-taking, shootings and arrests, we had entered the heart of Sumatra's burgeoning palm industry. Yet to keep us safe we had a secret weapon: Dendy had summoned the help of a shadowy figure known as the 'main man' round here. This was Mr Prakoso. Whilst we were with him, we were told, no one would give us much trouble.

We pulled into Prakoso's house, accidentally knocking down a small garden wall – not the start I was hoping for. Happily, he seemed unperturbed. Indeed, the 'main man' and his two teenage daughters were all smiles. A palm and rubber producer himself, with his own mixed plot of land, he is also a defender of the native forest.

Prakoso explained why the jungle matters to the local communities as well as to the elephants. 'The forest is a water-catchment area and we have to protect that,' he told me. 'The villagers rely on the forest for their water supply.' Native forest trees hold rainwater and release it slowly, thereby regulating the flow. As well as holding soil in place and controlling landslides, they play a vital role in preventing flooding.

'If we lose the forest, we will be facing drought. If there is no rainfall for two days, or if it rains for two days without stopping, we will get floods,' Prakoso said. A recent flood, linked to the destruction of local forest, had destroyed two homes. 'My hope is to see the degraded land rehabilitated, replanted with trees that can store water, like fruit trees,' he went on. Yet he feels that the outlook is bleak. 'The government is giving licences to palm plantations in the forest. I feel angry at the companies because of the impact they have on us; on the water and in terms of natural disasters.'

Heavy floods seem to hit the area every ten years. Working as a journalist, Dendy was stranded here by severe flooding in 1995. A decade later, the floods hit again. The community is now bracing itself, expecting more flooding soon. Only this time, with much of the forest gone, they expect it to be far worse.

Palm is not bad in itself; the problem is how the crop is produced. As part of a mixed landscape, palm can be beneficial to communities without destroying wildlife habitats or undermining essential eco-services like flood control. Yet palm in industrial monocultures brings all sorts of problems for people as well as animals.

If the villagers have their own land, they'll mix palm with different types such as fruit trees, I was told, making for a more balanced plantation. Large companies armed with heavy-duty kit like caterpillar machinery prefer to scale everything up, and plant rows of monoculture. 'Big companies are bulldozing wisdom,' Prakoso told us with a sigh.

The villagers here have had enough. They don't want more of the jungle opened up for this industry. Once the native plants have been felled, there's no going back. The workers move in, then their families, and shops to serve them, and before you know it a whole village has sprung up.

I heard how they had felt tricked out of their land by a big company and taken matters into their own hands. Prakoso was jailed for nine days in 2012 for burning a bulldozer in protest. He was not alone. Two hundred people joined the protest, nine were imprisoned.

Prakoso took us to where the locals fought their pitched battle with the palm company. Teeming rain made the going treacherous as our four-wheel-drive headed up steep dirt tracks and our driver wrestled with the wheel. The bumpiest tracks were now as slippery as an ice-rink and our truck lurched to and fro, bumping against the banks on either side. Sheer drops came and went. It was impossible not to think about the very real possibility that we would plunge down, never to be seen again. Palm fronds slapped the windscreen. We were being tossed around like some crazy fairground ride without the safety features.

Eventually we reached the top of a hill named Titi Akar, where we found a scene of devastation. A black eagle uttered plaintive cries as she flew over the depleted forest, landing in the last tall tree standing. On a barren hillside, where the vegetation had been razed by fire, young palms poked out of plastic sheeting designed to stop the jungle fighting back. The only remains of the once-mighty forest were burned black stumps.

This used to be jungle with a treasury of trees and plants. Soon it would be cloaked in monoculture. Swallows and swiftlets weaved low, taking advantage of newly bare hilltops. Workers with yellow suncream on their faces were busy planting a rampant creeper to stop the soil being washed away. The slope ahead of us had just been felled. Logs and fallen branches were strewn down the hillside. A nearby patch of forest was still standing, but not for long. The appetite for palm would soon consume what remained.

I was joined by Tezar Pahlevie, a 27-year-old conservationist. Tall, with chiselled features, he used to work for the local government but was now regional manager for a lobbying group, Forest, Nature and Environment Aceh (HAKA). 'I felt really frustrated working with government,' he said. 'You'd tell them what needs to be done, but they'd do nothing.'

Pahlevie had recently found signs of elephants around here. 'I feel sick, totally sick,' he told me, looking out across the deforested hillside. 'With such little remaining forest here, the elephant cannot survive . . . The elephants cannot live in a monoculture plantation like this. They don't have any food to eat,' he added.

For a host of reasons, palm plantations and elephants don't mix. When the jungle is cleared, chemicals are used to protect the young trees. Porcupine and wild pigs partial to a bit of palm are poisoned. Sometimes, elephants pay the ultimate price too. 'Yesterday, villagers found a dead adult elephant in an oil-palm plantation,' Pahlevie said. 'They say he was poisoned.' With just 500 elephants left in Aceh, this was the second report I'd heard of an elephant killing on palm plantations inside a week.

Pahlevie had also spotted orang-utans in this area. Three families were thought to be living in the area with their babies. But surveying palm-filled valleys and tree-plucked hillsides brought us both to the same conclusion: like the elephants, those baby orang-utans had no future.

## CONSERVATION DRONES TO THE RESCUE

Graham Usher stood over a glass table which encased a display of seeds, leaves and skulls collected from Borneo and Sumatra. With a flourish, he produced a long box, out of which, magician style, he pulled a polystyrene airplane – his secret weapon in the fight against palm plantations. 'This,' he declared proudly, 'is the drone that's mapping the forest.'

Living in Medan, Usher is one of a new breed of conservationists here in Sumatra; highly knowledgeable and using up-to-the-minute technology. Originally from Ipswich, England, he came to Indonesia in 1979 and never left. His view is that Indonesia has some good planning and environmental legislation. In theory, the Leuser ecosystem has been officially designated a national strategic area for environmental protection. 'If that was enforced, that would go a long way to ensuring the long-term survival of those species,' he said. 'Currently it's pretty much being ignored. It's as if it didn't exist.'

By flying drones, Usher gauges the state of the forest, mapping how they are being nibbled away. The drones – or unmanned aerial vehicles (UAVs) as he prefers to call them – give better images with a higher resolution than satellites, and cost less.

'We started experimenting with UAVs about three years ago. It's a very different story when you go to a government official with a high-resolution photograph and put it in front of him. He'll say: "Oh yes, I can see exactly what you mean." They can see exactly what's going on.'

Usher conceded that palm is a very attractive industry for those who stand to make money from it, because it grows fast and is productive. It requires much less land to produce the same volume of oil than the chief alternatives. Soya is claimed to be about ten times less productive per unit of cultivation, while rapeseed is around five times less.[24] 'In terms of production per hectare, theoretically it's a wondercrop!' he said. 'But the problem is the expansion and how it's expanding.'

When industry figures talk about the rapacious development of palm plantations, they like to use the word 'sustainable'. The phrase is designed to make everyone feel better, but all too often it is virtually meaningless. I am painfully familiar with the way that this word is wheeled out as a cover for unfettered expansion of insidious types of agricultural production.

When talking about 'sustainable' palm oil or 'sustainable' anything, what needs to be borne in mind is the capacity of the

Earth to deliver. Global demand for palm products is expected to triple by 2050. It's hard to see how this could possibly be met without massive environmental consequences.[25] There's nothing very complicated here: quite simply, if you fell vast swathes of rich jungle and replace it with one type of vegetation, you kill the rich array of plant and animal life that virgin forest would otherwise sustain.

Much of the current expansion is into lowland jungle, because palm oil tends to be grown in the lowlands. For one thing, lower, flatter terrain is easier to cultivate with big machinery. However, these are '*the* most biodiverse forests', according to Usher. 'It's where your big iconic species are. In Sumatra, we're already down to a few per cent left of what fifty years ago covered a lot of the surface area of Sumatra.'

He pointed to a satellite image showing patches of green that marked remaining forest areas in Sumatra. A lot of it is uplands where elephants don't go. His assessment of the outlook for the elephant is 'very grim'. 'They have nowhere left to live,' he said simply.

Usher showed me some aerial footage taken by his drones that highlighted evidence of land clearance, burning and drainage. 'It's rather depressing. Just about everywhere I've flown, I've seen a lot of indications of a continual nibbling away at the forest. In some areas, not just nibbling, but big gulps being taken out of the forest.'

The erosion is almost incessant. People open up a patch and are allowed to have that land. Then five years down the line, they move in a bit further. 'OK, we'll draw a new boundary. And the line is always moving, the goalposts are always moving,' Usher said. 'No one is drawing the line and saying: "*No*, no further."'

What effect is this having on the Sumatran elephant? 'It's like me coming bulldozing your house, simple as that. They're gonna have nowhere to live.'

While I was there, I also met Mr Iskandar (he didn't want to give his first name), head of the forestry department for the East Aceh local government. I wanted to hear the official line. He was in Tangahan searching for solutions to conflicts between elephants and communities, perhaps through establishing more elephant patrols.

Speaking through an interpreter, he told me that the government was genuinely concerned about the decline in elephant numbers. Aceh is thought to have lost half its elephants in the last ten years. From a population of a thousand, there are now estimated to be 500 left. The national picture is even worse. Losses have been put at 70 per cent in the last decade, and experts I spoke to now estimate that as few as 1,700 individuals remain alive in the wild.

'The local government in East Aceh totally supports and really cares about the conservation of elephants,' he claimed. 'Elephants this year are a high priority to save, because we realise that the deforestation is really making elephant lives difficult – that's why conflict is happening.'

Sumatra's palm industry is now thought to be driven by large and middle-sized operators with a tendency to flout the rules, thought to often clear more land than their licences allow.

'We are not too worried if the land clearance is by villagers to open plantations, because mostly villagers only open small areas of land,' Iskandar said. 'What I am more focused on are the big companies that are sometimes doing things which are not good, like opening up more land than they are given. So for the future, we will have clear lines between what can be opened and the areas to be saved.'

It sounds positive – but not everyone is convinced. The government's track record is poor.

'The laws of the land need to be enforced,' Usher told me. 'We know we're not going to save every last remaining patch of forest, but if the rules were enforced as they should be, a lot of the areas would be protected. It comes down to governance, a lot of it. Right now we have an anarchic situation with a completely dysfunctional governance situation.'

## FROM PALM TO INDUSTRIAL FARM

My final day on Sumatra brought a last surprise. We were standing in one of the endless plantations and a young man was fetching us a palm fruit, using a long pole with a knife at the end. He jabbed and slashed at the canopy above us until at last a knobbly fruit the size of a pineapple crashed to the ground with a thud.

I picked it up and was surprised by its weight – perhaps 15 kilos or more. It was also crawling with ants, which went careering up my arms and inside my shirt.

As I was inspecting the fruit, there was a loud rustle overhead. I heard shouts and crashing, and more out of instinct than anything else, I ran for it. As I turned tail, the sound of cracking tore down towards us, culminating in a deafening crash that was followed at once by a powerful slap across the back of my head. I'd been clipped by the canopy of a falling sengon tree, which must have been dislodged somehow as we harvested the fruit. I just avoided being flattened.

Once it was clear nobody was hurt, I returned to cut the fruit. There beneath the fleshy stuff was the pearly-white nut – the so-called palm kernel – now propping up industrial livestock operations around the world.

The market is booming. In 2013, palm kernel was a $3.4 billion industry, with every 7 tonnes of palm oil producing 1 tonne of kernel. In recent years, demand has soared. The value of Indonesia's kernel trade alone rose tenfold between 1990 and 2013. A ready market for kernel as industrial animal feed adds about a tenth to the income from each palm fruit, offering further encouragement to the growth of the industry.

The European Union is the world's biggest importer, with a growing hunger for palm kernel to feed its farm animals. Some 3.6 million tonnes of palm-kernel meal was imported in 2012, an increase of 50 per cent since 2000. However, the market for this commodity is also growing in China, where imports have rocketed 100-fold during the same period. New Zealand's use of the stuff has increased 2,500-fold, mainly to feed its industrialising dairy industry.[26]

Environmentalists generally consider the Roundtable on Sustainable Palm Oil (RSPO) the only credible source of environmentally friendly palm products. The organisation tries to work with palm-production companies to reduce incursion into natural habitat. It requires all new plantations to be sited on land that is not defined as 'primary forest', native trees undisturbed by human activities, or important to conservation.[27] Companies signing up to what RSPO calls its 'responsible palm pledge' essentially promise not to take part in any activity that kills more elephants.

Sadly just one-fifth of the world's palm oil, and even less of its kernel, is covered by the scheme. 'Unfortunately, we know that only a small number of the players are RSPO members, and you now have this massive mid-layer industry in Indonesia that doesn't follow any rules at all,' said Graham Usher.

In any case, RSPO is not without its critics. A report by Greenpeace, entitled 'Certifying Destruction', stated that current standards are so low that those who sign up to the pledge remain 'free to destroy forests', and claimed that the scheme fails to protect international household brands from the risk that the palm oil they use is 'tainted with deforestation'.[28]

Whatever the truth about the level of success so far, I was keen to find out more about what consumers and companies buying palm products could do to help. Usher is upbeat about consumer power. 'Consumers in Europe and North America do make a difference,' he said. 'They are listened to . . . the political impact of pressure groups and consumer concerns do make an impact on decision-making here. It doesn't change overnight, it's a long process to make these changes. The question is, do we have enough time?'

What role can ordinary shoppers play in reducing the market for palm kernel? After all, how many consumers in Europe even know that milk or beef could come from animals fed from the ashes of former elephant habitat?

Concerned consumers can look for pasture-fed beef and lamb, and organic dairy that is more likely to have come from animals fed grass rather than concentrated feeds that may contain palm. Shoppers could also ask questions of their supermarkets to find out whether meat has been produced palm-free and thereby elephant-friendly.

In Britain and the Netherlands, the animal-feed industry has set targets to be certified fully sustainable. These moves are led by Nevedi, the animal-feed association in the Netherlands, and by the Agricultural Industries Confederation (AIC) in the UK. The animal-feed sectors in other countries, including Germany, Norway, Sweden, France, Belgium and Denmark, are not yet thought to be involved in sustainable palm initiatives.

Yet why feed farm animals on palm kernel in the first place? Europe's appetite for cheap meat from industrial farms is already known to gobble more than half of its cereals and 30 million tonnes of imported soya, not to mention vast quantities of fish. Now Sumatran palm can be added to the list of environmentally damaging industrial animal feeds, despite the many viable alternatives that this book will explore.

The worry is that palm kernel helps drive more factory farming; as a readily available feed source, it tempts farmers to take animals off grass and into confinement feeding. It's a particular concern in relation to cattle, for which a greater proportion of the diet can be made up of palm than for other types of livestock. Wouldn't it be so much simpler to feed cattle grass, as nature intended? As I hope I showed in my previous book *Farmageddon*, and we'll explore further later, this is not a pipe dream.

Right now we have a vicious circle. The increasing availability of palm-kernel meal as feed drives industrial animal farming. In turn, factory farming drives demand for more cheap feed like palm kernel. Vast tracts of land are being lost to monocultures producing fodder for animals, rather than food for people. Among the losers in this equation are Sumatra's dwindling elephants.

The palm industry may claim with some justification that palm kernel is just a by-product of its main game: peddling palm oil. Perhaps better that it feeds animals than that it goes to waste. In addition, it may be difficult to reduce demand for kernel without first reducing demand for palm oil. But that is no excuse for inaction.

Furthermore, as we explore in subsequent chapters, there is no cover story to justify the many millions of acres of other crops like corn and soya grown primarily to feed intensively reared farm animals.

In far-flung lands, spectacular species like elephants and tigers are being driven to extinction, but the effects on the countryside much closer to home are no less serious.

# 2

# Barn owl

High above a hilltop woodland, shapes are dancing in the darkening sky. They are supremely graceful and somehow prehistoric-looking, like giant butterflies. There are about forty, a silent flurry of swirling wings and tails. With a flap and a glide, they melt away among the trees of oak, birch and pine. They are red kites at their winter roost, on the outskirts of the village where I live in Hampshire, England.

As they disappear for the night, I catch a glimpse of a ghostlike figure: the white of a barn owl drifting silently along the hedge-row, his piercing dark eyes scanning for breakfast. In this single winter scene, birds of both day and night come together in the last moments of daylight.

I feel privileged to witness such scenes on my doorstep. In Britain, red kites used to be very rare. When I first started watching wildlife in the 1970s, there were only about forty red kites left in the country, every one of them in remotest Wales. Now, these magnificent raptors have made a dramatic comeback.

Here in the South Downs, barn owls are doing well too, with several pairs nesting within walking distance of our cottage, but in the wider countryside, all is not well. Barn owls have always had their ups and downs, but 2013 was their worst year on record. The cold spring killed more than ever before.[1]

It would be easy to see it as just one of those things – after all, we can't do much about the weather. But over much of Britain's farm-land there is something else at play, making it harder for wildlife like the barn owl to find food and nesting sites. As they struggle with these basic needs, they become more vulnerable to other chal-lenges they face.

Birds have been my passion since I was seven years old. I have always been particularly fond of barn owls, and I'm not alone. Enigmatic but easy to recognise, they've been voted Britain's favour-ite farmland bird.[2]

I remember as if it were yesterday the very first time I saw one. We were on a family holiday in Norfolk and Dad had dropped me off for the day at a nature reserve run by the Royal Society for the Protection of Birds (RSPB) called Titchwell Marsh. Fascinated by the reedbeds and lagoons that made up what was to become one of the RSPB's flagship nature reserves, I spent ages looking for bearded tits – tiny birds with long tails and immaculate features. I listened to the cries of ducks and shorebirds. I heard the evocative call of the male bittern, deep and throaty, like someone blowing over the top of a bottle.

I felt a sudden jolt of excitement as through the heat haze I clapped eyes on something brilliant white: the unmistakable spec-tre of a barn owl. I peered intently, hardly believing my eyes, as the bird hovered and glided before settling on a post. Surely there was some mistake? I was watching in broad daylight through shimmer-ing heat, and owls are nocturnal. Were my eyes playing tricks?

By now the distant bird was staring back at me, daring me to believe. Happily a passing reserve warden came to the rescue. Sensing my nervous excitement, he smiled and confirmed what I longed to hear, that yes, my bird *was* a barn owl. That was the moment I learned how these birds of the night can sometimes be seen during daylight hours, especially when they are feeding chicks.

When I close my eyes more than thirty years later, I can still see that bird and feel that same excitement. That barn owl fuelled what has been for me a lifelong fascination with the natural world.

I was born in 1965 and grew up in the Bedfordshire market town of Leighton Buzzard, best known as the site of Ronnie Biggs's Great Train Robbery. Together with my younger brother and sister, we lived in a modest 1930s semi near the centre of town. During school holidays, we used to stay at Grandad's little bungalow in Bedford. For a boy with a growing interest in wildlife, it was bliss: his lawn was always covered in birds. For me, one of the greatest treats was putting out bread for sparrows – and back then there were always loads of them. I remember being curious about all aspects of their lives – where they nested, what they sounded like, how males and females would stick together or not, and whether their beaks had saliva like our mouths. I remember watching a sparrow pick up a tiny pebble in Grandad's garden and turn it round in her beak before dropping it. I ran out and touched the pebble, eager to see if it was wet.

Mum taught me a wider appreciation of nature. I remember her encouraging us to be kind to ladybirds: 'They've done you no harm,' she used to say. I remember her getting annoyed when the government suggested some half-baked attempt to deal with over-fishing by launching a seal cull. 'They're the seals' fish too!' she exclaimed at the telly.

She kept house while Dad was busy running the local social centre for elderly and disabled people. He was active in the community in all sorts of ways: organising the local carnival, working with the local St John ambulance brigade, and sitting on the bench as a magistrate. He was committed to the Church and in later life became a vicar.

As in many households back then, we didn't eat meat every day. I remember one day when Dad was out shopping, he was given the wrong change – fifty pence extra, which seemed a lot back then. On the way home, he put it in a charity box. Mum was furious. I can still remember her indignation as she shouted that we didn't have that much money – we couldn't even afford meat!

Mum and I started keeping birds in a big aviary at the bottom of the garden. We had finches, canaries, budgerigars and tiny quail. We loved to see them make their nests and rear their chicks. Over time, we got really good at getting them to breed. I'd spend hours just sitting in the aviary watching them fly around my head or pecking beside me. It's not something I would do now, as I don't agree with keeping birds in cages, but I saw things differently in those days, and our aviary was pretty spacious in any case.

When I was off school for a couple of weeks with chickenpox, Mum gave me my first bird book. We were big bird-feeders in our house, putting out all manner of scraps: leftovers, stale bread, peanuts. I remember how that winter was particularly cold, but we managed to attract a gorgeous, brightly coloured little bird to feed on our flowerbed – a dainty seed-eater with bright red facial blaze and flashing gold wing patches. The mystery visitor was a goldfinch. I'd never seen anything so beautiful. They were rare in gardens back then, much more a bird of the farmland countryside.

Fired with enthusiasm, I became a budding schoolboy conservationist. I loved to look at sticklebacks in the river near home, and yearned to see bigger creatures like badgers, deer and barn owls. I would spend many a day walking local woods and cycling to lakes in search of wild things.

I dreamed up schemes to raise a few pennies to help buy nature reserves. In my childhood mind, I thought that if only it were possible to raise enough money for more nature reserves, wildlife would be safe. I hadn't figured out that most of Britain's countryside is farmland – three-quarters of all available land in fact – and that actually, the way this land is used is the crux of the problem. It was not until I was much older that I made the connection.

Back then, farms fascinated me as wildlife habitats. I didn't give a great deal of thought to the pigs, chickens and cows. For one thing, they seemed to have more to see and do in those days. Of course, there might have been an element of nostalgia on my part – summer days seemed to roll on for ever back then – but the truth was that farm animals were literally disappearing from fields, to be reared inside. The birds I loved were also vanishing. In my lifetime, Britain has lost 44 million birds at the rate of a pair every minute.[3]

My interest continued to grow. I joined the local group of the RSPB, setting off on coach trips to far-flung places with exotic names like Minsmere and Gibraltar Point. I must have been thirteen years old when I first started going on outings with forty or so pensioners and middle-aged folk. They were all bird enthusiasts, with astounding knowledge of their subject, and I wanted to be like them. I'd join them in my anorak, with a packed lunch and cheap binoculars that, looking back, weren't much better than peering through a pair of milk bottles.

At school, I dreamed of becoming a nature reserve warden. I bunked off classes to cycle over to local reservoirs to watch birds and volunteered to act as a warden in a local wood. I even made wildlife the theme of my school A-level projects wherever I could. I remember one – the study of birdsong in relation to 'photoperiod' – which, in less pompous speak, means seeing how many birds were singing in our local wood as the days got longer.

Thanks to an elderly couple called Mr and Mrs Edgar, I had my own woodland nature reserve for a while. They owned the land and seemed to like having me and a pal pottering around. We watched woodpeckers, dug a pond and cleared away old brush. In truth, I'm not sure we added much, but it got us out and active, and we loved it. To this day, I still hanker for my own nature reserve – a patch of ground I can transform into a haven for wildlife. It's never happened yet, as land in Britain doesn't come cheap, so I have to content myself with making our garden as attractive to wildlife as possible. But maybe one day, when I retire – who knows?

I took biology A level in the hope that it might be useful, but drew the line at dissection. I couldn't see the point of animals being killed just for us kids to cut up. I remember leading a classroom boycott on the day we had to do a horrible experiment to show the beating heart of a living frog. Looking back, it seems extraordinary that we were asked to perform vivisection. To me and most others in the class, it was beyond the pale.

Shortly after I left school, dissection was dropped as a compulsory part of science teaching in Britain, but there have been moves recently to reintroduce it as a must-do element of courses, thirty years later, which seems a shame.[4]

After I left school, I decided to spend a few months devoted to watching birds and volunteering on nature reserves. That was how I came to be a regular hitchhiker to Norfolk, a Mecca for birdlife. I became very skilled at cadging lifts for the hundred-mile journey, usually making it in eight hours. Once I took the train, only to find it took just as long and cost a fortune.

I would hitch in all weathers. The days when it was throwing it down with rain were the worst, because people didn't really want to pick up a passenger who looked like a drowned rat. But even then, someone would eventually take pity and offer a lift.

Once, a shiny red Porsche pulled up. The driver flung open the passenger door, declaring it my lucky day – as indeed it was. He was a slick young 'yuppie' as we called them back then: upwardly mobile and flash with it. He seemed to love showing off to me about his car and how fast it could go, throwing me back into my seat as he floored the accelerator. Another time I hopped into a truck to find the driver covered in blood – an alarming vision. Panicking, I thought I was being picked up by an axe murderer. It turned out that he worked at the local slaughterhouse.

I always enjoyed chatting to the people who picked me up. After all, they would often be looking for company for what might otherwise be a long and tedious ride. Many were intrigued by the lengths I'd go to for wildlife. Some of them no doubt dined out for weeks on stories of how they picked up a 'bird nut'.

Nothing deterred me in my quest to spot birds. I slept rough on park benches, sometimes in bird-watching hides, hoping desperately not to get caught by the warden. I also spent many memorable nights bedded down in the coastal shelter of a nature reserve. I would be kept awake by the blood-curdling shrieks of a male barn owl flying around advertising for a mate. Good job I knew it was a bird making that noise, or I'd probably have fled in a panic!

My wildlife apprenticeship really got going at Cley on the North Norfolk coast. Barn owls patrolled the marshes. There were masses of pools with every kind of duck and wading bird. The adjoining shingle spit of Blakeney Point, famous for its breeding seals, would hold migrating birds in the sueda bushes. I was thrilled when I found a scarce migrant from America called a pectoral sandpiper.

I became a regular in Nancy Gull's café, the epicentre of the British bird-watching universe in the 1980s. A phone in the corner of this humble greasy spoon would ring constantly: birdwatchers from all over the country calling to check on the latest rare sightings. I whiled away many a rainy hour nursing a mug of tea and answering those calls, the voice at the other end, invariably asking the same question: 'Anything about?'

Then came a six-month stay at the RSPB reserve at Titchwell, where I'd seen my first barn owl. I dug ditches, planted trees and pulled wind-blown roofs from bird hides out of the marsh.

Titchwell was heaven for an aspiring naturalist like me. I was able to spot really special birds like bitterns, marsh harriers, and even tall white spoonbills with their thick spatulate bills. We put out dummy spoonbills in the reedbeds to tempt the real thing to breed. They came and went but didn't breed. Evidently they were unconvinced by our replicas.

I spent many a night guarding the nests of rare breeding birds like avocets, all black and white with their long upcurved bills, and parrot crossbills, which are strange-looking red finches with overlapping beaks.

I began to notice how rare birds like avocets were starting to do better, while common birds like farmland sparrows, finches and barn owls were suffering. Part of the problem for owls was the disappearance of the habitat that gave them their name: tumbledown barns had become rich pickings for property developers.

I remember 'Bob's barn' as we called it, home to the barn owls that would fan out across Titchwell Marsh and enliven my night-watches as they hovered overhead. How I loved to see those steely eyes looking down at me. Sadly, the barn has long since been converted.

Another peril is cars, a danger brought into sharp relief for me when I had an all too close encounter with a bird whilst at the wheel myself. I was driving along country roads in the dead of night when a ghostly figure appeared above the car. I don't know if I hit it – I've always hoped not – but in all likelihood that bird went the way of thousands of barn owls in Britain every year, killed by cars, their habit of flying low bringing them into fatal collision.

Yet it is changes to farming that have presented perhaps the gravest danger. Once upon a time barn owls were a common sight over fields and farm buildings. Most farms had a pair. Now just one farm in seventy-five has a nesting pair of barn owls.[5]

David Ramsden MBE, head of conservation at the Barn Owl Trust, said: 'Farmland wildlife will continue to decline as long as we farm the vast majority of the land intensively. What we need is different systems of farming.'

I met Ramsden at his eco-friendly office on the edge of Dartmoor just above the small town of Ashburton. Outside, a barn was lined with nest boxes of all shapes and sizes. It acts as an owl hospital: some two dozen patients a year are treated and released. Owls of any kind are welcome. A fluffy brown tawny owl fledgling picked up near Dartmoor Prison had the inevitable name 'Porridge'.

Dressed in functional country garb, David and his wife Frances looked as if they were ready to rescue another owl at a moment's notice. He told me he has always been fascinated by flight, whether it's archery arrows, aircraft or birds. It was wildlife declines in the 1980s that prompted him and Frances to set up the Trust.

'Everybody loves barn owls,' he told me, adding that people who catch an unexpected glimpse of one of these magnificent creatures often remember it for life. He talked about an elderly gentleman who had recently told him about a barn owl he'd seen, describing every characteristic in great detail. When Ramsden asked him when he spotted the bird, he replied that it had been in the summer of 1947.

The irony is that barn owls do a great service to farmers. Like flying cats, they scoop up large numbers of voles, mice and rats. They hunt mainly at dusk or during the night, with their sensitive eyes and even more impressive hearing. They can catch prey in total darkness guided by nothing more than rustles and squeaks.

'Barn owls are incredible birds,' Ramsden agreed. 'They have the most sensitive hearing of any animal ever tested, are able to fly in almost total silence, and of course, are amazingly beautiful to look at.'

Ramsden explained how UK barn owl numbers have dropped to about 4,000 pairs. They have good years and bad years, in response to extremes of weather and fluctuating numbers of prey.

'The long-term trend is mainly determined by food availability, which in turn is determined by land management,' he told me. 'As we know, the vast majority of farmland is intensively managed. Very little land is managed primarily for small mammals, which simply make do with whatever habitat is left, The switch from lightly grazed unimproved pasture to intensively managed ryegrass, and the switch from spring-sown cereals to winter cereals, have both caused huge reductions in wildlife.'

He showed me first-hand how farmland can be managed for wildlife. We walked into a field called 'Kiln Close', part of a 26-acre site bought by the trust with a legacy gift.

'This used to be short ryegrass,' he said. 'The combination of intensive grazing and artificial fertiliser allowed the ryegrass to outcompete all the native grasses and wildflowers. In terms of wildlife, there was virtually nothing here. So-called "improved" grassland is certainly not an improvement for wildlife!'

When the Barn Owl Trust bought the site in 2001, it set about recreating hedgerows that had been grubbed out in the 1970s. Cattle now graze in summer. Mixed native hedgerow shrubs like blackthorn attract scarce brown hairstreak butterflies. Stitchwort, celandine with its shiny buttercup-yellow flowers, and masses of primroses were bursting to life on the steep slopes where orchids bloom.

'The fundamental problem with intensive farming is that there isn't enough cover,' Ramsden explained. Barn owls are specialists, they need small mammals to eat. But their main prey, the field vole (also known as the short-tailed vole), doesn't generally burrow underground, and thus relies on being concealed by its habitat to survive. Without rough grassland, hedgerows and thickets, field voles have nowhere to hide.

We set off in search of rough grassland. A mass of wildflowers coloured the sunny bank: marsh thistle, hemp agrimony, foxgloves, bluebells and primroses. Then we reached a stretch of grass which he said provided cover for voles and other creatures barn owls feed on: 'So in rough grassland you not only find a lot more small mammals, there's also a lot more invertebrates than in a short sward of ryegrass, even more than in a traditional hay meadow.'

The key thing about rough grassland is the litter-layer. Grass grows up in spring and summer and dies back the rest of the year. If it's not removed, the previous year's grass becomes a litter-layer through which new grass grows and provides the cover the field voles need. This sort of habitat is becoming ever more scarce as the countryside is increasingly intensively managed.

'You can tell if it's good "rough" grassland because it's springy underfoot. That's caused by the dead grass litter-layer underneath,' he explained.

He crouched down and soon spotted a vole's hole in the grass, a tiny round gap no wider than a two-pound coin. In no time he spotted several more. I got down on my haunches to have a look for myself. Once I got my eye in, I realised that the long grass was teeming with them. It was a vole town.

Intensively grazed landscapes, where fertilisers are used on the grasses, have certainly affected wildlife. However, the way crops are produced these days also has a lethal impact. The switch from spring to autumn sowing, using varieties that have a longer growing season, has been a significant factor.[6] Traditionally, with spring sowing, fields would be left as stubble in winter. Stubble was a wonderful habitat for small mammals and birds, providing them with food all winter long, and cover to keep them safe.

The widespread modern practice of growing cereals over winter has marked the end of those beautiful golden stubble fields – and the loss of vital food for creatures like mice and voles, on which owls feed, and seed-eating birds, which have suffered drastic declines.

'Now we have winter cereals, so there are very few stubble fields in winter. In a bare field or a field of very young cereal crop, there's no food for wildlife,' Ramsden explained. Hedges are a last refuge, but bigger fields mean fewer hedgerows. 'On intensively managed farms at least, it's in the boundary features where you still find wildlife, and in most landscapes there are a lot of those.'

We walked through the wooded Ashburn Valley, with its tributary running to the River Dart. In this beautiful place, a tangle of sycamore, ash, oak and hazel now provides food and shelter for masses of wildlife. Otters have returned to the river and dippers – dapper little thrushlike birds that swim underwater – nest under a bridge in a purpose-made box.

Ramsden applauds successful efforts by landowners and conservationists on behalf of certain species like cirl buntings, cranes or red kites, but is less optimistic about prospects for the wider countryside. 'My feeling is that the long-term trend will be the decline of wildlife, as long as we farm intensively,' he said.

For the time being, Britain's barn owls are holding their own[7] and red kites are on the comeback, but other once common farmland species have been decimated and remain at an all-time low. Birds including turtle doves, grey partridges, corn buntings and tree sparrows have declined by 90 per cent or more over the last forty years. The skylark, lapwing and even the common starling have dwindled by at least 60 per cent. In recent decades, 2 million pairs of skylarks and a million pairs of lapwings have simply disappeared.

These declines are not confined to Britain. European bird census results for 1980–2010 show that 'farmland birds have fared particularly badly', with 300 million fewer birds today than in 1980. Grey partridge and crested lark have been particularly hard hit, with declines of more than 90 per cent. Ortolan buntings, turtle doves and meadow pipits have seen their numbers slashed by more than two-thirds.[8]

In the US, where farmland birds are called 'grassland' or 'shrubland' birds, many species are also in deep trouble. Those suffering include eastern meadowlark, lark bunting, mountain plover, short-eared owl and burrowing owl.[9]

Again, industrial farming is largely to blame. Birdlife International says the declines in Europe are widely accepted as being driven by agricultural intensification and the resulting deterioration of farmland habitats.[10] US farmland bird losses are thought to be in response to the loss of small farms, declines of shrub habitat and expanding 'industrial agriculture'.[11]

'Chastening and difficult to comprehend' is how retired British farmer Michael Shrubb describes the situation. He believes that intensification has effectively rendered farmland 'lifeless'. Watching the changes first-hand from his West Sussex family farm, he attributes the loss of bird life to what he calls a 'collapse in the diversity' of farmland. 'The haven of mixed farming systems is being swept away and, as a result, farmland is no longer able to support the same number of species and individuals,' he concludes in his book *Birds, Scythes and Combines*.[12]

Mixed farming involves growing a variety of crops on fields and changing them from one year to the next while interspersing arable production with grazing animals. It has long been a more natural way to produce food, building soil fertility, improving yields and avoiding infestation by pests and disease. A classic rotational system would involve growing vegetables or cereals like barley for three years, followed by three years of grass, which would support a dairy herd of cows or other grazing animals.

This kind of farming dominated the British landscape until the last few decades, when it was usurped by a new chemical age of industrial monoculture. Mixed farms gave way to specialist factory-like farms churning out single crops of seed, plant or animal. Chemical fertilisers replenished tired soils and pesticides kept bugs at bay. Farming appeared to have been liberated from its age-old dependence on Mother Nature – on the face of it, a cause for celebration. Yet there would be a heavy price to pay.

Shrubb sees the mid-1970s as the period when the intensive revolution swept the land. Farm animals were taken off grass to be caged, crammed and confined on factory farms. They were fed cereals from the subsidised monocultures. A new breed of large-scale arable farmers, dubbed 'barley barons', emerged in Britain and elsewhere. Farming geared up towards growing single crops in large quantities.

Chemical herbicides wiped out weeds (plants that farmers didn't like) but they also wiped out the wildflowers that once graced the countryside. As they disappeared, so too did the seeds and insects that for so long had helped wildlife to thrive. Insecticides designed to eliminate bugs regarded as pests by agriculturalists often kill a much wider spectrum of species, decimating the insect population on which birds depend for food.

All in all, the common link to the desertification of the countryside has been the declining diversity of farmland.

The Founding Father of the United States, Benjamin Franklin, famously declared that there is 'a place for everything, everything in its place'. When it comes to birds, in recent decades this truism has been turned on its head. Those associated with wide-open farmland have been fleeing for the sanctuary of urban gardens. The beautiful goldfinch – so rare in our Bedfordshire garden in the 1970s – may well have garden bird-feeding to thank for its existence. Numbers of these fetching little finches seen in gardens have increased more than forty times over, rescued from what the British Trust for Ornithology (BTO) describes as a 'reduction in the availability of weed seeds, due to agricultural intensification'.[13]

To its credit, the UK government isn't trying to hide what's going on. It admits that the 'intensification of farming' is behind the declines. In its own report, the UK Department for the Environment, Food and Rural Affairs (Defra) cites the loss of mixed farming, increased pesticide and fertiliser use and the removal of hedges as having robbed birds of suitable places for nesting and feeding.[14]

The government's chief scientist, Professor Ian Boyd, has gone so far as to admit that we 'can't have farmland birds at the level they used to be with the agricultural system we have today'. It's a blunt assessment, and solving the problem clearly requires thinking big. Unfortunately, faced with the daunting prospect of changing 'the system,' it appears that ministers prefer to shut their ears to the consequences and carry on as before.

At a conference I attended in London on food and farming, the government's chief scientist was pressed on why there has been so little action in response to his stark warning. With a shrug, he replied that he provides information and asks society 'through their elected politicians to make that choice'. In other words, he's given MPs the facts: it's up to them to do something about it.

The status quo is bad enough, but the outlook is bleaker. The British government is actively promoting a new wave of industrial-isation in the countryside under the seductive guise of 'sustainable intensification'. Quite what is meant by this term varies according to who you ask. Former Prime Minister David Cameron strug-gled to define it. What is certain is that it spells no good for the countryside.

It is not as if it is impossible – or even that difficult – to protect wildlife as well as to produce enough to feed people. Graham Harvey, former agricultural journalist turned scriptwriter for BBC Radio Four's *The Archers*, puts it this way: 'In Britain, we are constantly torn between this thing that "you can have wildlife or you can have food" . . . this is absolute tosh. In fact you need the biodiversity there to show that the system works, to show that the soil is alive. If there is no wildlife on the farms, there won't be any nutrients in the crops they grow.'

I accompanied Harvey to a farm not far from where I live in the south of England where an alternative method of farming has been adopted: one that is far more favourable to wildlife. Pitt Hall Farm belongs to Tim May, who has known farming all his life. His 2,500 acres of land near Basingstoke, Hampshire, has been in his family for four generations. It's a big farm, ten times bigger than the UK average. At thirty-four years old, married with three small children, he's seen the farm go through a predictable transition, with hedges ripped out to make fields bigger for chemical-driven arable cropping. Now he's trying to do something different. Sheep and cattle have been reintroduced to the farm, grazing swathes of pasture on a rotational basis.

I stood gazing at what looked like a cemetery of scarecrows, buried up to their necks in the hillside. We were overlooking

Watership Down, that wonderful pasture made famous in Richard Adams's classic story about rabbits.

May pulled up one of the heads, all orange and green, and set about it with a knife. 'Here . . . try that,' he said, handing me a sliver. 'Tastes good doesn't it?' I nodded, and tried it, rather gingerly. It was sweet and watery, somewhere between fruit and salad. 'It's fodder beet, we feed it to the sheep,' he explained. Sheep are back after a lengthy absence on what was an intensive arable farm. May feels that he has brought the farm back to life, or as he puts it on his website, 'back to the future'.

Barn and little owls are taking advantage of the more favourable conditions, with field margins designed to be bird-friendly. As we took a tour in his truck, a host of birds whizzed in and out of hedgerows and copses: yellowhammers, chaffinches, sparrows.

Talking to May and touring his farm underlined what I have known for some time: farming has become hopelessly detached from the fabric of the countryside. 'The really sad thing about me as a farmer is that I can't tell you anything about birds,' he said. 'It's one of my biggest regrets. As farmers, you're just taught if it's not a crop, you don't need to worry about it. That connection with the environment just doesn't exist with the farming community. I think it's actually shocking that I can walk into a wood and not know what I'm hearing. I don't know many farmers who would know much.'

His candid admission rather summed up for me what's been going wrong.

For decades, farmers have been encouraged to focus on production, seemingly at any cost. The general view is that if it isn't producing more per hectare, then it's failing. It may sound cost-efficient, but there is plenty of evidence to the contrary, not only in terms of the wider cost, but even in terms of the bottom line for individual farmers.

May describes what he's now doing as multi-cropping or 'multi-culture'. 'We decided we should be grazing our cereal crops so we could make money from having livestock on that area as well, not just the eventual crop harvest,' he explained.

He plants the cereal seeds early so that they grow really lush, then lets sheep loose on the ground. Over the autumn and winter, the sheep feed well on the green shoots of the growing cereals. Come the spring, they'll be taken off so that the barley can grow up properly, ready for harvest. This kind of innovation seemed to me to represent the future.

In switching from intensive arable to mixed land use, he has been able to reduce the amount he spends on expensive chemical pesticides and fertilisers. Previously his bill for these totted up to £700 a hectare. Now, he keeps most of the chemicals in the shed and the money in the bank.

The change has also transformed his relationship with wildlife. 'We're getting out of our tractors a lot more now . . . we're actually in the environment more.'

But when the system is stacked toward intensification, to go against the grain can be hard. 'It's almost broken me . . . I've been waking up in shivers, it's been terrible . . . big anxiety problems, stress . . . The whole transition has been much more about me than it ever was about sheep and grass, because they know how to graze and grow without any interference,' he admitted.

He told me that he had done much soul-searching through the process: 'I've had to learn to understand myself, as well as other people, and how to manage change. That's been by far the greatest challenge.'

I asked if he ever felt like giving up, and he replied that occasionally he had.

'What pulled you through?'

'Having that vision,' came the reply.


MIXING MUCK AND MAGIC

Duke and I were out walking early on a sunny October morning. We'd just heard the first thin 'seep' calls of redwings returning from Scandinavia for the winter. As a chunky mixed-breed, Duke needs plenty of exercise. Our dog walks often take us past an old mill beside a chalk escarpment that rises over the pasture like the shape of a beached whale.

I brought Duke to heel on the side of the road as a familiar black truck pulled alongside. It was my neighbour George Atkinson who, wearing his trademark baseball cap, wound down the window. He was keen to share some news.

'We had two pairs of barn owls breed successfully this year!' he said with glee. 'A pair of kestrels too.' The barn owls were the highlight of our banter about local news – the fate of our local cricket team, my wife's pink hair, and the comings and goings in our village. He was bringing me up to date on a conversation earlier in the year.

Tall, energetic and always on the go, George had dropped by for breakfast at our riverside cottage. Leaving his wellies and overalls at the door, he settled in for the longest conversation I'd had with him in years. (Most of our exchanges are snatched moments as he drives past in his pickup or over the garden fence.) He told me he'd just been talking to the local RSPB about why bird numbers have turned round here on his farm despite continued declines across the country. 'So what's the secret?' I asked. 'Well, Philip, it's not rocket science.' He sipped at a big mug of tea. 'Mixed farming in my view. We're lucky we're in an area where you've still got a lot of mixed farms, so consequently there's a huge spin-off for wildlife. It's about putting fertility back into the soil. Then there's all the massive spin-offs in feeding animals outside – insect life and everything else that grows in the crop.'

His farm in the South Downs has been described as an impressive example of how to produce quality food and still find room for nature. He grazes sheep and cattle on a mix of arable and permanent pasture on 1,200 acres of land (five times bigger than the average UK farm) that's been in his family for a hundred years. Twice finalist for his conservation efforts in the national Nature of Farming Award, a competition for wildlife-friendly farmers, run by the RSPB and the *Telegraph* newspaper, he derives huge pleasure from spotting egrets in the mornings, kingfishers by the stream and wild brown trout.

Thanks to a recent survey, he knows all the species on his land.

'I have a record of absolutely everything,' he told me. 'We've got thirty-two different types of butterfly [more than half the total number of species in the country]. . . we've got an orchid and then all the birds and everything else. That kind of excites me.'

He believes that creating a sympathetic environment for wildlife should be part of a modern farmer's role: 'If we can put hand on heart and say, yes, part of your remit as a farmer is to provide food, but also to create an environment that people want to live in or walk on, then that's just as much food for the body as what we put in our mouths.'

He talked about his experience of driving through large parts of the countryside and not seeing any farm animals at all, a sure sign that things are under the steely grip of intensive farming. Does he see a time when farming might get beyond this twentieth-century mode of thinking?

'You are losing the generation that just had to produce food in the Seventies and Eighties . . . It's all about education and people understanding that the two [food production and wildlife] can work together and must work together,' he said. 'I was always brought up to believe that you should try and pass the land on in better heart, and that means everything that goes with it. For the next generation.'

As for the barn owls, 'We've got three around at this time of the year, which is good. My father fortunately had two that nested above his dog kennels for a number of years, and they would raise young, which was amazing.'

Every time I see the flash of a barn owl, whether in a barn, flying over the road, or at the red kite roost, I remember those words and can only agree: Amazing.

# 3

# Bison

'Welcome aboard,' said the sugary-voiced air stewardess over the tannoy. 'We're going to West Yellowstone. If you do *not* want to go to Yellowstone, please let me know.'

Crossing eight states in as many days, I was embarking on a journey to understand how millions of bison on America's Great Plains had given way to cattle and corn. In the days that followed, I would get lost in a sea of genetically modified crops (weirdly disorientating), become infested with cattle ticks (seriously itchy), and find myself swimming in one of the world's largest dead zones (surreal) – water so polluted that it can't support life.

My quest was to see for myself the iconic bison which, along with the bald eagle, has now been designated a national symbol of the USA.[1]

Wild bison were saved from extinction by the establishment of Yellowstone National Park in 1872. It was America's first and is still its largest national park, and its formation coincided with a new concern for conserving the natural world. Encompassing more than 3,400 square miles of subalpine forest, mountains, canyons and river valleys, today the park is home to wolves, bears and eagles and attracts nearly 4 million tourists a year.[2] Located primarily in Wyoming, it extends into Montana and Idaho, and is the centre-piece of the largest unspoilt ecosystem left in the temperate north part of the planet.[3] I was drawn to this unique location on a hunch that the plight of America's bison might shed light on what can happen when industrial farming takes hold of the countryside. Coming at a critical point in the history of America, their demise marked the birth of factory farming.

The tiny airport of West Yellowstone lies in the shadow of great mountains and dense forest, under huge Montana skies. The arrivals hall was small and compact, more like a village hall than an airport. They'd been expecting us – this place has only a couple of flights a day at most. I was handed the keys to our hire car and guided outside to the awaiting vehicle. As I stepped onto the tarmac and sniffed the air, fresh and infused with the smell of pines, I found myself surrounded by mountains and forest, big sky and cool breeze, and was suddenly questioning the wisdom of coming for a couple of days when a week or a month wouldn't do justice to this fantastic place. I am always excited arriving in a new place, but this was something else.

I drove from the airport to the town centre, such as it was. It serves a population of fewer than two thousand.[4] Perhaps it's for the tourists, or perhaps it's how the tiny population of West Yellowstone would have it, even if no outsiders came to this little place, but the businesses lining Main Street looked as if they'd been plucked from a theme park. I wandered past shops and restaurants with names like Beartooth Barbecue, Gray Wolf Inn and Buffalo Spirit. Soon I found the Park visitors' centre, an impressive-looking double-storey chalet. Inside, the walls are adorned with stuffed elk, deer and bison heads. Outside, the American flag flutters proudly in the wind.

'If you're looking for bison out there, be real careful,' the park ranger cautioned. 'Tail up means charge or discharge.' According to her crash course in bison body language, a raised tail either means they're irate or about to poop. 'You should have bear spray with you at all times,' she added, pointing to pepper spray in what looked like a small fire extinguisher. 'Peace of mind in a can.' I couldn't see a downside to arming myself accordingly, and gladly handed over $50 for it.

By now it was mid-afternoon, so I decided to spend some time getting familiar with the place. To help get my bearings, I drove into the park and past endless pines and mountain vistas. Yellow warblers darted in the trees ahead and a Townsend's solitaire, a grey bird with a long tail, sat proudly on an old pine stump.

I drew up quietly beside a hot spring known as Fountain Paint Pot geyser. The earth all around was scorched black, the trees long dead. It looked like a smoking battlefield. Every now and then, the simmering waters would explode with spitting fury, steam streaming away on the wind. The setting sun shimmered through the steam like burning magnesium. This was fire and brimstone all right!

Yellowstone's thermal spring areas are notoriously unpredictable. A thin crust may be all there is above boiling water, and they're not to be messed with. According to the sign boards, more than a dozen people have been scalded to death and many others badly burned. Boardwalks and no-nonsense signs keep tourists from many a lobster's fate.

A little before first light the following day, I sallied forth in the car, armed with my pepper spray, on my quest to find bison. They're big, I thought – about six feet tall and weighing about a tonne each – so it shouldn't be too hard. As a birdwatcher, I'm used to struggling to find tiny little brown jobs in bushes, so spotting a bison would be no sweat. Then again, there was a vast area to cover.

The roads were narrow but well kept. I drove past forests of long pole pine and Douglas fir, the Gallatin Mountain Range etching the skyline. The landscape was extraordinarily varied. Dead pines, stripped to bare bones of trunk and branches, reared up from flat, boggy ground like grey skeletons.

Further along, I saw more hot thermal springs – geysers – that boiled like kettles, the steam gathering in wispy-edged puffs before disappearing into the cool air. A bald eagle with an unmistakable white head flew low over the Madison River. It was not yet dawn. Tiny cinnamon teal dabbled in the shallows. Elk browsed as the first glimmer of sunrise brushed everything with an orange glow.

Eventually, the endless trees gave way to pasture; my bison hunt was on. Just south of a village called Canyon, the moment I'd been waiting for finally arrived: there, grazing contentedly on the grass-land, were two bull bison so close I could hear them munching. Steam streamed from their backs in the early morning sun and puffs of breath dissolved in the cool air as they focused on the serious business of breakfast. They had strongly triangular outlines: tapered at the back and big at the front, accentuated by that charac-teristic massive hump at the shoulders. Their heads were unfeasibly broad, their coats matted and curled. They moved like big bearded men walking on their knuckles. It was a formidable sight.

As I gazed at them, relieved to have found what I'd come all this way to look for, the animal nearest to me suddenly raised his tail. I remembered the ranger's mantra. I wasn't under any illu-sions: I would not be messing with a ton of raging bull. Was he angry? Would he charge? Had he been looking at me with an air of menace, I wouldn't have hung around. As it was, I figured he was more likely to discharge than charge, and thankfully I was right.

North America was once home to several species of bison or 'buffalo'. When threatened, the larger ones tended to react not by running away but by turning on their aggressors using their sheer size and power to defend themselves. This natural instinct served them well for millions of years, but as human weaponry became ever more deadly, what had long been the right thing to do, confronting the hunter head-on, made them very easy prey. They were wiped out.[5]

The bison (*Bison bison*) we know today is more likely to run away than stand and fight. Despite their size, the animals are quick on their feet and can run at speeds of up to 40 miles an hour.[6] They are smaller and more agile than their ancestors. When their ancestors were wiped out, they inherited the Great Plains, endless grasslands that once spanned the continent. Yellowstone boasts the largest public herd of bison in the United States – an estimated five thousand individuals, according to National Park authorities.

Having found two lone males, I went in search of more. I knew there must be a herd, but with so little time and such a vast area to cover, I could not be sure of finding it. I knew the herd might have travelled some distance by now for the mating season, called the rut.

I followed the Yellowstone River through Hayden Valley till the tall pines that escorted me everywhere felt claustrophobic. At Alum Creek they melted away into a beautiful river valley lined with rich pasture. A pair of pearly-white pelicans splashed in the creek, huge orange beaks with pouches like shopping bags collecting fish.

And then an awesome sight that few in North America are lucky enough to see: a magnificent herd of about two hundred bison, grazing by a stream. Calves at foot, they snorted, jostled and rolled in the dust. The coats of the young were ginger, in contrast to the adults' darker brown fur.

It was a glimpse of a bygone age.

A century ago, travellers wrote of seeing countless bison on America's Great Plains. 'I know a million is a great many, but I am confident we saw that number yesterday,' wrote one newspaper editor about bison he had observed from a stagecoach in 1854. During the Civil War, Texas rancher Charles Goodnight described the whole country as being covered with what appeared to be a 'moving brown blanket, the length and breadth of which could not be determined. The number of animals it contained was beyond the human mind to estimate.'[7]

According to historical estimates, around 30–50 million bison once roamed the Great Plains, together with countless elk, deer and other grazing animals.[8] The bison alone weighed, in total, about the same as North America's entire human population today.[9]

Feeding in dense herds and constantly on the move, they were sustained by nothing more than sunlight, rain and grass, returning the nutrients they took from the prairie back to the soil through their droppings. Out on the plains, they seem to have lived harmoniously with humans for millennia. Native Americans hunted them on foot for their meat, hides and bones – but never threatened their numbers.

In the late nineteenth century, however, the teeming herds were depleted to near-extinction within little more than a decade. Slaughtered wholesale by outlaws and military men, they were caught in the crossfire of the battle between the European settlers and indigenous Native Americans. In the eyes of the authorities, as one commander put it, 'every buffalo dead is an Indian gone'.[10] The army armed and protected 'buffalo runners' or 'hide hunters' who used large-calibre guns to shoot as many bison as possible. These market hunters hit the plains en masse, taking hides and tongues. They killed millions, hastening the end of the buffalo on the southern plains by 1877 and the northern plains by 1885.[11]

General Custer, an American cavalry commander during the civil war, and famous for his Last Stand at the Battle of the Little Bighorn where he was killed, was seen as one of the worst bison slaughterers. He earned a reputation for being the 'most ardent and wasteful buffalo hunter'.[12]

'Today the hide hunt and the hide hunters seem utterly foreign to most of us,' writes Dale Lott in his natural history of American bison. 'We wonder what they could have been thinking – no, feeling – that allowed them to kill and waste on that scale.'[13] Lott really summed up for me what was on my mind: how abhorrent it now seems to go wiping out countless millions of large mammals within just years, bringing the animals to the brink of extinction, for no good reason.

By the turn of the century, the last survivors held out in sanctuary refuges like Yellowstone, where they were either protected or hard to find. Out on the Great Plains, they were quickly replaced by cattle. At first the new arrivals grazed freely, but over time they were shunted into feedlots, as the cowboys and wide-open ranches gave way to the plough.

Driven by an ethos of expansion and a sense of autonomy from nature, early ranchers and farmers ploughed up vast areas of prairie. They paid a heavy price for the desecration. By the 1930s, light soils, low rainfall, and high winds had made for a destructive combination. When drought struck, the soil lacked the stronger root system of grass as an anchor. The winds picked up loose topsoil and swirled it into dense dust clouds, called 'black blizzards'.

Dust storms wreaked havoc in America, choking cattle and pastures and driving many off the land.[14] Even the streets of

Washington DC were affected, darkened by a dust cloud that blew up just as Congress prepared for a crucial debate on soil conservation.[15]

High grain prices during the First World War had encouraged farmers to plough up millions of acres of natural grass cover to plant cereals. They worked hard to produce record amounts of crops and animals, creating a surplus that led to a crash in prices. Farmers responded to low prices by producing even more to pay off their debts, taxes and living expenses. By the early 1930s prices were so low that many went bankrupt.[16]

The government was forced to step in with a package of subsidies for struggling farmers during the Great Depression. In 1933, the first Farm Bill was introduced, a multi-billion-dollar deal which included a government scheme to purchase surplus grain for a rainy day. It propped up prices and fuelled production for decades to come.[17] Bolstered by government support, the corn industry boomed and sought new markets. If people couldn't eat more corn, what about their cattle? Cheap, plentiful, and in steady supply, it began to replace grass as the staple diet for farm animals. Instead of grass out on the prairie, cattle would eat the crop that replaced them on the plains – corn.

Early crops grew in soils enriched by many years of natural fertility, leading to bumper harvests, but with bison and cattle gone, and the land increasingly farmed with just one type of crop, the soil quickly became depleted. Fertilisers came to the rescue. Today, those swaying cornfields in the Midwest remain super-productive thanks to heavy doses of fertiliser, mostly from a chemical plant rather than a cow or bison.

More and more cattle have been moved off pasture into so-called feedlots: muddy paddocks, dusty and shadeless in summer, squelching with filth and mud in winter, not a blade of grass in sight. After the Second World War, Britain and Western Europe followed a similar route, pouring billions of taxpayers' money into subsidising agriculture, much of the cereal going to animals reared indoors or in close confinement on industrial farms.

'This tragic sequence has been repeated over and over again in Britain and around the world,' wrote the former agricultural journalist Graham Harvey. 'Sustainable grasslands producing healthy foods are ploughed up in the great global [pursuit] of cereal cropping.'[18]

Yellowstone was an evocative place. And to see so many people getting a real thrill out of seeing bison, wolves and other charismatic wildlife – that was just something else. But my exhilaration was tempered by the realisation that the bison that once roamed the Midwest plains in countless millions have been reduced to refugees in a national park. Just as I had envisaged, it highlighted the way in which the evolution of factory farming traces back to the demise of the Great Plains bison. The herds were wiped out, giving way to cattle and then corn. For millennia, a wonderful, continent-wide, array of flora and fauna was sustained by nothing more than the perennial harvest of the plains: grass. Then it was carpeted with chemical-soaked corn, largely destined to feed cattle, not people. Is that really progress?

## CHILDREN OF THE CORN

Giltner, Nebraska. I was wading through a vast field of GM corn. After a while I became disorientated. The lanky plants towered about my head, sown so densely that I couldn't see anything else ahead of me, or behind. Underfoot, there was no sign of life: no beetles scurrying to avoid my heavy tread, no glimpse of a startled field mouse or vole. Nothing but square mile after square mile of chemical-soaked flat earth.

'I see a flowing green ocean of corn,' said 41-year-old Brandon Hunnicutt as we climbed into his hulking great John Deere tractor. Its tyres were 6 feet tall. His description of the view was flattering. Where he saw a flowing green ocean, my mind's eye saw an environmental catastrophe.

A self-confessed tech-geek, Hunnicutt tapped away at his tractor's computer, allowing it to steer itself. These days, some agricultural vehicles have more software than early space shuttles.[19] 'Some people listen to music in the tractors, others drink wine, watch movies,' Hunnicutt explained.

He and his wife Lisa live in a clapboard farmhouse with their seven children and Rockstar the dog. While we were talking, his dog cocked his leg at my bag. 'Well,' I said with an awkward smile: 'At least I can say it's been peed on by a rockstar!'

Hunnicutt guffawed apologetically – he's used to rough-and-ready.

The 2,600-acre farm has been in his family for over 100 years. Today, all those acres are dedicated to soya and corn. 'So where are all the buffalo?' I asked playfully. He laughed: 'They're long gone.'

The cornbelt state of Nebraska is America's third-biggest corn producer. The industry is worth $7 billion dollars a year.[20] 'It kind of encompasses everything . . . It drives the economy of the state,' Hunnicutt told me. He spoke with the authority of one who sits on Nebraska's Corn Board.

A third of the world's corn is produced in the US, with much of it going to feed pigs, poultry and cattle.[21] More than 90 million acres of the US are blanketed in corn crops, mainly in the Midwest heartland states including Iowa, Illinois and Nebraska.[22]

'There's been this long-standing love affair with cattle in the state,' said Hunnicutt. They're part of the 'golden triangle' in Nebraska: ethanol, corn and cattle. He estimates that some 40 per cent of the crop is fed to cattle, and about the same amount goes on ethanol biofuel for the new grain-guzzling kid on the block – cars. 'Gas' stations (petrol stations to Brits) in the US now commonly have petrol pumps where the fuel is mixed with bioethanol from corn. 'Total use of corn and corn products for cattle is a little bit higher than it is for ethanol,' he told me. About a fifth of what is produced in Nebraska goes to the human food market, proportions that are similar for the entire national crop.[23]

Nearly all corn production here is genetically modified. I asked about the benefit of GM over conventional corn. 'Using GM to feed the world really allows us to concentrate on making sure we're producing high-yielding, high-quality crops,' Hunnicutt enthused.

It wasn't the first time I'd heard 'feeding the world' as the justification for industrial farming. The claim always makes me wince.

It's something I've heard time and again from industry leaders
and their spokespeople far and wide, so no wonder it's become
so ingrained. Yet it's all too easy to cite platitudes about the challenge of feeding the burgeoning human population as a cover for
business as usual, or even more industrial farming. The suggestion that increased production will safeguard future generations
from the hunger and malnutrition that already ravages parts of the
world seems highly questionable. Particularly when hunger today
is primarily a result of distributional problems, yet is relentlessly
trotted out by food producers and policymakers who have too
many vested interests, or simply don't ask if the suggestion bears
scrutiny.

Putting the rocket-boosters under production worked in the
1960s, a time when there was a genuine mismatch between agricultural supply and demand. As I've heard Olivier De Schutter argue
when he was UN Special Rapporteur on the right to food, policymakers at the time had three options: address population growth;
tackle runaway consumption, particularly in the West; or look to
technology for answers.

Wary of being seen to be telling people what to eat, Western
policymakers preferred not to have a debate over consumption.
Nor was there any appetite for a debate over population control,
a political taboo. Technology was seen as the lone saviour – and it
delivered spectacular success, to the point where far more food is
produced today than is needed.

De Schutter, a strong proponent for the need for a different food
system without industrial agriculture, was explaining why things
worked out in the 1960s but may well not do so again if we simply
try to address today's problems with the thinking of half a century
ago. The production-centred approach from the 1960s has been
'locked in' by the plethora of business interests that stand to benefit: chemical companies peddling fertilisers and pesticides; drug
companies with their growth-promoters and disease-suppressants;
breeders, grain traders, supermarkets, fast-food chains, and of

course equipment manufacturers like John Deere. The company's eponymous founder invented the steel plough in 1837, replacing the old-fashioned wooden or iron ploughs that had always struggled with the rich, sticky prairie soils of America's Midwest. This new piece of kit aided migration to the Great Plains.[24]

Fast-forward to today and we find ourselves in a world still struggling to feed everyone. Of a global population of over 7 billion, about a billion still go hungry. With numbers expected to increase to 9 or 10 billion by mid-century, it's easy to see why some put their faith in making the production wheel spin faster. With greater production comes more demand for agricultural chemicals, veterinary drugs, machinery and so on.

Yet, as I showed in my book *Farmageddon*, and as we'll explore in a later chapter, we already produce enough food for twice the human population today: more than enough for everyone both now and in the foreseeable future.[25] The trouble is that much of it is wasted.

In developing countries, it happens not out of choice but out of sheer poverty, like the inability to invest in a decent grain store to stop cereals rotting, or a transport system to get food to market before it's past its best. In the developed world, food is wasted in our homes, in our supermarkets and restaurants. All the way along the food chain, we seem to have fostered a throwaway culture. Tristram Stuart, a leading authority on food waste, points out that up to 40 per cent of UK fruit and vegetables are rejected even before they reach the shops – mostly because they do not match the supermarkets' pointlessly strict cosmetic standards.[26] We're not much better when it comes to meat; EU countries alone waste the meat equivalent of nearly 2 billion farm animals a year – reared, slaughtered and binned.[27]

Yet the biggest single area of food waste on the planet is the diversion of arable crops fit for human consumption to industrially reared animals like cattle. The amount of global land currently used to grow grain crops like corn and soya for farm animals is equivalent to a single field covering half the land surface of the USA, or the entire European Union. Worldwide, if the grain-fed animals were restored to pasture and the cereals and soya went to people instead, there would be enough for an extra 4 billion folk.

In a sense, we could have our cake and eat it: animals kept on pasture, where they can forage, turning something we can't eat – grass – into something we can – meat, milk and eggs. With pasture covering about a quarter of the Earth's land surface, there is plenty of scope for doing this, bearing in mind that there is nothing 'space-saving' or efficient about housing animals in barns and then taking food to them, often over distances of thousands of miles.

In the conversion to meat and milk, much of the food value of grain is lost by animals in the simple act of living. Some two-thirds of the potential food value or calories of grain is lost in the process of converting it, through animals, to meat, milk and eggs.[28]

Beef has the worst conversion rate. According to a study by the University of Minnesota, for every hundred calories fed in the form of grain, as little as 3 per cent are returned in the resulting meat.[29] The picture in relation to protein is little better. The same study found that for every 100 grams of grain protein fed to animals, we receive only about 43 grams of protein from milk, 35 from eggs, 40 from chicken, 10 from pork, or 5 from beef.

The UN Food and Agriculture Organisation (FAO) has said: 'When livestock are raised in intensive systems, they convert carbo-hydrates and protein that might otherwise be eaten directly by humans and use them to produce a smaller quantity of energy and protein. In these situations, livestock can be said to reduce the food balance.'[30]

The phrase 'reduce the food balance' is political speak for 'wasted'.

And so, more than two-thirds of the available calories of huge tracts of land are being lost. These fields are industrial farming's 'ghost acres'. That's not to say that we should all turn vegan. Instead, farm animals like cattle could be kept on the pastures that cover so much of the land's surface, leaving precious arable land free to grow food rather than animal feed.

Such change requires looking at agricultural efficiency in a different way. Researchers at the University of Minnesota recently produced a paper calling for a rethink in the way production is measured. Instead of assessing efficiency in terms of the amount produced per unit of land (tonnes per hectare), they argue that efficiency should be measured in terms of how many people are being fed by a given piece of land, the number of people fed per hectare. When they assessed how many people are currently being fed per hectare, they concluded that the figure is far smaller than it could be: six per hectare, against a potential ten.[31] In the USA, the spiritual home of industrial agriculture, croplands produce enough to feed as many as sixteen people per hectare. Yet in these terms, America is one of the least efficient producers, feeding less than six.[32]

The balance of food in these examples is lost in converting grain to meat and milk in much the same way as food is lost if we throw it in the dustbin.

A recent paper by the think tank Chatham House describes feeding cereals to animals as 'staggeringly inefficient'.[33]

This view is echoed by the International Institute for Environment and Development, which says that using cropland to produce corn and other crops for animal feed rather than direct for human consumption is 'colossally inefficient'.

Olivier De Schutter, former UN Rapporteur, has called for feed grains to be reallocated for consumption by people, arguing that 'continuing to feed cereals to growing numbers of livestock will aggravate poverty and environmental degradation'. Yet the trend is toward keeping more animals in grain-fed confinement rather than less, as I saw when I travelled across the Great Plains.

I saw numerous factory farms along the way from Denver, Colorado. I counted a dozen grubby warehouses alongside the Interstate Highway – all lined with giant fans. They were most likely home to tens of thousands of caged hens. I also passed endless sage brush and rough pasture with barely an animal on it. Further along the route we hit mega-dairy land – farms with a thousand or more cows. The animals we saw were black and white milk machines as thin as hat-racks, jostling for space on grassless, muddy paddocks. Crowded together in a long line, they munched listlessly from a feed trough.

By mid-afternoon I'd crossed the state line into Nebraska, part of the once Great Plains of Midwest America. Here the land was flatter and the road worse. Nebraska is America's biggest state producer of so-called feedlot cattle – animals reared for beef in confined feeding operations. Some two and a half million cattle are fattened on grain, rather than grass, in this way.[34] At $12 billion a year, the state's cattle industry is even bigger than corn.[35]

I had seen it all before in Argentina, a country with a worldwide reputation for producing wonderful steak, when I was researching my last book, *Farmageddon*. That reputation is largely built on a lie, for what the beef restaurant diners imagine comes from animals that once grazed freely on the pampas, often comes from those raised on the equivalent of battery farms.

It wasn't long before I had my first taste of the Nebraskan version of these farms – which were much the same as those I'd seen in South America. A thousand cattle stood motionless in muddy paddocks. An eerie hush hung over the place, as if in a hospital ward, broken only by the odd cough, sneeze or wail. Some were big, some were small. Clear shiny fluid ran from the nose of a coughing black calf. I noticed some of the animals discharging strangely runny cowpats. All stood in the hot sun, without an inch of shade. Desperate for relief, they tried lying in each other's shadow. The stench was overpowering, a heady mix of cow dung, mud and corn. Although this was an open-air feedlot, the smell soon caught the back of my throat.

The signs around here suggested this was 'cowboy' country. Yet there was no need for Stetsons on horseback, no roundups required. These cattle were going nowhere fast.

And why are the cattle kept this way? Essentially, to make them grow faster.

Further up the highway, I came across another feedlot. Confined cattle stretched along the road for half a mile. Again they were eerily quiet, and swarming with flies. Whenever the herd shuffled a little, the mass of flies around their feet went crazy, zigzagging like a thick dust cloud. I wasn't there long, just watching from the roadside, but as I drove away, I found myself crawling with ticks.

It had been a depressing drive. These days, most consumers know something of the misery of battery cages for hens, but there is little public awareness of the appalling conditions in which factory-farmed cattle live out their lives. I couldn't help feeling that beef from cattle reared in this way should carry the same stigma as battery-produced eggs. Reflecting on how farming trends starting in the US often make it across to Britain, I decided to stop at a roadside convenience store for some sort of refreshment. I was about to learn a lesson in regional variation.

All I wanted was a bottle of plain old water and an ice lolly. As there was no one else in the shop, I thought I'd just check with the shopkeeper that I'd chosen the right thing:

'Is this *still* water?' I asked, checking it wasn't carbonated.

'*What?*' he asked irritably.

'Is this water flat?'

'What *do* ya mean?' he said, sounding even more annoyed.

'Has it got gas?' I asked evenly, doing my best not to sound as if his tone was getting to me.

'Gas? We got *plenty* of gas!' he said, pointing to the petrol pumps. 'Do ya want some?'

'No, no, just water . . .' I sighed.

'That's OK then', he said, sounding relieved. 'That's what ya got . . .'

Two nations still occasionally divided by a common language . . .

Outside the gas station were clusters of space-rocket-like steel grain silos. Gleaming in the sun, they would not have looked out of place on the set of a Bond movie. I saw them all over rural Nebraska, but they were dwarfed by what I was about to encounter.

A feedmill by the railway in Gothenburg, County Dawson, Nebraska was so enormous and complex it might have been a NASA installation. Cylindrical towers as tall as a high-rise block of flats loomed over the biggest grain silos I'd ever seen. Against the setting sun, they were an awe-inspiring sight, giants next to the standard-sized warehouses and silos which sprawled away from the railroad.

Nearby, a monstrous long snake of a goods train waited for the weekend to end. As another train passed with an ear-piercing klaxon blast, I clambered up the ladder on a stationary carriage for a better look. This was what Hunnicutt had described as a 'high-speed load-out facility' train.

As I walked through the deserted agri-industrial complex as the sun went down on a Sunday evening, I found it strangely atmospheric. That dusty smell of grain hanging everywhere. A tributary of railway line bent away through scattered storage buildings. This, I thought, is what keeps it all on track. Corn, soya, wheat and so on, distributed from here through the nation's arteries, much of it to satisfy the world's hunger for cheap beef.

## BISON, BEWARE OF THE BURGERS

'A cold wind blew across the prairie when the last buffalo fell . . . a deathwind for my people,' said the legendary Native American chief Sitting Bull. He had led the Sioux tribes in their bitter struggle for survival on North America's Great Plains following the discovery of gold in the Black Hills of South Dakota in 1874. At first he was successful in the Great Sioux Wars, which culminated in the battle of the Little Bighorn in 1876, in which he and the legend-ary tribal chief Crazy Horse and a confederation of tribes saw off federal troops. Eventually, however, he and his people were forced onto a reservation, and Sitting Bull himself was shot dead by US forces hell-bent on maintaining control of the land.

The demise of the Great Plains bison is a poignant chapter in this fascinating period of American history.

Today bison appear to be bouncing back. According to the National Bison Association, there are now some 340,000 in North America.[36]

'Saving wild bison requires humans to learn to eat wild bison,' according to Yellowstone's bison project leader, Rick Wallen. He isn't alone. Most people with whom I spoke while on this trip felt that eating them was a good idea.

On the face of it, it sounds like a win–win solution – particu-larly as bison meat is reputed to be healthier. The American Heart Association lists lean cuts of buffalo meat amongst its 'healthy eating' choices.[37] But scratch beneath the surface, and you find that by far the most bison meat sold for consumption in America today comes from animals reared on farms and ranches, of which there are more than 2,500.[38] There are only around 15,000 truly wild bison in North America – meaning that the species is approaching threatened status.[39]

'Very few bison burgers come from wild bison,' Wallen admitted. 'There is a huge industry to produce bison.'

Some are reared on huge ranches where they can roam in much the way nature intended, but others are reared like cattle in feedlots. Andrew Gunther of the American-based food assurance scheme Animal Welfare Approved has told how these wild animals are fundamentally ill-adapted for life in the captivity of an industrial farm. They have not evolved for such conditions. 'I saw thousands of these undomesticated animals react as their natural behaviour dictated they should to any threat,' he reported. 'They stood unmoving in defensive circles. When they did move, only to eat and drink, the closely packed feedlot left them unable to fight off any parasitic challenges and many required pharmaceutical treatments.'[40] They were fed corn.

Knowing whether bison burgers come from a ranch or a feedlot is a mug's game. More often than not, there's no way of telling from the label. Food labels in the US don't have to say how the meat was produced. The same is true in Europe. So unless there's a specific phrase on the packaging, like 'pasture-fed,' 'grass-fed' or 'organic', the assumption should be that it has been intensively produced. After all, farmers who have invested in rearing animals more naturally have no reason not to proclaim it on the packet.

Everywhere I went in the Midwest, bison was on offer. With its distinctive bison logo, the most conspicuous outlet was Ted's Montana Grill. According to the menu, they serve the largest selection of bison dishes you'll find anywhere. Bison nachos, bison meatloaf, bison short ribs, bison chilli and, of course, the ubiquitous bison burger. All served 'bold and unapologetic . . . no matter what'. The company website boasts how its founders 'pioneered the effort to preserve the American bison by returning it to America's table', saving the species from extinction. They make much of their environmental credentials, and how hard they work to 'do the right thing for our guests, our people and our planet'. The company website says that 'sustainability' is 'intrinsic' to the food it serves and talks about 'leading the way in solar energy', and how bison are a natural part of the North American ecosystem, therefore 'bison ranching can also be beneficial to the environment'.[41]

However, I was unable to find out how the bison that went into Ted's Montana Grill's food products were reared, despite scouring the menu, looking through their website and contacting them directly. Instead, the company responded to my query about whether the meat on their menu comes from wild bison, or those raised in pasture or grain-fed in feedlots, by referring me to the National Bison Association. According to the NBA's Executive Director, Dave Carter, all the bison meat in the marketplace comes from 'commercial' ranches rather than genuinely wild herds. About a quarter of the animals are estimated to be purely pasture-fed; the rest are fed grain.

The general suggestion that eating bison saves the species therefore seems questionable. Especially as some bison burgers come from 'beefalo', bison cross-bred with cattle. In any case, rearing these animals in the misery of feedlots is a dismal way to safeguard their future. I can't help feeling that if they're farmed, they're no longer wild – and thus the system is essentially preserving a different type of beast, wholly for the purposes of consumption.

'Why on earth do we want to put bison in feedlots just to make it more like beef?' Gunther has asked. Given the consequences of forcing domesticated animals into unnatural industrialised farming systems, he wondered, 'do we seriously need to do the same to a wild animal?'

Where they do remain, wild bison can come into conflict with communities and cattle ranchers. The oldest and biggest wild bison herd in Yellowstone is a case in point. Ranchers who work land that borders the park worry that they pose a risk of disease to cattle, specifically the nasty bacterial condition brucellosis. About half Yellowstone's bison are thought to have been exposed to this disease, probably from cattle that once grazed there. The condition can cause miscarriages in cows, but has been virtually eradicated in the cattle population surrounding the park. 'Brucellosis-free' status means that ranchers can sell cattle across state lines without tests, quarantine or vaccination, and is thus highly prized.

Understandably, ranchers get particularly exercised when wild bison stray beyond the park's confines. Yellowstone is tiny relative to the wide-open pasture their ancestors roamed. These habitual wanderers are now shoehorned into a park of pine forest, mountains and woodland pasture. When the grass is growing, the pickings are good enough. Come winter, however, food stretches thin, and the animals often head north and out of the park in search of food.

'Truant bison are harvested on sight,' one cattle rancher told me, using a sanitised word for killed. He'd seen off several bison himself in recent years. 'We shot 'em,' he said bluntly.

As well as allowing ranchers to shoot those that stray onto their land, Yellowstone operates a formal cull to keep numbers in check, based on a long-standing management plan hammered out between federal and state wildlife agencies and agricultural interests. This sets the target of the Yellowstone population at about 3,500 bison.[42]

'The need to cull Yellowstone bison is a testament to how successful we have been at restoring wild bison to this landscape,' Rick Wallen told me. Sporting a big beard and clad in a khaki ranger's uniform, complete with brimmed hat, Wallen was standing outside his grand stone office flanked by bear statues in Mammoth Hot Springs. He explained that bison numbers were managed primarily by hunting individuals that wander outside the national park. 'But we need to supplement hunting with actual capturing and removal,' he told me, referring to the way in which several hundred bison are caught by the Park at its Stephens Creek facility and shipped for slaughter.[43]

The cull divides local opinion, as I found out when talking to people in the area.

'These buffalo are pretty docile, but they do cause damage. My son had his car damaged [by a migrating bison],' said Don Laubach who runs a local business making hunting equipment.

Other locals see it differently. Talking with photographer Chris Thomas in his shop, he explained how he's uncomfortable with wild bison being killed simply because they are following their instincts to search for food, as they have done for thousands of years. 'They're heading towards their winter ground, but they're not going to make it. It's sad to see,' he said.

Yellowstone's bison seem to have become an example of big-country claustrophobia: a troubling state of affairs in which wide-open spaces are no longer big enough to sustain charismatic megafauna. I saw this in South Africa's national parks, where vast wilderness supports a surprisingly small number of large animals. I saw it here in Yellowstone, where really small numbers of bison – a tiny fraction of the original herd – remain under constant threat of cull.

I couldn't help thinking that the bison in Yellowstone were more like refugees or museum pieces than part of the landscape. They were holed up in the sanctuary with nowhere else to go. And in their plight lies a bigger lesson: that if we're not to look back on a world where the wild things were, then we'll need to learn to live better with them side by side, to make them part of living landscapes where wildlife and food production coexist to the benefit of all.

## TAKING CARE OF THE LITTLE GUYS

In the shadow of Yellowstone and the Centennial Mountains the sweep of the intermountain grassland stretches as far as the eye can see. It is rich pasture with a riot of different grasses, herbs and wild flowers under a limitless sky. From my vantage point by a dirt road taking a break, I could see a single homestead – a pretty, wooden affair – by a fishing lake. In the distance were hills, swathed in forest.

I was now in Rexburg, Idaho, not far from Yellowstone, to find out more about how bison, cattle and corn can coexist harmoniously on today's Great Plains.

Jim Hagenbarth, a lifelong cattle rancher whose family has worked this land for well over a century, prides himself on looking to nature to provide all the food his animals need.

'This is good summer country,' he tells me. 'Very good grass, you put a lot of weight on the cattle.'

Today, the 66-year-old and his brother raise 5,000 cattle for standard beef, rather than the premium types like organic. Although they use hormone-growth promoters to boost the growth rate of the cattle, mainly for economic reasons, in every other respect they feel they're doing as much as possible to rear the animals as nature intended.

Hagenbarth greeted me warmly in his straw Stetson and was soon telling me off for referring to his land as a farm.

'It's a ranch. You don't have ranches in England because you don't have the wide-open space,' he teased.

He's been putting the cattle here 'back to work', converting grassland into meat. They are given very little supplement – just hay. I asked if they were ever given grain on his farm, and he shook his head scornfully. 'They get heavy enough without grain,' he replied.

Hagenbarth is big on rotation and light on chemicals. His land is sprayed with herbicides once every two decades at most. 'This hasn't been sprayed for forty years,' he told me proudly.

He showed me a field on which black cattle with calves at foot grazed happily. It was a mass of mountain sage, wildflowers and grass. The fluttering orange of a monarch butterfly caught my eye.

The space and wide-open grassy vistas were so different to the feedlots in Nebraska. I was disappointed when Hagenbarth told me he sends some of his cattle to feedlots for 'finishing'. The industry seems to be in a tangle, dumbing down some of the best pasture-fed ranch beef on corn before it ends up on supermarket shelves. It's the way the industry is set up now and few seem to question it. He goes with the flow because that's what makes the economics work for his business. No wonder consumers are confused.

For all his small part in it, Hagenbarth remains worried about the corn culture: 'I'm very concerned about the stature that corn has taken in our society today. It's almost at the point where they're destroying some of the most fertile soil we have using fertilisers on hybrid corn to feed cars and cattle instead of raising food for people.' It's 'unfathomable', he said. 'We need sustainable agriculture. We don't need to be pouring all these fertilisers on to burn the soil, destroying it.'

Corn needs a lot of nutrients. In the monocultures of today's Great Plains, there are no bison or cattle to replenish the soil, so artificial fertilisers fill the breach. And there you have a dangerous cocktail. Lots of nutrient fertilisers on tired soils leaves them vulnerable to heavy rain washing both soil and nutrients into rivers, lakes and streams. As we will find in the next chapter, this often has devastating consequences.

When the Great Plains were covered in grass, the root system was sufficiently thick and complex to equip the earth to cope with both drought and flood. It allowed plants to root further down when times were dry, and held water like a sponge when there was a deluge. This made the terrain very resilient. Now we have swapped millions of bison on a self-sufficient landscape for millions of feedlot cattle dependent on corn monocultures.

Some argue that returning free-ranging bison to the plains is a step too far, especially as there's so little left that's free from either crops or fences. However, there are more and more calls for farming to coexist with wildlife, for nature to be part of the farming system rather than banished from it. Whilst it may be too late for bison, there is still time to save birds, bees and smaller mammals from the same plight.

Hagenbarth sees great importance in what he describes as the 'little guys'. We both poked at a cowpat with a big stick. Dung beetles – all black with russet stripes – scuttled away. They'd been hard at work fertilising the soil with poo. 'These are "the little guys" that make things work,' he told me, referring to insects, birds, bees and the like. 'We don't pay enough attention to them. And if we lose those, we're done.'

In the nineteenth century, nature was seen as a fount of endless bounty, an untamed wilderness that needed bringing under control. Wild animals became a source of sport and fascination. Those that weren't shot were put into zoos.

The twentieth century saw a rising awareness about the need for conservation. Society began sensing the limits of nature: that if not properly stewarded, things would die out. Species were lapsing into marked decline and habitats disappearing. Buying up parcels of land to conserve national treasures for some became quite fashionable. As a schoolboy conservationist, I was very taken with the idea myself.

Huge efforts were made to preserve endangered species in nature reserves as if they were living artefacts in a museum. Most energy was expended on unusual habitats and rare species that rely on those unique environments. The logic was that common creatures didn't need any help – after all, they were common.

History proved the approach that took 'common' species for granted was fundamentally flawed. Over the last half-century, populations of many previously common species have crashed. As industrial farming spreads across whole landscapes, the way it has done in the American Midwest, wildlife – whether it be birds, bees or bison – has inevitably been squeezed out.

The truth is, we've underestimated the impact of agriculture on everything else. After all, it has always *sounded* so benign. People imagine swaying fields of barley, cows in buttercup meadows, farmers at the heart of our green and pleasant land, selflessly providing the nation with 'natural' 'wholesome' food. The myth is entirely outdated, but it suits the industry to perpetuate it. Furthermore, some of the most insidious aspects of industrial agriculture – growing a single crop on vast swathes of land, over and over again – may not jump out to the untrained eye. Casual observers can be forgiven for thinking that endless fields of golden corn are a thing of beauty. Driving through the English countryside, or looking out of the window while whizzing along by train, who can see that soils are tired or that fertiliser is running off into rivers? Who can tell that those gorgeous chocolate-brown ploughed fields that look so rich and fertile are sown with seeds laced with chemicals that kill birds? Who notices that there are hardly any farm animals except sheep and horses left on the land?

When agricultural activity dominates much of the land mass of countries and continents, what happens on that land matters to so much else. Only now are we truly coming to realise that those animals and plants are integral to an ecosystem on which we all depend.

# 4

# Shrimp

New Orleans was hot and sticky. I had expected it to be humid – that stifling feeling of a brewing thunderstorm you sometimes get in Britain on the hottest of days – but I wasn't quite prepared for the sultry sweatiness of the Deep South. It was gone nine o'clock in the evening and I had just arrived off the plane from London.

Nighthawks, shadowy night birds, croaked like frogs above a Walmart car park where I'd stopped to pick up something to eat. I wasn't expecting much if anything to be available at the cheap hotel where I was to be staying with Katie and Leah, my crew for the trip.

Though I was excited to be in New Orleans, there was no time to visit the tourist hot spots. Grabbing some snacks from the supermarket, we headed past a succession of neon-lit drive-throughs and diners and finally pulled up at our shabby budget motel. My companions were unimpressed. The night porter did little to improve our flagging spirits, laboriously scanning our details on the computer as if it were no matter whether we all whiled away the whole evening standing at the front desk.

'Where's Tina?' he asked eventually, fixing me with a critical stare.

'Not here,' I replied patiently. 'She's my secretary and made the booking but she's not with us.' He looked at me sceptically, then took my passport and stared for another age at his computer. A guy behind us in the queue advised us not to take it personally: 'He's always like this. Slow.' I tried not to let the irritation show, but it had already been a very long day. I could feel my hackles rising.

Eventually, we made it to our rooms. I was too tired to care about the absence of creature comforts, and crashed out into jetlag dreams. Two days later, our instincts about this grotty place proved right. Our camerawoman returned from a day out in the field to find her room door wide open, lights on. Luckily, we knew better than to leave anything worth stealing in such a place.

The drive from the motel to the harbour where I was to pick up a boat was unremarkable, but not so the sea. Soon I was 15 miles out in the Gulf of Mexico looking at something that resembled a construction site. All around me were oil rigs. Some were huge tangles of scaffolding and metal beams; others resembled small cities. It was blistering hot and the sea was eerily quiet as our boat lilted gently by the yellow and rust of one of the rigs. Every few seconds, a foghorn blast jolted the senses. I felt as if I were on a film set.

I'd heard a lot about this place in the media: somewhere out to sea where nothing lives. It is called the 'dead zone', an expanse of water so polluted that nearly all the oxygen is gone. This liquid symbol of what happens when efforts to prevent, mitigate or contain environmental damage fail represents the worst-case scenario: the marine 'end of days'. Sadly the dead zone in the Gulf of Mexico is not unique – they exist all over the world – but among biologists, marine scientists and conservationists, it is among the most notorious.

Against my better judgement, I was preparing, quite literally, to get down and dirty. My plan was to see the dead zone for myself – and not from the nice clean comfort of a boat. Snorkel fixed, I steadied myself and slipped into the water, clad only in trunks and a snorkel mask. Treading water, the pleasant cool of the ocean was sweet relief from the searing heat. At surface level, the pea-green sea looked nothing out of the ordinary, though I wasn't exactly thrilled when I accidentally took a gulp of the water.

'I hope it's not polluted!' I spluttered lamely, then ducked below the waves.

I slipped a few metres through the water, peering into the gloom below. Almost as soon as my eyes adjusted, I could see fish – in hordes. Through the murk I detected shoals of grey angel fish – spadefish – darting in and out of the rig. Smaller fish flitted happily amongst the barnacle shells, looking perfectly at home. A whirling shoal of silver tiddlers right above me splashed through the surface. Why all these fish in a dead zone? And why were those silver ones moving so fast? Then the terrifying shape of something bigger hove into view – a shark, or so I thought. I held my breath, braced for what could come next. Was I going to end up dying in a dead zone?

By now I was anxiously bobbing on the surface. A fellow diver cried out: it was a cobia, not a shark! To the untrained eye of a nervous British snorkeller, the elongated creature with its pointy nose and jagged grey and black fins had looked alarmingly like a man-eater. I hadn't thought to check if there were sharks in these waters. It was a dead zone after all.

As I swam to the surface, the water around me seemed very much alive. Had there been some mistake? Were we in the wrong patch of water? I ducked below again, holding my breath this time, and swimming down. Now things started to grow clearer – or rather not.

A few metres beneath the surface, everything changed. The water was cooler, saltier, and far more murky. Already I could see very little, and without diving kit I could go no further. I wouldn't reach the dead zone itself, for it was far, far below, coating the bottom half of the water in a suffocating blanket. Swimming in the actual dead zone was an experience I could live without – I had already learned a lot from my dip below the waves. My plan was to accompany someone who knew what they were doing on a dive into the deep.

Nancy Rabalais, executive director and professor at Louisiana University's Marine Consortium, was the obvious escort for such a trip. Marine ecologist and 'Gulf champion', she has spent decades mapping the dead zone that forms off Louisiana's coast, and was the first scientist to document its evolution. Her work is seen as having been critical in focusing attention on this important environmental issue. She has made countless visits and knows this region better than anyone else.[1]

'When you dive down through the dead zone in summer you find it greenish on the surface, murky brownish at the bottom and clear in between,' she told me.

In all, Rabalais has been diving for forty-six years, and has been taking samples of the water here since the mid-1980s, a decade before fishermen and scientists began noticing the seasonal bouts of death by suffocation amongst marine life.

I joined her and her dive team for the day, setting sail for one of her monitoring zones in a 12-metre catamaran called the *Gadwall*. As she pulled on her wetsuit I couldn't help noticing a scar running down her spine. She told me how it happened: a few years ago, she had broken her back in a swimming accident. Undeterred, she set herself the goal of diving again within a year, and she did. Today, she takes that same determination into the Gulf where she is pressing for urgent environmental change.

The dead zone starts 4 miles or so offshore. On the way out, we zoomed past a couple of shrimp boats, perhaps a hundred feet long with outrigger booms. The Gulf is a major fishery for shrimp and other marine life, and provides about a sixth of the total US seafood catch. The shrimp fishery alone is worth half a billion dollars a year and some 5,000 boats rely on it for a living.

Nutrients in the ocean feed the microscopic phytoplankton eaten by shrimp and the small fish, which are in turn eaten by the big fish, but something is upsetting this ancient food chain, and the fragile balance of nutrients that makes the area so productive. In recent decades, levels of nutrients in the Gulf have been rising, causing phytoplankton to 'bloom' – to multiply and die in such vast quantities that their decay sucks nearly all of the oxygen out of the water. The gathering body of oxygen-depleted – 'hypoxic' – water forms a barrier to life, killing just about everything that can't flee in time.

The Gulf of Mexico now boasts the world's second-largest area of oxygen-depleted water (the Baltic hosts the biggest in the world).

It's a squalid claim to fame. The zone emerges every year, without fail, from February to October, stretching all the way from the
shores of Louisiana to the upper Texan coast.[2] Covering an area the
size of the states of Connecticut and Rhode Island combined (or
nearly the size of a country like Wales), this lifeless bottom layer of
ocean has made the Gulf synonymous with the term 'dead zone'[3]
as it loses the oxygen below and drives anything alive towards the
surface. It is as if there were a city packed with high-rise apartment
blocks, and every year their bottom halves were gassed and subject
to emergency evacuations.

As the dead zone spreads, some bottom-dwelling fish are forced
to the surface, where they are vulnerable to predators; some may flee
the area; and the rest just die. 'Some fish live on the surface, others
normally live on the bottom,' Rabalais explained. 'The bottom-
dwellers are not down there today' – she pointed over the side of
the catamaran. 'They're either near the surface or gone. I've been
on shore before on a small boat and seen schools of stingrays at the
surface, not where they normally live but at the surface, as if they
are moving inshore to get out of the way of the low oxygen. I've
seen animals swimming at the surface that shouldn't be . . . trying
to escape the low oxygen. Some of them don't make it.'

As bottom-dwellers, shrimp take a heavy hit. Shrimp trawlers
use 'tickler' chains to disturb them from the seabed and into their
nets, a practice whose assault on the seabed has been likened by
environmentalists to 'harvesting corn with bulldozers that scoop
up topsoil and cornstalks along with the ears'.[4]

There are no shrimp in the dead zone, and so the trawlers mass
along the edges, to catch fugitive survivors. The anoxic barrier
disrupts the shrimp's migratory patterns. Normally, they head back
to the ocean when their food supply on the coast runs out and
continue to grow at sea until ready to breed. Thanks to the dead
zone, however, some are forced out into deeper colder waters, where
they grow slowly. Others are held at bay in the shallower warmer
bays, where they overeat their food supply.

With a huge section of the Gulf now a shrimp no-go zone, the
environmental onslaught is hitting the fishing industry where it

hurts. Shrimpers must travel further to find their quarry. The catch is declining and fishermen have been forced out of business.[5] 'You just gotta keep going miles and miles and miles, and hopefully you'll run into something,' one shrimper told CNN. 'The fuel costs are so high, it's just not feasible to get out there unless you can catch a boatload.' In the same report, a Louisiana seafood processor told how his livelihood has been affected by the growth of the dead zone: 'This is the prime shrimping ground in the country right here, and it shut us down. It just shut us down. It's unreal.'[6]

The US government's scientific agency, the National Oceanic and Atmospheric Administration (NOAA), estimates the dead zone to cost US seafood and tourism industries $82 million a year, a significant blow to the Gulf Coast economy.[7] But for all the pain it is causing, since the first dead-zone action plan was hammered out in 1981, the problem has continued to escalate. In 2015, the area of low to no oxygen water or 'hypoxia' covered 6,474 square miles, three times the 1,900-square-mile goal set by the Hypoxia Task Force in 2001.[8]

And the main culprit? Fertiliser. According to the NOAA, the source of the problem are those 'flowing green oceans' of corn I saw in Nebraska that also carpet the rest of the Midwest. In a report entitled *The Causes of Hypoxia in the Northern Gulf of Mexico*, the NOAA describes this part of the USA as 'an area of intensive corn and soybean production, where large amounts of nitrogen from fertiliser and manure are applied to soils every year'. The agency report explains how excess nitrate is washed into rivers and streams and ends up in the Gulf; it describes the scientific evidence as 'overwhelming'.[9]

In May 2015, some 104,000 metric tons of nitrate and 19,300 metric tons of phosphorus flowed down the Mississippi and Atchafalaya rivers into the Gulf of Mexico.[10] It is as if a flotilla of more than 4,000 shipping containers or 3,000 heavy goods vehicles headed downriver in just one month, fully loaded with pollution.

Since the authorities agree that agriculture is fairly and squarely to blame, why not do more to curb the industry's excesses?[11] 'Oh, that's just history,' Rabalais shrugs, with a hint of frustration.

'I mean, that's what feeds the world [intensive corn and soya], right? Only they're not feeding the world, they're feeding chickens and hogs . . .'

Of all people, I need no persuading, but Rabalais spelled out how problems in the Gulf are linked to the food on our plate. If we eat more meat, then there's likely to be more corn grown for animal feed, more fertiliser use, and a worsening situation in the Gulf. 'I'm not asking everybody to become a vegan, but there are choices you can make . . . lower meat, less beef, less pork, even chicken . . . just less meat,' she urged. 'I'm not a vegetarian but I don't eat that much meat.'

While the Gulf of Mexico has become the most notorious dead zone linked to nutrient runoff from agriculture, it is by no means alone.[12] In the upwards of forty dead zones around the coast of the USA, the role played by agriculture is increasingly well documented. The executive director of the UN Environment Programme (UNEP), Klaus Toepfer, has suggested that mankind is engaged in a gigantic global experiment as a result of inefficient and excessive use of fertilisers and the disposal of other sources of pollution like untreated sewage. 'Nitrogen and phosphorus from these sources is being discharged into rivers and the coastal environment or being deposited from the atmosphere, triggering alarming and sometimes irreversible effects.'[13]

Scientists have only recently begun to understand how nitrogen cascades through ecosystems, creating environmental problems along the way. Worldwide, humans create more than 160 million metric tons of nitrogen each year, far more than the environment has had to cope with through the ages.[14] It is accumulating faster than our capacity to break it down.

There is no doubt that it increases crop yields. The difficulty is that plants do not fully absorb it, so that more fertiliser and animal waste is often added than the plants need. Hence, only a fraction of what is applied to the soil ends up in the crops. In some regions, the absorption rate is less than 20 per cent. The rest is on the run – to places like the Gulf.[15]

With fertilisers so heavily implicated in the environmental horror that is the Gulf dead zone, I was keen to get a sense of the scale of the industry. That was how I ended up at Baton Rouge aerodrome, where for a few dollars I could take a flight in a light aircraft to see the industry from the sky. I had learned that an aerial view can offer a very different perspective.

For the last fifteen years, Paul Orr, a river-keeper, has been monitoring the state of the lower Mississippi, and he knows only too well how the fertiliser industry affects his patch. Softly spoken, with a neat beard, he had arranged for us to head up in a four-seater Cessna plane so small it felt almost as if we were strapped directly to the wings, they were that close. From here on, I knew the routine. We squeezed in, shut the doors and donned our headphones as the pilot fired up the engine. The propeller sparked into life, throwing a welcome breeze through the open windows.

'So what are we going to see?' I asked. I told him what I expected: various warehouses with impressive pallet-stacks of fertiliser bags. Orr gave a wry smile. The reality was very different. When we flew over a small town of sprawling industry – silos, towers and tangled metal – I asked: 'So which bit's the fertiliser plant?'

'All of it,' he replied bluntly. But that was not it: there was also a waste-water lagoon the size of a small reservoir, and an enormous quarry-like feature, filled with a chalky white substance. It was a mountain of gypsum – a type of soft mineral often used to make building plaster. I reckoned the pile was about 100 ft tall and maybe twice as wide. It towered high above the surrounding trees, all chalky white: a waste product from making fertiliser. Against the huge stack, the dumpster trucks waiting to cart it away looked as small as toys.

So where was all this white stuff headed? Perhaps to be buried, or processed for some other use? Not so. I learned that the plan was simply to dump it in the river until environmentalists stopped it from happening.

To our pilot, it was an old story. 'I see this a lot. It's very disturbing to see how many there are,' he sighed, as we swooped low over another fertiliser facility. Behind was a patchwork of fields, each as big as a fertiliser park. I never saw a farm animal the whole flight; only crops. We flew over a tight row of towers connected to a tanker being filled with a mass of dusty grain. 'Grain dust is the worst,' Orr remarked.

'OK, so are we going back now?' I asked, thinking we had seen it all. 'No, no . . . there's more,' Orr replied.

Beyond a paper mill that filled the plane with the pungent smell akin to boiled cabbage, we found more fertiliser plants, each one a complex of construction and all perched, handily for disposal purposes, right beside the winding banks of the Mississippi. We saw four such plants in the space of as many square miles. A massed flotilla of fertiliser barges headed upstream, crossing with container ships full of grain coming down. It was all part of the criss-cross matrix of farm activity seen by so few consumers.

As river-keeper here, Orr clearly had his hands full. His patch includes what he described as one of the biggest concentrations of petrochemical industry in America. I asked him how he felt. 'On the one hand, that's the way it is,' he replied philosophically. 'But I've learned how things have changed, how the forest has gone and been replaced with industry. I wish there was more of how this amazing environment used to be.'

Despite the sigh in his voice, I could sense that Orr was far from giving up. He told me how he used to always be out with his father in this area, along the rivers and swamps. I could see he wants to do all he can to ensure that the next generation can enjoy the waters round here like he did when growing up.

This river drains land from more than thirty states, making it far and away the largest drainage system in North America. The broad S-bend sweep of water is a funny red colour, unfamiliar to the British eye. Like the dead zone in the Gulf, the fertiliser factories weren't immediately obvious. They weren't exactly hidden from view, but we had to take to the air to see them properly. In so doing, I discovered that those two words, 'fertiliser factory', entirely fail to convey the sheer scale of this hidden part of the industrial farming jigsaw.

I reflected that while fertiliser is hardly a sexy subject, what it does should exercise anyone who cares about nature, and the future of plant and animal life. Quite simply, our hunger for cheap meat from animals fed on cheap corn grown on chemical-laced fields is poisoning and driving out precious species, creatures large and small, from birds to bison and shrimp. Does the dead zone need to spread from sea to land, before policymakers wake up to this catastrophe and act?

## FORGOTTEN GULF DISASTER

The Gulf of Mexico hasn't been lucky of late. Ravaged by hurricanes like Katrina and Rita, and saddled with one of the world's largest dead zones, 2010 also saw it damaged by the largest marine oil spill in history. *Deepwater Horizon*, an oil rig under contract to BP, exploded and sank, gushing millions of barrels of oil into the Gulf. The bodies of eleven workers were never found and the environmental disaster affected countless livelihoods. Despite a massive rearguard action to protect beaches, wetlands and estuaries along the coast from the black stuff, there was no stopping the devastation. Months of gushing oil wreaked havoc with the local fishing industry, as well as tourism and of course wildlife.

BP's then chief executive, Tony Hayward, caused outrage when he told Sky News that the environmental impact was likely to be 'very, very modest'.[16] The gaffe-prone mogul seemed more exercised by the personal nuisance he suffered than by the gargantuan crisis for which his company was responsible. 'There's no one who wants this thing over more than I do. I would like my life back,'[17] he told reporters wearily.

Among the mass of people and organisations on his back at that dreadful time was a 72-year-old grandmother called Wilma Subra, who was to become Hayward's nemesis. Her phone began ringing the morning after the explosion on the *Deepwater Horizon*, with calls from friends and neighbours who had men on the rig or were suffering as a result of the oil fumes. Members of Congress were starting to ask Hayward about reports that workers had fallen sick. Subra was already on the case. She and the Louisiana Environmental Action Network used the courts and political connections to compel BP to provide respirators and other protective gear to workers out on the boats fighting the spill. Her lobbying earned her such a high profile that soon she was being asked to meet Obama administration officials visiting the Gulf. Later, she was asked to testify to a Congress committee investigating the spill.[18]

A long-time environmental campaigner with blue eyes and tied-back hair, she is an authoritative-looking woman with a kindly headmistress look about her. We met at her home office, a small bungalow in rural Louisiana. Her village seemed a sleepy sort of place, with the dangly, moss-laden trees so typical of the area, and fields of sugarcane opposite. The houses were pretty but none too fancy, as the locals would say – the kind of place you could imagine settling down to retire.

Inside, a large pine table was stacked with papers: legal briefs, chemical lab reports, government memos and other evidence she uses when fighting her environmental corner. Her work has earned her enemies as well as friends. It was soon apparent why the windows on her bungalow, rather than cloaked in curtains of rose-print and lace, were covered with metallic netting. The target of repeated intimidation and burglary, she even endured a drive-by shooting when, one cool June evening, someone in a passing car fired a single shot in her direction. The bullet lodged in a brick a few feet from where she was sitting.

But the campaign of intimidation had failed. 'It actually strengthens my resolve, because what I'm doing is helping communities,' she told me with a determined look in her eye. 'And if they keep harassing me and I stopped doing this, they would win . . . I can't let them win.'

A trained microbiologist and chemist, Subra was one of the first scientists to identify the Gulf dead zone during routine sampling back in the early 1970s. She told me how she first realised something dreadful was happening.

'You know, we'd go on a cruise and we'd do it every month,' she said, recalling her days working at a local research institute. 'We were doing a research project around the oil and gas rigs. We were taking samples in the entire water column and we found this milky layer . . . right near the bottom.' The water turned out to be low in oxygen but high in nitrogen and phosphorus. That was way back in 1972.

She started talking to local shrimp fishermen who were noticing that they were having to go further and further out to sea to make a catch. Nets were coming up full of dead organisms. 'We didn't know what, but we knew something was going on. As it turns out, the nutrients [causing the problem] were coming down the Mississippi River from the Midwest states primarily . . . from the fertiliser,' she recalled, observing how the problem continues to grow with the relentless expansion of Midwest corn production.

'The more corn they grow, the more fertiliser runs off into the river and comes down and makes the dead zone even larger.'

She is troubled by the disconnect between what goes on in the Midwest and its effect in the Gulf. On a basic geographic level, it allows Midwest farmers and policymakers to carry on doing what they do in convenient ignorance of the impact downstream: out of sight, out of mind. 'The issue becomes how much destruction will be allowed to continue when we know what the source is and the source keeps coming down and impacting the Gulf,' Subra said.

Taking on the Midwest corn culture is a daunting prospect. It's a deeply embedded and powerful vested interest, and enjoys a deluge of tax-dollar subsidies from the US Farm Bill. The taxpayer gets whacked twice, once for the farm subsidy, and a second time for the environmental clean-up costs and lost livelihoods.

Subra wants Gulf fishing communities and Midwest agricultural interests to collaborate to devise ways to reduce runoff. However, she acknowledges the need for support at a national level, because, as she puts it, 'the emphasis on more and more corn' is coming from the top.

Since the BP disaster, the dead zone has struggled to attract much attention. Five years on, and after many billions of dollars in settlements and costs, BP claims the environment in the Gulf is returning to pre-spill conditions.[19] Media focus on the dead zone used to be 'huge', but *Deepwater Horizon* displaced it, and reviving interest in nutrients coming downriver – a quieter story – is hard. From an environmentalist and conservationist point of view, the worry is that this type of agricultural pollution starts being viewed as if it were the weather – a fact of life to be accepted with a shrug – as opposed to a man-made travesty that would be entirely preventable if the will were there.

Dead zones are now emerging around the world. Since the 1960s, the number of dead zones worldwide has almost doubled every decade.[20] There are now more than 400 coastal dead zones in the world, affecting a total area of some 95,000 square miles – about the same size as New Zealand.[21] The affected areas range in size from small stretches of coastal bays and estuaries to huge swathes of the open sea, where they can reach tens of thousands of square kilometres. Most are found in temperate waters, off the eastern coast of the United States and in the seas of Europe. Some are brewing in the waters off China, Japan, Brazil, Australia and New Zealand. The world's largest dead zone is in the Baltic Sea, where nutrient-enriched runoff from farms has combined with nitrogen deposition from the burning of fossil fuels and human waste discharged directly into the sea's waters.[22] Nitrogen and phosphorus levels are thought to be still increasing in places like Chesapeake Bay, Long Island Sound, Puget Sound, the Rhone Delta, the North Sea and the Adriatic.

For now, at least, dead zones are reversible if farmers and policy-makers can be persuaded to stem the flow of nutrient pollutants into lakes and coastal areas – and that is a sizeable if. As the Gulf of Mexico illustrates, when there are powerful agricultural interests involved, all too often it's a case out of sight, out of mind.

# 5

# Red junglefowl

## FACTORY FARMER SPEAKS OUT

Midnight under a starlit summer sky. The North Carolina country-side was alive with the buzz of cicadas and distant bullfrogs. I was in a Chevrolet four-wheel-drive, parked unobtrusively among some sheds on a poultry farm. As we waited patiently for something to happen, my companion joked that, in hanging out with me, he was hobnobbing with an eco-terrorist. He was teasing, of course. When I'm on duty with Compassion in World Farming (CIWF), which my wife would probably say is most of the time, I usually cut a rather corporate figure, suited and booted for the many meetings I have every day with politicians, media and leaders in the food and farming industry.

That night, however, I was kitted out for a long uncomfortable stint of waiting and watching. There was no quick and easy way to see what I wanted to see. We were lying low so as not to blow our cover by being seen by workers, on high alert for unexpected sounds or the flicker of distant headlights. Yet despite the subversive feel, there was no fear of being caught by an angry farmer – because he was sitting right next to me in the driving seat.

Earlier that day, Craig Watts had opened the doors on America's secretive poultry industry. It's big business in North Carolina, a broiler-chicken state that churns out 785 million birds a year. The business is worth $3 billion a year.[1]

Watts decided to blow the whistle after becoming uncomfortable about certain industry practices. He was concerned at the way in which cheap chicken was being advertised to the public and had grown disillusioned with the company to which he was contracted. He wanted to tell his story. He said he did his homework on my organisation, CIWF, and felt we were willing to listen and not just to blame the farmer for what was going on. A journalist friend put the two of us in touch.

I arrived with CIWF's US director, Leah Garcés, to find Watts sitting on a bright orange lawnmower outside his white clapboard homestead. Ruggedly handsome in a sleeveless T-shirt and dungarees, with a thatch of greying hair and engaging brown eyes, he was welcoming and jovial.

Watts married his childhood sweetheart Amelia in his twenties. He went into chicken farming because he wanted to be his own boss, and soon found out he was anything but. Now with two young sons and a daughter, the 48-year-old farms chickens on a large scale. His contract is with Perdue, one of the biggest poultry-processing companies in the US.[2] Like an army of so-called contract growers across the country, he feels he has been running to stand still on the debt treadmill, beholden to a processing company he feels holds all the cards.

He invested around half a million dollars in four state-of-the-art buildings – long, low-slung warehouses – for raising chickens for the meat market. Watts provides the sheds, land and labour, whilst Perdue provides the chicks and the feed, and specifies how they should be reared. The chickens remain the property of the company, who take them back once they are big enough for slaughter.

Rearing enough chickens to repay all the loans he took out to set up his premises has meant decades of work. We hopped into Watts's truck: he had offered to show me the kind of conditions that all too often lie behind the appealing-sounding labels like 'all natural' or 'farm raised' that you find on food in supermarkets and smaller grocery stores.

We drove along quiet pine-lined roads. 'That's where I was raised' – he pointed to a small homestead nestled amongst the trees. Further along, we drove past his grandmother's place. Watts was no disgruntled Johnny Come Lately in these parts. The farm has been in his family since the 1700s.

We arrived outside four industrial-looking buildings with no windows, each one home to 30,000 chickens. Watts beckoned us from the blinding midday sun into the dusty gloom of the chicken shed. A caustic slap of ammonia-ridden air thwacked the back of my throat. My eyes adjusted to the darkness before focusing on a carpet of motionless white birds. They covered every available inch of what seemed like a giant corridor – covering 20,000 square feet – with huge whirring fans at each end. 'I told you, a sea of white,' he said.

I scanned the flock. It was a miserable sight. Most were squatting and panting. 'They waddle to the feed, they waddle to the water and that's about it,' Watts explained. Some ran awkwardly and flapped round. They enjoyed the space we'd created by parting the sea of birds. Watts estimates that each bird has about the same amount of floor space as a standard sheet of typing paper. Ironically, they'll get more space in the oven.

This is hothouse rearing: intensive farming with a breed of bird genetically selected to grow super-fast and fed a rich diet. They sounded like giant chicks, making a throaty, high-pitched 'cheep'. At less than six weeks old, that's exactly what they were: chicks. They grow from fluffy Easter chicks to grotesque parodies of their ancestors in a matter of weeks. And the strain showed.

'He's a hopper,' Watts said as a bird flapped furiously past, dancing on one leg. I noticed one bird lying with a leg sticking backward. She finally struggled to stand, her splayed feet digging sideways at the ground in a desperate attempt to move before she flopped down under the feeder, panting and dishevelled.

Even the ones in better shape looked unsteady, bloated bodies that tottered around, anchored to the filthy few inches of ground they stood on by their hopelessly weak legs and obesity. Their dark eyes were tiny spots on a blanket of white feathers.

'How long could you stand for if you had twice as much body weight as you're supposed to have?' Watts asked me as I picked up one of the birds. Her raw pink breast was hot to the touch. She cheeped and blinked a little then, as I put her down, limped away. Another bird lay dead, a dismal little bundle of feathers on the compost floor.

Watts has no control over the health or genetics of the chicks he's delivered. Bound by contract, he told me, he can't even give them fresh air or sunshine. 'It's a moral dilemma,' he sighed. He knows it isn't right. 'What disturbs me most is the way it's being portrayed; it's so far removed from reality,' he said.

So what would he do differently if it weren't for the contract?

'I would absolutely do away with solid walls. I would give 'em back sunlight. Let the sunshine and fresh air in. Number one, the birds love it, and number two, it's better for me.'

I asked him what he sees as the future of the industry.

'I think it's almost going to have to be a start over. I think we're past the rewind button here. I think this has gone too far.'

In a promotional video, Jim Perdue, chairman of the company for whom Watts's chickens are destined, boasts about treating the chickens humanely. He calls it 'doing the right thing'.[3]

The company's labels carry a seal of approval from the US Department of Agriculture asserting that the birds are 'raised cage free'. The company has also used food labels on some of its chicken saying the meat has been 'humanely raised', although this latter label has since been withdrawn in settlement of a lawsuit brought by the Humane Society of the United States (HSUS).[4]

Watts knows that by flinging open the doors to his production unit and speaking out he's taking a big risk. He worries about having his contract torn up. Yet at the end of his tether, he felt he had to tell his story. If he were axed by Perdue, what would he do? 'Polish up my career as a trophy husband,' he joked.

That night, Watts, Leah and I sat quietly in the pickup truck with the lights out. We were waiting for the catching gang to arrive. The long corrugated poultry-shed roof disappeared in the gloom. Giant tin cylinders filled with chicken feed stood on stilts outside like sentries. Dusty grass fluttered furiously beside fans as big as family hot tubs. They were working overtime to keep the tens of thousands of occupants cool enough for their last journey. The now familiar sea of white was softly visible through the blur of rotating blades.

'We're not parking by those fans, they stink,' Watts said.

Just before 2 a.m., headlights appeared at the far end of the shed.

'They've arrived,' Watts announced.

The view through the fans went hazy as dust levels rocketed. Suddenly the seething mass of birds, formerly so still, jerked alive in panic, flapping and running as a member of the catching gang waved a flashlight to move them toward the catching machine. He moved among the flock as if walking through 2 feet of water, birds splashing up in front of his feet. For the final scene, the lights went out.

I heard how the catching process has improved since the days when chickens were just chucked into crates and the doors slammed shut, sometimes on their heads. 'You used to see chicken heads all over the place,' Watts told me. I suppose he and the poultry-catchers must have become desensitised back then, or at least felt forced to accept things in silence.

Now it's all automated. The catching machine works its way through the pitch-black shed, sweeping up chickens like cabbages before depositing them via a conveyor into crates. These get stacked ten-high on the back of an articulated truck for the journey to the slaughterhouse where they are killed, plucked, gutted and wrapped in cellophane.

The slaughter plant rises out of the South Carolina border, an industrial mountain of a building as bleak as its function. A billboard by the roadside crassly proclaims that 'Chicks dig soy: Animal ag is your number one customer'. It reminded me of the vast monocultures of soya I saw in Argentina, sprawled like a desert of green on what used to be lush pasture and forest. And of course, chicks don't 'dig soy'. What they 'dig' is foraging for natural food: ideally grubs, worms and seeds.

It was lunchtime before the last bird was crated – over one hundred thousand in all had been packed off to slaughter. Back at the farm, Watts looked relaxed. He was in his dungarees watering vegetables. His demeanour had changed, an insight perhaps into how it feels to be a contract chicken farmer.

'I'm happy today,' he told me with a smile. 'A day without chickens is like Christmas. I'm happy but tired.'

These conditions are by no means unique or unusual. I've been to intensive chicken farms all over the world and they're remarkably similar to each other. From US industrial parks rearing nearly a million birds at a time to what look like Bedouin tent encampments in the sandy deserts of Peru, featuring conditions so cramped the birds can barely move, and all too often accompanied by an overpowering stench of ammonia. I've seen chicken sheds on stilts in the Philippines; large low-slung warehouses in South Africa; massive cramped barns in Taiwan; huge windowless sheds in Britain.

Whether they house a few thousand birds or tens of thousands, the story is the same. I challenge anyone who sees or learns what goes on behind closed doors in these places to feel the same way about buying bargain-basement supermarket chicken as they did when they were blissfully ignorant of the conditions that produce them. How did chicken meat come to be so highly valued by society, but the birds themselves considered so worthless?

## HOW CHICKENS CAME TO FUEL THE WORLD

The chickenisation of the planet owes its origins to a bird from tropical forests known as the red junglefowl. The male of the species is an impressive-looking creature: slim and athletic, with a fine golden mane, yellow, orange and chestnut feathering, and a resplendent tail of metallic green.

Roosters like to fight: programmed to compete for status. I have watched these skirmishes, marvelling at the way they puff out their neck feathers and spread their wings to make themselves as big and impressive as possible. They go at it with an instinctive tenacity exploited by cock-fighters all over the world. When the fight is over, the loser will slope off to nurse his wounds, while the victor will shake himself off, throw back his head and let out

a triumphant cry, a throaty version of the familiar cock crow of
farmyards and fable.

Where they end up in the hierarchy may owe as much to their
parentage as to how well they fight. Scientists think genetics are
instrumental in determining who ranks where in the pecking order,
with offspring from top roosters most likely to grow up and lead
the group. Hens play a part too, actively deciding who they want to
father their chicks by retaining sperm from dominant roosters and
rejecting it from others.[5]

Red junglefowl naturally inhabit the forests and mangroves of
Southeast Asia, where they have long been hunted for food. They
were first domesticated by the Indus Valley civilisation during the
Bronze Age around the third millennium BC.[6] Since then, travellers and explorers have taken them wherever they have trekked
or voyaged. Chickens arrived in northwest Europe and China by
1500 BC.

Early Pacific seafarers took them on sea voyages in search of
undiscovered islands, where they even found their way to remotest
Easter Island. Here they were kept in stone chicken houses known
as *hare moa*. Were it not for the more impressive stone sculptures
with which this far-flung place is now widely associated, perhaps
Easter Island would have subsequently become known to tourists
as the island of stone chicken coops.[7]

Today, the junglefowl's domestic descendants are the most
populous bird on the planet. The world has some ten thousand
species of bird. Why has this one unassuming forest dweller soared
from jungle obscurity to chicken supreme, and what does its dubi-
ous modern status as the world's most populous farmed animal
mean today?

It is the elaborate fighting rituals of the male birds that appear
to have caught the eye of ancient tribes. Their innate reluctance
to fly made them easy to keep; their readiness to eat pretty much
anything – foraging for food and eating scraps – made them an ideal
species to domesticate; and their meat and eggs made a good meal.

However, it was probably the ease with which different strains
of chicken could be produced through selective breeding that shot

them to the heights of farm animal par excellence. The proficiency with which scientists have been able to tear up the original jungle-fowl and create new chicken models based on the old blueprint but engineered for maximum meat and egg production efficiency has kept consumers all over the world supplied with cheap white meat. Globally, around 60 billion chickens a year are now churned out for meat, a tenfold increase on half a century ago. It has come at a terrible cost for the farmed birds, and is a source of serious human health and environmental concern.

Animals and plants go to extraordinary lengths to breed. Sir David Attenborough has observed that if you watch animals objectively for any length of time 'you're driven to the conclusion that their main aim in life is to pass on their genes to the next generation'. It is after all what drives evolution: the passing on of genes and the slow adaptation of the species through the survival of the fittest. This is how species adapt to cope with changes in the environment. But what if this subtle process of natural selection is hijacked?

On one level, chickens could thank their lucky stars they were chosen. After all, *Gallus gallus* now populates the world in a way otherwise impossible for a near-flightless non-swimmer. We now see billions of chickens inhabiting just about every corner of the Earth. But there are downsides to such a stratospheric ascent.

According to the UN, four-fifths of the world's meat chickens are reared in what they describe as 'specialised broiler systems': factory farms. International companies with multi-billion-dollar turnovers have developed to specialise in broiler chickens. These food-production giants are known as 'integrators' because they tend to own almost every aspect of production but the farm. They own hatcheries and feed mills, supplying the chicks to the farms or 'contractors' before buying them back in time to be slaughtered in their purpose-built 'processing' plants.

Among the biggest companies of this type are Brasil Foods, Tyson Foods Inc, Pilgrims Pride and Perdue Farms. The US is the birthplace of these 'specialised' broiler systems. After China, it is the biggest producer of chicken in the world, and the white meat is now more popular than beef.[8] Despite its size and clout, the US chicken industry is wary. It has good reason not to welcome outsiders to its premises. As a result, few people get to see first-hand what 'chickenisation' means for the birds and the people who rear them – as I did thanks to the principled Craig Watts.

Four-fifths of commercial chickens reared for meat globally come from some three breeding companies[9] whose business is to specifically breed strains of bird that can be converted from living creatures to chunks of meat in as short a time frame as possible. The quest to accelerate growth, particularly of the chicken's breast, inflicts suffering. The fast-growing white chicken gains weight at the expense of its heart, lungs and legs. It is a painful experience. Scientists in Europe have found more than half of commercial chickens to have problems just walking.[10] Some die from serious heart and lung problems before they reach the age of six weeks. They rarely see daylight. Crowding is the norm. The breeds of bird used commercially are now sold globally, meaning welfare problems associated with them are likely to be global too.

If someone were to take a live chicken into a big public space – say Trafalgar Square in London – and treat her to the ordeal experienced in a factory farm, it would cause a public outcry. The culprit would most likely find themself in court, on charges of animal cruelty, and rightly so. On farms, that kind of suffering attracts no attention or penalty whatever.

Nicolas Kristof of the *New York Times* observed: 'Torture a single chicken and you risk arrest. Abuse hundreds of thousands of chickens for their entire lives? That's agribusiness.'[11]

More and more farmers are being relegated to the role of contract grower for big integrated chicken companies. Perdue alone has some 2,100 poultry producers on its books.[12] The contractor carries the risk inherent in rearing hundreds of thousands of chickens. If they fall sick or die, it's the contractor's problem. This basic model is spreading across the globe.

It was a coup to find someone like Watts willing to speak out. Few contractors dare. Most in the industry are either doggedly defensive or head-bowed in silence. Very few will let the likes of me around their sheds, never mind the general public. I remember being the after-dinner speaker at a local gathering of the British poultry industry, where I firmly but politely told them what I thought of factory-farmed chicken rearing. Indignation raged – 'How dare you talk about what we do when you've not been to our farms?'

Poultry farmer after poultry farmer stood up to challenge me to come to *their* farm and see for myself how much better it was than I claimed. What they hadn't reckoned on was me jumping at the offer. In the heat of the moment, the pack mentality had kicked in: teeth were bared. At the first opportunity, I asked the chairman to connect me with my challengers, but the cold light of day found them less keen to welcome me onto their premises. Every one of those who had thrown down the gauntlet failed to honour their invitation.

Accessing these places is so difficult that I normally only see what's going on inside by looking at footage brought in by whistle-blowers or undercover investigators. Now and again the odd farmer wants to engage – I've known a handful of such individuals and visited their premises – but never in the US. Watts was the first.

British celebrity chef and food activist Hugh Fearnley-Whittingstall came up with an imaginative way to show consumers what goes on behind closed doors without the help of this highly secretive industry by building his own factory farm on television. He crammed 2,500 live chickens into a tiny shed for thirty-nine days, depriving them of sleep for twenty-three hours a day to encourage them to eat non-stop. The resulting sight and stench was so bad that it made fellow TV chef Jamie Oliver feel physically sick.[13]

In Britain, Fearnley-Whittingstall's campaign led to a big consumer swing away from factory-farmed chicken. The supermarket giant Sainsbury's pledged to move away from intensively reared birds. When individuals without the public profile of Fearnley-Whittingstall and Oliver try to blow the industry's dirty secrets, however, all too often they are crushed by far more powerful players. After Watts's revelations were aired via a video release from CIWF to the media, Perdue seemed to suggest that it was all his fault, not theirs. They showed up the next day to do an animal-welfare audit and suggested that he had failed to follow their guidelines on rearing and animal welfare. Naturally, this ploy infuriated Watts, who is adamant he follows their guidelines meticulously.

'That response was as predictable as the sun rising,' he said wearily. 'Was it insulting? Yes. Was it surprising? No. That's what they do; they divert and deflect. They'd rather fix me than fix the system. I'm only one man. They can kick me to the kerb tomorrow.'

When CIWF released Watts' story to the media, the accompanying video was featured by the *New York Times*, quickly went viral and was seen by millions.[14] Although Watts felt under pressure from the company following his admissions, Perdue also started to show signs of exploring better ways to keep its chickens.

By July the next year (2015), Jim Perdue was quoted in the *New York Times* saying 'We need happier birds.' The company's senior vice president in charge of food safety and quality was reportedly dispatched to Europe to learn more about animal-welfare standards there.[15]

A year later, Perdue made a huge announcement: it was to be the first major chicken company in the US to publish a detailed policy on animal welfare.[16]

The statement included a commitment to add windows to poultry houses in a bid to increase activity amongst the birds, and to connect with outside stakeholders with an interest in animal welfare. At least animal welfare is now on the map and some birds will soon see natural light.

As for Craig Watts, he is no longer a contract poultry farmer for Perdue. Instead, he's been investigating other business ideas, including the option of using his chicken sheds to grow vegetables.

Having blown the whistle, Watts has undoubtedly sparked off change within part of the chicken industry. However, the fact remains that factory rearing is still the commercial norm for the majority of the world's chickens.

## CHICKENISATION

The chickenisation of the planet has been one of the most remarkable livestock stories of the twentieth century. The system has been stunningly successful in producing what looks like ultra-cheap food – the price of chicken has fallen by three-quarters in real terms since 1930. But at what cost?

In many ways, chickens are the ideal farm animal for the industrial age. Relative to pigs or cattle, they are small and easy to handle. They can be kept in huge numbers and grow much quicker. Modern intensive chickens can be ready for slaughter in just six weeks. Pigs need six months, beef cattle up to two years. Factor in the versatility of chicken meat as a fairly bland base for the latest sauce or topping, and it seems you are on to a winner.

The emergence of specialist breeds of chicken designed to produce either meat or eggs has played a key role in the remarkable growth of the industry. The development of fast-growing birds is linked to the development of high-yielding varieties of corn. 'Hybrid' chickens – higher-yielding birds – started to appear in America during the 1940s, when the administration was keen to develop a market for surplus corn and soya and ran competitions to promote faster chicken-growth rates. The winner was the farmer who could produce the fastest-growing bird with the finest breast meat.[17]

The Atlantic and Pacific Tea Company (a supermarket in those days) sponsored contests for the 'chicken of tomorrow', first on a county basis, then at state level, and finally at federal level. The subsidy system in America and Europe also played its part. Though chicken production isn't directly subsidised, intensification depends on access to affordable feed grains (up to 70 per cent of production costs relate to feed), and subsidies for arable farming help assure the supply, cushioning corn farmers who expand production from the risks involved in scaling up. Cheap and reliable supplies of grain created the ideal conditions for intensive poultry production. In turn, increased demand for feed incentivised grain production – usually in environmentally damaging monocultures – in a not-so-virtuous circle.

For some time now, white meat has been marketed as a healthier alternative to red meat, but the mask is slipping. Industrially produced chicken today is nearly three times higher in fat and has a third less protein than the chicken of the 1970s. To achieve the same level of nutrition requires eating a lot more fat and calories.

Free-range chicken tends to be significantly better – the average intensively reared chicken can have up to twice the saturated fat of birds that have been allowed to move as nature intended.

There can be a misconception about keeping animals indoors: that it is somehow safer and healthier for the animals, and so for the consumer. The very opposite is true. Industrial production of poultry for meat or for eggs can increase the risk of disease, and could thereby threaten consumer safety.

Super-fast-growing breeds of chicken are strongly associated with the food-poisoning bug campylobacter, which can cause severe diarrhoea, weight loss and even death. Two-thirds of supermarket chickens in the UK have been found to be contaminated with the bug, and the latest science suggests a link with the way chickens are kept. As the growing birds suffer stress, campylobacter flourishes in their guts. It then gets passed out in their droppings and permeates the flock. As fast-growing birds are more susceptible to it, now it can pass through the wall of their guts and into their bloodstream and muscles. Once this happens, active food-poisoning bacteria are inside the body of the bird and the subsequent carcass, enhancing the risk of it reaching the end-consumer.[18] Birds kept free-range are generally slower-growing, so have better immune systems in healthier conditions, and are therefore less likely to cause food poisoning.

Poultry meat and eggs are a major source of infection from another serious food-poisoning bug, salmonella. Keeping chickens in large flocks or in cages can dramatically boost the risk: studies have shown that caged hens are up to ten times more at risk of salmonella than birds kept free-range. Again, keeping animals in stressful conditions lowers their immunity, making them susceptible to infection.[19]

Farmers routinely attempt to safeguard their birds against such bugs by dosing them with antibiotics. Factory farms dish out lavish amounts of these drugs, with their precious potential to save human lives. Indeed, half of all the antibiotics produced in the world are fed to chickens, cows, pigs and other farmed animals. In the US, farm-animal use can be as high as 80 per cent of total use

92

of antibiotics. In Britain, nearly 90 per cent of farm antibiotics go
to poultry and pigs, the species most intensively farmed.[20]

Antibiotic use in livestock is acknowledged by the World Health
Organisation as a factor in the rise of so-called superbugs: bacteria
resistant to antibiotic treatment. The WHO fears the world may be
on the cusp of a post-antibiotic era where once-treatable diseases
will once again kill. It is pressing pharmaceutical companies to
develop new antibiotics, but this will do nothing to tackle the root
cause of the crisis, which is the wholesale use of such drugs.

'Chickenisation' is wasteful on multiple levels, but perhaps the
most egregious waste derives from discarding chicks. The routine
mass slaughter of newly hatched birds – the cute fluffy yellow things
we fete at Easter – is a facet of factory-farming that would surely
repel consumers if they knew.

Half a century ago, chickens were dual-purpose. They would be
kept for eggs until they stopped laying, and then for the pot. Most
cockerels went straight to the table. Specialisation throws up a
dilemma: what to do with the male chicks of the egg-laying breed.
After all, these breeds have been designed as egg-laying machines:
they don't put on weight, whether they are male or female.

Obviously the male chicks can't lay eggs. Does this mean that
billions of them grow into cockerels, to live out a pleasant if unproductive life somewhere; or perhaps to be used for meat? No. They
are killed at a single day old. In a practice concealed from consumers, male chicks are simply gassed or dropped live into mincing
machines, and then binned like shredded paper or polystyrene
package-fill.

Battery or free-range, it's just another dark side of the industry,
and one that producers will go to great lengths to keep quiet. Over
the past twenty-five years working as a specialist in farm-animal
welfare, I've made it my business to see just about everything that
goes on first-hand. The wipe-out of male chicks is one sight I've
not witnessed. In truth, I've not gone out of my way to see it,
because I know it would be awful to watch and I'm not sure what
I would gain from seeing it first-hand. To me, killing chicks at a
day old because they're not female isn't so much a welfare issue as a

moral obscenity. That said, in my time in the animal-welfare business I've never known a door to be opened, an opportunity offered, to observe the process. It's an utter taboo.

Until recently, nobody has shown much interest in finding an alternative to the killing machines. In a ground-breaking statement in 2014, however, the global food-manufacturing giant Unilever declared that it wanted to solve the problem once and for all. The company pledged to find ways to 'eliminate the culling of male chicks in the industry', probably through sex determination of the chicks before they hatch.

According to Unilever's senior external affairs manager, Willem-Jan Laan, researchers are making good progress and are 'optimistic' that the technology could be available commercially as soon as 2018. He told me how Unilever is working with other companies who want to solve this problem too, and considers it important for politicians to back the move by banning the killing of male chicks. 'We have eliminated [barren] battery cages by EU regulation,' he said. 'Could we take the hurdle and also eliminate the practice of culling one-day male chicks in the future?' In what some see as a sign of the food industry starting to fall out of love with eggs altogether, Unilever has also started looking at ways to replace eggs as an ingredient in some of its products.[21]

As someone who keeps a cockerel myself, I am reminded every day of the sheer waste of life and resources involved in killing and binning day-old chicks. It's a situation brought on by a decades-old decision to develop 'specialist' breeds of poultry for eggs and for meat. Now there could be a breakthrough. Technology could bring an end to male chicks being gassed or minced alive. And on that day our free-range eggs, whether boiled, fried or scrambled, will taste so much better.

## A CAGE IS STILL A CAGE

*Beware of the chickens'* warns the sign on the five-bar gate. A handful of hens scratch and peck under some young fruit trees. If they look up from their foraging they will see a medieval manor built by the bishop of Winchester, and the spire of a Norman church against the steep grassy slopes of a chalk escarpment. The song of skylarks fills the air and the odd red kite drifts overhead.

I've whiled away many a moment looking over that gate. On the safe side – for the chickens at any rate – is our modest cottage, which dates back to at least 1802. Half a dozen chickens live in our hexagonal chicken coop. They have straw on the floor and a ladder up to nest boxes and a roosting area. They're a mix of breeds, all of them taken in when they needed a good home: Louis the bantam Silky cockerel, and several commercial hens adopted when they were no longer profitable and facing slaughter.

We give our eggs away to local people in exchange for donations to the local hospice. Many of our neighbours also keep a few hens: there's a small flock at the manor house, and some in the nearby cow fields. Plenty of people living in cottages in our village keep them too – you can tell by the sound of celebratory clucks marking yet another newly laid egg.

In the wild, junglefowl will lay five or six eggs in a nest, once, perhaps twice a year, tucked away under a bush or in clumps of bamboo.[22] Today's egg-laying hen can pump out over 300 eggs in a year – a grossly unnatural surge that leaves them exhausted. It's hardly surprising that they have a very short lifespan. Yet still it is not enough for the industry – some have set their sights on a super-hen capable of laying an amazing 500 eggs in little more than a year.[23] It's an ambition that seems to start with the premise that animals are machines to be tweaked and twiddled to enhance performance. This approach does not acknowledge either natural or humane limits.

Of the 7 billion laying hens in the world – one for each person – nearly two-thirds are kept in battery cages – bare wire boxes so small the hens can't spread their wings, and a very far cry from the forest floor. Here they stay for life – usually little more than a year, maybe two, before they are slaughtered and their worn-out bodies sent for soups, pies or pet food.

Only when I started keeping hens myself did I fully grasp how unnatural it is for hens to live out their lives the way they do on factory farms. One thing you learn pretty soon when you have hens is how busy they like to be. They are arch-foragers, always on the lookout for something fresh and tasty to eat. They scratch with their strong claws then peer at the freshly turned earth, sometimes having a peck with their sensitive beak. They love variety. They also delight in demolishing leftovers, and will get through a pile of waste food with an enthusiasm that is a joy to see. Hens are the ultimate recycler, taking grubs, worms and waste food and converting it into wonderful fresh eggs.

These traits they inherit from junglefowl that have a marked daily routine. They roost up in trees, typically a favourite one, and then in the morning they all come down and forage, usually for worms and insects. Later they'll 'dust-bath' – a preening activity designed to get rid of parasites. It involves shaking dirt particles up into the feathers, and helps to keep the feathers in good condition, which is important, since they generally only get one set a year. Towards the afternoon activity peaks again; more foraging, then mating, then back to roost.

If hens could build their own house, it would have at least three rooms and a spacious garden, with the bedroom or roosting area upstairs – hens are programmed to perch high up at night to avoid predators like foxes. They would also choose to have a separate nesting area, somewhere dark and secluded where the expectant bird can slope off and be undisturbed until that perfect shell is laid. The third room would be the dining and lounging room at ground level, covered with straw or other material to scratch around in search of extra scraps.

A big garden would also be a must – only then can a hen really feel like she is exploring. To top it all, a hen needs a spot that catches sun, for relaxing after eating. When they bask in the rays of the sun, hens take on a whole new look – their eyes bulge and their wings spread. You can see the pleasure it brings them. It is remarkable how quickly caged hens will take up these innate behaviours once they're released.

Despite a lifetime in a barren cage with little to see but lots of other bored chickens, a newly released hen will walk for the first time, tentatively at first, then walk and walk and walk . . . How my wife and I have felt like weeping with joy to see a hen that has never before felt the sun on her back lie down and spread her wings in sheer pleasure. Pretty quickly – within days – she will be doing the full repertoire of behaviours found in much more experienced free-range hens.

This is because such behaviour is hard-wired, a genetic inheritance: no amount of selective breeding to make the bird more 'efficient' as an egg- or a meat-producer can take away the features that make a hen a hen. To deprive a hen of the ability to 'be a hen' will make her suffer, just as it would for other creatures.

We named one of our hens 'Huckle' after the harsh throaty noise she made when she first came to us. Huckle came from one of the last of Britain's barren battery cages before they were banned. She had spent a year with nothing but bare wire in a space too small to even stretch her wings, crammed in with four or more fellow inmates. This bird might never have walked in all her life. When she got to us, she was featherless. Bored companions had pulled her coat out. What little they left was stripped bare as a result of constant rubbing against the cage sides.

She took to a life of freedom with great joy. When we opened her carrying pen onto the lawn, it took her a while to step out. She did so gingerly at first, an experimental walker. Before we knew it, she was walking the length of the garden, then into our cottage, flying up onto the windowsill and peering at bemused passers-by.

Within six months, she was dead. A virus killed her. Our other hens were fine; coming from free-range farms, they had stronger immune systems. Huckle's was shot to bits. That year in a cage had taken its toll. I was pleased we had given her life before her death, joys that so few caged hens ever get.

Those barren battery cages are now banned across Europe, a welfare reform for which I like so many others am proud to have campaigned. These days there are so many more hens than there would otherwise have been, living free-range, enjoying fresh air and sunshine on farms. However, one travesty of that ground-breaking law is that it still allows so-called 'enriched' cages. These are a bit bigger, with rudimentary features meant to mimic things that hens need, like a nest. In truth, they are little better than barren battery cages, although I'm sure the extra space is a blessed relief.

The 'enriched cage' was designed by scientists. I know some of them personally. Good people, well-meaning, but perhaps blinkered by their own professional myopia. Having examined every aspect of the wants and needs of a hen, it seems they studied everything and learned nothing. For no hen I've ever encountered would choose to live in such conditions.

## BREEDING TO EXTINCTION

While 'chickenisation' sweeps the world, the red junglefowl is quietly slipping towards genetic extinction. The biggest threat to the survival of the species in its purest form comes not from the usual suspects – hunting or habitat destruction – but from genetic contamination with its domestic brethren. Through cross-breeding with their domestic cousins, genetically pure junglefowl are dying out. They have already disappeared in some areas where they once thrived in Southeast Asia.

In the National Parks of Thailand, red junglefowl still live alongside elephants, leopards and even tigers. We think a lot about conserving exotic big creatures, but what about something as humble as the junglefowl? Tom Pizzari, professor of evolutionary biology at the University of Oxford, who has been studying junglefowl for a decade, believes that to save it is 'hugely important'.

'From an ecological perspective the less charismatic species are just as important to the resilience of that ecological community as the ones that are more charismatic,' he told me. Losing the genetically pure wild junglefowl has implications beyond the regret intrinsic to seeing any species disappear for ever. Some experts fear it could jeopardise the ultimate health and welfare of domestic poultry.

'We, as a human society, rely so much on domestic chickens that we can't really afford to lose their wild ancestors. At the moment most of the domestic chicken population in the world is produced by two global companies, so the risk of monopolising this and losing a huge amount of genetic diversity and genetic lines is very high,' Pizzari said.

He believes that 'pure' populations of chicken could hold the key to resolving problems facing the poultry industry in the future. Without them we lose an important and irreplaceable genetic benchmark for comparing the modern-day chicken. To put it simply, following such relentless selective breeding might make it difficult to know what a chicken is really 'supposed' to be like.

'We're gathering more and more information about the genome of the domestic chicken,' Pizzari explains, 'but we really don't know enough at the moment about how domestication has changed these birds, so losing pure populations now would be a real disaster. Domestication has resulted in a loss of genes that nowadays would make the difference between the extermination of a domestic flock or not.' As he sees it, the process has made chickens 'incredibly vulnerable' to disease. By contrast, most wild junglefowl are almost entirely immune to the highly virulent avian flu strains now ravaging poultry flocks in Europe, Asia and North America. Some strains even pose a threat to human health.

In the face of a rising tide of disease, the intensive poultry industry has responded by vaccinating birds, dosing them with drugs, and warding off the environment by keeping them indoors. Pizzari thinks this means fighting a losing battle – 'Clearly in the long term this is progressively less and less achievable and costly.'

Ultimately, consumers must decide whether animal suffering and the extinction of species are a price too high to pay for cheap chicken.

# 6

# White stork

SO WHERE DO THE SUBSIDIES GO?

Tucked along the banks of the Thames is the stately home estate that inspired Kenneth Grahame to write *The Wind in the Willows*.

In the children's classic from 1908, Ratty, Mole and Badger band together to persuade the flamboyant and self-destructive Toad, who has a penchant for the latest shiny things, to see the error of his ways. First he goes a bit crazy with a horse-drawn caravan that ends up in a ditch, then there's high jinks and reckless driving in a motorcar, and finally he ends up in jail, where he comes to learn the value of what he had before and almost lost.

Toad was modelled on Sir Charles Day Rose, a banker, Liberal MP and early pioneer of motoring, crazy about flash gadgets and status symbols and particularly fond of his 1904 Mercedes Benz, which he liked to drive at high speed to the nearby village of Whitchurch. He blew his horn, 'poop-poop', just like Toad, heedless of anyone luckless enough to find themselves in his way, and sending pedestrians scattering as he careered along country lanes.

His sixteenth-century Elizabethan home, Hardwick House, was Grahame's inspiration for Toad Hall and now belongs to his great-grandson, Sir Julian Rose. Set against a steep hillside covered in beech wood, the mellow red-brick house is surrounded by wild-flower meadows that have never been ploughed or treated with chemical sprays. They are all part of the estate, which is lovingly managed with nature in mind.

When I met Rose for the first time in twenty years whilst giving a conference lecture in Oxford, I knew him at once; he hadn't changed a bit. A tall, stately fellow with neat beard and a jovial look, he invited me over to 'Toad Hall' to catch up. Which is how, on a glorious spring morning, I found myself crossing the quaint toll bridge through the old village of Whitchurch-on-Thames in Oxfordshire and up to the gates of Hardwick, which bore a sign: 'GMO-free zone'. Inside, I passed a 'veg shed' packed with enticing produce, and marvelled at how the Thames glistened in the sunlight like a silver line running through pasture.

I headed for the estate office, where Rose greeted me warmly and offered me coffee. He had lots that he wanted to talk about and even more he wanted to show. We were soon touring the house and grounds, chatting as we went. Originally a farmhouse, Hardwick House became gentrified in the sixteenth century. I marvelled at the Toad Hall library, unaltered for the best part of a century and packed with enough reading for a thousand years. The drawing room was something else; during the mid-1500s, Hardwick hosted Queen Elizabeth I on one of her many grand tours of the kingdom. To mark this royal visit, the Queen's bedroom was richly decorated with magnificent plasterwork cameos.

Outside, as the sun beamed down, we walked towards the river through a corridor of lime trees, which attract masses of bees in the summer. There was a dazzling display of daffodils first planted by Sir Julian's grandmother. Eventually we reached a flat grassy bank with willow and ash overlooking the gentle meander of the Thames. A pair of swans drifted by as Rose explained that this was the place where Kenneth Grahame used to sit while he was writing the story that came to be loved by generations of children.

'My grandmother remembers that he went down to the river and sat and mused among the willow trees and watched the river flow whilst he was writing the chapters of *Wind in the Willows*,' Rose told me. 'He put together a story about how these creatures of the waters of the Thames plotted to get into this place. He called it Toad Hall. And there's no doubt that this is it. And my great-grandfather, the mad old Sir Charles, was Mr Toad!'

Like his great-grandfather before him, Rose is a pioneering spirit. He turned his estate organic in 1975, long before it became fashionable. In 1997, he took on the forces of homogenised food and opposed government plans to ban raw unpasteurised milk.[1]

He has long been a fierce critic of industrial farming, which he considers to be as reckless as Toad's driving habits. Unlike his great-grandfather's fictional character, he is fundamentally sceptical of the new-fangled – at least when it comes to farming – arguing that the technological advances that make it possible to go on squeezing high yields from depleted soils or accelerating chicken growth do not amount to real progress, but are instead an exercise in short-termism.

'You can't see farming in the same light as you see Ford motorcars and microchips,' he told me. 'Farming is about managing the land and nature.'

I had not seen Rose since the mid-1990s when he was involved in pushing for reform of the Common Agricultural Policy (CAP), the European Union's monolithic subsidy system. I was a rookie back then, a new boy at Compassion in World Farming (CIWF), whereas Rose, now in his late sixties and a baronet, was in the vanguard of the campaign.

For two decades we lost touch, until that chance meeting at a conference in Oxford. It was then that I discovered his special interest in rural Poland, and the impact of the CAP on the Polish countryside.

His long-standing interest in the country started with a headline in the British farming press in 1989 which read: 'Poland up for grabs'. He told me how much it had upset him that such beautiful countryside could be seen in such colonial terms. His affinity with Poland and the plight of its countryside was cemented years later when he met Jadwiga Łopata, a Goldman prize-winning environmentalist who campaigns to preserve the countryside.

She and Rose met at a London conference in 2000 as Poland was preparing to enter the European Union. He was with Patrick Holden, founder of the Soil Association, a pioneer of the organic food movement and close friend of HRH Prince Charles, another early adopter of the cause. She had newly established a body to fight for the Polish countryside.

These days, Rose and Łopata are a couple and run a non-governmental organisation called the International Coalition to Protect the Polish Countryside (ICPPC), based in Stryszow near Krakow. They switch lives every few weeks between Stryszow and Hardwick House. People in Stryszow wonder why Łopata hasn't simply upped sticks to England to live the good life of an aristo-crat, and why an aristocrat should want to live in rural Poland. The answer is that they both adore the Polish countryside. They are also deeply worried about what has been happening to it since the country joined the EU.

Brussels lavishes some 50 billion euros on farm payments every year, accounting for about 40 per cent of the entire EU budget.[2] In the past, the bountiful handouts so distorted the market that farmers produced far more than could be consumed, resulting in the notorious butter mountains and wine lakes of the 1980s. While the days of exorbitant production linked to CAP payments are over, the system is now equally reckless in other ways, driving small farmers out of business, and incentivising mass production on industrial farms.

To keep the green lobby at bay, these days Brussels officials make much of the 'sustainability' of the system, claiming that the CAP now places a significant emphasis on producing food in ways that support farmers and harmonise with the landscape. Sadly, rhetoric and reality are at odds – and nowhere more so than in Poland, as Rose explained:

'With the advent of Poland joining the European Union in 2004, you've got enormous pressure on this country to modernise as they see it, restructure; get involved in the global marketplace; get rid of this peasant farming anachronism and move on. Enormous pres-sure from corporations and from government, from the European Union and from the World Trade Organisation, everybody – and they want a stake in Poland.

'Unfortunately there are all sorts of other regulations too which make it very difficult for the small farmer to survive. So what we've

been doing, Jadwiga and myself, is to raise the voice of these people
for them, help to promote their way of life, and show they are not
behind. If anything, they are ahead of the game and everyone is
eventually going to have to come behind them if we are going to
have a planet which is sustainably managed in the future.'

As a recent entrant to the EU, this part of Eastern Europe
illustrates how quickly and fundamentally the CAP can alter the
countryside. The subsidy system has been integral to agriculture
in the original member states for so long that it is far harder to
identify cause and effect. In Poland, where it has had a highly
detrimental effect on wildlife within a decade, the relationship is
easier to see.

I took up Rose's offer to see things first-hand and found myself
careering around the Polish countryside squeezed in the back of a
dented Ford Fiesta driven by an English aristocrat. It was not quite
as flash as the motorcars driven by Sir Charles, but the experience
had shades of accompanying Toad on the road.

I was sitting in the back of the car, with Rose at the wheel, flanked
by Łopata. When they are not at Hardwick House, the couple live
in the soft-peaked Beskidy Mountains, part of the Carpathian
range which borders Poland and Slovakia. Called Małopolska,
'Lesser Poland', this part of the country is full of small villages, with
Krakow the region's capital. The area has a reputation for obstinacy,
as the communists discovered when they tried, and failed, to estab-
lish farm collectives following fierce resistance from smallholders.
Today, the average farm size in the region is still as small as two and
a half hectares.[3]

These small farmers still work their land in the traditional way:
no chemicals, rotating crops and animals, and using manure as
fertiliser. 'They never waste anything,' said Rose. 'You could say
they are the best model we have of low-carbon-footprint, benign
agriculture.'

They were keen to show me the highlights of the Polish countryside. Our whistle-stop tour reached Kiczory, a village in
southern Poland close to the border with Slovakia. In the shadow
of a peak known as Witches' Mountain (Babia Góra, in Polish),

the area harbours lynx, wolves and brown bears.[4] Schoolgirls
with old-fashioned satchels on their backs headed home through
pastures profuse with wild flowers. Chickens ran free in the yards
of crimson-roofed houses. Cows grazed beside a babbling brook
whilst ravens cawed overhead. I could see why Rose and Łopata
loved it so much – it was idyllic.

We talked to some local farmers. A lady called Stanislawa, who
owns land in the area, told us: 'The big difference is in the quality of the food we produce here compared with what we can buy.
We have fantastic woodlands, clean air, the stream is unpolluted.
It's a charming place.' We were standing outside her Górale-style
farmhouse, which had three gables and a roof designed to be steep
enough for the snow to slip off in winter.

'Any white storks?' I asked.

She confirmed that there were – apparently they like the frogs
in the brook.

On the horizon, the Tatra Mountains seemed to levitate above a
line of pine trees. As if on cue, the streamlined figure of a white stork
wafted into view, black and white wings beating in slow motion, drifting above the stream. Long red beak and red feet outstretched, she
rose on the afternoon thermals. With a few lazy flaps, she was gone.

White storks are one of Poland's best-loved wildlife treasures.
The species, which is struggling elsewhere, thrives in this part of
the world, so much so that Poland has long boasted a quarter of the
world's nesting population. They nest in old trees, behind rocks, on
rooftops and even in tall chimneys. The Polish love them and treat
them with reverence: some people set up webcams to watch their
nesting progress.

They are also seen by conservationists as a good indicator of the
overall health of the countryside. Every ten years, a census is carried
out across the country to assess numbers. In Poland, thousands of
volunteers are drafted in to count stork nests and questionnaires are
sent out to village mayors asking for details of stork populations in
their communities.

Paweł Sidło of the Polish Bird Protection Society describes
Poland as a 'paradise' for this species. Hunting storks is forbidden,

so one of the biggest bearings on their future is how the country-side is managed. In an interview with Radio Prague around the time Poland joined the EU, Sidlo talked of 'indirect threats' to white storks – a reference to the dramatic changes to agriculture he expected to go hand in hand with EU membership.

'When we implement very intensive farming and convert small farms to big ones . . . then the species is endangered indirectly because they cannot find food,' he said simply.

As Poland prepared for EU accession, conservationists warned of unprecedented declines in Europe's farmland birds. Industrial farming methods were cited as the biggest threat, particularly in the UK, with much of the rest of Western Europe close behind. Talking to BBC News Online in 2001, Dr Paul Donald of the Royal Society for the Protection of Birds' (RSPB) claimed that falls in farmland bird populations in Western Europe were 'most severe . . . where the Common Agricultural Policy has fuelled agricultural intensification'.[5]

As EU enlargement approached, so fears grew for the Polish countryside. 'I became spellbound by the issue,' Rose recalled. 'The way they manage the land in Poland is still traditional, so you've got the crop rotations, you've got reapplications of farmyard manure, you've got people working with small tractors . . . And they take enormous care and detail over what they do.'

Rose believes that small farmers have been hardest hit by the CAP. His novelty factor as an English aristocrat in Poland opened many doors, but some of what he discovered behind them was deeply disturbing. As Poland was being prepared for entry to the EU, he urged Polish authorities not to follow Western Europe in changing agriculture in favour of industrial farming, fearing that Poland would simply repeat their mistakes.

'They are the guardians of the countryside. Yet the Commission seems to want rid of them,' he said.

In Brussels, Rose and Łopata met the government committee setting conditions for Poland's entry into the EU. As he recounts in his book, *In Defence of Life*, out of twelve committee members, none were Polish. Rose argued that in a country in which more than a fifth of the population live off the land, the majority on small farms, new rules and regulations should work differently from the system in more industrial nations, where even some of the best farmers have been lost to large-scale monocultures. The room went silent. After an awkward pause, the commission chairwoman cleared her throat and leaned forward.

'I don't think you understand what EU policy is,' she said condescendingly. In order to achieve the EU's objectives, 'old-fashioned' Polish farms would need to modernise so that they could compete on the global market, she explained. 'To do this it will be necessary to shift around one million farmers off the land.'[6]

It's hard to conceive of another sphere of society where policymakers could speak so casually about effectively removing the livelihoods of a million families and get away with it. Yet, throughout Europe in recent decades, farmers have gone out of business as if farming were a thing of the past. Now Poland looks set to follow that same future.

Sadly, some of Rose's fears have come about: since joining the EU, hundreds of thousands of Polish farmers have gone out of business. Yet about a million and a half remain.[7] With an average holding of less than ten hectares,[8] one EU Commissioner expressed 'frustration' to Rose at Poland's small farmers appearing to survive against the odds.

Rose explained that these small operators don't need subsidies; they simply need to be able to sell their produce direct to local communities. I spoke to one such farmer from the village of Skawinki. Tadeusz produces potatoes, grain and cattle for beef and dairy. He also keeps three pigs which he slaughters himself, and sells the meat locally. His cattle graze lush grass in an apple orchard. The calves stay with their mothers, suckling for as long as the cow will allow it. He feels he's only survived by trading locally, selling direct to consumers. As a small farmer, he needs a decent price. High-volume sales are not an option. Indeed, people want what he has to offer precisely because it's not mass-produced.

Direct sales to consumers are a lifeline for a small farmer such as Tadeusz. As it stands, they lose out on both the domestic market and on exports. There is no doubting the demand for local produce from small or chemical-free farms. However, the EU is slapping stacks of restrictions on direct sales, making life hard for those who wish to do business in this way.

Prices for Tadeusz's products have fallen since Poland joined the EU. Although he now receives direct subsidy payments, the system has pushed up the price of his materials such as fertiliser and machinery, leaving him worse off, on balance.

'We struggle to keep up, as it's expensive,' he told me. He has two small tractors. He can source cheap spares for the vehicles in the Czech Republic and has the skill to do repairs himself. If he bought expensive Western John Deere-type tractors, he tells me, he'd have to pay someone else to do the work if anything went wrong.

This traditional way of supplying local food is breaking down. As in America and other parts of the EU, animals are disappearing from the land, and small fields with a variety of crops are giving way to vast monocultures. A new wave of regulation has swept Poland since joining the EU, making it harder, and more expensive, for farmers to sell their produce direct to consumers. New hygiene rules may sound consumer-friendly, but because small farmers can't afford to meet them, they skew the market towards bigger players.

'Small farmers can't process the meat and milk into sausages and cheese for sale without paying for expensive registration, and the regulations often require separate premises for these products,' Łopata explained.

'Now the best Polish food is illegal,' Rose said.

I met a man called Krzysztof Kwatera who runs a project offering shared facilities to farmers to help them sell direct to local consumers while staying within the law. It enables them to overcome what might otherwise be prohibitive costs of meeting EU hygiene rules. 'Farmers can rent out the kitchen by the hour, as well as storage facilities,' he explained. I was told that the local government in Małopolska wants to develop this type of kitchen in every district, but it is as yet unclear that this will suffice to save struggling small farmers. All too often, any government support they receive is hopelessly ham-fisted. Locals tell the story of a farmer who asked for some simple advice and received a 200-page manual in response.

For the moment, the 'illegal' local food market still survives. But the trend is clear: small producers are being squeezed out.

Since Poland and its Central and Eastern European neighbours joined the EU in 2004, small farms have disappeared at twice the average EU rate. Between 2007 and 2010, the number of farms in Poland fell by more than a third.[9]

Meanwhile agricultural chemical use has soared. Soon after accession, fertiliser and insecticide use shot up by 80 per cent; herbicide use tripled.[10] Single farm payments based on farm size mean that small farms get peanuts. At the same time, rising land prices and input costs are eating into already minimal returns.

By the Commission's own evaluation, only a fraction of each subsidy euro given under its Rural Development scheme was reflected in net family farm incomes in Poland – less than 14 cents.[11] In other words, for most farmers, the money Brussels dishes out is making next to no difference to the bottom line.

I met a southern mountain farmer called Maria whose seven cows graze the slopes of Jablonka, near the border with Slovakia. We stood talking in her barn, where three calves were resting on straw while their mothers grazed. Sunlight streamed through the windows. Next door was her micro-dairy, kitted out with shiny aluminium churns bought before Poland's accession to the EU.

Maria wore a plain green jersey with blue tunic. She told me how she struggles to get a decent price for her milk. Before Poland joined the EU, she used to have more cows and the milk fetched a decent price, but no longer. 'Mineral water is now more expensive than milk in the shops,' she said. It's a complaint I've heard many times from dairy farmers in other countries, not least Britain. It's just one of many branches of the industry that have seen prices fall to a level where it's a struggle to make ends meet.

None of the small Polish farmers I met were optimistic about the future. 'The subsidies for cows are going down,' Maria told me. 'We spend the subsidy payment on fuel and fertiliser.' I met her son Robert, who hopes to take over the farm. However, with such depressed milk prices, it will not be economical. 'The future is very uncertain,' he admitted.

Ten years on from joining the EU, these mountain farmers are already dependent on subsidies just to keep going. Before, they were able to get better prices. What they've gained on the subsidy, they've lost on the price. It seems that Poland is being sucked willy-nilly into a global market that drives down prices paid to farmers whilst dismantling the means to sell produce locally. As elsewhere, the nation's farmers are under rising pressure and many are getting out.

Where is the sense in billions of taxpayers' money going into a system that no longer seems to be working for the very people it's meant to support: farmers?

## CAP'S LAW OF UNINTENDED CONSEQUENCES

The party was in full swing. As the drink flowed, polite small talk gave way to raucous laughter and frivolity. The Roberts family had gathered at their cottage in rural Hampshire, England, home since their farming days more than forty years ago. Now in her eighties, Anna, the matriarch of the family, was sitting beside me sipping tea and enjoying the late spring sunshine. We were all outside enjoying the warm weather, and I was on my best behaviour because I was engaged to her daughter, now my wife. That's when it happened. I glanced up from my tête-à-tête with Anna and saw the unmistakable shadow of a white stork drifting low above the cottage. I could scarcely believe my eyes.

'Sh*t! Sh*t! White stork!' I exclaimed. In a flash I was hopping around the garden, grabbing for my trusty binoculars.

'What did he say?' Anna asked indignantly. It was hardly the sort of language to use in front of a future mother-in-law.

'Damn, sorry . . . white stork!! Oh, sh*t!' I spluttered, even more flustered now.

So much for my carefully constructed clean-boy image! But in the sort of bird-induced panic only a twitcher can appreciate, I was glued to the sky, watching as the long red beak and legs of our surprise visitor circled then disappeared.

When I explained how rare they are in England, Anna forgave my outburst. It was only the second stork I'd found here, the first being thirty years ago, when I was a schoolboy. As a wildlife-lover herself, she understood my enthusiasm. She and her late husband Peter had farmed this area during the dawning of the CAP. They had seen how government policies and subsidies were driving farming towards intensification. It's what led them to give up the farm and set up the charity for which I now work, CIWF.

The CAP was established at a time when post-war food shortages were strong in the collective memory. The objectives were to increase production, protect a fair standard of living for the agricultural community and assure the availability of food supplies at reasonable prices.[12] These goals were enshrined in 1957 by France, West Germany, Italy, the Netherlands, Belgium and Luxembourg in the founding Treaty of what is now known as the European Union (EU).

European countries were already subsidising agriculture. However, if agricultural produce was to be included in the free movement of goods while maintaining state intervention, national intervention schemes had to be made compatible across the Community. The aim was to protect European farmers from international competition and support prices by buying and storing surpluses and subsidising exports.[13] As more countries joined, so their farm support was swept into the CAP. Britain, for example, had its own subsidy scheme enacted by the 1947 Agriculture Act, and wasn't to join the Common Market until 1973. In the decades that followed, the EU expanded from six nations to the twenty-eight member countries of today, and the CAP became a behemoth.

Quite how the UK's referendum decision to leave the EU will play out in terms of influencing future agriculture policy remains to be seen. UK farmers have been used to receiving £3.6 billion of subsidy every year via the CAP and will want the UK taxpayer to give them a similar amount. At the same time, Brexit may provide an opportunity in the UK to at least make a fresh start and direct some taxpayer support towards protecting the environment and improving animal welfare. British agriculture, with its high land and labour costs, isn't best placed to compete with other countries on price. This may focus minds on quality rather than quantity, which would mean a shift away from industrial agriculture. However, the government's pre-referendum strategy for agriculture was very much about more industrialisation for decades to come.

For the EU, CAP remains the dominant item on the budget sheet. These days, much of the CAP budget goes directly to farmers to support their incomes. Farmers are getting a higher price for their goods than the market price, and this difference is being funded by taxpayers.

Paying farmers to maintain prices regardless of supply and demand does have benefits. It acts as a kind of insurance scheme against bad harvests or other uncertainties that might undermine food supply. Indeed, the mammoth US subsidy package now describes its main subsidies as coverage for 'agricultural risk' and 'price loss'.[14] However, the effect is to rig the market. Instead of operating naturally according to the laws of supply and demand, the agricultural industry is shaped as much around subsidy incentives as customers. This can yield distortions in both the quantity and the type of products produced.

On the face of it, that the CAP fuels intensification is not self-evident. Direct subsidies for rearing farm animals have historically been targeted at more extensive forms of animal production, namely grazing sheep and cattle. Meanwhile, pigs and poultry have long been the most intensively farmed and receive no direct subsidy. However, their feed – primarily cereal – has been heavily subsidised. Payments designed to enhance animal welfare further confuse the picture. While these bonuses sound animal-friendly, the reality is that they constitute just a tiny fraction of the entire CAP budget and, as we shall see, they are hardly effective in any case.

Following the excessive production of the 1980s, the CAP was reformed, and new incentives introduced to encourage environmental conservation. The Commission claims that it has numerous schemes to encourage what it calls 'modernisation' whilst helping farmers improve their land and sell their produce 'using more sustainable, environmentally-friendly farming methods'.[15] The reality is very different.

Another local farmer I talked with in the Śląskie Voivodship region of Poland told me that villages in her area were slowly dying. She and her husband Szczepan were proud to show us the single cow they own, a solid brown and white house cow with stubby horns. She grazed on lush grass, strolling from one patch to another on a long chain wrapped benignly round her horns.

Before joining the EU, every house in that area would have had two or three cows, and these afforded much the same living as working for the national railway. Now it is getting unusual even to keep one cow. I heard how prices were more reliable before joining the EU, so a family could plan its finances better. Border controls and tariffs protected the local market. But not any more. 'Agriculture is dying in this area,' Helena said sadly.

In the old days the CAP paid farmers direct subsidies to produce more, a system that helped larger arable farmers the most. In recent years, subsidies have been largely decoupled from production; direct payments to farmers are based on the area farmed. The bigger the farm, the greater the subsidy. Only 3 per cent of the EU's farms exceed 100 hectares, yet these account for half of all the farmland.[16] They swallow the lion's share of subsidy outlay. About two-thirds of farms in the EU are smaller than 5 hectares.[17] The smallest – under 5 hectares in England, under 4 hectares in France, or under half a hectare in Italy and Poland – are not even eligible for direct subsidies.

'This is not agriculture, this is destruction-culture. It's nothing to do with real farming, with real food, or caring about the environment, with caring about people or about animals. It's just a disaster,' Łopata said.

I tried to make sense of the economics in play here. By supporting production, taxpayers' subsidies cause farm prices to drop, whilst the price of inputs – fertilisers, pesticides, machinery and so on – rise, because demand for these is so high. Much of the subsidy gets soaked up by the input providers. Once that happens, farms are stuck on a treadmill: pedalling faster and faster to produce more at lower cost. It's not long before they grow totally dependent on subsidy to stay afloat. They learn to hate Brussels but need the hand-outs. The subsidy system (whether or not intentionally) becomes a tool for maintaining the status quo of intensive chemical-based farming, with all its expensive inputs.

Couple this with subsidy payments based on farm size, and you have a driving force for farms to expand.

As small farmers go to the wall, food-processing giants like Smithfield and Danish Crown have entered Poland and captured the market. Rows of metallic buildings replace rustic smallhold-ings. They lurk behind high fences and locked gates that hide hundreds, perhaps thousands of animals – usually pigs or chickens, in cramped, squalid conditions.

Defenders of this regime, particularly those set to benefit, like fertiliser, pesticide and drug companies, may view this as progress – a banner flown to justify all sorts of evils. Personally, I struggle to see how such change can be characterised in positive terms.

On factory farms, pigs lead as wretched a life as chickens. As intelligent as dogs, on intensive farms they are often kept in the most barren conditions.[18] With little else to do but grunt and nuzzle each other, they often resort to biting off each other's tails in sheer frustration. The industry's neat solution: cut off their tails. This painful mutilation is frequently carried out without anaesthetic on whole herds of pigs, despite an EU-wide ban on the routine dock-ing of piglets' tails.

Sows suffer a ruthless cycle of pregnancy and suckling. Often they must rear their young in so-called 'farrowing' crates, stalls so narrow and restrictive that sows can barely stand up or lie down. For weeks on end, they cannot even turn around. This cruel system is designed to prevent mother pigs inadvertently trampling their offspring. Yet it seems to me that the misery it inflicts, day in, day out, is unacceptable, especially as well-designed alternatives can also avoid piglets being crushed.

As with chickens, such conditions also promote disease. Masses of drugs are doled out to keep the inevitable bugs at bay. These days, 68 per cent of Poland's use of antibiotics goes to farm animals, largely to ward off the infections associated with intensification.[19]

The European Commission admits that its subsidy system has encouraged intensification. 'In its early years, the CAP encouraged farmers to use modern machinery and new techniques, including chemical fertilisers and plant protection products,' it says.[20] What is not so clear is how farm animals got hijacked by factory farms as a result.

The answer, as we have discovered elsewhere in this book, relates to the availability of cheap feed.

During the life span of the CAP, pigs and poultry have been the most intensively farmed animals. They also happen to be the biggest consumers of grain. And whilst those sectors receive no direct subsidy, they have been supported indirectly through payments to the cereal sector. One estimate puts the amount of indirect subsidy received in recent years by industrial livestock in England alone as high as 400 million euros.[21] Quite simply, the CAP has ensured the flow of cheap animal feed.

Graham Harvey reports how all this has played out in Britain following the passing of the Agriculture Act in 1947, which introduced a subsidy system in pursuit of greater production. 'When the government took over agriculture, following the Agriculture Act, small farms became a problem' he said. 'They were seen as inefficient and we had to get them out – like Poland now. So we end up with big farms that can't make a living without the subsidy. We have this arable model where you have to get bigger and bigger to spread your overheads, sustain a business and milk bigger and bigger herds and get more and more, and still you can't make decent money out of it.'

The knock-on effect on rural communities is significant. Crop monocultures are highly mechanised and require much less labour. Pesticides and weedkillers eradicate farmers as well as bugs. Before too long, villages cannot sustain local post offices or schools.[22]

The CAP subsidy regime does pay heed to animal welfare, in theory at least, with producers having to comply with minimum welfare legislation. Under its rules, for example, routine tail-docking of pigs is illegal, as is keeping the animals in barren pens. The law requires them to have some straw or other 'manipulable' material as opposed to cold concrete and slats.

Yet in Poland and the rest of the EU, such practices still prevail. Clearly the law doesn't work, and a toxic combination ensues: a system that encourages farmers to confine animals in sheds and feed them cheap cereals (or soy) whilst failing to protect the animals from the insidious effects of their new living conditions. In the ten years since the EU's animal welfare rules were introduced, the number of pigs reared in illegal conditions in Europe has been estimated at 2 billion animals.

The CAP also cites animal welfare as a priority for funding under its so-called Rural Development programme, which earmarks about 50 million euros a year for animal welfare payments. That sounds like a lot, but amounts to a tiny proportion of the CAP budget – about 0.1 per cent. The payments are available to farmers who make animal-welfare improvements that go beyond normal requirements – as when giving animals more space, more comfortable flooring and better bedding material, or even allowing them outdoors. It's designed to encourage moves toward less intensive production, but there is scant evidence that it is having a positive impact. Quite the reverse.

In March 2015, Phil Hogan, the EU Commissioner for Agriculture and Rural Development, tweeted about a pig farm he'd visited in Romania. The photo he posted showed the proud recipient of Rural Development funds: an intensive pig farm with barren conditions and no straw bedding. The animals had their tails docked – contrary to EU law. On his blog, Commissioner Hogan described the farm as a 'perfect example' of the 'CAP supporting local development in rural communities and the economic opportunities for agriculture within the EU member states'.[23] To me, this says it all.

In Germany, a study by two research centres found that the proportion of dairy farmers keeping their cows shut permanently indoors actually increased by 5 per cent as a direct result of Rural Development money. A 2009 study pointed out that at least some of the farms are likely to have increased the number of cows kept after investing subsidy money, so the increase in the number of animals deprived of access to pasture may be even greater.[24]

The same German study found that the proportion of pig farms using harsh, fully-slatted floors – thereby probably breaking the legal requirement to provide pigs with enrichment materials like straw – soared from 50 to 73 per cent after funding. When experts measured the welfare of the pigs by monitoring their behaviours, they found a drop in well-being on no less than 40 per cent of farms.[25]

In the Czech Republic, more than 500 million euros in Rural Development funding went on new animal housing, with no due assessment carried out on how the cash would improve animal welfare. So tumbledown facilities – or open spaces – may well have been replaced with shiny new premises on which conditions for livestock are actually worse.[26]

In England, a nation of animal lovers, the government appears to lump animal welfare in with health and disease control. They do not coincide. Yes, the welfare of animals suffers if they are sick or diseased, but that's not the end of the story. An animal's welfare includes its physical and mental well-being. Policymakers need to consider whether, for example, broiler chickens have been designed to grow so fast that they suffer as a result; and whether it is wise, or humane, to support high-yielding breeds of dairy cow which produce so much milk they are worn out and sent for slaughter after just three lactations. More balanced breeds can go on for many years more.

Then there is mental well-being. Can animals express their natural behaviours, or is this impossible, as it is for hens in very small cages? Just keeping animals 'disease-free' tends to mean that only the welfare aspects relevant to production are accounted for – getting the animals to grow fast enough and stay alive long enough before slaughter. For a true appraisal of animal welfare, a whole lot more needs to be considered. As for Poland's Rural Development plans – well, they do not once refer to animal welfare.

All too often, then, good intentions fall short – leaving animals worse off than they were before.

It was my last day in the Polish countryside. Before me lay a patchwork quilt of little fields, defiant to monoculture rule. The soft peaks of the Beskidy Mountains, carpeted in forest, melted away in the distance. I stood admiring the view in glorious sunshine as a breeze sent ripples across the seeding heads of tall grass. At my feet were golden buttercups. I could hear the quasi-mechanical trill of a grasshopper warbler.

According to the European Commission, farming is 'not just about food'. Explaining the CAP, the Commission acknowledges that it is also about 'rural communities and the people who live in them. It is about our countryside and its precious natural resources.'[27] Yet under CAP, farmers in Western Europe have gone out of business as if the days of making a living from the land are over and done. My time in Poland had given me an insight into how subsidies have distorted the industry. I now had a better understanding of the forces that have historically shaped the landscape in Western Europe, turning mixed farms into monocultures.

While the CAP has evolved over the years, the basic premise stands: support production, promote 'modernisation', keep prices low. Poland offers an insight into what happened to the original EU member states half a century ago. It also provides real-time perspective on whether we've learned anything from the mistakes of the past.

While I was there, an announcement on national radio caught my ear: Poland had just lost its status as world leader in white storks. The story was that the stork population has dropped by up to 20 per cent in just a decade.[28] Compared with the previous census carried out just as Poland entered the EU, numbers declined by 15–20 per cent across the country.

The birds were hardest hit in the west of the country, where numbers fell by up to 40 per cent. Experts connected the trend with the start of intensive farming. Marcin Tobolka, of the Institute of Zoology in Poznan, a researcher involved in the study, said simply: 'Storks disappear from Western Poland because more intensive agriculture enters.'[29] He told the government-funded website Science in Poland that the birds were struggling to find food among monocultures of rape and corn. 'Where storks are doing quite well, traditional agriculture is still dominant, with its wet meadows, pastures and boundary strips,' he said.

As the CAP speeds across the Polish countryside like Toad in his motorcar, it takes a heavy toll.

# 7

# Water vole

Some of the best things in nature are understated. Take the chalk-streams of England, for example. These fragile river systems meander quietly through undulating countryside before disappearing into the sea. Look closer and you find another world. Beloved by fishermen down the ages, chalkstreams are fascinating river systems where everything grows in abundance. Fed by babbling springs, they have their own ecosystem, so unique and biologically productive that experts have come to call them the nation's rainforests.[1]

I am lucky enough to live near some of the most beautiful chalk-streams on Earth. Our cottage stands just miles from the source of the Itchen, a river that attracts anglers from all over the world because of the quality of its fly fishing. We also overlook the Itchen's 'Cinderella' sister, the Meon, which usually trickles past our cottage, but sometimes gushes by in torrents after heavy rain.

There is something quintessentially English about the clear, chattering waters of chalkstreams. The gentle verdant banks that wind away through tranquil fields evoke memories of village greens, cricket pitches, long summer days with the chink of china crockery and cream teas. The community of life that thrives in these jewels of the countryside has been the subject of much prose, not least in Simon Cooper's charming *Life of a Chalkstream*, where he describes discovering 'his' river: a 'fast clear stream with huge rafts of waving green crowfoot, the banks lined with sedge grasses and margins festooned with semi-aquatic plants like rushes, water-cress and wild mints that provide the "perfect home" for the insects which sustain a rich web of life'.[2]

I am mesmerised by these magical waters. Duke and I go on long walks along the stretch of chalkstream near us. He loves to run and splash and drink in the shallows, biting the water and near-choking himself, then doing it all again in the way that dogs do. We're always on the lookout for surprise: wild trout sheltering beside a bridge, a heron or little egret staring motionless at the passing water, the vibrant flash of a kingfisher.

There are little more than 200 genuine chalkstreams in the world, and 160 are in England. All along a band of calcareous rock that slants across the country from northeast to southwest, they bubble out of thousands of underground springs, ripple over gravel beds and meander through valleys toward the sea. They are typically shallow and crystal-clear, with alkaline water purified and filtered through chalk to emerge at a constant temperature come summer or winter, providing thriving conditions for wildlife like the mayfly, trout and the water vole.

Water voles were once a familiar part of life. Riverside rambles would be punctuated by the sound of these sweet furry brown creatures jumping into the water with a 'plop' and swimming away. To the untrained eye, they look a bit like rats (they inspired the character 'Ratty' in *Wind in the Willows*), but in fact they are quite different to their much-despised cousins. They are smaller, their tails are furry as opposed to hairless, and they have short blunt snouts rather than a pointy nose. Their ears are almost concealed by their fur. Unlike rats, they have no links with the spread of disease and they cannot be found in cities, around sewers or up drainpipes. Indeed, they need pristine, pollution-free rivers and riverbanks to thrive – conditions harder and harder to find.

During my childhood in the 1970s, they thrived along the canals and rivers in my native Bedfordshire. I'd hear them more often than I'd spot them – a liquid plop in the water, then a string of bubbles: they must be somewhere just below the surface. I'd sometimes watch them sitting on their hind legs, preening and scratching their little round faces before they scurried along the bank. If I sat quietly enough, I'd catch an occasional glimpse of them coming and going from a burrow tucked away in the river bank, just by the waterline.

They were unremarkable back then. Today, the water vole is one of Britain's most endangered creatures. Though I have whiled away countless days by riverbanks and among the marshy reedbeds of Titchfield Haven and other south coast sites – areas that should be teeming with water voles – I haven't seen one for more than two decades.

My neighbours on the Meon remember their cat bringing in the last water vole they can remember way back in 1982. My own last sighting of a water vole in England was in the 1990s, at the late Sir Peter Scott's Slimbridge reserve in Gloucestershire, an oasis for ducks, geese and swans. Despite now living in the heart of England's rich chalkstream country, I haven't seen so much as a whisker.

The water vole has become Britain's fastest-declining wild mammal. The extent of the decline is staggering. In the Iron Age, there are thought to have been some 6.7 billion.[3] Over the last forty years in Britain their numbers have plummeted by 90 per cent, a state of decline as fast as that of East Africa's black rhino.[4] In 2008, along Hampshire's Meon Valley, they were considered extinct. The decline of their chalkstream habitats and the destruction of bankside sanctums has hastened their demise. Yet the final nail in the water vole's coffin has come from an overseas interloper in the form of the American mink.

The mink now patrolling Britain's waterways were originally brought from America to be farmed for fur in the 1920s. The industry peaked in the 1950s, when 400 or more farms confined these active wanderers to tiny cages. They were first confirmed to be breeding in the wild in 1956. By December 1967, feral mink were present in over half the counties of England and Wales, and in much of lowland Scotland, taking advantage of the ecological vacuum left by the demise of the otter. Today, mink can be recorded in every mainland county of England and Scotland and are fast colonising some of the many offshore islands of Scotland – a very real threat to internationally important seabird colonies.[5]

Unfortunately, they are successful and opportunistic predators with a voracious appetite, particularly for water voles. Darren Tansley from the Wildlife Trusts said: 'Mink have a devastating effect on water voles and our wildlife. They are super-efficient predators. Once a female sets up territory along a river course the majority of prey species will be totally wiped out. Mink eat just about anything they can catch, and they can catch just about anything – ground-nesting birds, small mammals, frogs and crayfish all prove easy prey.'

Water voles escape predators in three ways: diving into the water, disappearing into thick vegetation or shooting down their burrows. None of these loopholes work against mink, which pursue them both through water and above and below ground. Sadly, if mink move into water-vole habitat it's curtains for Ratty.

The Game and Wildlife Conservation Trust describes it as a 'widespread modern misconception' that the American mink in the wild in Britain originated from mass releases from fur farms by animal-rights activists. Escapes and perhaps deliberate releases by fur farmers had been occurring for decades before the industry became the subject of public protest.[6]

On fur farms, mink were generally kept in tiny battery cages, a highly restrictive lifestyle for an animal that would naturally cover large distances in the wild. In such alien conditions, many resorted to pacing back and forth in their cages. They would grow stressed to the point of self-mutilation. Eventually, the British government became persuaded that the industry was inhumane, and in the year 2000 farming of mink for fur was banned on animal welfare grounds.

While the source of the original invasion has gone, however, the problem remains. The animals spread successfully over much of the country, leaving conservationists with a stark choice: either leave the mink to thrive, and seriously jeopardise native wildlife, or start a colossal and doubtless highly controversial campaign to remove them.

In 2003, plans were drawn up by conservationists for the biggest-ever cull of mink in Britain. It followed a series of local culls that led to a remarkable and instant recovery of the water vole, prompting hopes that the animals could be saved, though experts warned that total elimination of the mink would probably take 100 years to complete.[7]

Some, like the animal rights organisation Animal Aid, objected to the cull, claiming that mink had become a scapegoat for the decline in native British mammals.[8] They had been blamed for the dramatic decline of the otter, though evidence now indicates that it was pesticides and persecution by hunters that put the species under so much pressure. Now that hunting is banned, otter numbers are recovering in cleaner rivers. And where otters do well, mink numbers decline just as spectacularly, indicating successful competition by the otter.[9]

In any case, mink are not the only villains of this piece. Arguably, it was the impact of intensive farming in destroying much of the riverbank habitat on which water voles relied that made them even more vulnerable to the furry invaders.

In his book *Farming in the Clouds*, the former Conservative MP Sir Richard Body describes the chain of events he witnessed from the 1970s on the River Pang, a tributary of the Thames. First trees were felled, including the willows, and then came dredgers to straighten and deepen the rivers until they looked more like canals than meandering chalkstreams. Body describes how millions of pounds of public money was used in this way to lower the water table and fit the land for arable crops like wheat, barley and oilseed rape, which now dominate the flanks of England's chalkstreams. A beef farmer himself, Body felt that taxpayers' money was being lavished on arable farmers at the expense of grazing animals.

'We need a high water table to enable the grass to grow well all through the dry summer months,' he wrote. 'Some of the wild-flowers have gone, others are markedly fewer. Of the birds, the snipe, the peewit and the kingfisher are seen no more and the mallard and the moorhen are many fewer. Removal of the cover along the river bank has taken away the habitat of the otter and the water vole – Kenneth Grahame's "Ratty".'

As the rich variety of plantlife that provides grazing animals with both flavour and nutrition was depleted, he began to notice that the quality of the beef being produced from his animals

was being diminished.[10] These concerns are echoed by Graham
Roberts, now retired Water for Wildlife officer at the Hampshire
and Isle of Wight Wildlife Trust, who told me how the straighten-
ing and dredging of rivers and excessive drainage of land for arable
cropping has had a drastic effect on the water vole: 'In continental Europe, water voles live much more on land. In Britain, due
to long-standing intensification of the fertile free-draining flood-
plains, they are much more confined to the riparian fringe where
farm meets water. A classic example of the problem is in Kent
on sections of the Medway, where intensive farming with arable
crops comes right up to the river. The edge is flailed and cleared,
and the moment the river rises, the banks break away. As the bank
collapses and falls away, so too does the water vole's home, clog-
ging the river with silt,' he told me.

The Environment Agency's Paul Smith concurs, identifying
intensive farming as a key source of the threat to water voles. 'Their
habitats [have] suffered from heavy engineering work for flood-
defence and land-drainage purposes.'[11]

Chalkstreams are naturally rich in nutrients, which is why they
are so great for wildlife. But they are fragile ecosystems, easily
upset. Pollution causes weed to grow and algae to bloom, smoth-
ering flowering plants, coating the riverbed an unsightly green
and sucking oxygen out of the water. When gravel on a riverbed
is coated in a slimy brown fur, it is a sure sign of pollution, often
linked to phosphorus and nitrates from fertiliser. In the River Avon
in Hampshire, levels of nitrates – mainly from agriculture – have
doubled, and levels of phosphates have trebled since 1950.[12]

One major source of pollution is nearby farmland under intensive arable cropping. England's chalkstreams have more arable land
in their catchment areas – nearly half of all surrounding land –
than other types of river.[13] Since the 1970s, there has been a heavy
shift towards growing maize in Britain; the area under cultivation
has shot up from 1,400 to 160,000 hectares, much of it grown for
livestock feed and for the biofuel business.

Maize (corn) crops are particularly blamed for polluting rivers.
Maize is a tall crop with widely spaced stalks, leaving relatively

large areas of soil exposed and therefore vulnerable to erosion and nutrient runoff throughout the growing season. It is a 'needy' crop, requiring relatively high inputs of pesticides and fertilisers. During heavy rain, water runs off the surface of compacted fields, taking some of these chemicals with it, causing rivers to become polluted and at greater risk of flooding.[14]

A change in the way that farmers manage their crops has also had an impact on rivers. Farmers have been ploughing land that was previously untilled and switching from spring to autumn sowing, a practice that leaves the soil bare during the winter rainy season and susceptible to erosion and runoff.

A scientific paper in the journal *Soil Use and Management* found that surface water runoff in southwest England had reached a critical point due to this wholesale change in the way the land is cultivated. At 38 per cent of the sites investigated, the water, instead of percolating into the ground, was pouring off compacted soils.[15] In many of these fields, soil, fertilisers and pesticides were being washed away too. In three-quarters of the maize fields in the southwest, the soil structure has broken down to the extent that they now contribute to flooding.[16] Six weeks after this paper was published, the Somerset Levels in the southwest were hit by devastating floods.

All of this can be bad news for wildlife as well as for people affected by floods: water voles can fall victim to algal blooms associated with agricultural pollution;[17] invertebrates like the mayfly, which feed fish and drive the entire river ecosystem, are also affected by pollution. Delicate riverbeds can become silted up with soil, robbing fish and other species of vital breeding habitat. Experts fear that water voles are unlikely to survive in many of the habitats they currently occupy.[18]

All in all, the future looks bleak for Ratty.

## RATTY'S RETURN

The Meon springs up near our cottage and reaches the sea just beyond the marshy harbour setting of Hampshire's Titchfield Haven.

I often stand on the flintstone bridge over what is the highest of all chalkstream springs in the UK. I gaze at the water as it chatters from beneath a ramshackle copse before heading slowly downriver for 20 miles through downland and coastal plains. As I look into the chalky hollow, I frequently hear the fluty chimes of hidden teal – tiny grey and red ducks with exquisite emerald head stripes. Buffy-green chiffchaffs search for insects among the woody kindling strewn along the edges of the shimmering river. Further along, I sometimes see the flash of brown trout.

Wildlife and fly-fishermen are not the only beneficiaries of chalkstreams. They are a primary source of freshwater for household consumption. More than two-thirds of the water supply for the southeast of England comes from the chalk aquifer, with an average family of four using the water equivalent of 60 metres of river each year. However, these beautiful streams are showing signs of strain from increasing demand for water abstraction.

Fed by springs that come up from calcareous hills with tremendous water-holding capacity – more than any manmade reservoir[19] – chalkstreams help maintain domestic water supplies. The springs release purified water in a steady flow, even in the driest summer, but they are being stretched to the limit. A third of England's rivers generally are at risk of damage from over-abstraction. Nearly three-quarters of the Meon's flow is syphoned off, raising concerns over long-term sustainability.

In 2004, a UK government Environment Agency report found England's chalkstreams in a 'fragile' state. It warned that they are at risk of being 'damaged forever' and cited mounting pressure from water abstraction, urban development, effluent discharges and agriculture. Without careful management, it said, these activities threaten the chalk-river resources upon which so much wildlife and so many people depend. A third of rivers were found to have deteriorated to the point of being described as 'poor'.[20]

Matters did not improve as a result of this blunt warning. A decade later, in 2014, WWF-UK found England's chalkstreams in a 'shocking state of health'. The organisation classed less than a quarter as 'good', and found one-third in a 'poor' or 'bad' state.

It said that the chalk aquifer – the engine room of the chalkstream – was in poor condition, with elevated phosphate and nitrate levels at a point where they pose a real risk to drinking water.

Again, it warned that without dramatic change in the way these precious resources are cared for and managed, the outlook for England's chalkstreams was bleak. WWF-UK called for less abstraction, less pollution, habitat restoration and better river management.[21]

Speaking at the launch of WWF-UK's report, Charles Rangeley-Wilson, a passionate chalkstream conservationist, said: '[It took] millions of years to form the rolling chalk hills of England and tens of thousands more to form the chalkstreams these hills give rise to. Over centuries these gentle streams were enriched with the history of a living landscape. But now, in only a few decades, we have taken these unique rivers to the edge of existence. They are our very own burning rainforest. It is up to us to put the fires out.'[22]

Encouragingly, there is growing interest in restoring chalk-streams to their former glory. Otters are making a comeback and were recorded at two-thirds of the chalkstream sites surveyed – a huge leap since the 1980s, when they could be found in only 5 per cent. Significant efforts are also under way to support the remaining population of water voles. A number are being reintroduced to rivers across the country, including to the river Meon, five years after they were declared locally extinct. Hundreds were also released at one of my favourite places, Titchfield Haven, in summer 2013, once the whole catchment area of the river was considered mink-free.[23] Elaina Whittaker-Slark, ranger for the South Downs National Park, described it as a highly ambitious project.

'We hope that in the future we'll have water voles back and thriving from the source in the heart of the South Downs National Park, its tributaries and all along the length of the Meon Valley,' she said. Although this first reintroduction was 20 miles away, the prospect of seeing Ratty again on my local patch was looking up. Two years later, a further 190 water voles were released further upriver, just 10 miles from my home.

Whether they succeed in getting this far along the Meon Valley depends in part on some of my neighbours, George Atkinson among them. A regular on our local cricket pitch, where he's seen as a 'solid all-rounder', he takes that reputation with him when it comes to wildlife too.

Atkinson farms nearly 500 hectares of the rolling South Downs with sheep, cattle and crops, and has a strong belief in the ability of farmers to help restore the countryside for a variety of wildlife, including water voles. Where the Meon River runs through his land, he fences off banks so that they grow up and provide cover for water voles when they get here. 'In our wet meadows, water voles, snipe and barn owls are the main conservation priorities,' he said.

So if Ratty makes it this far up the valley, he could be in for a warm welcome – but we need many more farmers like George.

# 8

# Peregrine

## POISON SEEDS IN THE COUNTRYSIDE

In the days of the Magna Carta in the thirteenth century, England found itself fighting a series of battles with France. The monarchy faced a double threat, first from across the Channel, and second from treacherous barons closer to home. One family that became notorious for betraying the Crown was de Marisco, who took up residence on Lundy, a small island in the Bristol Channel.

In 1216 Henry III was crowned king and became known for his love of religious ceremony[1] and charity. He famously paid for the feeding of 500 paupers each day.[2] He also had a passion for falconry, a popular pastime in those days, so much so that falcons were worth more than their weight in gold.[3]

The king's bird was the peregrine, a fearsome hunter that catches prey on the wing, and the most prized of these came from Lundy. Around that time, Lundy was owned by the king but was under the control of William de Marisco, who was no friend of the monarch. The man was a ruthless survivor with a fearsome grip on the island and was on the run for murder and treason. With a family namesake born the illegitimate son of Henry I, he also had a dodgy claim to the throne and wasn't going to let things lie.[4]

Henry III's patience finally ran out when de Marisco sent a hitman to kill him. The king resolved to get his own back, and with it his island and prize peregrines. A Norfolk baron by the name of William Bardolf was ordered to capture de Marisco and bring him back to London. Accompanied by two knights and a dozen sergeants, he set sail for Lundy. By now, de Marisco had become a fearsome outlaw who was terrorising passing ships, launching pirate raids from Lundy. He knew they were after him, so had taken steps to ensure that any visitors suffered a painful welcome.

Bardolf landed on the bay, the only weak point in the island's otherwise impenetrable buttress of cliffs. On a good day, any approaching vessel would be spotted well before it became a threat, but Bardolf had set sail when Lundy was shrouded in mist, hoping to land unobserved. Instead, he was spotted. Through the murk, a lone watchman saw him and his men. Had the alarm been sounded, the adventure would most likely have ended with Bardolf and his men being pelted to death by rocks. But the alarm never came. The watchman was being held prisoner on the island and was only too happy to betray his captor.

Through the cold mist that had cloaked their landing, Bardolf's men made their way up the steep cliff along a narrow windy path. They couldn't believe their luck. Against the odds, they reached a desolate grassy plateau, and headed to the sheltered area known as 'Bulls Paradise'. Here was de Marisco's residence, a stronghold enclosed by granite walls 7 feet thick.[5] He was dining in his fortress, unaware that his defences had failed him. Taken by surprise, he and his sixteen men were captured and taken to London to stand trial.

On 25 July 1242, still protesting his innocence, William de Marisco was taken from the Tower of London and hung, drawn and quartered.[6] King Henry III was rid of his sworn enemy.

By regaining his island, the king also regained control of Lundy's peregrine eyrie, reputed to house the very finest falconers' birds. So prized were they that Henry would now and then use them as special gifts for those he wanted to honour or thank. A 1274 Crown Juror's assessment of the island listed among its attributes 'the esteemed peregrine eyrie'.[7] Lundy is the earliest known nesting site in Britain for these dashing falcons.

Peregrines are muscular birds with scimitar wings that streak through the air like a flying sickle. They spend hours perching and watching over their territories. Slate-grey above and white below, with delicate barring, they have a distinctive black facial mask and moustache. A peregrine's eyesight is eight times more acute than our own.[8] Henry III would have been impressed by their sheer power and speed. When they close their wings and 'stoop', a hunting bird will knock the living daylights out of any unsuspecting pigeon. Lundy's reputation for producing the very best and most successful hunters persisted well into the twentieth century. In 1937 the falconer Colonel Gilbert Blaine described how birds from its eyrie had long been considered the best by his professional colleagues.[9]

Now fully protected by law from nest-robbers, falconers and guns, the island remains a prime spot for seeing peregrines. I visit most years to see them, sometimes staying in the very castle Henry III built after getting rid of De Marisco. It is now managed by the Landmark Trust, which has converted the old building into unique self-catering accommodation. The granite fortress, ironically known as Marisco Castle, is the oldest surviving building on the island and has stunning views.

Perched on sheer cliffs several hundred feet high, it provides the perfect viewpoint for watching the Earth's fastest animal. (Cheetahs are the fastest land animals, running at speeds of up to 75 miles per hour. Peregrines can beat that, flying at speeds around 200 miles per hour.) There can be few more impressive sights than these magnificent birds of prey, with their dark hoods and angular grey wings, cutting through the sky. They hurtle like jet planes and can pull 6G – six times the force of gravity.[10]

Yet Lundy's peregrines have a chequered history. During the Second World War they were declared a public enemy because of the threat they posed to carrier pigeons. Thousands of Britain's pigeon fanciers had volunteered their birds to help the war effort by acting as messengers for the army, RAF, Home Guard and police. Birds of prey along the coast were culled in an attempt to create safe passage for pigeons bringing messages home.[11]

In the event, none of Lundy's famous falcons were destroyed, due perhaps to the secret protection of local people. By 1950, the death penalty had been lifted and peregrines were once again declared breeding on the island. Having dodged government bullets during the war, however, they were about to face a far more deadly threat: toxic farm chemicals.

By the 1960s, agricultural pesticides were beginning to devastate bird populations. Robins and other songbirds eating pesticide-laden worms were dropping dead en masse. Residues of organochlorine insecticides started to build up in larger birds like falcons and hawks at the top of the food chain. The chemicals interfered with the bird's reproductive functions, causing adults to lay eggs with unnaturally thin shells that would break under the weight of the parent bird.[12] The peregrine population plummeted.

In June 1963 an adult male peregrine was found dead on his nest on Lundy. Its liver was contaminated by a lethal mix of chemicals – DDE, dieldrin, heptachlor, BHC (lindane) – evidence that farming's new chemical age was now killing adult birds. By the late 1960s, as in many other parts of Britain, Lundy's peregrines were wiped out.[13] However, from 1975 peregrines returned to breed there. They also started bouncing back across Britain. The early excesses of chemical-soaked intensive farming seemed to have been curbed. The worst offending chemical – DDT – was withdrawn worldwide from agricultural use.

Sadly, however, new threats are being faced by peregrines and other birds associated with farmland. Whilst the chemicals that destroyed the eggs of peregrines have been banned or restricted, rural industrialisation grinds on. Populations of once common farmland birds like the skylark, still abundant on Lundy, have collapsed across the rest of the country.

For birds and other wildlife, the countryside has become a hazardous place. Chemical herbicides obliterate the flowering plants that provide seeds to eat. Chemical insecticides wipe out their insect food. Vast prairies of single crops swamp habitat. And while the main damage from pesticides comes from industrial monocultures and the associated lack of wild seeds and insects, there is another deadly threat: crop seeds coated with pesticide.

I first learned of this hidden facet of industrial agriculture when I heard about the plight of Lundy's population of house sparrows.

They had been wiped out by grain laced with rat poison. It was the winter of 1996/97 and farmers had been using a new type of rat poison called difenacoum, which is highly toxic to both birds and mammals. Until then, the birds had been happily eating warfarin-baited grain with no ill-effect, because they have a high natural tolerance to the substance. The new generation of rat poison proved lethal. The flock was wiped out, to the point that new birds had to be imported from the mainland.

The Lundy sparrows had been part of a long-term study of evolution in this isolated population, which was disrupted by the poisoning. In spring 2000, Nancy Ockendon, a researcher at the University of Sheffield, caught forty-nine adult sparrows from Yorkshire and took them to the island. Although some flew off back to the mainland, more than half of the newcomers stayed and the study has since continued.[14]

Efforts have been made to produce grain-baited rat poison that does not do collateral harm to birds. If you look around office buildings or railway stations, you'll often find weird-looking plastic boxes with a hole in the front big enough for a small mammal to get in. Rats and mice are attracted to the grain in these boxes and get a fatal dose of poison.

Yet rat poison continues to contaminate wildlife habitats. Owls are regularly adversely affected by rodenticides, as are other species that eat rodents. Rat poison has even been found in peregrines – and they eat birds, not rats.

Whilst Lundy's sparrow kill was a terrible accident, the story of poisoned grains doesn't end there. Shocked by that incident, I investigated whether poison-coated seeds do damage elsewhere, and was horrified to discover that they remain common in the countryside today.

Seeds are planted with a coating of pesticide to give early protection, but some are inevitably spilt and may be found by seed-eating birds that spend a lot of their day foraging, such as sparrows and finches. Just one and a half beet seeds treated with a commonly used neonicotinoid pesticide called Imidacloprid would be enough to kill a house sparrow.[15]

Baiting funny black traps with rat poison is one thing; scattering pesticide-coated grains over great tracts of countryside, imperilling the bird population, is another. In theory, mechanised sowing drills such seed into the ground to ensure that it cannot be pecked out by birds. However, research suggests that about 1 per cent of chemical-treated seeds may remain accessible to foragers after planting. Every hectare sown can contain enough to provide a fatal dose for 100 grey partridges. (The grey partridge, a now rare but prized gamebird, only needs to eat a small number of neonicotinoid-treated seeds to get a fatal dose: 5 maize seeds, 6 beet seeds, or 32 oilseed rape seeds).[16]

A report in 2013 by the American Bird Conservancy found that even where manufacturers' instructions are followed, treated seeds remain readily accessible to birds. 'Seeds are never fully covered with soil, making them easy to find by foraging birds,' it said. 'Spills are commonplace with current machinery. And many species have the ability to scrape and dig for planted seed.'[17]

In the US, red-winged blackbirds can take just ten minutes to eat enough treated rice seeds to prove fatal.[18] In Canada's prairie region, nearly all of the canola (oilseed rape) seed covering 8.5 million hectares of cropland carries neonicotinoids: nearly half the region's cropland is treated with the pesticide.[19] After a Canadian farmer from the prairie province of Saskatchewan applied granules of carbofuran to control flea beetles in a canola field in 1984, he returned to find the bodies of several thousand Lapland longspurs, small seed-eating buntings, dotting the field. These Arctic migrants travel in flocks numbering tens of thousands. During migration they are vulnerable to pesticides used on farms, because they favour recently seeded fields and love to peck in search of food.[20]

It doesn't take many treated seeds to kill a songbird. Even low doses of pesticide can cause chronic and reproductive effects that would likely reduce the bird's ability to breed. A study by Canadian scientists into general pesticide effects found sixteen species of 'grassland' (farmland) birds dead in field trials. Among the species affected were birds of prey like northern harriers, burrowing and short-eared owls, all of which could prey on grain-eating birds and small mammals that had eaten pesticide-treated seeds. Other victims included species readily taken by birds of prey – larks, buntings, pipits.[21] All of this raises the spectre that peregrines too could be affected. After all, a peregrine could eat several small birds in a day, and birds sick or very weakened by poisoning will be easier to catch.

Pesticides work by disrupting a vital bodily process, such as photosynthesis in plants, or by destroying a major organ, such as a caterpillar's intestine. Organophosphates and carbamates, the insecticides most in use today, are described as 'cholinesterase-inhibiting' because they kill by interfering with an enzyme vital for nerve transmission. The question for those who care about the environment is the range of species vulnerable to the particular chemical used – that is, how targeted these chemicals are. The answer is not very. Pesticides don't actually 'recognise' target pest organisms. Instead, they are 'programmed' to affect a process or organ, and unfortunately, any organism with that process or organ can be affected. A pesticide may therefore be perfectly capable of killing species that people want to keep, as well as species labelled as pests.[22]

In a report published in 2015, an international group of scientists blamed neonicotinoid use for 'the catastrophic decline of insects across Europe' and the consequent decline of insect-eating birds.[23] They pointed to EU rules restricting pesticide use to treating known problems above a certain level and questioned whether the routine preventative use of seeds dressed with broad-spectrum pesticide in Europe was even legal.[24]

Caroline Cox, a US scientist and pesticide expert, writing in the *Journal of Pesticide Reform* has warned that pesticides will 'continue to kill birds, reduce their food resources, and disrupt their normal behaviours as long as pesticides continue to be used.'[25]

If they think about it at all, people probably assume that pesticides are generally sprayed onto crops to provide temporary protection from bugs. In reality, some pesticides are designed to be absorbed by the plant, making the whole plant, and not just its surface, toxic to wildlife. These 'systemic' insecticides are designed to diffuse throughout the plant, making it a danger to any susceptible species throughout its life. Neonicotinoids and many other seed treatments work in this way.

Neonicotinoids and related pesticides account for a third of the world insecticide market.[26] In the UK, about 90 per cent of all neonicotinoid pesticides are used to coat seeds before planting. And they have other uses: as bait for creatures like ants and cockroaches; sprinkled on pasture in granular form; sprayed on the foliage of plants.[27] Studies have also found that most of the active ingredient in seed dressings is not absorbed by the crop. A small proportion is lost as dust during sowing, but more than 90 per cent enters the soil, where it will contaminate the land for some time to come.[28]

Systemic pesticides can't be washed off the plant and may even contaminate the food on our shelves. Nearly half of the fruit and vegetables we eat in the UK are tainted with pesticide residues, often with more than one variety. Bread and flour are particularly likely to contain them. With the exception of organic crops, pesticide contamination of food is universal.[29]

Most pesticide residues found in food are below accepted 'safe' levels. But the tests used to set these levels cannot accurately take into account the long-term effects of low-level exposure, nor can they be expected to predict the effects of the changing cocktail of chemical pesticide residues we encounter in food, again possibly every day over years or decades. Even traces of pesticides banned decades ago – DDT and dieldrin for example – still linger in fish and other seafood, liver, burgers, milk and root crops as a result of long-term accumulation of these pesticides in animal fat, soil and water.[30]

In Cox's words: 'For the birds' own sake, and because, like the miner's canary, they can warn us when our own health or the health of our ecosystem is threatened, these effects are worth our attention and action.'[31]


### EATING THE VIEW

Lundy was bought by the National Trust in 1969. From the mainland, it looks as if someone has shaved a chunky 3-mile strip off Dartmoor and dropped it into the sea. The island is managed by

the Landmark Trust, and has a church, a shop, a pub and one thousand acres of grass-covered granite moorland. Visitors can stay in
historic buildings: everything from a lighthouse to a remote nautical lookout to the Marisco Castle perched high above the landing
bay. The Landmark Trust makes a point of retaining the historic
feel of this unusual accommodation: there are no televisions, radios
or telephones, no wi-fi, and the electricity is switched off between
midnight and 6 a.m.

Lundy just happens to be my favourite place in Britain. I've stayed
here with my wife, Helen, about a dozen times already. We are
slowly making our way round all twenty-three Landmark properties,
trying not to repeat any along the way. We recently stayed in 'Castle
Cottage', which is part of the Marisco Castle built by Henry III. This
particular property has an unrivalled view over the cliffs and landing
bay and is a divine place to spend a week or a fortnight.

Whenever I'm on Lundy, I get up with the lark and set off
searching for birds. I'll head down the east side where there are
bushes and places for tired migrants to shelter. I'll stomp around
for a couple of hours, searching for birds on land and sea, before
returning for breakfast of porridge, toast and several mugs of tea.
Helen and I then head off with our cameras, taking photos of the
buildings, the horses, sheep and goats, flowers, sunsets and pretty
much anything else that takes our fancy. For Lundy is one of those
very special places. It's the kind of place where, if you have to ask
'What's there to do on Lundy?', then it's probably not for you.
Walking and wildlife out in the wilds is what it's all about.

Then in the evening, without fail (and often lunchtimes too),
it's over to the Marisco Tavern, the centre of village life on the
island. Fitted out with nautical flags, life-rings and artefacts from
the island's long history of shipwrecks, it's the place where visitors
and the handful of locals meet to while away the evening. You can
dine on local produce and wash it down with ales, whiskies and
wines. The latter two are my tipple.

I've come to Lundy as a writer's retreat, for which it's fantastic –
the kind of place that allows you to clear your mind and go for it.
Most times though, we're here on holiday.

When I was on Lundy for a break in May 2015, I arranged to meet Beccy Macdonald, a marine biologist and Lundy's warden for the last two years. Naturally we met in the Tavern, where I found her sipping coffee.

She told me that Lundy's peregrine falcons were doing well, and the population far higher than the island's size might suggest. Macdonald had just finished setting up a number of live webcams on the island's puffin colony. It means that armchair puffin-watchers can now watch the birds from the comfort of their living room and can even help monitor their behaviour around their nesting burrows, all part of the sort of 'citizen science' – like the RSPB's Garden Birdwatch or the Big Butterfly Watch, organised by Butterfly Conservation – that is such a valuable resource for researchers these days.

The surrounding seas are protected as England's only marine nature reserve and support a thriving colony of seals. The cliffs are a wonderful breeding ground for all sorts of seabirds: puffins, guillemots, razorbills and Manx shearwaters. The cliffs on the east side of the island are sprinkled bright yellow with the flowers of the Lundy cabbage, a species that grows nowhere else in the world.

Macdonald described Lundy as a conservation showcase: a work-ing farm as well as a haven for wildlife. The menu in the Tavern testifies to its produce: Lundy lamb, Lundy venison, sausages from Lundy's own pigs, and the odd dish from the rare-breed Soay sheep which graze the heather moorland. There is also a thriving mail order business.

The farm balances conservation and agriculture. Kevin Welch, its farm manager, makes sure his sheep are moved around regularly to avoid disease and to keep the land healthy. His lambs are born and reared on the island without what the sales blurb describes as the 'pressure of modern intensive methods'. Lundy's animals are grass-fed, so they do not depend on cereals from fields miles away or the chemicals that go with these crops. Reared on traditional grasses and herbs such as yarrow, vetch, medick and clover, the animals enjoy a rich diet that not only improves their quality of life but also enhances the taste of the meat.

Animal welfare is seen as a priority, so much so that Macdonald has noticed how some vegetarians are prepared to eat meat on the island because they know the animals have been well cared for. 'They see the life it has and they're happy that it has had a lovely life, and therefore they're quite happy to eat it. I think that's testament really to the way that we farm,' she said.

Wandering among the sheep on Lundy, with swallows darting in and out and a peregrine shooting overhead, always gives me a sense of the way in which, in an ideal food-production system, everything fits together. Paying attention to the environment – working with nature rather than against nature – helps ensure it is safe and sustainable, promotes animal welfare and generates great food.

'It does show how nature and farming can work together, they don't have to be at loggerheads,' Macdonald agreed. 'I think a lot of farmers understand that looking after nature will actually help their stock in the long term.'

Farmers are not the only ones making these connections: big food manufacturers are catching on. That night, my wife Helen and I sat in the Tavern, as we have many times. Our meals arrived, piping hot and delicious. I reached for the mayonnaise – Heinz – and was pleased to see that it is made from free-range eggs.

That is just one example of how the groundswell of interest in better food from sustainable farming is changing the choices being made by manufacturers and consumers: quietly but surely, taste is shifting. A few years ago, almost all major manufacturers of mayonnaise used eggs from caged hens. Most supermarket shelves were stocked with boxes of cage eggs too. Compassion in World Farming launched a campaign to persuade big companies to think about the food on their shelves and the ingredients they select. Thanks to our work, and that of other organisations like the RSPCA, the big supermarkets started to dump battery eggs. They began exclusively stocking eggs from cage-free hens.

Around the same time, CIWF worked with Unilever to switch the flagship Hellmann's mayonnaises and sauces across Europe to free-range eggs. When the campaign came off, it felt like a massive victory. A switch like this can mean hundreds of thousands, sometimes millions of hens a year living free-range lives instead of cooped up in a cage. Since then, other brands of all sizes and profiles have been making the switch, including supermarket own-labels in Tesco, Morrisons and ASDA. The pace of change has been dramatic.

CIWF continues its crusade to persuade companies to offer better food. Working with over 700 firms in Europe, America, South Africa and China, we have helped create a better life for three quarters of a billion chickens, pigs and cows a year. Meanwhile the countryside and consumers also benefit.

Whenever I come to Lundy, I see people appreciating the island's working countryside – combining food, recreation and wildlife. It is such a contrast to agriculture elsewhere in Britain, ruled as it is by the drive for so-called 'sustainable intensification'. Could it be that we are being lulled into accepting a situation where the countryside as it should be can only be found in parks or reserves, like museums? It is said that islands are a microcosm; a world in miniature. How about a little of this everywhere, instead of a countryside rendered bland and lifeless?

It will take more than a little imagination. It will require governments, food companies, and everyone who shops for food to help bring it about. But what a future it could be. The result could be so much better for all of us. As I look out and see a peregrine hanging in the wind, it seems to me worth striving for.

## THE JOY OF BEING ALIVE

I've clung to perilous cliff edges, bobbed around in boats and spent hours crouching by rain-soaked rocks to watch peregrines on Lundy, but one moment stands out.

It was a raw morning in late May, with a stiff northeasterly wind. Emerging from our cottage beside the Marisco Tavern, I was wearing thick fleece and woolly hat and armed as ever with camera and binoculars. I wandered through my usual bird-watching routine: scouring the bushes for small migrants, past the marshy area where you can see ducks and the odd waterrail, before doubling back toward Millcombe Valley, a richly vegetated gorge that runs to the sea.

I made my way past the cricket pitch, along the horse fields till I reached the fence that runs along the top of Millcombe Valley. As I went through the gate, a flash of wings whooshed right past my face. Startled, I leapt backwards and grabbed my binoculars.

A dark angular shape rose sharply, twisting and turning. As the shape hung in the headwind, I could see it was a male peregrine, now motionless, wings like boomerangs, tail clenched and head swivelling. I watched in awe as the bird positioned himself to make the legendary peregrine 'stoop'. He closed his wings and plunged like a bullet. Boy, was he fast! I tried to keep him in my binoculars, but I just couldn't, he was that quick.

In an instant, he'd shot across the valley, soared high again and then dived steeply, to pull up within a whisker of the grassy hillside. He rose triumphantly, banked, and with a ripple of wings shot across the fields. A heartbeat, and he was out of sight. I was stunned.

I had just watched an adult peregrine at play. It seemed the aerodynamics were pure joie de vivre. He had no prey in sight, no hapless pigeon or puffin. He wasn't being chased. He dived in the wind apparently for the sheer joy of it.

This, to me, is where the environment and animal welfare meet.

Animal welfare, like a living countryside, is a positive state, a joyful one. It is an environment in which animals have the freedom to express themselves naturally, to behave naturally – to be themselves. Animal welfare is about a positive state of well-being. Yes, being free from disease or injury or distress is essential. These things should be a given on any decent farm. But the absence of demonstrable suffering is not enough. What really should shine through is the scope to do what comes naturally: grazing, scratching at the ground, or – in the case of the peregrine – closing wings and hurtling at utmost speed just for fun.

As that exhilarating Lundy peregrine reminded me, what's really important is the joy of being alive. Surely it's not too much to ask for farm animals too?

# 9

# Bumblebee

## BUZZING FROM THE FACTORY FARM

The shadow of a nuclear power station casts jagged shapes across one of Europe's most impressive spans of shingle. Sand stretches as far as the eye can see, punctuated by scrubby patches of marram grass. Some call this 21-square-mile stretch of open shingle Britain's only desert, while the salt air signals that the sea is not far away.

Down at the shore, waves pound the beach, dragging at millions of flinty pebbles. The stones crash and crackle as they heave back and forth with the tide. Seabirds wheel overhead, buffeted by squalls. Save for a smattering of simple wooden homes owned by fishermen and the old coastguards' headquarters, it is a barren and desolate-looking place.

This is Dungeness, a headland on the coast of Kent by the English Channel. The bleak landscape attracts television crews looking for other-worldly film sets, as well as walkers and tourists drawn by the solitude. For a century and a half, it has also been a military training site. With not one but two nuclear plants in the vicinity and periodic red flags warning civilians to keep out during live firing exercises, it seems an unlikely backdrop for a remarkable wildlife story – yet the area has long been renowned as a unique wildlife habitat.

Now it is also the site of an amazing experiment: the very first reintroduction of a bumblebee last recorded in Britain near the RSPB's nature reserve in Dungeness in 1988 and officially declared extinct in this country in 2000.

The Short-Haired Bumblebee Project began in 2009, with an ambitious attempt to capture queen short-haired bumblebees in New Zealand, where they still do well, and export them to the UK. It failed: genetic analysis showed high levels of inbreeding. Undeterred, the team – made up of various universities, bumblebee conservation outfits, quangos and charities – switched its focus to Sweden, which has a more robust population of short-haired bumblebees and a climate more like the UK's.

After an initial batch of the insects were successfully collected and shown to be disease-free, in spring 2012 eighty-nine queen bees were collected from southern Sweden and spent a fortnight in quarantine at the University of London. A total of fifty-one of the captives were healthy enough for release into the RSPB's Dungeness reserve. Since then, the team has been out to Sweden every spring to collect further batches of bees, and there are cheering signs that the new arrivals are slowly making themselves at home. Farmers, smallholders and other local landowners have thrown themselves into the project, helping to create 850 hectares of flower-rich, bee-friendly habitat within the project area of Dungeness and Romney Marsh, and further releases are planned in the years ahead.

One hundred years ago, short-haired bumblebees were common in south and east England, but numbers crashed in the later twentieth century. As farming became more intensive, the wild flowers and rich meadows that had supported bees were swept away, and with them went the insects themselves. By the 1980s the last survivors were disappearing from their remaining haunts. The last known individual bee fell into a trap set for beetles and drowned, and that was that.[1]

Although the bees themselves are small and simple to handle, their reintroduction has not been easy. In the past, Dr Nikki Gammans, the scientist leading the project, has worked on returning rare ants to sites where they have died out, but bees have proven far trickier.

For starters, the first thing they do when released is fly straight over the horizon. A queen bee can fly miles: in half an hour she could be 7 or 8 miles away, and in a few days, anywhere. It makes it extremely difficult to keep track of the insects – and most of those released, after months of meticulous planning and care to guarantee their health, simply disappear without trace.

Every spring since 2012, Gammans has driven her campervan to Sweden with a permit to catch a hundred short-haired bees and bring them back to England. Accompanied by a team of volunteers, she catches the bees with a net and pops them in a fridge in her campervan, where the cold makes them drowsy and easier to store. She then takes them home for quarantine. After a brief period of confinement, they are ready for release from the small cylindrical vials where they have been fed artificial nectar on cotton buds since capture. They emerge dozily – so much so that volunteers can stroke their striped yellow and black backs.

The work can be frustrating: queen bees that Gammans released in earlier years were never seen again. But she's confident that some are still out there somewhere. 'The queens that survived are going to be pretty tough and pretty feisty,' she said. 'They are going to be able to cope with anything in the future.'

In 2015, the news was more positive, with three short-haired bumblebee workers spotted at the RSPB's Dungeness nature reserve in Kent on four consecutive days.[2]

There are about 20,000 species of bee in the world. Honey bees get a disproportionate share of the attention. In the UK, three bumblebee species are now extinct and several more species have become very rare, disappearing from most of Britain. Harking back eighty years, it was normal to find a dozen species of bumblebee in every back garden pretty much everywhere in Britain. Now if you find six or seven, you're doing well. And the problem is not just in Britain: four species have become extinct throughout the whole of Europe. In recent decades, North America has also seen dramatic declines in wild bee populations.

I spoke to the scientist who first came up with the scheme to reintroduce bees in Dungeness to hear his take on why bee species are suffering.

Dave Goulson is Professor of Biology at Brighton's Sussex University and a leading expert on bee conservation and works on wild bees, which play a more important role in pollinating crops and wildflowers than honey bees.

'Admittedly, honeybees are the most abundant and widespread around the globe but nonetheless, the bulk of pollination is done by bees that nobody looks after, that have to look after themselves and have been quietly pollinating crops for millennia without any thanks from us,' Goulson explains.

Many are now in trouble. To some extent, the loss of wild bees is offset by the rise of domestically reared honey bees like those I saw in California on a previous trip. With wild bees all but gone, Central Valley's vast almond orchards are now pollinated by some 40 billion bees drafted into the state every year on the back of 3,000 trucks. Their hives are placed among the crops for six weeks; the honey bees do their thing; and the insects are then hastily scooped up and taken on to the next eco-stricken state. Beekeepers live with the constant anxiety that their charges will be poisoned by clouds of pesticides drifting towards the hives from neighbouring fields.

The industry generally uses tan-coloured bees without the archetypal yellow and black stripes most people associate with the insect. To all intents and purposes they are domestic animals, their fate more influenced by economics than ecology. It is possible to foresee a future point when it becomes impossible for beekeepers to keep colonies alive due to disease. For now, however, European and North American beekeepers can replace colonies lost in winter.

However, not all crops can be serviced by industrially reared bees. Meanwhile wild bee populations continue to decline.

Goulson puts at least part of the blame for the demise of Britain's wild bees at the door of one man – Adolf Hitler. The Second World War was the death-knell for Britain's flower-covered meadows. The celebrated drive for self-sufficiency – 'Dig for Victory' – saw millions of hectares of flower-rich grasslands, hay meadows, chalk downland and so on either ploughed up or given over to fast-growing grass for intensive grazing.

'We used to have an awful lot of flowery meadows, and now we have almost none, and that, from a bee perspective, was a catastrophe. It's compounded by herbicide use in modern intensive farmland which leaves very little room for anything but the crop,' he told me.

Today, if you take a walk beside a hedgerow in Britain, you are unlikely to see any flowers at all. Field margins are dominated by cow parsley, nettles and docks – tough but dull-looking plants which appear to be able to survive a chemical dousing. The problem is nitrate fertiliser running off fields to hedge bottoms, triggering what Goulson describes as a 'staggering loss' of diversity, perhaps the biggest long-term factor in the decline of bees.

Industrial bee-rearing began in the late Eighties, spurred by the economics of commercial tomato production. Until 1988, tomato-growers all over the world were pollinating their plants by hand using thin vibrating wands. Since each individual flower has to be touched by the tip of the wand if it is to bear fruit, the process is immensely labour-intensive, particularly as some commercial tomato farms cover hundreds of acres and have millions of flowers.[3] Around that time, it emerged that bumblebees could do the job more efficiently. Researchers in Belgium and the Netherlands worked out how to breed them and a new market began.

Today, there are bee factories in Europe, North America and Asia churning out nests of buff-tailed bumblebees. Only growers in Australia have been left out of the bee bonanza because of the country's strict rules on importing non-native species.

On the upside, from an environmental point of view, the switch to the use of bumblebees in the tomato industry has reduced pesticide use, for fear that the chemicals will kill the bees. But while industrially reared bumblebees are a cheap alternative to hand pollination, they also carry a major threat: disease.

'These factories are rearing bees at really high densities; they are feeding them on pollen they'd get from honeybee hives out in Europe which often have honeybee diseases, and they feed it to their bumblebees and then they ship the bumblebees all over the world. If you wanted to devise a system to spread bee diseases all around the world, you'd be hard pressed to come up with a better one,' Goulson said bluntly.

In 1998, factory-reared buff-tailed bumblebees were deliberately released in Chile with the full backing of the government. This European species is spreading across South America at the moment, carrying at least two European bee diseases that did not naturally occur in native bumblebees. Native species have little or no resistance to these diseases, and are now being wiped out.

Goulson is one of very few observers to have secured access to a bee-production plant. In a suggestion of nerves about bad publicity, the operators first made him sign a confidentiality agreement. In his best-selling book on the looming bee crisis, *A Sting in the Tale*, he describes the sheer scale of the bee production operation he saw: 'The scale of the operation is staggering. Imagine vast white rooms the size of football pitches, with tall stacked ranks of bumblebee nests on shelves in row after row stretching into the distance, tended by teams of technicians in lab coats sweating in the warm, sticky conditions.'

As industrialisation crept into beekeeping, so food production grew more complicated. Consumers might imagine that their tomato sauce comes from local plants bulging with ripening fruits in the sun. It is more likely to come from a factory in the Netherlands using tomatoes grown in Spain, pollinated by Turkish bees reared in a factory in Slovakia.

The British love bees. The insects have been identified as the number one endangered species Britons would save. Indeed, opinion polls suggest that many see it as more pressing than climate change.[4] A third of what we eat relies on these insects for pollination, yet numbers have almost halved in the past twenty-five years in England.[5] Researchers at the University of Reading believe that Britain has less than a quarter of the bees needed for the proper pollination of its crops, while Europe has only two-thirds.

'If these wild bee populations collapse there would be nothing to compensate for them,' the University of Reading's Dr Tom Breeze told *Farmers Weekly* magazine.[6]

To find out more about the role of bees in food production, I talked to Simon Potts, Professor of Biodiversity and Ecosystem Services at Reading University. Potts has worked with bees and other pollinators for a quarter of a century, focusing for the last fifteen years on the contribution they make to society. He has come up with a figure for the value we derive from pollinators, which he believes is in the region of £690 million a year in pollination services alone. Globally, he has calculated that they are worth somewhere in the region of £230 billion each year.

If wild pollinators disappear, replacement will be far from straightforward. One option might be to switch to crops that do not need insect pollination, which some regard as the easiest route for farmers. This would mean, for example, switching from oilseed rape that relies on insect pollination to a crop like wheat that is wind-pollinated. However, to jettison a catalogue of fruit and vege-table crops because they are too difficult or expensive to produce without bees seems pretty desperate.

'A lot of insect-pollinated crops are packed full of vitamins and minerals, and we can't get those from wind-pollinated crops at all,' Potts said. 'So farmers deciding not to rely on those insect-pollinated crops is not really an option for healthy diets.' In any case, such a move would have a drastic impact on millions of livelihoods, because so many of today's cash crops – coffee, cocoa, high-value soft and top fruits – are pollinator-dependent. 'So the option of switching away from crops that don't need pollinators doesn't work.'

Another option might be to breed crops capable of bypassing pollinators. This has been attempted, with minimal success. 'If it could have been done it would have been done,' Potts considers. 'I know lots of breeders have tried, but the problem is you tend to lose massive yield and quality benefits from trying to miss that [part of the process] out. So we haven't come up with a technolog-ical solution on plant breeding to cut pollinators out.'

Other potential solutions include hand-pollination and the installation of vast industrial fans to blow pollen around fields. But while hand-pollination is cost-effective in countries with very cheap labour, such as China, where armies of very low-paid workers are used to hand-pollinate pear blossom and other pollinator-dependent fruit trees, it is simply not economically viable in most developed countries.

Potts has worked out how much it would cost to employ thousands of individuals to hand-pollinate crops. He believes that even if workers were paid the minimum wage, the annual bill for hand-pollination in Britain alone would come to about £1.8 billion – more than twice what natural pollinator services are estimated to be worth to the nation.

'So it's utter nonsense,' he said. 'We couldn't afford to do it and it just wouldn't be worthwhile on any scale.' Thus far, then, there is no viable technological alternative to pollinators. 'The only real option is to safeguard and look after what we've got, because that is the only way forward really,' Potts remarked.

When it comes to the chief culprit for the decline in bee populations, the scientific evidence is clear: pesticides.[7] A major study by the Task Force on Systemic Pesticides – a group of global, independent scientists affiliated with the International Union for Conservation of Nature (IUCN) – found that systemic pesticides were a big reason behind the decline of bees.[8]

The analysis published in the journal *Environment Science and Pollution Research* found that neonicotinoids (neonics) pose a serious risk to bees. Neonics are nerve poisons and the effects of exposure range from instant and lethal to chronic. Even long-term exposure at low (non-lethal) levels can be harmful.

The study looked at the use of these, the most widely used insecticides globally, accounting for 40 per cent of world market sales worth over US$2.63 billion. It concluded that pesticide use causes 'significant damage' to a wide range of wildlife like butterflies, birds and earthworms, and is a 'key factor' in the decline of bees.[9]

According to Goulson, the majority of scientists believe there is overwhelming evidence that neonics not only harm bees but also pollute whole ecosystems:

'They are in streams and ponds and hedgerows and in the soil and everywhere in farmland, and they will be for years to come, even if we stop using them. And they are incredibly toxic to insects. So we've been studying where these things are in the environment and analysing samples of soil and pollen from wild flowers and so on . . . and pretty much everything comes up as positive, which is pretty depressing.'

Were you to take a walk on almost any arable farm in Britain, almost every bit of vegetation you would see would be tainted by a cocktail of neonicotinoids toxic to insects. Almost all insects and many other types of wildlife are vulnerable to poisoning: bees, butterflies, ladybirds, earthworms and birds.

It was not until I met Tim May, a fourth-generation family farmer from Hampshire, England, that I fully appreciated the scale of chemical use on intensive farms. Now in his mid-thirties, May runs a 2,500-acre farm that was once devoted to intensive arable production. Recently, he has begun transforming the business from an exclusive focus on chemical-based crops to rearing farm animals and operating rotational pastures.

He talked to me about the chemical arsenal he used to use.

'I took the seed straight out of the shed. We would normally dress the seed with a fungicide, then we'd put on an insecticide, then a pre-emergent herbicide, and then we might well put on an autumn herbicide and another insecticide,' he said. The process literally involved a shedload of chemicals and, in his words, a 'rough-load of expense'.

He explained that a typical intensive wheat crop might have nine chemical applications, including two or three doses of artificial nitrogen, phosphate and potassium, all racking up expense and inflicting untold damage on wildlife, including bees.

While he has not gone completely organic, discarding all chemicals, he has drastically reduced their use, and has found that fewer chemicals means more diversity on the farm, which, together with sheep and cattle grazing extensive grassland, has made the land more attractive to wildlife. So much so that the transition is being monitored by the Hampshire Wildlife Trust to see what the changes do for birds and bees. In the course of the transition May has learned a great deal about the fragile environment on farms, and now supports Goulson's view that modern farming uses far more chemicals than necessary for food production.

Bees have become emblems of what is going on in the country-side. Happily, they remain a common sight in most gardens, despite the declines. In fact, gardens are something of a refuge. According to recent research in Britain, there are now more bees, of more different varieties, in cities than in the countryside. While farms often plant swathes of one crop, gardens and allotments provide a mixed source of flowers all year round, creating a wonderful habitat for insects.

Bees could be seen as ambassadors for the ecosystem, and symbolise the high stakes involved in a reckless fixation on maxi-mising yields from single crops doused in chemicals at the expense of all other life on the land. A world without bees would mean no tomatoes, no chilli peppers, no courgettes, no blueberries, no raspberries, no runner-beans, no cucumbers – the list goes on and on. Even a tin of baked beans contains beans pollinated by bees in a sauce pollinated by bees too.

Could ambitious schemes to reintroduce bee species that have become locally extinct be the answer? The results from the Short-Haired Bumblebee Project in Dungeness are encouraging.

'The last two years, we've seen worker bees, so we know some of the queens managed to nest and produce offspring. We don't know whether those nests did well enough to produce new queens. The basic plan is to keep going until either the money runs out or we see these things thriving in Kent again,' Goulson told me.

More importantly, the way land at Dungeness and Romney Marsh is now being managed for bees benefits thousands of other precious species: birds of prey, songbirds, small mammals and butterflies. Some of the rarest of Britain's twenty-five bumblebee species are already thriving: the shrill carder and the ruderal bumblebee, once common in English gardens, have returned to Dungeness after an absence of more than two decades.[10]

Even if the reintroduction of the short-haired bumblebee does not work, the project has been a success in other ways. 'It's been a brilliant vehicle for lots of habitat creation for wildlife,' Goulson enthused. 'If you could just do that all over Britain without both-ering with a reintroduction, how cool would that be?'

But what can bees tell us about the overall importance of the natural world?

Goulson's answer is that: 'Bees are a really easy example to explain to people why they're important to us. For other biodiversity, the links may not be quite as obvious, but they are there. The human race wouldn't survive if it weren't for biodiversity.'

In other words, when it comes to survival, people and wildlife are in it together.

# 10

# Scapegoats

A crowd of a hundred people or more had gathered in the Hayden Valley of Yellowstone National Park, USA. More were perched on a slope overlooking the valley, armed with cameras and binoculars, pointing and staring into the distance. Children skittered around playing, as adults chattered and munched on sandwiches between bursts of shouting directions at each other. It was quite a party atmosphere.

As the late afternoon sun bore down, a shout sent a ripple of excitement through the crowd: someone had glimpsed something. Slipping between the trees skirting the grassy river basin was a wolf. Although I was there to watch bison, I couldn't help getting caught up in the excitement of 'wolf watch', a feature of the tourist season in the park. My heart lifted at the sight of so many people coming together in the hope of spotting a creature that is sadly all too rare these days, and I left in no doubt which creature Yellowstone's 4 million visitors a year consider the star of the show.

What a turnaround in fortunes wolves have had in these parts. A century ago these charismatic creatures were driven to extinction around Yellowstone by government 'predator control' programmes. In 1995, after a battle that dragged on for decades, grey wolves were reintroduced into the park, where more than a hundred now roam. Yellowstone has become one of the best places in the world to see this elusive species. They generate $35 million for the park's economy every year.[1]

Stories of ecosystems destroyed or devalued are two a penny. In Yellowstone, biologists have a highly unusual opportunity to document what happens when an ecosystem becomes whole again: what happens when an important species fallen locally extinct is added back into the mix. Wolves kill, but as the experiment in Yellowstone has shown, they also bring new life.

Reintroducing the wolf as a so-called apex predator – the one at the top of the food chain – has helped balance the elk population, reducing overgrazing of vegetation like aspen, willow and cottonwood. The wolves have also controlled the coyote population, allowing animals further down the food chain to flourish again. Beavers have bounced back, the number of rabbits and mice is rising, and this in turn is boosting survival rates among hawks, weasels, foxes and badgers. The scheme has even changed the physical nature of the rivers running through Yellowstone. The regeneration of trees and vegetation has helped reduce soil erosion, which makes river banks more stable and brings further life back into the landscape.[2]

Ed Bangs, wolf-recovery coordinator for the US Fish and Wildlife Service, has been genuinely surprised by the explosion in life linked to the return of the wolf. 'I call it food for the masses. Beetles, wolverine, lynx and more. It turns out that the Indian legends of ravens following wolves are true – they do follow them because wolves mean food.'[3]

Today there are almost 1,600 wolves across greater Montana, Idaho and Wyoming, yet the reintroduction of these magnificent creatures has been highly controversial. While conservationists celebrated, hunters fretted about competition for their game and ranchers feared for their livestock. *Beef* magazine summed up the mood among many sheep and cattle farmers with a headline that read: 'Western ranchers fight the curse of introduced wolves'. The magazine castigated the comeback, saying: 'The wolves were supposed to stay in the backcountry and eat elk, but the wolves apparently didn't read the fine print.' It went on to blame them for a catalogue of livestock kills.[4]

While they remain within park boundaries, wolves are protected from hunting. Stray outside, however, and it's a different matter. During the winter 'wolf harvest' of 2014–15, more than 400 were trapped or shot in the neighbouring states of Montana and Idaho.[5]

Carter Neimeyer, a veteran wildlife service trapper and wolf expert, believes that some responsibility for whipping up wolf hysteria sits with the media. 'The media is definitely guilty of keeping it polarised,' he says, 'because killing wolves whether we are hunting them, trapping them, or removing a problem wolf periodically really shouldn't be news any more. We don't announce every time someone shoots a coyote or someone kills a mountain lion or a bear. Wolves are not weapons of mass destruction.'

Neimeyer feels that people 'almost wanted them to be a problem', pointing to the widespread opposition to returning wolves to the Rocky Mountains.

Aside from longstanding public antipathy amongst some, there's another reason wolves may be blamed for the death of livestock they didn't kill: a compensation scheme under which ranchers receive payouts if their animals are attacked. Neimeyer is far from convinced that wolves are killing anything like the numbers of livestock they are blamed for. He spent many years working for the government in the Rocky Mountains, inspecting suspected wolf kills as part of the compensation scheme. The evidence was that ranchers were submitting claims for far more attacks on their animals than were actually warranted.

'Once the media started putting out the information that wolves were in the landscape, nearly all the reports coming in were assumed to be wolf damage and so the assumption was that wolves were causing a lot of problems,' he told *The Ecologist*. 'But there are many things that killed them besides wolves. You have disease and birthing problems and a multitude of things that kill livestock.'[6]

It appears that bad weather, poor health and getting into trouble when giving birth without assistance kill far more livestock on ranches than wolves do. Of the many reasons ranchers lose their animals, Neimeyer reckons that wolves are responsible for well fewer than 1 per cent of sheep and cattle deaths. 'I think you are talking a quarter of one per cent at the current kill rates,' he said.

A recent study has shown that waging war on wolves is the wrong way for ranchers to protect livestock. Researchers from Washington State University looked at twenty-five years of data on how the removal of wolves affects levels of livestock attacks in Idaho, Wyoming and Montana. The results were surprising: far from protecting farm animals, shooting individual wolves makes them *more* vulnerable to attack. In fact, the odds of a rancher finding his sheep or cattle hurt or killed rose by 4–6 per cent once a predating animal had been eliminated.

So the actual impact of wolves on livestock is very small before ranchers start shooting at an individual animal, the net result of which is to exacerbate the problem, but to a relatively modest level.

Where ranchers go on a wolf-killing spree – as sometimes happens when word gets around that wolves are marauding in an area – the consequences are even worse. The study found that if twenty wolves are killed, the number of attacks on livestock can as much as double.[7]

How so?

The findings mirror earlier research by two scientists called Rob Wielgus and Kaylie Peebles, who found lethal control of cougars can also backfire. It appears that killing individual animals can disrupt the pack and the natural structures of family groups to the point where younger, less disciplined animals attack more livestock.

Wielgus did not expect to find the same result with wolves.

'I had no idea what the results were going to be, positive or negative. I said: "Let's take a look at it and see what happens." I was surprised that there was a big effect,' he said.

Wielgus believes that if one of a dominant pair of wolves is killed, it can trigger uncontrolled breeding among their offspring. As several pairs breed at once, they become tied by their less mobile pups to one area. They can no longer roam so freely after elk and deer, and so turn their attentions to otherwise less attractive but more static prey: livestock.

However, he continues to stress that the proportion of livestock deaths attributed to wolves is tiny relative to other factors. He estimates that they are responsible for between 0.1 and 0.6 per cent of all livestock deaths. 'A minor threat compared to other predators, disease, accidents and the dangers of calving,' is how he puts it.[8]

According to Wielgus, non-lethal methods such as guard dogs are the best way to deal with 'problem' wolves. Other means of control include 'range riders' on horseback, fluttering flags, spotlights, and simple avoidance measures such as keeping grazing animals away from areas in which they are likely to be attacked.

Rancher Becky Weed, who is based in Bozeman, Montana, agrees. Her enormous guard dog Max is her main asset in deterring wolves from her property. Speaking to the *Ecologist* magazine, she described the animal as 'unbelievable, our main tool'.

'We also use pasture management strategies,' she said. 'We don't just let the sheep wander all over the place . . . so it's really a matter of vigilance and adaptability . . . wolf predation is not the biggest problem that ranching in Montana is facing right now.'[9]

Max is part of a new method of ranching that enables her to sell 'predator-friendly' certified wool to markets at home and abroad. Her 'live and let live' mentality is now being adopted by other ranchers who can see the logic in finding better ways of tackling the problem than simply loading their guns. A number of Montana landowners concerned about the future of the spectacular open countryside in this American state have come together to form a community project they have called Blackfoot Challenge. Between them they are preserving and enriching some 90,000 acres of land. The ethos is to encourage livestock keepers to coexist with predatory wildlife.

'If you're just "damn the wolf" and wolves make you mad or whatever . . . that doesn't get anything accomplished,' one of its members, Tracey Manley, told the *Ecologist*. 'You're still losing livestock, so why not try to build a corral or build an electric fence around your lots and see what works . . . just banging your head against the wall saying "kill them all" isn't going to happen.'[10]

There was a time when grey wolves ranged throughout the entire lower forty-eight states of America. Over the years, they have been systematically driven out of just about every environment in which they have thrived. A partial recovery has been made possible by wolf reintroductions and government protection under endangered species legislation. Now they inhabit a few patchy areas in the Big Sky states of Montana, Wyoming and Idaho; sometimes nearby states too.

It's a far cry from the original picture. Two centuries of shooting, poisoning and trapping have taken the heaviest of tolls, and it will take considerable time to restore the population. The Center for Biological Diversity estimates that wolves now occupy less than 10 per cent of their historical range.[11] Yet even these pockets of recovery are under threat. Having been 'delisted' from federal protection in 2011, wolves are once again the target of sport hunting and government predator controls. In 2014, some 20,000 licences were said to have been issued to folk wanting to hunt and trap wolves in Montana alone.[12]

Wolves incite deep divisions within society. Many see their return as a cause for celebration, a symbol of success, of determination to repair broken ecosystems. As I saw that afternoon in Yellowstone, the slightest glimpse can be a source of huge excitement to those who do not have to worry about the safety of cattle herds. Others resent their return, feeling it has been foisted on them by high-minded types who don't understand the realities of life in remote places. What is sometimes lost in this emotive debate is the extent to which wolves can prop up local economies by attracting visitors who buy ranchers' products in local shops.

To me, wolves have always evoked a natural world in balance. They symbolise so much of what it means to be wild: running with the pack, with heightened senses and a fierce will to survive. They are also a perfect illustration of the risk that, if we are not careful, much of the natural world around us might just slide into folklore. Many of us grow up on a storybook diet of 'the big bad wolf', a reputation earned in a bygone era. Some exploit the stereotype for their own ends, which is a pity. Will short-term self-interest prevail over the long-term interest of preserving a planet worth our children inheriting? I can't help but wonder if future generations will have the opportunity to experience these magnificent creatures only in their mind's eye.

Love them or fear them, wolves are a powerful example of the disconnect between food and the way it is produced. They are a potent symbol of how modern society has yet to learn to live with wildlife without razing habitats or taking up a gun. All too often, they are an easy scapegoat for livestock losses. Ranchers would often do well to look closer to home for levels of livestock deaths that might otherwise be seen as unacceptable on animal-welfare grounds. It's so much easier to blame a bloodthirsty yellow-eyed predator for the unexplained death of one or more of their animals, than look to their own animal husbandry.

### DEADLY DUCKS OR POULTRY TRUCKS?

Police in fluorescent jackets watched over men in masks and protective clothing as they moved from shed to shed, grim and businesslike. At first glance, it was not obvious that there were animals involved: the place looked like a brownfield industrial site. In fact, it was an intensive breeding farm for ducks, never a pleasant environment at the best of times – and on this occasion, a biohazard. Officials from the Department of Environment, Food and Rural Affairs (Defra) had seized control of the premises, following an alarming new outbreak of disease. The place was now cordoned off like a crime scene, and 6,000 unfortunate birds were being carted off for slaughter.

An otherwise quiet corner of Yorkshire was now in lockdown, having been hit by Britain's first incidence in six years of highly pathogenic bird flu.

At Westminster, the minister for agriculture was swift to assure everyone that on this occasion at least, the outbreak represented a minimal risk to human health. But with potentially deadly strains involved in previous outbreaks, no one was taking any chances. Poultry farmers in the surrounding area feared for their livelihoods. Biosecurity became the mantra, keeping poultry locked in and disease locked out.

The media was quick to speculate on the original source of the scourge, identifying the number-one suspect as wild birds. After all, it was November, around the time of year when migrating birds arrive from the Continent, or so the logic went. An ITV news headline firmly pointed the finger, declaring: 'Wild bird may be behind bird flu outbreak.'

A reporter dutifully poked around country lanes, breathlessly announcing the discovery of free-range hens and geese in the neighbourhood. 'We're just a hundred yards or so from the farm where the outbreak was discovered. And look, in this smallholding we found hens in the hedgerows and in the yard here there are turkeys and geese wandering freely in the mud. And then of course, there are wild birds . . . all over the place . . .'[13]

He made it sound more like a scene from a Hitchcock movie than an ordinary snapshot of country life.

Meanwhile, a similar outbreak was reported at Hekendorp in the Netherlands.[14] The official response there included mass slaughter of birds in affected areas and a ban on the sale of any poultry that might be diseased. Some 150,000 birds were killed in efforts to contain the outbreak to the premises where it was thought to have originated – a battery egg farm.[15]

Despite a paucity of supporting evidence, the theory that wild birds were somehow responsible quickly gained currency. In reality the disease had struck on factory farms, where flocks were reared solely indoors. The BBC dug out a quote from the head of the World Animal Health Organisation, Bernard Vallat, suggesting that poultry feed at affected farms might have become contaminated by wild migratory birds. 'If feed is not protected and a wild bird comes to eat it, it's enough to contaminate the feed and then those that eat that feed,' Vallat was reported as saying.[16] Yet operators of intensive farms tend to keep feed bins – and shed doors – firmly closed. The explanation did not stack up.

Whatever the cause, the outbreaks in Britain and the Netherlands were serious. Both were part of a global wave of infection by a new and highly pathogenic strain of avian influenza known as H5N8, which was first noted in Korea in January 2014. By April of that year it had reached Japan, and by the end of the year it had made it to Europe, affecting farms in Germany and Italy as well as the Netherlands and Britain. By the following year, farms in Taiwan had been hit.

At the same time, a different bird flu strain (H5N2) was affecting commercial farms in Canada. The stakes were high: the massive global poultry industry was under siege by a deadly aggressor moving unseen from farm to farm. Wild birds continued to be blamed – including by the European Commission.

'The fact that the three recent outbreaks in Germany, the Netherlands and the UK have occurred in proximity of humid areas with wild birds and the absence of any other possible epidemiological link between them point towards wild migratory birds as a possible source of virus,'[17] they claimed, in an official statement.

Yet hard evidence that wild birds were the vector remained elusive.

In the Netherlands, the best they could come up with was duck poo infected with the virus around the same time as the outbreaks, but it was discovered some 50 kilometres from the affected farms. Even the best prosecution lawyer would have trouble making that case stick. In Japan, scientists found faeces from a swan infected with highly pathogenic bird flu, but not until six months after the initial outbreak. Two infected ducks were found in China and Russia, but neither country reported an outbreak among poultry.

While novice commentators drafted in to pad out TV and newspaper coverage of the outbreak hyped up the drama, a credible smoking gun was nowhere to be found. A classic case of sensationalism over analysis. Global surveillance of wild bird populations failed to turn up any instances of highly pathogenic bird flu until after it was discovered in poultry. In fact, as time went on, the evidence pointed firmly to the virus originating in poultry before infecting wild birds.

This was not the first time that wild birds had been the scapegoat during a bird flu outbreak. In 2007, a Bernard Matthews turkey farm complex was hit by H5N1. Both the British government and poultry industry were quick to point the finger at wild birds. Yet surveillance of wild birds in the UK at the time found nothing, and Defra later conceded that spread by wild birds was 'highly unlikely'.[18]

Although the cause of the outbreak was never fully determined, the Food Standards Agency concluded that the problem might well have started with infected meat imported from the company's operation in Hungary. There was an outbreak of exactly the same strain of H5N1 in parts of Hungary at the time.[19] Traffic in turkey meat between the company's UK and Hungarian operations was regular and large-scale. In the month leading up to the outbreak, twenty-four consignments totalling 256 tonnes of turkey meat from Hungary were delivered to the UK processing plant close to the turkey sheds.[20] According to news reports at the time, the regular trade was even more complex: the UK operation sent hatching turkey eggs to Hungary to be reared and then slaughtered, and the turkey meat then returned to the UK for extraction of the breast meat before returning again to Hungary for manufacture into sausages.[21] This is an example of the extraordinary and overcomplicated trade patterns that no doubt enrich big business but of which consumers are blissfully unaware.

In the past decade, most outbreaks of highly pathogenic avian flu have struck farms with intensively kept poultry. Operators of these grim places like to boast that they are 'biosecure' because the birds are kept permanently locked indoors, 'protected' from threatening natural elements like fresh air and sunshine, and the dangers of potentially disease-ridden wild birds. Yet in the quest to identify the source of disease, wild birds turned out to be a red herring. Veterinary scientists who analysed outbreaks of bird flu in Thailand found that large commercial (intensive) farms were four times more likely to suffer an outbreak than smaller farms and chickens kept in backyards.[22]

Another study found that killer bird flu was more likely to spread along transport routes than migratory flyways.

Then there is the mismatch between the sudden rise in serious bird flu outbreaks and the decline of wild bird numbers in the countryside. If wild birds were the source of the problem, one might expect them to be spreading it about when there were more of them on and around farms. Yet farmland bird populations have been in serious decline in Britain and across the European continent for decades. Why would outbreaks of disease from deadly bird flu rise at exactly the time wild bird populations have crashed?

The answer appears to be factory farming. In late 2014 a United Nations task force set up to investigate the problem announced that outbreaks of bird flu were 'most frequently associated with intensive domestic poultry production and associated trade and marketing systems'.[23]

Under normal circumstances, avian influenza is a run-of-the-mill disease that can affect any bird, wild or domestic. Birds get it in much the same way as people get colds and flu. In nature, birds do not live their lives crowded together indoors as they must in a poultry shed. So a virus in natural conditions often behaves rather as a parasite does, and avoids being too virulent so as not to wipe out the hosts it needs to survive. The poultry industry has changed this and made it viable for flu viruses to be very deadly, because there is always another host very close by in the poultry shed for the virus to infect. It can move through densely packed flocks rapidly, benefiting from warm, often filthy conditions.

As the virus spreads it can mutate, sometimes recombining with genes from other viruses sloshing around in the infected population. Without the natural limit to how virulent the virus can become, deadlier mutations can emerge. During the 2007 bird flu outbreaks, the UN Food and Agriculture Organisation (FAO) said: 'Much of the scientific evidence suggests that domestic poultry provide a favourable environment for the entry, spread and shift to high virulence of influenza viruses.'

Once a new and deadly strain of virus has emerged, the UN suggests it then gets spread rapidly by the poultry industry itself, whether through the transport of live birds; or through the meat; or unclean cages or dirty egg crates.[24] As to where it all started, the FAO declared: 'The origin of the current outbreak of avian influenza can be traced to East/Southeast Asia, home to an estimated six billion domestic birds . . .'

Clearly, more needs to be done to prevent such disasters. Scapegoating doesn't help. After all, it's not as if we don't know where to find the culprit.

### HATED HAWKS

The man who inspired me to become a birdwatcher in my teenage years was sitting in his front room, surrounded by piles of old vinyl records, beneath walls lined with showbiz memorabilia. The room was an Aladdin's cave of colourful ornaments from exotic trips: wooden masks, carvings of animals and tribal figures, as well as more regular showbiz fare like a full drum kit and supporting cast of guitars. Through the window, sparrows, great tits and other birds peeked at us as they pecked from garden birdfeeders.

I was at the leafy Hampstead home of the TV personality and celebrity naturalist Bill Oddie. He originally shot to fame as one of the Goodies, a surreal 1970s comedy trio, but is now more likely to be introduced as a 'wizened godfather of nature' (as one journalist once put it). Sporting his trademark beard, glasses and cargo trousers, the 74-year-old birdman was bobbing up and down with enthusiasm as if back on the couch of TV's *Springwatch*, as he regaled me with stories about how he has been sticking up for wildlife in what he sees as a countryside under siege.

Naturally what keeps him awake at night is the devastating decline in bird populations – not only in Britain, but all over the world. Although rare birds like red kites are doing well, as we have seen, numbers of common birds over most of the country are plummeting.

'It's more than worrying,' he told me sadly. 'I find myself looking back to when I was a teenager. I was in Birmingham and would cycle to the edge of Birmingham, which was to all intents and purposes farmland. I parked my bike by the side of the road and, depending on the time of year, chances are there would be . . . linnets, yellowhammers particularly and tree sparrows . . . a big mixed flock. Lapwings – once you got to spring and there were open fields with not too much cover, you'd see them in every field.

Same thing would happen at the other end of the year . . . great big flocks of lapwing and great big flocks of skylark and golden plover following them.'

Not any more. 'I just haven't seen anything like that for so long,' he said.

We talked about how some blame declines of farmland birds on sparrowhawks, buzzards and other birds of prey. Bill rubbishes the theory. 'I think all those things are complete nonsense. I really do. Nature finds a balance,' he said. 'It's proven time and time again that it's not in the interest of the predator to eat all its prey.'

When it comes to scapegoats, birds of prey have long been an easy target. To Victorians, they were always villains, spoiling a good day's shooting by taking the odd gamebird or two. Hawks, eagles and even owls were disparaged. Indeed, Victorian Britain declared war on anything with a hooked beak. After two centuries of persecution by gamekeepers, landowners, sportsmen and egg collectors, Britain's birds of prey were decimated. By the early twentieth century, five species of breeding bird had been driven to extinction, including the osprey, honey buzzard and white-tailed eagle.[25]

Barn owls too were persecuted, indiscriminately trapped and shot. They ended up hanging on the keepers' gibbet alongside tawny owl, weasel and the hated sparrowhawk.[26] Persecution and pesticides hit birds of prey so hard that by the time I started birdwatching in the mid-1970s, it was years before I saw my first buzzard or barn owl, let alone an eagle.

As we chatted in the fading light of a December afternoon, Bill recalled how he'd seen his first barn owl in North Norfolk, along the coastal road near Titchwell, the same part of the world where I saw mine.

At least owls – or at any rate, images of owls – are fashionable. In 2015, they seemed to be everywhere: emblazoned on clothes and stationery, cushions and hot water bottle covers, tableware and crockery. If their brief moment in fashion's starry firmament drew even a little extra attention to their plight, so much the better. Other birds of prey – such as sparrowhawks – have a less sympathetic image.

These little woodland raptors, which eat songbirds, have long been vilified. Historically, they have often been seen as vermin.[27] In the nineteenth century, they – and anything unfortunate enough to look like them – were trapped and poisoned with great zeal in a campaign of persecution that lasted unbroken for well over a century.

The two world wars brought temporary reprieve as gamekeepers were conscripted to the frontline. Numbers of sparrowhawks rallied to their highest point since the 1800s. Then came post-war intensification of farming and the widespread use of organochlorine pesticides; what gamekeepers had tried doing for a century or more was accomplished in a few short years with chemicals. Sparrowhawks were poisoned and virtually wiped out.

As a boy, I longed to see one of these yellow-eyed predators, but it didn't happen for ages. After several years of birdwatching, I eventually saw my first sparrowhawk during an RSPB local group coach trip to Aberton Reservoir in Essex. When I close my eyes, I can still remember that bird. It was a cold, windy and overcast day in early February 1981 when I tramped round England's fourth-largest reservoir marvelling at how it teemed with ducks and other waterbirds. That's when a large brown female sparrowhawk flitted from trees like an enigma. I was elated.

Now protected by law, sparrowhawks are making a comeback, helped by the withdrawal of the worst-offending pesticides. Their revival has been a double-edged sword, however, for they are once again being scapegoated for farmland bird declines.

I remember a lively discussion on this very point with National Farmers Union (NFU) vice-president Guy Smith. It was 2014, not long after my book *Farmageddon* had been published, and we were both invited to the prestigious Hay literary festival to talk in front of a live audience about the future of agriculture. The discussion was about whether we should be farming intensively or not. Inevitably, the subject of wildlife declines came up. I pointed out that numbers of once-common farmland bird species have fallen to an all-time low. I talked about the evidence linking the decline to intensive farming practices, and the fact that even the government admits it.

As usual with representatives of the NFU, however, Smith gave no ground. He was adamant that, when it came to the disappearance of sparrows and other small farmland birds, sparrowhawks were to blame. In a lame attempt to suggest it's what predators do – wipe out their prey – he quipped: 'If they were vegetarian, they'd be called marrow-hawks!' I laughed it off along with the audience, but inside, I wasn't impressed by yet another attempt by vested interests in the food and agricultural industry – in this case, the NFU – to deflect attention from the real reason for farmland bird declines: industrial farming.

Bill Oddie agrees. 'I don't think there's any question that the actual quality of the countryside has deteriorated enormously in terms of how much it can support food for small birds. That means the knock-on effect that there are not so many wild flowers, not so many insects, and so on and so forth. And I would say that pesticides must be very high on the list . . . We don't even know the half of it,' he told me as we sat talking that afternoon.

As farms have grown less hospitable to wildlife, various bird species have taken refuge in suburbia,[28] particularly in winter. According to Dr Tim Harrison of the British Trust for Ornithology (BTO), this is 'because of changes in agricultural practice . . . there is less food available at the end of the winter' for birds on farms. 'You end up with the "hunger gap", leading to species like reed bunting, lesser redpoll, bullfinches and yellowhammer coming into gardens more and more.'[29]

As more birds amass in towns, so they inevitably attract the attention of a sparrowhawk or two in search of easy pickings. For bird lovers, this can be distressing. It's no fun watching the lavish spread of avian treats you've laid out to attract little songbirds turning into a scene of carnage as a sparrowhawk pounces. I wince at the occasional shrill sound of a young starling being throttled on our garden lawn. But for sparrowhawks, our cottage garden, like so many others, has become a happy hunting ground – and that's nature.

When David Lack, one of the greatest post-war ecologists, studied the impact of sparrowhawks on songbird populations, he

noticed that when gamekeepers in the late nineteenth and twentieth centuries reduced sparrowhawk numbers drastically, there was
no evidence of a surge in the number of songbirds. He concluded
that the population of small birds was more likely to be constrained
by availability of food. In his view, sparrowhawks might actually
have helped overall numbers, by reducing competition for food in
winter. Harsh though it may seem, in a sense, sparrowhawks were
doing the sparrows a favour.

At the end of the summer, there are more sparrows and other
small birds than at any other time of the year. They then face
winter, when food becomes harder to find. When some are lost to
predators, usually the weak or less wary, the remainder are more
likely to get through the winter. There is only so much food to go
round, and the reduced competition amongst songbirds for food
helps avoid a wider famine. This more than offsets the numbers
taken by sparrowhawks.

Lack's theory involves the idea that a balanced ecosystem means
predator numbers being controlled by available prey, not the other
way round. If it were any other way, the whole foodweb – big
things eating little things, which eat even smaller things, and so
on – would quickly break down.

His theory was supported by a long-term census of thirteen
bird species between 1949 and 1979. All the species involved
were known to be eaten by sparrowhawks. During the 1950s and
1960s, when sparrowhawks had been wiped out by pesticides, none
showed a spike in numbers.[30]

More recently, the biggest-ever study of its kind carried out
between 1967 and 2005 found no evidence of large-scale population declines among songbirds linked to increasing numbers of
sparrowhawks and buzzards. According to the study, the main
factors affecting farmland birds were 'agricultural change', including loss of nest sites and a lack of food.[31] The study reinforces the
point that predators are regulated by the availability of their prey,
and the need not to eat themselves into oblivion.

All of this points to the real reason for farmland bird declines:
decline in the quality of the countryside itself. The evidence is

overwhelming. Persuading policymakers and vested interests to accept it is another matter.

Long after dark, Bill and I were still sitting in his cluttered front room, trying to figure out how to overcome the huge collective resistance to acknowledging what to us seems so obvious. The way food is being produced is slowly but surely destroying the countryside, and the precious wild flowers, hedges and woods that make Britain so beautiful. As ancient habitats disappear to make way for intensive crop production to feed incarcerated farm animals, so birds, insects and mammals are vanishing. To the untrained eye, much of England's countryside may still appear as green and pleasant as it looked to William Blake when he wrote 'Jerusalem'. Little by little, however, the land Blake knew, and the wildlife that depends on it, is dying. A dark, quiet revolution is gathering pace. How long before there are just a few quaint relics left?

11

# Jaguar

When I think of jaguars I imagine them skulking through grassland or slinking through the dense vegetation of a tropical rainforest, so when my quest to see one of these iconic big cats in the wild took me to a flat and featureless expanse of soya in Brazil's agricultural heartland, I couldn't help feeling I must be in the wrong place.

I had flown from São Paulo to Goiania in the country's Midwest region, where I'd picked up a Chevrolet 4x4 hire car for the journey through mile upon mile of undulating cattle pasture. Travelling through the state of Goias towards neighbouring Mato Grosso, the land finally flattened out into endless crop prairie, mind-numbingly dull.

I followed the straight, gently undulating highway west for several hours. Every now and then, a collection of skeletal towers would loom on the horizon as we passed a grain mill and yet more fields of soya. Signs on some of the fences every few hundred metres advertised the latest crop trial or GM invention that otherwise would be growing anonymously by the roadside.

At one point, half a dozen brilliant blue parrots flapped lazily across the road, almost as if in slow motion, long tail streamers trailing behind. It was my first sight of blue and yellow macaws, a declining species of the region's forests and savannah,[1] and provided a flicker of excitement on the long tedious journey.

Grinding on through prairies of monocultures that seemed to go on for ever, as I was beginning to lose the will to live suddenly a copse of eucalyptus trees came into sight. It was the landmark I'd been looking for. Relieved that more than a day's travelling was over, I pulled off the road and up to a bamboo fence and security gate. Finally I'd arrived at the ranch of someone I'd been calling 'the jaguar man'.

I could tell at once that I had come at a bad time. The man I'd travelled all this way to meet – Leandro Silveira, a Brazilian biologist with a lifelong passion for big cats – looked distracted. It was clear he had something on his mind. His beige T-shirt was smeared with mud where he'd just wiped his grubby hands, and though he wasn't exactly rude, I could tell that we were an awkward diversion.

Flustered but trying to be welcoming, he extended a hand and a faint smile.

'Give me half an hour and I'll be back,' he said briskly, before disappearing in his pickup, so I sat in the open-sided barn beside his house, sipping the coffee he'd left me. It came out of the dispenser already sugared, which I wasn't used to, presumably to take off some of the bitterness of the local coffee. Nevertheless, I liked it and, still weary from the journey, I poured some more.

He returned cradling a pink towel like a proud father. Peering in, I saw the tiny black head of a newborn jaguar blinking back at me. I was amazed at how small she was, like a not-so-large kitten. Gingerly, I stroked her head. It was still damp to the touch. I watched her shiny black eyes squint then go wide again. She was almost completely black, with the slightest tinge of purple around her ears and mouth. As I gazed at her, overawed, she yawned and her eyes swam as if she was fighting off sleep. She couldn't seem to decide whether to snooze or to survey the new world in which she suddenly found herself.

'It was a bit of a surprise, as I didn't even know the mother was pregnant!' Silveira said. Apparently a black jaguar he had adopted as an orphan had sprung the surprise cub on him just as we were arriving. No wonder he had been so distracted.

'Oh my goodness!' I exclaimed, thrilled. 'I'm sure from your point of view we couldn't have timed that any worse, but from ours, it couldn't have been any better.'

That made him smile.

Silveira was my first port of call on what was to be an epic journey through Brazil investigating how its wildlife is faring in the face of breakneck agricultural expansion. The remorseless march of soya – fuel for factory farms – is gobbling up the rainforest, ravaging a once rich and varied landscape. There is precious little left for the wild animals whose habitats have been sacrificed.

I had expected Silveira to rail against the misery wrought by the machines and the chemicals, to despise every aspect of the new monoculture. I was in for a surprise.

Brazil has the richest biodiversity in the world,[2] and is on the global frontline in the bitter clash between the activities of multinational 'Big Ag', local economic interests and efforts to save endangered wildlife. Famed for the Amazon rainforest, it is a vast and contrasting countryside, from the expansive wetlands of the Pantanal to the savannah grasslands, known as the Cerrado, which have long covered much of the Midwest region.

The fifth-largest country in the world by land mass, it has a population of more than 200 million. Now the world's third-largest agricultural exporter overall, Brazil is ranked fourth for pigmeat exports, and is the undisputed number one when it comes to exports of poultry meat and beef.[3]

Sadly, for pigs and poultry it is a giant in the factory-farming stakes. Nearly all of the country's pigs are kept in industrial systems, with breeding pigs kept in narrow 'gestation crates' where they can't turn round for months on end. An estimated 95 per cent of the country's egg-laying hens are kept in battery cages.[4]

It also has a spectacular array of wild plants and animals, perhaps none more striking than the jaguar, the third-largest feline in the world (after the tiger and lion). Today there are still some 15,000 of these big cats left in the wild – but for how much longer?[5] Historically, jaguars could be found from the Grand Canyon of the US through the Amazon all the way to Argentina. Now, the species

is much more restricted and found largely in the Amazon.[6] Home
to half the world's remaining jaguar population, Brazil holds the
fate of this iconic species in the palm of its hand.

The pace of agricultural expansion in this rapidly developing
nation is unlike anything I have seen in the world. When people
think of deforestation they tend to associate it with logging, or
with felling trees to make way for housing and crops for human
consumption. In fact, the real driver is farming of soya and corn –
much of it destined for farm animals – as well as sugar (mostly for
people) and beef. Vast areas of rainforest and savannah are turned
over to these industries.

As their habitats are razed, jaguars are being driven out. Seen as
pests by cattle ranchers, when they venture onto open land – for
want of anywhere else to go – they are often shot on sight. 'All of our
jaguars are orphans that came from the wild as a result of a conflict
with ranchers. Mothers get shot and the young are left behind,'
Silveira told me. Referring to the day's new arrival, he explained:
'It's not our goal to breed jaguars. There's so many orphans coming
in all the time, it doesn't make sense to breed them.' Evidently, he
has enough on his hands.

Known as the 'dean' of Brazilian jaguar biologists,[7] 45-year-
old Silveira seemed the obvious person to talk to about what the
future might hold for the species. He was a fit-looking man, with
green eyes and cropped hair. Together with his wife Ana he has
studied jaguars and other carnivorous mammals in the Cerrado
grasslands for over two decades, founding the Jaguar Conservation
Fund in 2002. Its mission is to promote the conservation of the
jaguar as well as of its natural prey and habitat, throughout the
species' natural geographical range – 'as well as its peaceful coexistence with man'.[8]

As I was about to find out, the objective of achieving 'peaceful
coexistence' underpins the charity's approach to the competition
between wildlife and big agriculture.

Having tended to the newborn, Silveira relaxed. We sat chatting
beside brightly coloured hammocks hung between the thick-
chiselled wooden pillars of his veranda-style barn. An old wooden

dresser was crammed with ornaments: a china tea service, an ornamental miniature milk churn, an old-fashioned sewing machine. Beside long bench-style tables designed for convivial evenings, I could see an enticing-looking stonebake pizza oven. This was clearly his space for entertaining gatherings of the jaguar faithful.

With his nine-year-old son busily driving the white Mitsubishi 4x4 round the grounds, Silveira showed me his office. Jaguar skins – perhaps as many as forty – were piled high on a freestanding table like old rugs. Some were silver, others deep yellow, some nearer brown, and all with a faint musty smell. I touched one skin, all golden and spotted. It felt exquisite, like the coat of a sleek, short-haired dog. These were skins confiscated by government officials from the Amazon.

Silveira studies their DNA and age profiles and has identified most of them as coming from young cats, not quite fully grown. Most have been shot before they were able to reproduce. 'This is the sad story so familiar for jaguar in ranchland these days,' he sighed. He picked one up. 'This one was a six-month-old cub. Most likely shot with the mother.'

He believes the real threat to their future is less the march of crops, and more the intensifying conflict with cattle ranchers. Once worshipped by the ancient Maya and other civilisations like the Aztec and Inca, jaguars are now considered vermin by these farmers, who resent the loss of the occasional animal being reared for beef.

The jaguar is an opportunistic hunter, feeding on whatever's most abundant in its ecosystem. It has an unusual method of killing large prey. Whereas lions, tigers and leopards kill with a throat or neck bite, jaguars often kill by biting through the skull between the ears.[3]

In some regions of Brazil, they feed mainly on large mammals such as peccaries (wild pigs), capybara and tapirs. In other regions, they eat reptiles such as turtles and caiman. In areas where they live next to ranches, cattle can become part of their diet, especially when more natural targets like deer and peccaries are hard to come by.

According to Silveira, affected ranchers can lose an average of 1 to 4 per cent of their cattle to jaguars. He thinks these losses could be offset by better husbandry.

Looking around his office, I couldn't help noticing a long-barrelled pistol.

'Hey, is this for unwelcome guests?' I joked nervously.

'It's a dart gun,' he replied. He uses it to sedate jaguars before fitting them with GPS tracking collars. It's just one of many ways to keep tabs on them.

Silveira's property borders the Emas National Park, a UNESCO World Heritage Site with 130,000 hectares of grassland studded with trees: a remnant of Brazil's once great Cerrado. It is the largest and biologically richest savannah in the world, stretching across the Brazilian Midwest – but less than 10 per cent of it remains in a natural state.[10]

Silveira monitors jaguar movements in the national park and surrounding farmland using an array of camera traps. He deploys some 500 recording devices to track anything that moves, whether it's giant guinea pig-like capybara, pumas or jaguars. We set off together in his pickup truck so that he could show me how it's done. Where I'd imagined jungle, or at least grassland, he made for a plantation of sugar cane. He seemed unfazed by my confusion, almost enjoying it.

'People are starting to see jaguars here on the sugar-cane fields,' he told me, sounding more cheerful than I thought he should.

Camera trap number 32 was mounted on a handy fence post overlooking neat rows of verdant sugar cane. The crop looks less exotic than it sounds. With its thick rhubarb-coloured stems that shoot up into long green fronds, it grows to 10 feet tall and provides good cover for animals. Silveira's cameras, equipped with heat and movement sensors, can monitor comings and goings twenty-four hours a day for about a month before the batteries run out.

Later that day he showed me some of the footage he has collected. His cameras had revealed a wide variety of wildlife moving through the sugar cane: armadillo, tapir, howler monkeys, puma and white-lipped peccary. Then what we'd been waiting for: a female jaguar with her four cubs – evidence, to Silveira, that breeding jaguars are using the sugar cane.

It transpired that he is a passionate proponent of the idea that jaguars can coexist with intensive farming, as long as the crops are mingled with natural habitat. This idea is known as 'matrix conservation' or 'countryside biogeography'.[11]

'The larger the farm, the better it can be for jaguars,' Silveira told me. 'Yes, it gives a bad impression – visually, it's very dramatic when you see a huge soya-bean field and say to yourself: "Where is everything, where is the forest, where are the animals?" But you have to remember, when you see a large tract of soya-bean field, you can also ask the question: "Where is the reserve?"'

By 'reserve', Silveira was talking about the legal obligation on landowners in Brazil to preserve an amount of their land for nature. The regulation has been in place since as far back as 1965, when the country's original Forest Code established that a proportion of rural land should be maintained permanently as forest (Legal Reserves), and also banned the clearing of vegetation in sensitive areas such as on steep slopes and along the margins of rivers and streams (Areas of Permanent Protection).[12]

But the law has proved challenging to enforce. As global demand for beef and soya for animal feed increased in the early 2000s, annual deforestation in the Brazilian Amazon surged to more than 20,000 km$^2$ per year, prompting global outrage and a redoubling of efforts to ensure that the law is applied.[13] In 2012 it was updated, and Silveira hopes that the new terms will spur farmers interested in jaguar conservation to do something extraordinary.

He explained how landowners in Cerrado are now obliged to preserve 20 per cent of their land for nature. The proportion they are required to set aside rises to 35 per cent in what's known as the 'Legal Amazon' area, where Cerrado meets Amazon. In the Amazon itself, four-fifths of land owned has to be set aside for biodiversity.

'The larger the farm, the larger the block of twenty, thirty-five or eighty per cent, so fragmentation on this land is much less,' he said, returning to his thesis that large-scale crop farms can be an acceptable habitat for jaguars. Silveira believes the animals are adapting to survival in a changing landscape and that jaguars and big agriculture can coexist if things are managed carefully. His view is that monocultures that are not heavily worked by machinery and labourers – meaning that they are relatively undisturbed for much of the year – can offer a reasonable environment to big cats.

He talked more about his jaguar-monitoring, and how the big cats were now moving across the fields. I could see that he has had to learn to live with the vast swathes of soya, corn and sugar cane that have come to dominate the landscape here. But I couldn't help wondering if he wouldn't have far fewer records of jaguars, or anything else for that matter, if he didn't have Emas National Park on his doorstep.

Keen to demonstrate why he sees things the way he does, Silveira offered to take me on a tour of the area. The entrance to the national park is only a mile or so from his ranch, its gate adorned by giant statues of classic Cerrado wildlife like the rhea, an ostrich-like bird. Home to puma, ocelot, Brazilian tapir and many other species, the park also supports a small jaguar population, perhaps about ten to twelve animals.[14]

Founded in 1961, Emas National Park is one of the few large tracts of natural habitat in Central Brazil that haven't been converted into farmland for mechanised agriculture. In the 1970s, naturalists described it as 'the Brazilian Serengeti'.

'Had the park not been founded before the soya bean came to the region, it probably wouldn't exist. Politically, no one would have wanted this to be a park, because it's very good agricultural land,' Silveira explained.

Emas offers a sense of what virgin Cerrado looks like. Earlier in the day, I walked through waist-high grasses interspersed with thin gnarled trees and low bushes. Insects sprang up or scuttled away as I passed. A big black bee buzzed by. The air was fresh. On the other side of the road the land was barren: a vast flat prairie of uniform farmland, little else but big sky and bare fields of reddish-brown soil. No hedges, no field boundaries, just one crop after another. I'd seen these monocultures from the highway, but Silveira was keen to take me back-stage to show me what I wouldn't otherwise notice.

To the untrained eye, there was little on the horizon but yet more crops. But along the river valley it was different, and that is what he was trying to say. The land left to nature on these farms was down in a dell, out of sight from the road. Here, it was interspersed with cropland too: once it was pointed out, I could see forests, pasture and a mosaic of different crops. A dozen great rheas picked their way across a field in much the same way as deer do back home. I was thrilled to spot several red-legged seriemas, birds with lanky long legs and outstretched necks. Dense gallery forest clung to the valley, forming a corridor along the river where a lot of Silveira's camera traps were located.

We drove up a ridge of the reddest soil I'd ever seen. A dozen or more turkey vultures loafed, black and dishevelled, waiting for a sign that one of their fellows had found something to scavenge.

Though we hadn't driven very far, perhaps 3 miles, the landscape here was completely different. I was now looking across the headwater basin of the Araguaia River, which divides the states of Goias and Mato Grosso. I could see a patchwork of eucalyptus trees, soya beans, sugar cane and corn, strewn mosaic-like with native vegetation amid blocks of untouched land, known as refuge corridors, set aside for nature.

'For me, this is the big prize,' Silveira said. 'This makes me very proud. We have jaguars breeding down in this forest. This is big-scale agriculture and big-scale conservation.'

If they are big crop farmers, there's no cattle conflict. 'There's no noise, no people. I caught a mother jaguar and her two cubs out here and put radio collars on,' he enthused. I was starting to see what he meant.

'Five years ago, we talked to the owner of this land,' he told me. 'He owns the Araguaia spring. We talked to him about the importance of connecting the Araguaia basin to the [Emas] park. He gave seven hundred hectares of prime soya-bean land for conservation. This is an example of how farmers can give very effective support to environmental causes, if you involve them.' The farmer's neighbour is considering doing something similar.

Silveira's dream is to reconnect as many of Brazil's jaguar populations as possible by providing corridors of continuous habitat running right across the country. Jaguars use natural corridors like river valleys to visit different zones. It's nature's way of making sure the big cat population doesn't become inbred – a real threat to survival. If the animals can't mingle, Silveira fears that some jaguar populations will become genetically isolated and could die out within fifty years.

Scientists now recognise the importance of 'genetic connectivity', the idea that the survival of the jaguar relies on its ability to interbreed. The species was once much more widespread. Fossil evidence from England, Germany and Spain indicates the presence of jaguars into at least the middle Pleistocene in Europe. Experts have discovered that isolated populations are weakened by the expression of what they call lethal recessive genes. Once travel pathways or 'corridors' between seemingly disparate populations are severed, isolated jaguar populations, even in large areas, are prone to extinction.[15]

This is the thinking behind Silveira's most ambitious project: the Araguaia River Biodiversity Corridor, which aims to reinstate a corridor along the river valley running from Emas in Brazil's central south, all the way along the Amazon delta to the north of the country. To make this happen, he needs to recruit what he describes as 'jaguar-friendly' farmers and ranchers all along the 2,000-kilometre corridor. He knows it is a long shot, but he is cautiously optimistic. 'Farmers aren't the problem, they're part of the solution,' he said as our truck slipped and slid in the mud formed by overnight rain. 'This is a lifetime project. We need a lot more jaguar-friendly ranches.'

As we drove on past the reserve along the headwater banks of the Araguaia River, he pointed out tapir tracks in the mud beside green and golden soya plants, as well as signs of rooting peccaries. We passed a group of guys emptying big sacks of fertiliser – it looked like white and green bathsalts – into a tractor trailer. Four combine harvesters with tyres 10 feet tall stood by.

A beautiful blue and yellow macaw struck a discordant note amid a newly harvested field of soya. The lone bird was nibbling on a piece of stubble. Silveira saw this as evidence of wildlife adapting to a changing landscape. For a bird at home in forest and wooded savannah, I just saw it as desperate stuff.

In three hours' driving, we'd crossed the properties of four different landowners, following the corridor and the continuous mosaic of mixed land use.

Silveira seemed satisfied. 'This is the ideal model for a jaguar-friendly ranch, where you have the predators, you have the prey, and the law is being obeyed,' he said. 'If you see a large tract of agricultural land, they have to have twenty per cent reserved for nature. We've tracked our jaguars moving through this land.'

Yet I was still wrestling with the idea that the monocultures of soya, corn and sugar cane now carpeting what was once rich grassland and forest are somehow good for wildlife. After all, soya croplands are expanding by hundreds of thousands of hectares every year, while jaguars are shrinking in both number and distribution. Something didn't add up.

I pressed him further on the interplay between 'Big Ag' and wildlife habitats.

'When you deforest the land, and remove their prey species, even if you're doing farming of soya bean and corn . . . you're directly affecting the cat,' Silveira admitted. 'You are silently wiping out the species but you don't see it. Jaguars in some areas of Brazil are doing OK, but in some areas they are virtually on the line of extinction.'

He sees the corridor as a lifeline to save the species for a future when land-use policies may be more favourable. He knows time is running out, but for now he's taking a pragmatic approach, using existing rules to enlist farmers to his cause, rather than treating them as the enemy. The strategy is to make the best of things the way they are.

'We're going to have a bigger reduction [of jaguars]. They are going to be extinct in some areas . . . That's why we need to think about large-scale corridors, because we can always think about jaguars coming back [in the future], of recolonisation,' he told me.

I asked him about the future of jaguars in the face of the agricultural frontier moving further into the forest. 'I am pessimistic,' he replied bluntly.

There's no doubting his passion for jaguars, or his dedication to conserving the species. His Araguaia Corridor project is hugely important in preserving the genetic integrity of the species. I felt he has come to realise that, in a country with rapidly expanding agriculture, he will need the good will and cooperation of farmers – and lots of them – to make his corridor dream come true.

I could see the merit in his approach and sincerely wish him well with it. Jaguars need all the help they can get. However, my instincts were telling me that expanding monocultures were more the problem than the route to a solution.

Whichever way you look at it, the rapid expansion of cropland in the Midwest region of Brazil, as I was about to discover, pushes the agricultural frontier, and cattle ranches, deeper into the forest: straight into conflict with jaguars.

### LOSING THE LUNGS OF THE EARTH

Cuiabá, the capital city of the state of Mato Grosso, stands at the exact central point of South America. Founded in 1719, this former gold-rush city is now the trading hub for the state's dominant activity: agriculture. Squeezing into an 11-seater Cessna plane, I headed for São Felix do Araguaia in the state's northeastern region, known to locals as 'the end of the Earth'. I was off to spend time with one of Brazil's many indigenous tribes and to hear how the nation's agricultural revolution was affecting them.

Reaching its cruising altitude of 10,000 feet, the plane moved in what felt like slow motion, providing an amazing bird's-eye view over the Brazilian countryside. When the clouds dispersed, they revealed massive blocks of brown prairie – newly ploughed fields – rolling on as far as the eye could see. Pink veins around their periphery divided the tracts of land: dirt tracks for big machines to reap what they sow, most likely crops of GM soya. A yellow plane flew low to the ground, followed by a trail of vapour, probably giving crops their latest dose of pesticide.

I peered through my binoculars in disbelief: for mile upon mile, there wasn't a single hedge or treeline. The cattle that had been our constant companions as we drove through the rugged savannah grasslands to see Silveira were nowhere to be seen. They had given way to cropland. Some fields had been sown in wavy patterns; some were planted in a criss-cross shape; others in simple straight lines.

I remembered Silveira telling me to 'look for the reserve', but where I could see patches of forest, they were like small islands in a sea of crops. It was all the same plant: soya.

Where I live in England, seeing one combine harvester is a big deal. In the Brazilian Midwest of Mato Grosso, the vastness of the landscape lends itself to half a dozen combine harvesters trekking through the crops in formation like an aerobatics display team. Peering down from the plane, I saw several such teams at work, the giant machines working their way methodically across the fields. Trucks waited out on the sidelines to receive the harvest and deliver it to feedmills.

This was on a scale like nothing I'd seen before. My mind was in overload. A curtain of low cloud came, providing some respite. It felt like the interval in a particularly intense theatre play. Eventually, the view returned and forest followed the wavy line of a wide, meandering river. I could see the white dots of some cattle, and in the distance, wilder land of forest and savannah. For now, the agricultural frontier was behind us as we headed toward the Amazon.

As the journey went on, I got chatting to a fellow passenger who turned out to be the mayor of Confresa, a city of 40,000 people in Mato Grosso. Gaspar Domingos Lazzari wore a blue business shirt and gold chain. He was proud to tell me how his parents were the first people to live in Confresa, and he was its first mayor.

Our conversation gave me a renewed sense of the sheer scale of land management here. He told me there were two huge farms in the area, the largest covering 1.2 million hectares, the other rearing

110,000 head of cattle (one of the largest beef producers in Britain boasts little over 3,000 cattle).[16]

'Where we're flying now is mostly soya,' he said. 'Deforestation started here about thirty years ago and became more intensive ten years ago.' Three-quarters of the cropland is under soya, with corn and rice making up the rest.

This was all on the edge of the Amazon, the transition zone where savannah meets forest. Everywhere I looked there were chocolate-brown blocks with tan stripes where combines turned ripened soya into stubble.

Lazzari pointed out a bright orange dirt road between fields and forest leading to a reserve occupied by indigenous people. The area set aside for these ancient tribes was hemmed in on all sides by agriculture. Adjacent to the reserve, a cluster of six green combines had harvested a single soya prairie while five more were still hard at work in the next 'field'. But the word 'field' does nothing to express the scale here, for there is almost no beginning, or end. It was just a vast continuum of crop, broken up, barely perceptibly, by dirt tracks giving access for machinery.

Lazzari told me he thought farmland in this part of Mato Grosso had pretty much reached the limit of expansion, gobbling up all the land readily available. As the plane approached Confresa, he pointed out his farm. He's proud of what's happening here and his part in its development, but aspects of the rapacious development worry him.

'It's a big concern for me, because we have the Amazon here, which is the lung of the world. So the more it is preserved, the better for everyone,' he acknowledged.

As he left the plane at Confresa, we parted with warm hand-shakes: 'You've had the very best guide on this flight, and all for free!' he said cheerfully. I sat in the aerodrome, feeling quite mindblown. The monopoly of monocultures I'd just witnessed was on a scale and a starkness that I'd never seen before. As I have seen in other parts of South America, particularly Argentina, it's all about soya.

Brazil is second only to the USA in soya production, and is the world leader in soya exports.[17] Mato Grosso alone produces nearly a tenth of the global soya bean harvest, accounting for nearly a third of Brazil's soya output[18] in an industry worth nearly US$7.3 billion a year. Soya production continues to expand by hundreds of thousands of hectares every year in Brazil, largely into existing cattle pastures that have already been deforested.

In Mato Grosso soya production increased by a third between 2011 and 2016,[19] with industry sources suggesting that the area of soya could double again by ploughing up pasture to make way for yet more of the crop.[20] But ploughing up pastures for soya doesn't mean an end to deforestation. Researchers have found that, in Mato Grosso, conversion of pasture to soy production has been displacing cattle farmers further north, where they fell trees to create new grazing land for cattle. So while new pasture may be the direct reason for deforestation, soybean production is the major underlying cause.[21]

Of late, cattle farmers have found it lucrative to sell their pasture to soya producers and move somewhere cheaper, which usually means into the forest. Land prices in the Amazon rocketed during the global soya boom in the early 2000s. In some parts of Mato Grosso, values shot up tenfold. The land rush allowed cattle ranchers to flog their fields for enormous profits and buy land further north to expand their herds. Newly (and illegally) deforested land was relatively cheap.[22]

Scientists in America have come to describe the deforestation process between cattle and soy as a 'land-use cascade'. They calculate that reducing soya expansion would have a disproportionately large effect on the amount of rainforest that can be saved. According to the study, for the 2003–8 period, a 10 per cent reduction of soy expansion into old pasture areas in the Amazon would have reduced deforestation in the Amazon by as much as 40 per cent.[23] This reflects rising land values and the fact that cattle farmers displaced by selling their land for soya can buy – and therefore clear – so much more in the Amazon.

Flying over Mato Grosso gave me a much greater appreciation of the sheer scale of deforestation in this part of the world. I could see the forest frontier and the extraordinary extent to which soya dominated the plains. Reflecting on the scale of landscape change, I remembered something written by WWF's vice-president in the US, Eric Dinerstein:

> Few field biologists bother to check the daily price of soybeans or palm oil. This is an oversight because the market value of these commodities – along with beef, corn, sugar, and coffee – may, over the coming decades, define the future of rare species more profoundly than any other driver of habitat loss will.
> At present, nowhere is the conversion and fracturing of rain forests by industrialised agriculture in the world's most precious ecosystems more evident than in Southeast Asia and Brazil.[24]

Dinerstein goes on to explain that almost 70 per cent of the greenhouse gas emissions released annually from tropical forests come from just two parts of the world where the forest has been turned over to agriculture: Sumatra and the edge of the Brazilian Amazon in the state of Mato Grosso.

In theory, soya is a wonder crop. It contains all the essential amino acids needed for human nutrition,[25] making it one of only a handful of plants that provide a complete protein. Yet only a fraction of it goes to feed people. The vast majority is for animal feed. Most of the soya beans (85 per cent) are crushed to give oil and soya meal. Oil makes up less than a fifth of the pulped beans and largely goes for vegetable oil, with small amounts finding their way into soaps or biodiesel. Nearly four-fifths of the pulped bean becomes soya meal destined for the feed troughs of intensively farmed animals like pigs, chickens and cattle.

When defenders of factory farming suggest that cramming animals into airless barns 'saves space', they fail to take into account that the business model is wholly dependent on large amounts of 'space' elsewhere. This is what happens if you keep animals indoors, and bring food to them. It has to grow somewhere – and often that place is Brazil, which exports much of its soya. The European Union imports about 35 million tonnes of the stuff every year, nearly half coming from Brazil. Some 13 million hectares of South American land – an area roughly equivalent to the size of Greece – is dedicated to growing soya for the EU, much of it to be consumed by Europe's industrially reared farm animals.[26]

Feeding soya to farm animals means they are taken off the land and, in the process of turning soya to meat, waste most of the available energy and protein in conversion. Putting whole landscapes to the plough for the burgeoning trade in animal feed seems deeply questionable, particularly when that land could be used much more efficiently growing food directly for people.

My plane ride to São Felix was one of the most eye-opening experiences of my life. Nothing quite prepared me for the sheer scale of the animal-feed industry's takeover of the Amazon. I had long thought that the US boasted the biggest, most industrial agriculture on the planet. When it comes to soya production, I now see it has a serious rival.

As I stepped out of the plane at São Felix do Araguaia, the 'end of the Earth', I couldn't help reflecting on how much of the world's factory farms are powered by the deforested plains of Brazil. How many people imagine, when they eat cheap meat, that their bargain-basement chicken nuggets and pork chops reach their plates via the felling of rainforest trees?

## WARRIOR WARS

I was standing by a disused airport runway watching an extraordinary spectacle. Two dozen tribesmen dressed in little more than black and red body paint and cottonwood bow-ties had congregated on the hardened earth ahead of a competition. Split into two teams, they were about to go head-to-head in a fierce warrior contest known as *Wai Uhi Uwede*.

Hooting like owls and kicking up clouds of dust in the 40-degree Centigrade heat, the Maráiwatsédé tribe of the indigenous Xavante people, hunter–gatherers from the forests of Brazil's Midwest, were embarking on a race to manoeuvre a 70-kilo chunk of tree trunk back to their camp some 4 miles away. I watched as team members took turns to grapple with the thing, attempting to stagger along with it on their backs until, exhausted, they had done their stint, and could pass it on to the next man.

The contestants, lean men of indeterminate age with thick black hair (long at the back, and heavily fringed at the front), had already had quite a day of it, participating in various fighting competitions before the tree-trunk finale. If they were exhausted, it didn't show.

A misunderstanding with my Brazilian driver – who, perhaps rather fancying himself as the official race car, sped off without me, but with our photographer in the back – meant that I was left behind among running, grunting warriors. There was nothing for it but to join the race. I ran as fast and as far as my legs would carry me, at one point getting tantalisingly close to the car, but the driver didn't spot me, and sped off once again, leaving me sweaty and defeated.

I was soon beaten by the intense heat – and I wasn't the only one. Spectators from the tribe, their backs glistening with sweat, piled on the back of any vehicle slow enough to enable them to hop onboard.

After what felt an eternity, my driver finally twigged that I wasn't with him and slowed down to pick me up. Watching the race from the comfort of the car was a short-lived relief. Before the contest was out, our Mitsubishi 4x4, a big beast of a vehicle, went down an even bigger rut and got well and truly stuck.

That was how I came to walk the best part of 2 miles in blistering heat with a nun who had accompanied me on the visit and an elderly member of the 1,000-strong Maráiwatsédé tribe. By the time I stumbled into the village, I was exhausted and dehydrated, my face glowing bright red. I arrived just in time to see the triumphant team in a circle, hands clasped and heads down, feverishly chanting their victory song. That night, they would celebrate with a special cake made of corn.

'This is the new generation that will fight to keep this culture alive,' I was told by a tribesman speaking through an interpreter.

I soon came to realise that the warrior ritual wasn't just for show: the Xavante people have fought a long-running battle for the rights to their ancestral land. They remain determined to preserve their unique heritage.

Traditionally nomadic hunters and gatherers, they live in the state of Mato Grosso in a central Brazilian region of upland savannah interspersed with narrow bands of riverside forest. Divided into a number of distinct tribes, they live in horseshoe-shaped villages on the grassland, cultivating corn (maize), beans and pumpkins. Traditionally they have hunted tapir, deer, peccaries and birds, and gathered roots, nuts and honey.

Until the 1930s, when the government of the day embarked on a failed attempt to take over the land in the name of boosting the economy, they lived in relative isolation not far from the Araguaia River. The battle brought them prominence in Brazil, but their victory was short-lived.[27] In 1966, the Maráiwatsédé tribe of the Xavante people were forced off their land, 165,000 hectares about an hour's drive from São Felix do Araguaia in the northeast of Mato Grosso. The Brazilian government drafted in the air force to move the tribe in a brutal displacement that saw more than a hundred natives die from disease.[28]

Down but certainly not out, the Maráiwatsédé tribe began a fifty-year struggle to get their land back. In 1992 they took their case to the United Nations Earth Summit in Rio de Janeiro. The land had by this stage passed into the hands of an Italian petroleum company, AGIP, which bowed to international pressure to hand it back.

But the battle wasn't over. A new struggle began between the tribes and the cattle and soya farmers who had been using the land and were hell-bent on retaining their commercial interest in it. The years had taken their toll: by now it had become one of the most deforested areas in the Amazon. In 1998, the Brazilian government made an official declaration that the land was owned by the indigenous people, but the legal wrangling continued for more than a decade, and so did the farmers' hold on the land. Finally, in 2014, the federal government stepped in to remove the remaining farmers and allow the return of the Xavante.

Their plight attracted a number of high-profile and distinguished figures, including a Catalan-born Christian called Dom Pedro Casaldáliga. Emeritus Bishop of São Felix do Araguaia, he is known in South America as a staunch defender of human rights. These days he is too elderly to be an active campaigner, but irate landowners still blame him for fuelling the resistance that eventually led to the indigenous victory.[29] Now eighty-eight years old, he faced numerous death threats and attempts on his life for his part in the struggle. As recently as 2012, federal police officers are believed to have whisked him away from his home in São Felix to a safehouse 1,000 kilometres away, following an intensification of death threats from disgruntled farmers.

The death threats were real. On one occasion a priest he was travelling with was shot dead by an irate policeman who mistook him for the bishop. Another incident involved a contract killer who has described how he was offered a small fortune to kill Dom Pedro. According to the killer's account, he set up the murder but, just before he took out his gun, Dom Pedro turned and looked him straight in the face. 'I just couldn't do it after that,' the would-be assassin said.[30]

My meeting with Dom Pedro was one of the most moving moments of my time in Brazil. The rain was hammering down in São Felix do Araguaia as I entered his simple stone house, which was festooned with religious artefacts and figurines of birds and other animals. Now suffering from Parkinson's Disease, he was slumped in a chair. He looked frail and spoke so softly that I struggled to hear him over the sound of the rain.

I held his hand as I listened to him talk about how 'big agriculture' was taking land from indigenous tribes in Brazil, forcing them out of their ancestral homelands. He told me how pleased he was that after a decades-long struggle, the human rights of indigenous people were at last being respected and their land returned. I shared with him some of my own background: my father was a retired clergyman; my late father-in-law had started his own decades-long struggle against industrial agriculture in Europe when he set up Compassion in World Farming.

I felt a huge sense of privilege when he offered me a blessing, which I was honoured to receive. Overcome, I started welling up. It was all so unexpected, and after what had been an overwhelming trip, I suddenly felt profoundly at peace.

The next day, I would meet the chief of the Xavante's Marãiwatsédé people. Needing to gather myself for the remaining challenges, I stayed overnight in Alto Boa Vista, a small town in the northeast of Mato Grosso, in the transitional zone where savannah meets the Amazon. My driver said the hotel, a basic affair with bars at the windows, was the best in town. He also said there was no crime in the area. I told myself that the bars must be to reassure nervous outsiders about security.

It was the rainy season, and it was soon obvious why the locals took their cars everywhere. Dirt-track roads ran sticky with red mud. As the rain continued to hammer down, I was glad of our 4x4; I had not brought enough clothes to get caked in mud every time I stepped out.

After dinner in a simple local restaurant, I couldn't wait to lay my head down, but sleep proved elusive. All through the night, dogs barked, music blared and cockerels crowed, and all as if through a megaphone. The place might be a backwater, but it wasn't a quiet one. By 6 a.m. I had long ago waved the white flag and got blearily up. The place teemed with locals, getting on the school bus, whizzing around on motorbikes, making a cheerful din. Outside the hotel, a few men were hosing down a tractor.

In my tiny bathroom, a large brown bug lay on the floor, its elongated antennae having long ago twitched their last. That was when I discovered that the shower boasted a highly unusual feature: a clear glass window that looked right on to the street. Now, a window to the outside world is normally no bad thing. Through it, I could see the people on the schoolbus, the bikers having a chat, and the guys hosing down their tractor. But when you're having a shower, a window to the outside, nice as it may be, also means a window looking in. Both out of bashfulness and because the water was freezing, I didn't hang around to take in the scene.

I was soon downstairs and ready to join my driver to pick up the nun who would be accompanying us on a return visit to the settlement of the Xavante people. I had been told that the Xavante were fundamentally wary of outsiders and were more likely to accept my visit if it was arranged by someone they already knew and trusted. Thankfully, a local nun who was working with them volunteered to act as a go-between and oversee the visit.

Sister Dulcineia Dos Santos of the National Council of Brazilian Bishops was a petite black lady with a megawatt smile. She had been working with the Xavante people and other indigenous tribes in the area for the last two years, helping, among other things, with the children's nutritional health. When she first started going to the village, eighty of the children in the tribe were suffering from malnourishment.

'For me, it was very sad,' she told me. 'I had never experienced people with malnutrition before. They had very sad eyes. I was very touched. They welcomed me and started calling me "Africa". I was keen to stay' – that big smile shone. Happily it is now a problem of the past.

One reason for the children's plight had been tribal culture, which dictated that adults and the elderly were fed first. The tradition looks back to their heritage as warriors ready to hunt and fight at a moment's notice. But the real reason they were going short of food lay elsewhere: the land on which they had long depended had been stripped of edibles.

'There wasn't enough food for the tribe because the whole area was deforested by cattle farmers,' Sister Dulcineia explained with a sigh. 'But now it's starting to recover. They've planted fruit trees and are encouraging the forest to regrow.'

It is a slow process. The indigenous people are growing corn, cassava and rice without pesticides, but the mega-farms near their reserve grow soya, corn and cotton using pesticides, which contaminate the rivers in the reserve, and kill fish.[31]

Professor Wanderlei Pignati, Doctor of Toxicology at the Federal University of Mato Grosso, has been conducting research on chemical contamination around the Xavante settlement, and has confirmed the link. 'In this whole area, there are soya and corn farms. The pesticide runoff goes into the rivers, which kills the small fish and destroys the whole food chain. So the Xavante don't have fish to catch,' he told me.

I arrived back at camp early the next morning to hear chanting coming from a large village hut. Inside the simple domed structure, I could see young warriors in their cottonwood bow-ties dancing. I noticed that the older men sat very still. They had sticks as thick as pencils through each earlobe. Behind them was a giant panoramic painting of the camp, complete with domed homes, mother and child, and watching macaws.

Waiting for me in the shade of a mango tree was Damiao Paridzare, chief of the Maráiwatsédé people. He was wearing a traditional headdress of blue and white macaw feathers, his forehead painted red with the crushed seeds of a forest fruit. He fixed me with a stern stare. If I was meant to feel intimidated, it worked.

Speaking through an interpreter, I decided to break the ice by telling him about my meeting with Dom Pedro and what a special experience it had been. He broke into a smile. 'Our greatest ally is Dom Pedro,' he enthused. 'He is our greatest friend and we are fighting together.'

Paridzare was a young boy when the Xavante were forced from their land.

'Those were very troubled times. We felt we were being cheated. When I was a boy, my dream was to try to fight to get our land back. We fought and we won,' he said with feeling. 'When we came back here, the whole area was deforested. What we found was just pasture for cattle. Things that used to feed us have now vanished. We shouldn't have to buy meat, we should be able to feed ourselves from fruits and hunting.

'But the habitat of the animals has been destroyed . . . we don't have animals to hunt any more. All we have is grass. We don't have birds, we don't have monkeys, everything has just disappeared . . . and that's a big, big problem. Our rivers are also contaminated and we can no longer find fish here because we have a lot of soya farms in the neighbourhood and pesticide is getting into the rivers.'

Facing serious food shortages, the Xavante have been trying to plant crops.

'You see the soya fields now – they used to be forests . . . Because of the pesticides they use, we are being forced to breathe polluted air and to swallow contaminated food too,' the chief said.

I remembered seeing the warriors getting ready for the race yesterday. As they prepared to demonstrate their strength on the end of that runway, I had noticed a steady stream of soya trucks passing along the road behind them. Sadly, it will take more than the indomitable spirit of tribal warriors to stop the spread of Brazil's soya juggernaut.

### RAINING POISON

I was visiting a school in the heart of Big Ag country, Rio Verde, about 260 miles from the capital of Brazil. As I approached the cluster of buildings, I could hear the chatter and laughter of children. The walls of the compound were decorated with painted handprints of all sizes and colours, each accompanied by the name of the child it belonged to. Inside, youngsters from tots to teenagers were crammed into classrooms, taking in their lessons.

The headmaster of the rural municipal school of São Jose Do Pontal met me at the gate. A tall black man with fine features, Hugo Alves Dos Santos welcomed me with a smile and a friendly handshake. He wore a striped shirt and chinos – light attire for the sticky heat. In the playground, groups of boys were showing off their football skills. Some, from better-off families I suppose, wore football boots, or something like them. Others played in bare feet. A group of girls were deep into a game of table tennis.

My visit had generated some excitement: the children weren't used to visits from foreigners. As they thronged around me, eager to hear a snatch of my English accent, I noticed a plaque on the school library wall commemorating the proud sponsorship of one of the world's biggest chemical companies. What an irony, I thought – for I had come to the school to hear how, in May 2013, it had fallen victim to one of the most notorious incidents of aerial spraying with chemical pesticides.

The day had started normally with children outside playing during breaktime. Crops were growing in the surrounding fields. I heard how some of the children were eating outside when a small yellow plane appeared out of nowhere and started spraying. It flew low over the school – four times, according to Dos Santos.

'I was covered in a liquid, but didn't realise it was harmful. The kids also thought it wasn't harmful. They started playfully running after the plane,' he recalled. He told me how he took off his shirt and waved it at the pilot, trying to signal to him to get out of there. He sensed that no good could come of the plane flying so low, so near the school.

Dos Santos soon had trouble breathing and had a raging sore throat. 'I was feeling really bad; I thought I was going to die,' he told me.

One of the teachers raised the alarm, saying that some of the children had also fallen ill. They had breathing difficulties and their skin was itchy. Some were so uncomfortable that they began stripping off their clothes in the playground. Panic and chaos ensued, with kids screaming and passing out. As well as the intense itching, they were vomiting, suffering severe headaches and dizziness.

'The children were desperate, they didn't know what to do,' Dos Santos said. 'That was when I called the emergency services.'

Some forty-two students and teachers ended up at the city hospital, with twenty-nine admitted for in-patient treatment. So overloaded was the hospital that it was forced to take over part of a nearby school as a makeshift ward.[32] In the weeks and months ahead, some children made as many as eighteen return visits, and some feel that they still suffer from ailments linked to the incident, as I discovered when I spoke to a number of their parents.

Maria de Fatima, whose daughter was sixteen years old when it happened, said: 'My daughter suffered chronic stress and hormone problems and is still under treatment to this day.' On the day it happened, the girl's condition was so serious that she was taken by plane to the city hospital in Goinia.

Maria Aparecida de Oliveira first heard that her fifteen-year-old daughter had been affected when the teenager phoned to tell her that pupils had been poisoned. She arrived home to find her daughter and three other girls in such a bad state she feared they might not make it to hospital. 'They couldn't breathe,' she told me. 'Even today, my daughter isn't healthy. It's a really sad situation.'

The incident resulted in the school being closed for several days for cleansing,[33] and Professor Wanderlei Pignati, Doctor of Toxicology at the Federal University of Mato Grosso, believes it was no isolated episode:

'It's not only in Goias state, it also happens in Mato Grosso state . . . and Mato Grosso do Sol. Many schools in these places are surrounded by soya, corn and cotton fields, so these cases do happen very often.' According to Pignati, in the region of Rio Verde alone, pupils at eleven schools are at risk of harm from chemical spraying. 'Sometimes they stop classes during the spraying season. If it's not by plane, then big tractors spray the fields very close to the schools.'

The use of pesticides is regulated in Brazil, with a 500-metre exclusion zone required between aerial crop spraying and schools, houses, animal farms and nature reserves. However, the legislation is frequently ignored.

I asked Pignati whether pesticides could be used safely. 'There is no safe use of pesticides,' he replied bluntly, and told me how pesticides can evaporate, dispersing up to 3,000 metres away from where they are sprayed. They can also be absorbed into rainfall, and percolate into underground water, threatening drinking water. 'They can also contaminate many foods that we eat, such as soya and corn and cotton,' he added. 'If you're talking about people in the surroundings, then it's not safe.'

Brazil is now the world's largest user of pesticides, with consumption rocketing by more than 160 per cent between 2000 and 2012.[34] The nation's agrochemical market is worth over US$8 billion a year, and continues to grow. It now accounts for 20 per cent of global pesticide consumption,[35] their soaring use linked to the expansion of crop monocultures.

With its equatorial sunlight, steady temperatures and year-round harvests, Brazil is an attractive habitat for insects, fungi and weeds. Whereas crops grown in small and mixed farming systems are relatively well equipped to cope with pests, big monocultures are more susceptible to attack. As a result, farmers ladle on the pesticides.

To explore the issue further, I spoke to Professor Larissa Mies Bombardi from the University of São Paulo, who has been monitoring pesticide use in Brazil. 'Soya alone is responsible for forty-seven per cent of the consumption of pesticides in Brazil,' she said. 'It is the crop most responsible for the growth of pesticide use in Brazil.'

She told me that according to official data one person is poisoned by pesticides in Brazil every ninety minutes. She believes these figures only tell a fraction of the story, because only certain cases are recorded. She points to studies estimating that, for every notified case, fifty others are not registered, and asserts that between 2007 and 2014, 1,186 people in Brazil died due to pesticide poisoning. That means 'on average . . . every two and a half days in Brazil, one person dies from pesticide poisoning'.

This grievous mortality rate may be linked to the lax regulations on the use of the most toxic chemicals. A trade journal report describes how more than 400 chemicals can be used as pesticides here – including twenty-two that are prohibited in other countries. The twenty-two substances banned elsewhere (some are outlawed in the European Union and others in the United States)[36] are among the most commonly used in Brazil.

'We have pesticides that are allowed to be used here but have been banned elsewhere, including Europe. We are becoming a country where we produce less and less food – such as rice and beans – in favour of crops for export as animal feed. At the same time, we are seeing an increase in the use of pesticides, and that basically means that politically we are choosing to focus on agribusiness instead,' she said.

As monocultures continue their march across the plains of Brazil, evidently, jaguars are not the only ones at risk.

## CANNED CATTLE

Travelling through Brazil's Midwest, there was no escaping it: cattle are big business. They were everywhere I looked: across mile upon mile of pasture of the deepest green, in the valleys, on the hills, and everywhere in between. And they came in all shapes and sizes: white, black, tan, chocolate, grey, and pretty much every combination of those colours.

Every now and then, the grass would be ruptured by termite nests. They looked like giant molehills, a feature of the grassland savannah in Brazil. Thanks to agriculture, there is little left of the original pristine Cerrado.[37]

Four states make up the central–west region of Brazil: the Federal District (with the nation's capital, Brasilia), Goias, Mato Grosso do Sul and Mato Grosso. The Midwest grasslands of these four states are cattle country. They provide a cornerstone product – beef – for a nation that is now an agricultural superpower. The country is second only to the USA when it comes to producing beef.[38] As you might expect in a place so rich in land, most of the nation's 200 million cattle are reared on grass.

The Cerrado grasslands are not only home to a large cattle herd but have long been prowled by what remains of Brazil's jaguars. According to the International Union for Conservation of Nature (IUCN), which publishes a Red List directory of endangered species,[39] clashes with cattle farmers, as well as habitat destruction, now rank among the greatest threats to the species.

Given the sheer number of cattle involved,[40] it's hard to imagine even the most powerful killer cat so much as denting the bovine population. Indeed, ranches pose a far greater danger to jaguars than jaguars do to ranches. Despite being protected by law (they are currently classified as 'near threatened'), once they venture onto a farmer's land they are frequently shot on sight.[41]

As I travelled through the Midwest I was delighted to see so many cattle out on grass, but there were troubling signs of a new trend: the rise of feedlots. It was not long before I came across a classic of the genre, its reek long preceding it: hundreds of animals penned in together on a filthy square of mud, standing listlessly not far from the roadside. They looked filthy, and the stench caught the back of my throat, a mix of stinking muck and sickly-sweet corn.

The owner did not seem too bothered when I got out of the car for a closer look: it seemed he saw nothing wrong in what he was doing. The air felt thick and heavy as I made my way towards the animals, and it wasn't just the smell: it was also the swarms of flies.

Besides the flies, the main sound was the snorting of cattle. The glassy mucus streaming from their noses suggested that some were not well. As the sun beat down, a fortunate few crowded under a meagre tin-roof shelter, desperate for shade. The rest had no choice but to bear it, day in and day out. It was one of several I came across during my time in Brazil. Judging by the number of empty pens, this one was just stocking up. At full capacity, it could probably hold a couple of thousand animals. Given all the pasture available, cramming them into muddy enclosures seemed absurd.

The sign leading to the farm read 'Boa Esperanca' – 'Good Hope'. I could not think of anything less apt.

Later, I spoke to 36-year-old Carolina Galvani, a Brazilian animal welfare advocate working for the Humane Society International. Based on her family's 100-hectare farm in Barretos, some 400 kilometres northeast of São Paulo, she works with Brazilian-based companies to improve standards of farm animal welfare. Feedlots repel her.

'Most of the cattle in Brazil are pasture-based,' she told me, 'which is good. It basically means they are free-range. But there are still some practices widely used that are worrying for animal welfare. Things like hot-branding, dehorning, castration and long-distance transport.' Worryingly, she also told me that a number of cattle-industry figures and environmental groups are pushing the spread of feedlots as a way to curb deforestation. They are in fashion. In Mato Grosso alone, the number of cattle confined to feedlots increased fivefold between 2005 and 2008.[42] Nearly a million cattle can now be crammed into muddy paddocks across the state.

Galvani was critical of the idea that forests can be protected by taking cattle off grass. It may seem like a space-saving idea, she explained, but it overlooks the fact that the cattle still have to eat, and their feed has to be grown somewhere. 'I don't think advocates of feedlots are being very clever with mathematics,' she said wryly. To her mind, a more sustainable solution is required, one that keeps farm animals more freely in tune with the land, and where they don't depend on monoculture grain.

To me, it's just another industry dodge. Advocating a way of keeping farm animals that makes them reliant on feed crops (which displace forest, which in turn kills off wildlife) may benefit powerful vested interests. Everyone else – animals included – pays the price.

## PANIC ON THE PANTANAL

I was tingling with anticipation as I set off along the hundred-mile Transpantaneira road into the world-famous Pantanal, the largest continental wetland on the planet. I had heard so much about this place and its breath-taking wildlife and scenery.

The wetland spans the Brazilian states of Mato Grosso and Mato Grosso do Sul, and extends through Bolivia and Paraguay. To reach it, I would spend hours in a 4x4 hire car bumping along a dirt-track road barely worthy of the name, crossing more than 120 bridges – many of them alarmingly makeshift – until the road petered out. That is how I would know when I'd reached my destination: the tiny settlement of Porto Jofre beside the Cuiaba River, and the best place in the world to see wild jaguars.

I left the small town of Poconé, where I'd stayed the night, well before dawn. The sun rose like a fireball, sprinkling intense orange spits of light across a drenched and shimmering landscape. All around was an explosion of life. Nightjars performed their last flutter in the half-light, like half-seen shadows, before settling down to roost for the day. Kingfishers darted for breakfast as jacanas danced on waterlilies. Limpkins – like big brown herons – picked in the shallows. Family parties of the world's largest rodent, the capybara, wandered nonchalantly beside the car like giant guinea pigs. A caiman lay nearby, his leathery avocado skin glistening in the early morning light.

There was so much to see that I struggled to know where to look. Hard-pressed for time, I felt skewered by my own good fortune at being here with such a tight deadline.

The land was very wet. I drove past lilypads and bulrushes, saw tall trees and flooded pasture, bordered by lush vegetation. Huge yellow and pink blooms swayed on tall flowering plants. The rainy season had given nature a chance to recapture the place, and I was seeing it at its best. Come the dry season, much of it would be cattle country but now it was too wet for much grazing. As if to remind me, a lone white Brahminy bull stood stubbornly in the road.

As for the driving conditions – well, I struggled. Many of the bridges were so rickety that to cross them was a leap of faith. Every now and then, the road – such as it was – would drop away, forcing traffic to cross river fords whose depth varied according to how much it had rained. We lurched along for hours, our hired 4x4 trundling heroically over muddy bumps and ruts. Water levels on the Pantanal were high, and the surrounding farms were flooded. It grew more and more obvious that the road was near-impassable, but I only had a day to do this: tomorrow evening, I had to be back in Cuiaba, more than six hours away, for another stop on what seemed a relentless schedule.

Twice the 4x4 made it across fords far too deep to be a wise route for anything with wheels. On the third occasion, my luck ran out. The fast-flowing river had already claimed one victim, a flatbed lorry that was slowly sinking into soft mud. As his truck tilted onto one side, the driver could only wade around the water and wonder what to do.

With little room to pass, my car was soon stuck too. There was nothing for it but to join the other stricken driver in the murky water, and wonder how the hell we were going to get out of this one.

Bulbous little black fish swam around my feet. Piranha? I knew they could be found in the Pantanal. I had visions of flesh being torn from my legs and felt a stir of panic. Thankfully they didn't materialise, but just a stone's throw away a biggish caiman, a South American member of the crocodile family, was quietly watching . . .

After a long and anxious wait, a passing digger appeared miraculously and towed us out.

Overnight rain had transformed what was never more than a dirt track into an assault course. My driver fought constantly with the steering wheel to avoid sliding into floodwaters. I vowed there and then that if I were ever lucky enough to return, I would come by plane.

Despite further scrapes, we eventually made it to the promised point where the road runs out: Porto Jofre. And what an amazing place! With a population of just sixty people, no mains electricity and no landline telephones, it could barely have been more isolated. For fishermen, photographers and those seeking jaguars, it is the promised land at the end of the road from hell.

There was no time to waste. Soon I was in a 22-foot motorised pontoon, heading down the Cuiaba River that divides the states of Mato Grosso and Mato Grosso do Sul. Sebastian, the driver, warned me that jaguars were hard to see at that time of year. The rainy season meant they had plenty of watering holes, and less cause to venture to the river edge to drink. Still we pressed on, more in hope than expectation.

Heading upriver, we spotted macaques swinging through bankside trees, caiman gliding through the water, and a family of giant otter splashing and playing near the bank. With whistles, clicks and squeaks, the otters swam effortlessly before disappearing below the surface. The river was broad, brown and smooth-flowing. Dense vegetation lined both sides with thick stands of waterside flowers in yellow, pink and red. Elongated weaverbird nests hung from low branches. One trailed in the water, testament to the swollen river heights.

Bits of bark had been stripped from a fallen log beside the river bank – a tell-tale sign of jaguars – but wherever they were, they were lying low. Sebastian did his level best, we spent hours in the boat, in the full heat of the day – but we didn't get so much as a sniff of a jaguar.

Other tourists do better. Many have been lucky enough to see big cats in the area, thanks to enterprising conservation efforts that have transformed jaguars in this part of country from villains to money spinners. With more than 95 per cent of the Brazilian Pantanal privately owned, ecotourism has huge conservation potential, providing an alternative source of income for landowners and local communities.

I talked to one of the co-ordinators of Oncafari, a project promoting ecotourism in the Pantanal, getting people up close to jaguars and other wildlife.[43] When he's not out tracking jaguars with the project, Rogerio Cunha de Paula works as a government agent for the National Research Center for Carnivore Conservation (Cenap) at the Instituto Chico Mendes of Biodiversity Conservation within the government's Environmental Ministry. Currently its vice-director, 43-year-old Cunha de Paula has been working for the Institute since 2002.

'We see ecotourism as an important tool for raising awareness of the species,' he told me. 'We have started projects promoting tourism, promoting a better image for the species . . . associating a value with the species. For example, in the Pantanal, many people are working with tourism whereas before they were just shooting jaguars because of the livestock depredation. In the Pantanal, people are leaving cattle-ranching because they can make more money showing jaguars to foreigners, for tourists in general.'

I took the opportunity to ask Cunha de Paula about some of what we'd seen on our way through the Cerrado lands of Mato Grosso and Goias. He told me:

'Almost all the Cerrado has turned into agriculture, and this is a big problem. I see these vast areas of beautiful savannah, invaluable savannah in terms of ecosystem and natural balance, just ripped up and turned into purely pasture land or agriculture fields. I can't picture how the extensive monoculture lands could be turned into better places for wildlife,' he added, 'particularly for the species that have large home ranges like jaguar.'

At least in the Pantanal, prospects for the species are looking up. 'We're actually changing the jaguar's image, from that of an animal that causes only damage to one that brings profit for landowners,' he said.

I was heartened at the way ecotourism is throwing jaguars a life-line, at least in some parts of Brazil. It made me wonder whether, as a modern society, we appreciate nature more when it grows scarce. Perhaps the more elusive the animal, the more we value it.

Back at the lodge where we were staying in Porto Jofre, people were gathering for their evening meal. Around the main building was a cluster of chalets – one would be mine for the night. During the rainy season, they are largely frequented by game fishermen. In the dry season they are packed with tourists, hoping for a glimpse of a big cat in an area that has earned a reputation as *the* place to see jaguars.

I chatted to one of the enthusiastic staff members about what the big cats mean to the locals. 'They are very important to us because they bring foreigners here, and foreign visitors are what make the business profitable,' she said. Jaguar tours started ten years ago, before which it was only fishing. 'Nowadays, we do both and it's working very well for us,' she said.

In the dry season, as many as eight jaguars can be seen in a single day. Apparently, they relax by the river bank, drinking and playing with cubs. I wish I had witnessed that.

I loved it at Porto Jofre and felt as if I could have stayed for ever. Sadly, the next morning I would be back on the road from hell, heading for the city of Cuiaba and yet another plane flight.

All was not lost. While I had not seen a jaguar, I felt I now truly understood its prospects: desperate in some parts of Brazil, but in others looking up. I fell to wondering how many people realise that the reason the forest and savannah are disappearing – and wildlife with it – is to feed factory-farmed animals, often on other contin-ents. The bitter truth is that cheap meat in Britain, Europe and the rest of the world – whether it's beef, pork or chicken – is likely to have been reared on soya from the deforested plains of South America.

As I settled in for my one and only night on the Pantanal, the hotelier brought me a booklet about jaguars in the region. It featured a glossy centrefold picture of tourists in Porto Jofre photographing the big cats. Looking at the picture of the eager foreigners, I couldn't help wondering how many of them had arrived stoked up on cheap meat from soya-fed animals.

# 12

# Penguin

## NO MORE FISH IN THE SEA

Robben Island, South Africa, where Nelson Mandela was held captive for eighteen years, had a long and sombre history, as a prison, a place of exile for social outcasts, and a military base, before becoming a World Heritage Site and monument to the dark days of apartheid.

Sited some 7 kilometres west of Cape Town, it lies in a perilous stretch of the Atlantic for seafarers. Many a ship has been dashed on its reefs, the wreckage shattered and consumed by the sea as it pounds against the rocky shores. One casualty was a seventeenth-century Dutch vessel laden with gold coins meant for the salaries of workers from the Dutch East India Company. Today, the treasure would be worth tens of millions of pounds, but it was soon swallowed up by the waves, leaving only a handful of gold coins to be discovered by fortune hunters.

The word 'Robben' is Dutch for 'seal', but on 23 June 2000 it was another species that faced grave peril when a Panamanian cargo ship transporting 140,000 tonnes of iron ore from China to Brazil became the latest victim of the unforgiving waters.

When MV *Treasure* sank after developing a hole in her hull, she disgorged tonnes of oil into the sea, creating an environmental catastrophe that threatened an already endangered colony of African penguins on Robben Island and neighbouring Dassen

Island. The disaster could not have come at a worse time for the birds, who were in the throes of a breeding season, and were busy catching fish for their offspring when they became engulfed in the sticky slick.

As the oil spread, the stricken birds began assembling on the shores, just a few at first, then hundreds, then thousands. They stood shoulder to shoulder, black and bedraggled, hunched like miserable, dishevelled crows. These were the lucky ones: others did not make it to shore fast enough, and succumbed to hypothermia or drowning. The future of the African penguin, once the most common seabird in these parts, now hung by a thread. A hundred years ago, their numbers stood at 3 to 4 million. By the time the disaster struck, their ranks had already been depleted to some 170,000.

The tragedy triggered one of the world's greatest wildlife rescue operations. As news of the crisis spread, penguin specialists from all over the world headed to South Africa to join a 12,000-strong army of volunteers in a race against time to save lives.

Over 16,000 oiled birds were corralled, captured, boxed up, trucked, ferried and even flown by army helicopter to the mainland for treatment. The oiled birds were gathered in a massive disused train-repair shed in Cape Town, where they were fed and scrubbed clean by willing hands armed with toothbrushes and washing-up liquid. Thousands of traumatised penguins stood in stunned silence as the volunteers laboured amid an overpowering stench of excrement, oil, fish and human sweat.[1]

Nearly 20,000 birds were saved before they became oiled, but rescuers faced a dilemma: what to do with them. It turned out that the safest option was to transport them several hundred miles along the coast to Port Elizabeth, well away from the deadly slick, where they were released. They spent the next couple of weeks swimming back to their breeding grounds, buying precious time for rescue teams to disperse the oil.

It was a high-stakes operation, and it raised another headache: what to do with thousands of abandoned baby penguins. These would have to be reared by rescuers until they were old enough to look after themselves. Over 2,200 chicks were reared and released. Over the course of two months, volunteers worked round the clock, collectively putting in more than a century's worth of time. The operation, which cost nearly US$16 million,[2] became known as the world's largest, most successful wildlife rescue ever.

In all, 38,260 adult birds were saved.[3] By October, the last penguin was freed and the species saved from extinction. And yet within a decade numbers had plummeted again, this time by more than half, prompting them to be reclassified on the international Red List of threatened species in 2010 from 'vulnerable' to 'endangered'.[4] After all the hard work, it was a blow.

One of eighteen species of penguin worldwide, African penguins have been around for some 60 million years, resilient to the many threats of an ever-changing world. Now they appear to be in terminal decline – and industrial farming is at least partly to blame. The demise of the species is down to a range of factors including habitat destruction, climate change, pollution and disease. In South Africa at least, there is a relatively new threat: commercial fisheries. These are now targeting the same fish eaten by the penguins, and not to feed people, but for cheap feed for intensively farmed animals.

I was lucky enough to see wild African penguins in 2014 when I toured South Africa for Compassion in World Farming.

South Africa's farming practices had been changing. Over the last fifteen years or so, pasture-based farming where animals are kept on land has been giving way to a more industrial approach, with animals confined indoors and fed on cereal grains or soya. Poultry have been particularly hard hit, with more and more meat chickens and egg-laying hens crammed indoors in crowded sheds or imprisoned in battery cages. Cattle too are now being herded off pasture and forced to spend their last months crowded on feedlots where their staple diet is grain, not grass. As intensive or 'factory' farming has taken off, so local farmers have become more dependent on buying expensive inputs like chemical pesticides, and animal feed which uses ingredients that could otherwise feed people. As in so many other parts of the world, there is now a competition between farm animals and people for food.

I wanted to find out whether that competition had extended to marine wildlife, so I squeezed in a trip to Boulders Beach along the Cape Peninsula, where a colony of African penguins had recently set up home near to residential houses. The sandy shore is known as one of the easiest places in the world to get close to penguins. One side of the road to the beach was lined with derelict shanty houses, a throwback to a time when it was a less fashionable area. The other side was lined with attractive new builds in soft shades of green, orange and vanilla. Table Mountain dominated the skyline, its famous level plateau flanked by the jagged rocky promontories of Devil's Peak and Lion's Head. A chestnut horse grazed on the central reservation, while locals went about their business. I watched a woman lifting a brown hen by the wings and winced.

'There are chickens in there,' my driver told me, pointing at stacks of yellow crates by the road. 'They'll be standing there all day in the sun in those crates.' I turned away. In my job, I come across frequent cruelty to animals. My heart screams at me to get involved and sort things out there and then, to make it stop. Yet my head knows the reality – that change takes a lot of time and effort – and that's where I put my focus: on changing attitudes and systems that allow these things to go on. Hard as it is, I have to watch, document and then jam my hands in my pockets, knowing that, at that moment, I can do no more.

Half an hour later I was standing among the sheltered granite inlets of Boulders Beach, now a popular tourist stop. The penguins themselves have become a world-renowned tourist attraction, attracting some 60,000 visitors each year.[5]

They haven't always been here. A number of African penguins eloped to the beach in 1982 from their traditional island hideaways. It might seem an unusual place for such birds, which usually prefer remote islands where the sea offers protection from predators and the fish provide sustenance. In this area of the Cape, however, mainland predators have declined (a story in itself, I suspect), and fishing has stopped in the nearby bay, creating a refuge for a species in trouble.[6]

I walked along the immaculate wooden boardwalk, which had a fence on one side to protect nearby gardens from penguin invasion. I've seen penguins in the wild before, but only through binoculars and at long distance. This was something else! Soon I was eyeball to eyeball with three. They came unbelievably close, strutting nonchalantly along the beach, preening themselves as they went, handsome in their black and white dinner jackets. I noticed that their faces had a pale pink blush. Other tourists wandered past, chatting about problems at home or the merits of a new boyfriend as if the presence of these unique creatures was no big deal. It felt like a zoo.

I came to a stretch of lovely white sand where the boardwalk met the sea. Here about a hundred penguins were lounging in the sun. Some waddled past us tourists, setting cameras popping. Others floated playfully on the waves. Now and then they whirred their flightless flippers with comical enthusiasm. I felt relieved to spot some fluffy brown chicks among them. This new generation had hatched from rows of plastic urns buried in the sand as nest boxes by conservationists giving the birds a helping hand. And they need all the help they can get: declining fast, there are now only some 50,000 African penguins left in the wild.[7]

This colony now numbers around 3,000 birds, so here at least they are holding their own. The nearby visitors' centre sold everything penguin-themed: cuddly toys, bags, badges, brooches. A display board listed 'threats' to the species – *Spheniscus demersus*, to give it its Latin name – as a 'reduction of penguin food supply by commercial fishing (pilchards, anchovy . . .), pollution at sea, habitat destruction, viral disease . . .'

That bland phrase – 'reduction of penguin food supply' – encapsulates my big fear: that these birds are slowly being starved to oblivion.

After the Second World War, South Africa developed the first fishery on the continent dedicated to catching small pelagic fish and turning them into fishmeal. Pelagic fish are the same little fish that penguins and other seabirds need to survive. By the millennium the fishery was sucking 400,000 tonnes of anchovies, pilchards and red eyes out of the ocean every year. Most of it was turned into fishmeal to feed farmed poultry.[8]

This new threat came on top of immense pressure from commercial exploitation of their eggs and habitat. The rot set in a very long time ago when Europeans discovered that the rich mountains of seabird muck – 'guano' as it is known – on penguin nesting islands was a brilliant fertiliser.

For thousands of years, huge numbers of penguins had created homes for themselves and their offspring by burrowing into the dry claylike deposits of their own excrement. This material provided chicks, eggs and parent birds with protection from predators and shelter from the rain and baking sun. The penguin colonies were so extensive in those days that over centuries the guano reached depths of 80 feet.[9]

The lure proved irresistible. Decades of unregulated harvesting peaked in the 1840s when guano became known as 'white gold'. European and American ships clogged harbours and bays around penguin islands, scraping them down to bare rock. Islands off Namibia were particularly hard hit: at one point Ichaboe Island was surrounded by more than 400 ships as 6,000 men scooped up its wealth. As they went, they would also eat the 'goose' – the African penguin – that laid the golden egg. They stripped Ichaboe Island and made their way through other penguin breeding islands, wreaking havoc. Within just a few years, the deposits of centuries had all but disappeared.

The plunder went unchecked until 1967, when laws were belatedly passed to prohibit guano extraction. The penguins' plight had been compounded by nearly a century of egg harvesting, first as cheap protein for the poor, and later as a scarce luxury food.[10] Harvesting of both egg and guano is now banned. With their breeding grounds protected and oil spillages mercifully rare, the birds should be safe. And yet numbers are still in free fall– their fate, it seems, sealed beneath the waves.

For decades now, commercial fisheries have been targeting what they seem to assume are limitless shoals of fish off the southern tip of Africa. The plentiful fish stocks in this part of the sea stem from the wash of cool water from the Benguela current, the strongest coastal upwelling in the world. As this cold water rises to the surface, it brings with it a rich soup of nutrients that can support vast amounts of ocean life.[11]

However, the ecosystem relies on three small pelagic fish for food: anchovies, sardines and red-eyes. These species drive the rest of the ocean community, from the hake and yellowtail fish that eat the small pelagics, to the sharks and tuna that in turn eat those fish, to penguins, seals, dolphins and whales. They all depend on the little fish, known in fishery circles as forage, bait, prey, or 'trash' fish.

The so-called 'trash' – a derogatory term for a creature so vital to the rest of the food chain – can be super-abundant in these waters, making up for their tiny size by moving in massive shoals sometimes so large that they attract predators from thousands of miles away. Fishing vessels scoop them up in so-called purse-seine nets – they encircle the shoal then close like a purse before lifting the seething mass of fish aboard.

Now they are running out. In 1883, the British scientist Thomas Huxley notoriously declared that 'all the great sea fisheries are inexhaustible' and that 'nothing we do seriously affects the numbers of fish'.[12] A century and a quarter on, it is abundantly clear that he was wrong. The United Nations warns that South Africa's anchovy and sardine (pilchard) fisheries are being overexploited.[13] Slowly but surely, supplies are running out.

Because oil floats, and small pelagic fish swim well below the surface, the MV *Treasure* oil spill appears to have had limited impact on South Africa's fishing activity. In fact, by coincidence, South Africa's annual haul of small pelagic fish rose sharply in the four years after the spill, heaping pressure on the hard-pressed penguins. According to official figures, it increased by as much as half again – 611,000 tonnes.[14] The UN has questioned the reliability of Africa's catch figures, so the real figure could be even higher. For a depleted penguin population attempting to recover from the shock of the pollution disaster, the screw turned tighter with every additional fish haul.

Dr Lorien Pichegru, a leading marine biologist based at the Institute of African Ornithology, fears that within fifteen years, they could suffer the same fate as the dodo. 'Overfishing is a huge concern,' she said. 'Both fishermen and penguins are struggling because the fish population is also declining. It is very worrying.'

Her team fitted tracking devices to penguins and noted that overfishing was forcing them to swim further in search of food, affecting breeding rates. Efforts are being made by conservationists to save the penguins. Dr Pichegru is involved in a number of such projects.

'We built artificial burrows for them on their islands to protect them from heat waves or storms that can kill their chicks,' she said, adding that starving chicks are moved to a rehabilitation centre. Despite this work, numbers declined by a further 1,000 pairs in 2012.[15]

African penguins are seen by conservationists as the nation's marine sentinel, the 'canary in the coal mine' gauging the health of the ecosystem. As penguins feed almost exclusively on small pelagic fish, their decline is a sure sign there's not enough fish to go round.[16]

An experiment by the South African government in 2008 highlighted the direct link between the health of penguin populations and fish stocks. Fishing was stopped around one of a pair of islands in turn, St Croix and Bird Island, off the country's south coast. During the halt, researchers found that penguins did not need to expend as much energy sourcing fish for their chicks and were therefore more likely to survive. The experiment resulted in a decision to close fishing around these islands permanently. At the time, Johann Augustyn, secretary of South Africa's Deep Sea Trawling Industry Association, declared that the study had 'important implications for fisheries worldwide in competition with vertebrate predators'.[17]

Fishmeal is one of the tools of agricultural intensification. As demand for it escalates for industrial animal feed, so the stranglehold tightens around the neck of the remaining African penguins. Already, about a third of South Africa's entire cereal crop is being fed to farm animals, setting up the familiar competition between people and animals for food.[18] Now marine wildlife are in that competition too.

Turning small fish into fishmeal for farm animals is a wasteful process. Worldwide, the fish used in this way would be enough to provide a billion more people with a dietary supply of fish. Or, putting it another way, leaving them in the ocean would take huge pressure off hard-pressed fish stocks. A sizeable proportion of South Africa's catch is now exported to feed intensively farmed animals elsewhere.

Pablo Garcia Borboroglu, president of the Global Penguin Society, estimates that large-scale industrial fisheries have reduced the capacity of the Benguela ecosystem to support penguins to between 10 and 20 per cent of its scope in 1920. He believes there is a clear connection between the health of sentinel species like penguins and the health of the oceans on which people depend. 'Ocean conservation is crucial to life in the sea, the land, and to the quality of human life,'[19] he has said.

The African penguin is not the only penguin species hard hit by overfishing.

Peru had long been a place I had dreamed of visiting: it is one of the most species-rich places on the planet. I had heard so much about the seabirds and the guano islands; how walking onto those islands in years gone by would cause the sky to turn black as countless birds would lift off and blanket the heavens. These islands were once so densely covered in birds that their droppings would provide the economic backbone of the nation.

The opportunity to visit came in 2012, when I travelled to South America as part of my research for *Farmageddon*. We were on the second leg of a tour which had taken us to grim parts of Argentina to investigate industrial beef production and the mighty soya industry. It had been an intense and at times depressing trip and I was hoping that Peru might lift my spirits. As I flew into Lima, I was giddy with anticipation.

It wasn't long before I was heading south to the small coastal town of Pucusana, an hour or so's drive from Lima, in central

Peru. I was hoping to go out on a boat to the seabird islands off the coast where Peru's once famous guano harvest used to take place. The journey took me along the Pacific edge of the Atacama Desert, the driest place on the planet, where it's said never to rain. Sheer mountains reached the sky and telegraph pylons lined sandy peaks in a landscape that felt like the edge of the Earth.

I reached Pucusana to find dozens of artisanal fishing boats criss-crossing the bay. The air was suffused with the smell of seafood and boat fumes. Women cut and prepared fish beneath blue and white gazebos while elderly men passed the time of day chatting, drinking and reading the paper. I took a walk down the slipway, where a brindle Staffie dog rolled playfully on the beach. He reminded me of Duke, our rescue pup back home in England, who had at that time only been with us a few weeks.

I clambered into a glistening twin-engine boat, where I greeted the driver and a local bird expert, both of whom had agreed to take me out for the day. As we set off, I could see the bustle of the local fish market, with a row of refrigerated trucks taking trays of fish on board, destined for diners in the capital. A dozen pelicans flew over the harbour. As we headed out into the open ocean, I felt intoxicated by the deep smell of seaspray mixed with fumes from the boat's engine.

Motoring out of the bay, we passed an industrial purse-seine fishing vessel some 30 metres long, its rusting hull piled high with netting. It was just one vessel from what is the biggest single-species fishery in the world, all aimed at catching the Peruvian anchoveta, small pelagic fish that throng these waters in huge numbers thanks to the Humboldt Current. This cool ocean upwelling in the otherwise warm tropical sea provides the conditions for super-abundant sealife.

I spotted two Humboldt penguins, close cousins of the African penguin. They share the looks and mannerisms of the birds I saw in South Africa, and face the same type of threat. Listed as 'vulnerable' by the International Union for Conservation of Nature (IUCN), they too appear to be sliding towards oblivion.[20] They stood high against the sky on a rocky promontory as waves crashed below. I wondered how a flightless bird could climb so high.

Finally, we reached our destination: one of the fabled guano islands. Though in my head I knew better, in my heart it swirled with birds. So while I had tried to prepare myself for what I might find, it still came as a crushing disappointment to see it stripped almost bare, its famous bird populations ravaged by the struggle to compete with the rapacious anchovy fishing industry. It rose like a giant mound of Cotswold stone from the ocean, with so few seabirds they barely formed a tideline rim around the base. I felt heartbroken.

The boatman cut the engine, and we stayed awhile, looking at the island. As the cool water slapped the sides of the boat, the bird expert told me how, since the start of the commercial anchovy fishery, seabird numbers had plummeted by more than 90 per cent. The Humboldt penguin is just one of those to have suffered a devastating decline in numbers, from a million birds to fewer than 30,000 now.[21]

As we chugged back to shore, I noticed the low-slung outline of an industrial chicken shed on the clifftop. The dorsal fin of a dolphin broke the surface of the turbulent waters near our boat. So there it was, right in front of me: a scene that encapsulated the competition now raging between wildlife and farm animals for food. On the one hand, a beautiful dolphin, almost within touching distance of me; on the other hand, waters plundered of the little fish vital to the food chain. And there, on land, was visible evidence of part of the source of the problem: factory farms.

Though few consumers know of the practice, feeding fish to farm animals is nothing new. It appears to have raised concerns since at least the fourteenth century, when, during the reign of Edward III, in 1376, a petition calling for reform was submitted to the Westminster Parliament. The petition stated that in some places fishermen were taking so many small fish they did not know what to do with them, and were using them to fatten pigs, 'to the great damage of the commons of the realm and destruction of the fisheries'.

The big difference between those early misgivings and today is scale. Worldwide, over 17 million tonnes of small pelagic fish like anchovy, sardine and herring are removed from the ocean every year – an estimated 90 billion individual animals. This accounts for nearly one-fifth of all the marine fish catch globally, much of it for fishmeal.

Peru is the single biggest player in this game, producing a third of the world's total fishmeal for export. Much of it goes to feed industrially reared farm animals in Europe and China. The UK alone imports up to 100,000 tonnes of fishmeal a year, about a third from Peru.[22]

I soon discovered that the enticing images of Machu Picchu peddled by the tourist industry offer a false impression. Off the beaten track, Peru seemed a lawless place: even our German guide felt the need to carry a gun at all times. Like other aspects of this beautiful country, the fishing industry was clearly out of control. The United Nations Food and Agriculture Organisation (FAO) describes the Peruvian anchovy as the 'most heavily exploited fish in the world', due to continued 'gross' overfishing by the Peruvian fleet.[23]

The impact on other wildlife has been devastating. As the commercial fishery prospered, so seabirds and other marine life dwindled. Nothing was a match for the hungry new competitor hoovering up the same little fish other creatures rely on for food.

The Peruvian fishmeal industry seems to make little sense, particularly in a nation with a high rate of infant malnourishment. It is not as if anchovies can't be eaten by people – far from it: they are a rich source of protein. Yet four-fifths of the entire catch is ground down and shipped out to feed farmed salmon, chickens and pigs in the rich world. Much of the food value is then wasted in conversion from feed to farm-animal flesh.

The economics of the industry are questionable in any case. A recent study showed that while anchovies make up four-fifths of Peru's entire fish catch, it accounts for less than a third of the nation's revenue from fisheries. The anchovies are worth more as food than as feed.[24] Patricia Majluf, from the Centre for Environmental

Sustainability in Lima, and one of the scientific team responsible for the study, told *World Fishing*, 'There are far more economic and food security benefits to Peru to channel fisheries for human consumption.' Ms Majluf was also credited with launching a campaign in 2006 to encourage Peruvian chefs to incorporate anchovy on their menus.[25]

Yet still, the lion's share is shipped off to feed factory farms in distant lands. How does this stack up?

### FROM PENGUINS TO PUFFINS

My wife Helen and I were approaching a milestone birthday and had booked the trip of a lifetime to the Galapagos Islands. We had both long dreamed of a visit, and both turning fifty in 2015 provided the perfect excuse. We planned it for over a year, and got ever more excited as the day approached. The journey was an epic in itself: over two days, with an overnight stay in the Ecuadorian capital of Quito, high in the foothills of the Andes Mountains.

When we eventually touched down in the Galapagos, we still had two coach rides and two boat trips ahead to reach our hotel. It was worth the effort.

Lying 600 miles west of Ecuador and straddling the Equator, the islands owe their fame to Charles Darwin, who visited as ship's naturalist aboard HMS *Beagle* nearly two centuries ago. Darwin picked his way across the many islands of the archipelago, noticing the subtle ways in which animal and plant species had adapted to the unique surroundings of each individual island. He was a prolific collector and took back a host of wildlife specimens, the foundation for his scientific classic, *On the Origin of Species*. Published on 24 November 1859, the work became the foundation of evolutionary biology.

Darwin could not have foreseen that, even then, the Earth was moving into a new era that some now call the Anthropocene to describe a new period in which the activities of man are the greatest influence on the natural world and the sheer pace of change tests the adaptability of species to its limit.

One species on the brink is the Galapagos penguin. It is one of the world's smallest penguins, standing just 30 cm tall, and only about a thousand pairs remain.[26]

The day I had most looked forward to came midway through the trip, when we headed off from our hotel on the central Galapagos island of Santa Cruz for the day-long excursion to see penguins. We boarded a yacht called the *Sea Lion* bound for Bartolome, a relatively young volcanic island, formed about 200,000 years ago. It was a surreal place, with terrain like a moonscape. Mountains towered over jagged slag heaps of rock. A sloping cliff like melting chocolate plunged down to a bright orange-coloured beach. Nearby were other islets of varying shapes – one like a conical Chinese hat, another like a crumpled mass of intestines – all the product of natural lava flows.

From the comfort of our hotel's 70-foot yacht, we hopped into an inflatable Zodiac dinghy for the last part of the journey toward Sulliban Bay, James Island, close to the spot where we hoped to find penguins. Our guide, Mario Dominguez, told us that this island was one of the newest of all – a mere 150 years old. It looked like freshly cooled lava, all rippled and stippled, and appeared much like soft mud, but as I learned to my cost when I knelt down clumsily to inspect it, it was rock-hard and unforgiving – not a mistake I'll make again.

Next, we explored the surroundings of Pinnacle Rock, an impressive monolithic lava obelisk that might almost be mistaken for a piece of modern art. At the bottom of the structure were two blue-footed boobies – delightful marine birds with distinctive turquoise-coloured feet which they show off in a charming mating ritual. Nearby was a solitary Galapagos penguin. 'They like it here because the water here is the coldest of the islands,' Dominguez told us. Without warning, he held his nose and let out an extraordinary braying sound, like a donkey. Apparently, the sound attracts penguins – and sure enough, on hearing the noise, a tiny little penguin with a white chest hopped out of the water and shook himself, flippers outstretched.

We were dropped off by the Zodiac on Bartoleme Island in the shadow of Pinnacle Rock for swimming and snorkelling where the penguins live. Taking to the water, I headed towards two penguins I had spotted standing on a rock. As with so much of the wildlife on Galapagos, they took no notice of me whatsoever. Eventually, they slid into the water, bobbing buoyantly on the surface, little webbed feet splayed, heads peering down. I was thrilled when, a little later, they swam right past me within touching distance.

A UNESCO World Heritage Site, the Galapagos are guarded by multiple conservation laws protecting most of the islands' land surface. The waters around them are protected by the Galapagos Marine Reserve, one of the largest in the world, whose rich diversity of marine life also makes it attractive to illegal fishing interests. Overfishing and illegal industrial fishing are serious threats to the islands' delicate marine ecosystem. They deplete commercial fish, destroy marine environments and cripple local communities whose livelihoods and health depend on fish. According to WWF, almost all of the Galapagos's commercially important coastal species are being overfished.[27]

Once again, the fishmeal industry is a culprit.[28] In 2011 alone, Ecuador produced over 100,000 tonnes of fishmeal, more than South Africa.[29]

Producing that amount of fishmeal requires hauling out several times that weight in small pelagic fish, food that would otherwise be feeding endangered penguins and other marine life.

Galapagos is home to about 25,000 people, with nearly half living in the town of Puerto Ayora on the central island of Santa Cruz. Farming on Galapagos, one of the world's most protected areas, is closely regulated, with little heavy machinery allowed. Artificial fertilisers and pesticides are all but forbidden. A successful industry has sprung up in fair trade and organic fruit and other products.[30] Farmers on the islands used to be vilified for introducing invasive plant species and threatening the islands' unique ecosystems, but as the population of both residents and tourists soars, they have become a vital source of food that would otherwise be shipped in from mainland Ecuador.[31]

In recent years, Galapagos has seen another population explosion – chickens. As the industry takes off, so it brings a new threat
to the Galapagos penguins: disease. Geographic isolation is no
match for the 'chickenisation' of the planet, and farmers here are
now going down much the same desperate route as everywhere
else. By 2004 there were more than thirty intensive chicken farms
on Galapagos, each rearing up to 4,000 birds for meat. Although
modest in size by international standards, each of these farms rears
a bigger population of individual chickens than the entire global
population of Galapagos penguins.

As usual, rearing birds in large numbers in confined conditions
makes them more susceptible to afflictions like Newcastle Disease,
a highly contagious virus, and transmissible to humans. Newcastle
Disease outbreaks in 1992 and 2000 caused the deaths of 2,000
and 500 chickens respectively on Santa Cruz,[32] so the potential
for disease problems is a question of when, not if. Such viruses
threaten to endanger remaining penguins that have precious little
immunity to novel diseases.

Other rare species on the islands, such as the endemic flightless
cormorant and lava gull, are also highly vulnerable to outbreaks,
and there are nagging concerns that the islands could be hit by new,
more virulent strains of disease. Incubated through the pressure-
cooker effect of crowding lots of chickens together on intensive
farms, these could then spread very fast, wiping out swathes of wild
and domestic avians.[33]

Scientists from Ecuador, USA and the UK studying the risks posed
by chicken farming on Galapagos have called for viable economic
alternatives to high-intensity broiler production because of the
'ecological and disease threats' it presents.[34] To practise more natural
backyard chicken rearing could help, as birds reared this way are
more resistant to infectious disease. The same team of scientists are
also concerned that intensified poultry production on the Galapagos
Islands could cause what they describe as 'local ecological disturb-
ances', such as water and soil pollution. As if that weren't enough,
there are additional fears that these types of farms could become
breeding grounds for mosquitoes,[35] notorious carriers of disease.

While penguins are exclusive to the southern hemisphere, the problems facing seabirds are not. Around the coasts of Britain, Europe and the USA, puffins, guillemots and other marine bird species are experiencing similar pressures to southern ocean penguins.

The great auk, a large cousin of the puffin, known by sailors as the 'penguin of the north', is already extinct.[36] Millions of great auks once inhabited the seas from Norway to Newfoundland and from Italy to Florida. In many respects, they *were* the original 'penguins', a name that traces back to the Latin word *pinguis*, meaning 'fat', the moniker given by European sailors to the great auk. When sailors later discovered similar-looking flightless birds in the southern ocean, they gave them the same name even though they belong to different families.

Passing ships would kill the flightless birds for meat. Then industries grew up to exploit them for food, fish bait, feathers for mattresses, and fuel. They were wiped out from North America by 1800, and their rarity value became the final nail in their coffin. Rich enthusiasts seeking eggs and skins targeted them for burgeoning collections. In 1844, on the tiny island of Eldey, off Iceland, trophy hunters killed the last known pair.[37]

As a latter-day rarity-hunter – or 'twitcher' – I've chased many a sighting of an unusual bird, armed with my binoculars and a checklist of birds. It was during one such chase that I first became aware of the contest for food between factory farms and the common or Atlantic puffin.

It was late May 1995 and I had made the long trip from the south of England to Shetland in the hope of catching a glimpse of a black-browed albatross, the creature immortalised by Coleridge's 1798 *Rime of the Ancient Mariner*. Commonly found on the Falkland Islands, in South Georgia and on islands off Chile, this particular bird had left its home in the southern hemisphere, and become hopelessly lost. Having battled through the doldrums where the wind drops north of the equator – no mean feat for a bird that hates to have to flap those elongated wings – the hapless creature finally ended up on a remote cliff face off the coast of northeast Scotland, hanging out with a colony of gannets.

For more than twenty years, the albatross returned to his lonely vigil on Britain's most northerly tip at Hermaness almost every summer. It seems he adapted to life in the northern hemisphere, and spent the rest of his days roaming the seas during the winter in this part of the world before heading back to Hermaness for the breeding season. To the birdwatching fraternity, he became known affectionately as 'Albert Ross', which may say all you need to know about ornithological humour.

As soon as I heard about him being back that year, I made plans to travel to Shetland, setting off with my lifelong friend Richard Peach. We drove up from the English south coast to Aberdeen, where we took the overnight ferry to Shetland. The Shetland Islands are situated in the cool waters of the northern North Sea, a hundred miles beyond the mainland of Scotland. Their capital, Lerwick, is nearer to Bergen in Norway than to Aberdeen. The crossing was a joy in itself, studded with sightings of guillemots and their stunning northern counterparts, black guillemots, known in this part of the world as 'tysties'.

As soon as we arrived on Shetland, I fell in love with its rugged remoteness. The people seemed so friendly. Living appeared simple and traditional, a trip back in time, though I knew it was an illusion: there's nothing easy about living in these isolated, weather-battered parts. The humble crofts, fishing boats and relics from the Norse invasions of AD 800 ooze history. I was struck by the size of the place: when our guide Hugh Harrop picked us up and drove us the length of Shetland to the island of Unst, where Albert was residing, it was a journey of more than a hundred miles.

Our arrival on Unst coincided with the opening of a new visitor centre at the island's Hermaness nature reserve. Tragically, the previous one, a simple wooden affair called Watcher's Hut, had been blown away in 1991 during a ferocious storm remembered as 'the Hogmanay Hurricane'.[38] A Scandinavian couple were staying in the hut for New Year, having decided to sit it out there despite warnings of the approaching squall. When the storm abated, the man was found dead among the wreckage; the woman was washed up at the base of the cliffs some days later.

The TV personality and wildlife enthusiast Bill Oddie had been drafted in to conduct the opening ceremony for the new visitor centre, which is part of the former shore station of Britain's most northerly lighthouse at Muckle Flugga. Though I know him fairly well now, at the time we'd never met. I was thrilled at the chance for an introduction – he has long been a hero of mine. The one thing that worried me was the prospect of delaying our search for the bird we'd come so far to see. As it happened, however, our guide Harrop had been booked as the official photographer for the grand opening, so we didn't have much choice.

Muckle Flugga is a deserted place at the best of times, so it came as no great surprise when Richard and I were press-ganged into posing as visitors with birdman Bill. He was great fun and perfect company, joking and sharing stories as he went.

As soon as the photo-shoot was over, we pressed on with our quest to find Albert. Imagine our disappointment, when after our 850-mile journey, which took the best part of three days, we finally reached the gannet colony to find that Albert wasn't there!

'I knew we should have come straight here,' I said gloomily, not exactly hiding my frustration. Had the photo opportunity cost us the chance of a lifetime?

In my desperation to find the bird, I leaned just a little too far over the cliff, peering at the screeching, wheeling gannet colony below, detecting that familiar musty smell of long years of dried seabird droppings as the breeze buffeted my face. All at once I lost my balance, and teetered towards the deadly 200-foot drop. In a split second I managed to regain my footing, crashing backwards onto the grass. I was exhausted and annoyed. The atmosphere was tense, all three of us fearing we'd come all this way for nothing.

Determined not to give up, we persisted, scanning the water intently. Every passing bird got the once-over, just in case – a gannet, and another, then: 'Hold on, what's this? No. Another gannet.' By now, my patience was running out. I was having to suppress shameful thoughts of throwing our guide over the edge of the cliff to join those gannets! Until finally, his deadpan voice announced that the target was in sight.

'I've got him, sitting on the sea with seven fulmar,' he said calmly, as if we'd just popped out for a stroll from a nearby bothy and nothing was riding on it.

And there he was, just as Harrop said, bobbing around on the water. Perhaps he felt at home hanging out with the grey and white fulmar, which are in fact related to the albatross.

Boy, were we relieved! He looked like a huge black-backed gull, dwarfing everything else. We could see the white head and black brow that led into the characteristic heavy yellow beak of an albatross. What a moment! Suddenly, with several dramatic splashes of his unfeasibly long wings, he was airborne, treating us to the most breath-taking fly-past with barely a flap of those wings. It had all been worth it.

We were lucky in more ways than one, for it turned out to be Albert's last summer. While black-browed albatrosses have a natural lifespan of over seventy years, he may have been quite mature when he first started coming to Shetland. Maybe he got caught in a fishing net somewhere and drowned, or headed off somewhere else, away from prying eyes. Nobody knows – but he never returned to Unst. I would not see another albatross for the next two decades, until I saw a waved albatross on Galapagos.

Our time on Shetland was all too short, but we made the most of it, scouring the island for other birds like bluethroat and rosefinch as well as eider and puffin. I love puffins. I've watched them on Shetland, the Farne Islands and on the original 'Puffin Island', Lundy, in the Bristol Channel. They remind me of portly little gentlemen wearing dinner jackets and bright orange shoes which match the bright stripes on their multi-coloured beaks. I love the way they scurry about on the grassy terraced slopes above cliff edges, popping up and down disused rabbit burrows which make the perfect spot for a nest. From time to time, they throw themselves off the cliff edge and out to sea, where they shoot along on whirring wings. Landing again is far from easy for them. You have to wish them luck as they descend, orange legs splaying out before they crash-land back into the colony.

In Britain I've seen puffins grasping bunches of small silvery-thin fish in their beaks: sandeels. These little fish are rocket fuel for hungry puffin chicks, but they are in diminishing supply – and once again, industrial farming is in the frame.

While I was on Shetland, I remember hearing that the puffin population had periodic bad breeding seasons, a phenomenon that seemed to be dismissed in the popular mind as a consequence of climate change. When the water warms up, the small pelagic fish eaten by penguins, like sandeels, move too far offshore for birds to reach. But the shortage of sandeels is not only related to climate change. Just as anchovies are in Peru, so sandeels are being over-fished in the North Sea. Between 1994 and 2003, some 880,000 tonnes were sucked out of the water, a scale of catch that proved unsustainable. Subsequent sandeel catches fell to just 290,000 tonnes per year.[39]

In 2013 a joint study by the British Trust for Ornithology (BTO) and the Joint Nature Conservation Committee (JNCC) found a clear link between the intensity of industrial sandeel fishing in the North Sea and the decline of seabird populations. The study found that levels of seabird breeding failure were higher in years when more sandeels were harvested.[40] I remember a local on Shetland observing that poor breeding seasons seemed to coincide with big trawlers being in the area – which makes perfect sense.

Once upon a time, it was always pollution that was wheeled out to explain declines in seabird populations. Nowadays, the verdict tends to be climate change – that way no one in particular is to blame, and no one can be offended. Lately, however, the Marine Conservation Society (MCS) has dared to point the finger at the sandeel industry, which is responsible for 50 per cent of total fish landings in the North Sea. The organisation has said it is 'impli-cated in the decline of breeding success in seabirds'.[41]

Other authors have gone further, joining the dots more conclu-sively between overfishing and bird declines. A naturalist and author of the 1987 monograph *Auks*, Ron Freethy wrote how puffins are in 'direct competition with Danish trawlers catching sandeels'. He rated the chief long-term threat to puffins as 'food shortages caused by man's overfishing'.[42] More recently, a team of authors working on the authoritative *Handbook of the Birds of the World* cited fisheries that target small pelagic 'keystone' fish as the 'single most important factor influencing the future welfare of fish-eating auks' like puffins.[43]

And why are sandeels being scooped up from the ocean in such large numbers? To produce fishmeal and oil, with a lot of the fishmeal being used to feed farmed animals, not least farmed salmon.[44]

Europe's puffins are now classified as globally 'endangered' by the IUCN Red List and are predicted to decline by nearly 80 per cent by 2065. The major threat cited is climate-change effects, particularly where 'prey species are exploited unsustainably, leading to prey reductions and subsequent unsuccessful breeding'.[45]

In other words, when too many small fish are being hauled out of the sea.

The truth is that our wildlife is under multiple pressures and is increasingly being squeezed out of a world of ever-shrinking resources. Of course, climate change will have, and probably already is having, a big impact. However, it is hard to overstate the role of the sandeel fishery, and similar fisheries in Africa and South America, in turning the screw on already struggling marine wildlife species.

One might imagine that there would be places in the world where wildlife stands a chance of being left in peace. What about Antarctica?

Sadly even here, one of the world's last pristine wildernesses, penguins are in trouble. Like the Galapagos, the Antarctic continent is protected, yet the surrounding sea is under siege. In what is now a familiar theme, international fishing fleets are targeting the very small creatures – in this case, the crustacean, krill – on which seabirds depend, selling the 200,000 tonnes a year they catch for animal feed, pet food and fishing bait.

Krill are small shrimp-like creatures that live in shoals and feed on microscopic phytoplankton. They provide food for birds, fish, whales, seals, molluscs and many other kinds of life. They have already been badly affected by climate change, as melting sea ice disrupts their lifecycle. Numbers have plummeted.[46]

Today's catch may seem small beer compared with the amount eaten by wildlife, but, scientists warn that krill fishery is set to expand. Industrialised fishing methods are capable of reducing ocean biomass by as much as 80 per cent in just fifteen years.[47]

The outlook for another suite of penguin species – Adélie, chinstrap, macaroni and gentoo – is not good.

Seabirds are far from the only victims of the reckless looting of the world's oceans to feed factory farms: human food supplies also suffer. In the last half-century, about 90 per cent of the world's big fish – those we put on our plates – have been taken for food or discarded, leaving oceans close to collapse.[48]

In the blink of an evolutionary eye, fishermen the world over are coming to terms with the fact that the inexhaustible seas are anything but.

Scientists predict that most of the world's fisheries will be depleted by 2048.[49]

Herring, anchovies, sandeels and the like are a vital part of the food chain: the essential ecological link between microscopic phytoplankton and larger fish like cod and tuna. Put simply, the fish we eat rely on the small pelagic fish they eat. Trawling for small pelagic fish short-circuits the system – with devastating effects.

The ravenous fishmeal industry is just one of the tools of intensification that have captured farming over the last sixty years. Its true impact on iconic wildlife – and the ecosystem our society depends upon to survive – is only just coming to light. Terrible damage has already been done. But it is not too late. Sylvia Earle, a renowned American oceanographer and marine biologist, believes there is still time, 'but not a lot . . . to turn things around'. Should we carry on regardless, however, within our lifetimes there may be little to nothing left.

As Earle puts it, 'Business as usual' means that in fifty years there may be 'no commercial fishing, because the fish will simply be gone'.[50]

# 13

# Marine iguana

Tired, seasick and desperately missing home, Charles Darwin emerged from his cramped cabin below deck and fixed his sight on the approaching land.[1] The young Englishman had been at sea for four long years – twice the time originally planned – and was more than weary of life on board HMS *Beagle*, a British Admiralty vessel.[2] The sight and sounds of the Galapagos Islands, teeming with screeching seabirds, must have come as a tremendous relief. Terra firma promised respite from the relentless sway of the sea – and from what the young naturalist could see, there would be no shortage of curious creatures to chronicle.

This was to be no cheerful 'Land ahoy!' however. The terrain – endless black, jagged rock – looked inhospitable, and it was soon clear that there would be few creature comforts here. HMS *Beagle* was still a year away from home; these volcanic islands would be the last stop before a long month at sea. Already finding the journey both physically and mentally tough, and with his captain getting on his nerves, by the time he staggered ashore Darwin was in no mood to sit back and enjoy the company of the rest of the crew. Instead, he spent the weeks that followed amassing samples of the archipelago's birds, lizards, insects and plants.[3]

He could not know it but as he captured and labelled his specimens he was laying the foundations for the groundbreaking scientific discovery he was destined to make: the theory of evolution by natural selection.

Darwin and the Galapagos are synonymous with evolution. The islands remain a living laboratory of the natural world. They are also a microcosm of the challenges faced by flora, fauna – and people – in a warming and globalised world. As we shall see, his direct descendants are now trying to make their own contribution to preserving the riches of our planet.

Ironically, their famous ancestor almost didn't make it on the voyage of discovery for which he went down in history. He had planned at first to become a doctor, but found the lectures dull and performing surgery distressing, so he began to neglect his studies, choosing instead to pursue a growing interest in natural history. When he finally dropped out of his medical degree, his father hoped he would become a parson, and was unenthusiastic when, in 1831, the young Darwin asked whether he might join HMS *Beagle* as a self-funded passenger on an expedition to chart the coastline of South America.[4]

Nor was the ship's captain particularly keen. What Robert Fitzroy, a scientist and officer of the Royal Navy, was looking for first and foremost was a decent companion on what was likely to be a long and lonely journey. The vice-admiral had already seen what the sea could do to a man. The *Beagle's* maiden voyage had ended in disaster when its then captain locked himself in his cabin for two weeks before blowing his brains out. Fitzroy saw the tragedy first-hand and was determined not to suffer a similar fate. What he wanted was a gentleman naturalist, both to keep him company and to collect samples of fauna, flora and geology. His decision would transform the way mankind looked at the world.

Darwin nearly didn't get the job. He had competition and Fitzroy was taking no chances. Of all things, he took exception to Darwin's nose: slightly bulbous, which he suspected showed a lack of inner resolve. Nor were Darwin's competitors and facial features the only hurdles. He needed to pay for the trip, and his father was his only source of funds. Still wedded to the idea that his son would become a country parson, Darwin Senior took considerable persuasion to stump up the cash.[5] Against the odds, however, Darwin did join the *Beagle* on what proved to be one of history's most famous sea voyages.

As the ship's naturalist, his task was to collect information at a time when little of the natural world was known to science. Before he set sail, his mentor, a botanist called John Henslow, encouraged him to read a radical new book, Charles Lyell's *Principles of Geology*. It challenged the creationist dogma of the time, which attributed the origins of the universe and life on Earth to God.

Lyell's thesis caused a stir. He described the world's mountains, rivers and coasts as constantly evolving. The idea that they were in a state of constant flux, shaped by forces still in play today, ran counter to the established view that they were changeless and permanent, just as the Creator had made them.[6]

Darwin was intrigued. Soon after he left England, he started seeing evidence of this changing world for himself. He watched as volcanoes erupted in front of his eyes, and was even caught up in an earthquake. The Earth literally moved beneath his feet: 'the world, the very emblem of all that is solid, moves beneath our feet like a crust over a fluid,' he wrote.[7]

When HMS *Beagle* reached the Galapagos, on 15 September 1835, Darwin once again saw the natural world change in front of him. And he noticed something else: subtle differences in the animals on each island.

Despite popular myth, his first impressions of Galapagos weren't good. 'Nothing could be less inviting,' he wrote gloomily in his diary.[8]

Nor was he won over by his first encounters with the local wildlife. 'The black lava rocks on the beach are frequented by large most disgusting, clumsy lizards,' he noted, before labelling the creatures 'hideous looking . . . Imps of darkness'.[9] It was a damning description of one of Galapagos' most unique and intriguing species: the marine iguana.

Yet fast-forward nearly two centuries, and Sir David Attenborough uses those same 'imps of darkness' as the posterchild for his film series on the Galapagos. Standing regally on a submerged rock, a marine iguana stares out from the cover of a movie promising a 'gorgeous visual feast'.[10]

I've seen marine iguanas on the Galapagos myself, and found them fascinating. I watched as fellow tourists tried to capture them on camera, racing barefoot along the beach like paparazzi as they sought the perfect shot of a specimen swaying gracefully through the water (ungainly on land, they swim with much greater ease than they walk). I've studied 'iggies' sunning themselves on paths or rocks where boats dock to disgorge excited tourists, where they seem untouched by the attention. I've also seen them sit stubbornly in the middle of roads, making cars and bikes go round them.

Found nowhere else on Earth, the marine iguana is the only lizard that swims in the ocean. Iguanas are generally land-dwellers, found on mainland South America as well as throughout Galapagos. However, this marine variety has developed a unique trait: it can search for food below the waves.

Their land-dwelling ancestors come from the jungles of Central America, where they can still be seen in trees overhanging rivers or on rafts of reeds. Some are swept out to sea, most of them to perish, but long ago some enjoyed more luck. Cast adrift on floats of leaves or wood, their ability to go for days without food or water would have allowed them to survive until fate washed them up on the young (geologically speaking) volcanic shores of Galapagos.[11] In a barren land with little to eat, the survival of these Robinson Crusoe castaways would depend on their ability to adapt.

Darwin may have considered them ugly, but he certainly didn't find them dull. In those brief weeks on Galapagos, he started to notice the differences between these creatures and the many land iguanas he had seen elsewhere. Their unique seagoing characteristic set him wondering. He worked out that they were feeding in the ocean and began to examine what they ate. When he caught one and dissected its belly, he found that it was 'largely distended with minced seaweed'. A few more were caught and cut up with the same result. As there was no seaweed on land, he surmised that the vegetation grew 'at the bottom of the sea, at some little distance from the coast'.

He also observed that they did not jump into the water to escape. He found this puzzling, especially as they were so comfortable in water, swimming 'with a very graceful and rapid movement'. He caught one, and threw the unfortunate creature as far as he could into a deep pool. The hapless reptile swam straight back to Darwin, only to be scooped up and flung back again. This happened over and over. 'Perhaps this singular piece of stupidity may be accounted for by the circumstance, that this reptile has no enemy whatever on shore, whereas at sea it must often fall prey to the numerous sharks,' he wrote.[12]

Darwin was starting to notice that the Galapagos, where reptiles rule the roost, were unique. A near-complete absence of land mammals meant that lizards were the dominant herbivore – a situation rare since the time of the dinosaurs.[13]

The combination of the landscape changing before his eyes as a result of its volcanic nature, and creatures he had never seen before, made Darwin's mind whirr. As the homesick young naturalist wandered the islands, experimentally flinging iguanas into the sea, he grew more and more interested in what he was seeing in the sky.

At the time, he was baffled by the birds he came across, especially the finches. 'Amongst the species of this family,' he wrote in his Ornithological Notes, 'there reigns (to me) an inexplicable confusion.' He thought of them as 'samey' – which they are – but did notice that the size and shape of their bills varied. He collected thirty-one of what we now call 'Darwin's finches', and a range of other birds.[14]

Catching them was easy: the wildlife on Galapagos had an Eden-like quality, with little fear of humans – this persists. A dove was caught in a hat; a mockingbird alighted on the edge of Darwin's cup and sipped the water as he lifted it off the ground; and he pushed a hawk off a tree with the barrel of his gun.[15] Even today, the famous finches will feed from your plate; gigantic nesting seabirds will look straight through you; and sea lions are happy to sleep on beaches and memorial benches, places their counterparts elsewhere in the world would consider far too exposed.

By the time HMS *Beagle* returned home, Darwin had been elevated from obscurity to the status of reputed naturalist. After just a month or so on the islands, he had amassed quite a collection: reptiles, fish, snails, insects and hundreds of plants. However, it was birds with which he would become forever associated.

Some one to two million years ago, the common ancestors of Darwin's finches made their way across 1,000 kilometres of ocean to Galapagos. When they reached the islands, they did not encounter many competitors because the remote location prevented the frequent arrival of new species. Soon the finches dispersed to different islands, and eventually they diverged into distinguishable populations that adapted to different ecological niches. Over time, these adaptations led to the different species now known as 'Darwin's finches'.

Ironically, it was not Darwin himself who identified all of 'his' finches. It was not until some time after he left the Galapagos that he was struck by his theory of evolution, and much of what he collected during the voyage of the *Beagle* had to be reassessed. He sent his collection to the Zoological Society of London. There, the curator, a brilliant ornithologist named John Gould, worked out that Darwin's bag of 'samey' birds from Galapagos contained more than a dozen species of finch.[16]

As he began to formulate his theories, Darwin also realised that he had made a serious mistake. During his time on the *Beagle*, he failed to record the exact geographic origin of each bird. He had started to see Galapagos as a 'little world within itself'. If different islands in Galapagos had different species of finch, could it be that they came from a common ancestor, which had spread throughout the islands, and, over time, changed as it adapted to the particular environment in each place? Could isolation from other populations of its kind then have led to a single species evolving into more than a dozen different ones? Darwin became convinced that out of one finch had evolved thirteen. However, without knowing from which islands his specimens came, he could never prove it.

In the depths of despair, he approached his former shipmates who also collected specimens. There was still too little evidence to substantiate his theory. Again, Gould came to the rescue. He worked out that Galapagos had three different species of mock-ingbird. Fortunately, in this case, Darwin had noted where he had found each bird. As a result, it was possible to show that each species came from a different island.[17]

Darwin had been more diligent about labelling the geographic origins of his plant specimens. However, it was the eminent botanist Joseph Hooker who delivered the breakthrough. He sifted through more than two hundred plant species, and found half to be unique to Galapagos, and three-quarters confined to a single island. All of them seemed to be descended from species found elsewhere in the Americas. The discovery was the evidence Darwin needed to show that, rather than being static, unchanging creations, species evolve from common ancestors.[18]

What Lyell had done for geology – showing that the natural world was always in a state of flux – Darwin could now do for biology. Perhaps his greatest achievement was in identifying the mechanism behind evolution: survival of the fittest. He worked out that through natural selection, certain plants and animals developed the survival edge over their fellows and were more likely to breed successfully, passing on their superior traits to the next generation. This is how species evolve from a common ancestor.

The idea of evolution was hugely controversial in Victorian times, when creationism was rarely challenged. Darwin feared scandal, and held off publishing his findings for more than a quarter of a century. On the Origin of Species was finally published in 1859, as much to avoid being scooped as anything else. Alfred Russel Wallace, a collector selling to zoos and museums, had arrived at much the same conclusion and broached it with Darwin, who now faced a choice between publishing – and triggering uproar – or seeing the scientific credit for his great discovery go to someone else. He chose the former.

Perhaps as he feared, the reluctant parson turned scientist became known as the 'man who killed the Creator'.[19] The resulting controversy cast a shadow over the rest of his life.

## NOWHERE TO GO IN A WARMING WORLD

Wading through turquoise water, I felt like the first person ever to reach this beach. The white sand was warm beneath my feet as I scoured the mangrove-lined tidal lagoon in the middle distance. I was excited: sea turtles lay their eggs here, and I had been lucky enough to see several during my stay on the islands. Standing admiring the gently lapping shore, I spotted something thin and black shimmying along the surface of the water: a marine iguana.

Helen and I were on our big birthday trip. That's how we found ourselves on Las Bachas Beach on the central Galapagos island of Santa Cruz. We had the camera lens focused intently on the black scales and red gape of the world's only ocean-going iguana.

This collection of volcanic islands off Ecuador is perhaps the most pristine archipelago anywhere in the tropics, and one of the best places to learn about the process of evolution. Before Darwin arrived in 1835, most visitors considered it a grim place. The islands became a stopping-off point for whaling ships and pirates, intent on plundering whatever they could find. The giant land tortoises that gave the islands their name – Galapagos in Spanish meaning 'tortoise' – were a particular target. They were treated as mobile provisions, kept alive on board ships until they were eaten. Once upon a time, there may have been as many as a quarter of a million of these magnificent creatures, but by the time Darwin arrived, he was hard-pressed to find any.[20]

Today, the Galapagos are still widely considered to be almost untouched, but for how much longer? Drawn, as we were, by the uniqueness of this Garden of Eden, Galapagos now attracts about 200,000 visitors a year,[21] five times as many as twenty-five years ago. The influx has raised serious concerns about the very thing that brings many people to the place: its unspoilt nature.[22] The islands' national park authority does what it can to control tourism, with trained guides looking out to minimise the impact of the growing number of visitors.[23]

Climate change is a looming threat. Sea turtles on Galapagos nest in sand at the top of beaches, creeping ashore at night to lay their eggs. The same beaches are used for egg-laying by the marine iguanas. Their eggs are laid and incubated in burrows in the sand, which needs to be a certain temperature if they are to hatch successfully. Rising sea levels could threaten this delicate process.

Karin Kugele, a German biologist and professional guide who has lived on Galapagos for seventeen years, fears that as a result of climate change, iguana and turtle nest sites may vanish. 'The water will get higher and higher so the beaches will disappear,' she predicts, throwing into sharp relief what Darwin observed: the ever-changing nature of the world. However, evolution generally happens over long millennia, if not millions of years. Now, dramatic changes are taking place within human lifetimes.

The receding tide revealed black rock covered with green weed. 'That's what the iguanas eat,' she told me. Those early iguana castaways millions of years ago turned to the ocean bottom on Galapagos for the only available greenery, seaweed. Their tails flattened for better swimming and their pointed snouts grew rounded for grazing slippery weed.

'If the water warms, the algae dies, and that's a big problem for the marine iguana,' Kugele said. 'They have to stay close to the shore. Fish can swim away and find new food sources. The marine iguanas cannot.'

She describes them as endangered. Like many fellow scientists, she was quick to point out that we don't know exactly how things will change, but for marine iguanas the outlook is poor. If the sea warms, their food disappears. If sea levels rise, their breeding beaches disappear too. The Galapagos Islands are the only place these beautiful creatures exist. Before long, they may vanish altogether.

## THE PARABLE OF DARWIN'S FINCHES

On the second day of our holiday we headed to North Seymour, less than 2 square kilometres in size and named after an eighteenth-century British naval officer. Huge prehistoric-looking seabirds clung to a tangled mass of silver-grey palo santo trees while sea lions splashed below shallow cliffs. Formed when the seabed was lifted out of the water by tectonic activity below the Earth's surface, the flat-topped island is now home to a teeming mass of birds. It had an air of eerie stillness and a pungent smell of sun-baked seaweed and seabird droppings.

I stumbled over lava rocks and red sand and found myself among a mass of nesting frigate birds, which look like a cross between a gannet and a cormorant. The clamber, clatter and squawk of birds going about their business was the only sound. One of the all-black males puffed out the pouch beneath his chin into a bright scarlet balloon. Younger birds with hooked beaks and snow-white heads blinked with indifference. They showed no fear. Standing near-touching distance away, only a sense of privilege and the beady eye of our guide stopped me getting closer. This was a moment to savour: getting so close to such magnificent birds was one of my most magical bird-watching experiences.

As Darwin recognised, the Galapagos Islands are like a world in miniature. Each has its own flora and fauna, its own smell, its own colour. The red sand of North Seymour, the silver rocks and red carpet weed of South Plaza, the black of Santiago – all are at different stages of development and feature a unique collection of characters.

The tourist boats are a relatively new phenomenon.

Until as recently as the Second World War, the islands were closed to the wider world. Stung by the Japanese attack on Pearl Harbor, the US military was on the lookout for a base to defend the strategic lifeline of the Panama Canal. Galapagos was the perfect location. The US came to an agreement with the Ecuadorian government which owned Galapagos, and by April 1942 crushed lava had been covered with hot asphalt on the central island of Baltra to lay the archipelago's first airstrip. The way was now paved for the first commercial flights to reach the islands.[24]

After the Second World War the US turned the air force base over to the Ecuadorian government and dismantled the military buildings but left the runway.[25] Before giving up the territory, US President Franklin D. Roosevelt made clear how precious he considered the islands. 'These islands represent the oldest form of animal life and should, therefore, be preserved for all time as a kind of international park,' he told his Secretary of State. 'I would die happy if the State Department could accomplish something on it!' Sadly, he died a year later, his dream unrealised. In 1959, however, the Ecuadorian government declared much of Galapagos a national park, a century on from Darwin's *Origin of Species*.[26]

Even though long protected by a barrage of conservation laws, in 2007 the Galapagos was added to the UN Red List of endangered heritage sites amid concerns over the booming population, tourism, overfishing and the introduction of invasive species. In 1950 the islands had little more than a thousand residents. The human population has almost doubled every decade since,[27] and the Galapagos are now home to more than 25,000 people and armies of tourists.[28] Pollution, fuel spills and poaching, familiar elsewhere, are a serious threat.

As ever more people and provisions come and go, so the threat increases of accidental introductions of new plants and animals. Animals such as rats, feral pigs and goats threaten a habitat that evolved in isolation over millennia.[29] Introduced pets have caused birds and marine iguanas to flee some populated areas.[30]

Invasive plants also pose an increasing risk. It may not be long before introduced plant species outnumber native. If you travel north of Puerto Ayora you will see fruit trees everywhere: orange, grapefruit, lime, banana, lemons and coconuts – all introduced by humans. The scarlet blooms of introduced hibiscus contrast with the flowers of native Galapagos plants, which are all yellow. The limited range of pollinators on the islands historically rendered colour competition useless. Other destructive additions, like blackberry bushes, threaten to render the native vegetation into dense thickets.[31]

Farm animals have been increasing too. A sizeable chunk of the most fertile parts of Galapagos have been cleared or altered for farming. What remains has been badly affected by non-native flora and fauna.[32] On Santa Cruz, cows, the livestock backbone on Galapagos, are a familiar sight grazing on elephant grass, an invasive plant from Africa. Chickenisation is taking root. To the casual visitor, the abiding impression might be of chickens roaming free. From the road, we saw quite a few birds scratching among the trees. That is not the whole story, however. Tucked out of sight, there are now over thirty intensive chicken farms – that's more than one for every thousand human inhabitants on Galapagos. With each extra factory-farmed bird comes extra demand for scarce water and animal feed – plus the increasing threat of new diseases.

The sea around Galapagos is under pressure too, perhaps even more so than the land. The sea cucumber is just one species in real trouble. The authorities reacted to overfishing of sea cucumbers for the lucrative Asian market by imposing quotas. It prompted an outcry from local fishermen. Simmering tensions boiled over in the mid-1990s when disgruntled fishermen laid siege to the offices of the Galapagos National Park Service (GNPS). A rowdy stand-off ensued, involving Molotov cocktails and death threats, particularly aimed at the director of the GNPS. Unrest rumbled on for a decade, with fishermen and authorities clashing, until nature intervened with the collapse of the sea cucumber fishery.[33]

The government of Ecuador has had to work hard to remove Galapagos from the UN's world heritage list of endangered sites. Conservationists criticised the decision, announced in July 2010, insisting that 'threats from tourism, invasive species and overfishing are still factors and the situation in the Galapagos remains critical'.[34]

Despite the pressures, one of the archipelago's oldest endemics is still doing well, at least for now. In Cape Douglas on Fernandina, thousands of marine iguanas can be seen doing their morning warm-up routine. Across the Galapagos, more than 200,000 start the day by soaking up the sun, warming their bodies enough to take to the sea.

Walking along Divine Bay on Santa Cruz, we came across two dozen marine iguanas huddled in the sun, limbs entwined. Some – the bigger ones – had crusty frontal shields. Now and then, one of them would sneeze. According to our official guide, it is their way of expelling salt, a byproduct of their algal diet.

The natural inhabitants of Galapagos are used to the occasional hardship. The seas surrounding the islands carry cooling Humboldt and Cromwell currents, leading to an abundance of sealife. Every now and then, however, the cool water currents fail naturally – an event known as El Niño – with devastating effects. Our guide told us that El Niño kills large numbers of marine iguanas, sea lions, frigate birds and other species.

Native animals have developed a range of ways to cope with inevitable food shortages. The warmer waters of El Niño mean that the algae eaten by marine iguanas disappears or is replaced with brown algae which they find hard to digest.[35] To help them through lean times, marine iguanas have developed a remarkable adaptation. When food is short, the adults literally shrink their skeletons. When good times return, they grow them again. The ability to adapt can only take them so far, however. Increased pressure from the human population is making survival tougher.

Not all nature's troubles on Galapagos are man-made. As we headed back from North Seymour, our yacht sailed past the imposing volcanic crater island of Daphne Major. Treeless, with a rim 120 metres above the sea, this crumbling island has been the subject of intense study. For twenty years, British biologists Pete and Rosemary Grant, from the USA's Princeton University, came to this lonely rock for six months at a time capturing, tagging and taking blood samples of Darwin's finches. What they found was profoundly disturbing.

The local finches on Daphne Major rely on fruit from cactus plants to survive. The Grants discovered that something strange was happening to many of the cactus flowers: they were being rendered infertile as a result of the neat removal of the part of the plant that receives the pollen, the stigma. Without the stigma, the flowers don't fruit, and without fruit, finches could well starve later in the season.

Who was responsible for this vandalism? To their surprise, the Grants discovered it was the finches themselves. It turned out that some had developed an ability to pull out the flower and snip off the stigma so essential for pollination. They would then reach in to feed on pollen and nectar – food that was otherwise out of reach until the flowers opened.

In what has become known as the 'parable of Darwin's finches', a few stigma-snippers – apparently superior to their peers because they were smarter at collecting nectar – were destroying the flowers and effectively eating the island's seed corn. In so doing, they were making a quick gain at the long-term expense of the rest of the population. They were jeopardising future food supplies. Today, it appears that the stigma-snippers are still getting away with it. Should the population decline, they will undoubtedly do better than the rest – for a while. But only until they have driven themselves to extinction.[36]

## DARWIN'S UNFINISHED BUSINESS

When Charles Darwin died in 1882, having changed the way we look at the living world, he felt he was leaving unfinished business. 'I feel no remorse from having committed any great sin,' he wrote late in life, 'but have often and often regretted that I have not done more direct good to my fellow creatures.' Given his extraordinary contribution to science, his discomfort seems laughable. However, as we have seen, he was far from universally feted for his work during his lifetime.

What he felt was his unfinished business has now passed to his great-great-grandson, Chris Darwin. Chris is a 54-year-old professional rock-climbing instructor who has assumed a mammoth task in life: preventing the mass extinction of species. With a bent for breaking records, latter-day Darwin has already made it twice into the *Guinness Book of Records*. Hinting at his past life as a PR man, one record was for taking charge of a Peruvian mountain peak to host the world's highest dinner party. The only thing that marred the event, he told me, was the wine freezing and two of his guests getting hypothermia during dessert.

I spoke to Chris at his home in New South Wales, Australia. He lives in the Blue Mountains with his wife Jac and three children. We talked about his great-great-grandfather's time on the Galapagos nearly two centuries ago, and I asked him how it had felt to grow up as a descendant of the great Charles Darwin. I could imagine that being related to one of the world's all-time great thinkers might be something of a burden, as well as a privilege.

'Well, it hasn't always been fantastic. My nickname at school was "The Missing Link" and I did fail a biology exam at school,' he replied cheerfully.

Overall, though, he feels lucky to have such a distinguished ancestor.

'Charles had this extraordinary and clever way of thinking,' he reflected, referring to Darwin's belief both in verifiable evidence and in paying particular attention to things that challenge one's own belief. 'If you only read the stuff that supports your view, you'll never change your view . . . the chances are you're going to get left behind.'

I asked for an example. 'When I started coming into conservation,' he replied, 'I believed that the only way to stop the mass extinction of species was creating huge numbers of reserves around the world. Well, actually, I quite quickly realised that in fact that wasn't going to work.'

Of course, this resonated with me, because, as I've said earlier, when I was a teenager I used to take this view. I've since come to realise that I was wrong. Nature reserves play a valuable part, but something much bigger needs to change: what we are eating and the way we produce it.

While he still sees the benefit in having land set aside for nature, he believes in a more fundamental shift, a shift that requires us to change the way we look at one of the biggest drivers of wildlife extinction: meat. 'The greatest threat on land is habitat destruction; in the oceans it's overfishing,' he said simply.

Meat production is on the rise. If the entire world were to eat as much meat as the West, experts believe farmland would need to increase by another two-thirds.[37]

'I've come round to the conclusion that we need to reduce the amount of meat we're eating,' Chris told me. Had it not been for his ancestor's golden rule – always challenge your own beliefs – he feels it would have taken him longer to figure this out. There is a stark statistic here: wildlife numbers have halved in the last forty years.

Darwin's descendant believes that the world's insatiable appetite for meat is the chief driving force behind the decline of species, a decline that is sending some tumbling towards extinction. 'Trying to save species from extinction is a really hard thing to do,' he told me. 'It's much better to try and stop them getting there, and really what we do on an everyday basis, three times a day with our meals, is the most important thing you can change and there are many benefits.'

According to the UN Food and Agriculture Organisation, over the next thirty-five years, demand for meat is likely to double. A report by the organisation, published in 2006 under the title *Livestock's Long Shadow*, warned that the next few decades will see a huge explosion in farm animal numbers.[38]

Already, 70 billion farm animals are reared for food every year. Estimates suggest that in 2050 there will be 500 million more cattle, 200 million more pigs, a billion more sheep and goats, and 18 billion extra poultry on Earth than there were in 2005.[39]

Should we allow that to happen, the loss of wildlife will surely be incalculable. In addition to triggering the destruction of habitats, rising meat production is likely to accelerate one of the other big drivers of mass extinction: climate change. Farm animals already contribute 14.5 per cent of total greenhouse gas emissions, more than all the planes, trains and cars put together.[40]

The UN warns that global warming must be kept within 2 degrees Celsius by the end of the century or the consequences will be catastrophic. To do this, greenhouse gas emissions in 2050 will need to be 70 per cent lower than in 2010. Scientists working on how to reduce emissions from livestock – so called 'mitigation' measures – deem it possible to achieve reductions of up to 30 per cent. However, a recent paper by Chatham House concluded that 'technical mitigation measures' – altering the way animals are kept and managed – are unlikely to suffice on their own to prevent soaring greenhouse gas emissions.[41]

Expansion in agriculture is predicted to wipe away any 'mitigation' saving, and much more besides. As things stand, agriculture is set to near-double (up to 80 per cent) its total greenhouse gas emissions. So significant is the role of agriculture in this looming crisis that if things go on as they are, agricultural emissions alone could breach the 'safe limit' of a maximum 2 degrees Celsius temperature rise.[42]

Is climate change really so grave a threat to the world's remaining wildlife? The overwhelming weight of scientific opinion backs that view. The International Panel on Climate Change (IPCC) has said that : 'A large fraction of both terrestrial and freshwater species faces increased extinction risk under projected climate change during and beyond the 21st century,' especially as climate change interacts with other factors: 'habitat modification, over-exploitation [such as overfishing], pollution, and invasive species'.[43]

Polar bears, penguins, sea lions and other species highly adapted to cold climates, whether they are on mountain tops or unique and fragile environments like the Galapagos, are likely to find they've nowhere left to go. The seasons are already changing in the northern hemisphere, disrupting the synchronisation between breeding species and their food. Species' ranges are shifting. More floods, droughts and general weather disruption are likely to create havoc for both people and animals[44] – we are seeing this already. Devastating floods in the northwest of England and massive droughts in Africa are but two examples of extreme weather events which have been linked to climate change.[45]

Meat stands accused. Most livestock products – meat, milk, eggs – put out far more greenhouse gas emissions per unit of protein than plant products such as grains, vegetables and pulses.[46] The Chatham House study underscores the point that global temperature rise is unlikely to stay below 2 degrees Celsius without reducing consumption of meat and dairy.[47]

That's why Chris Darwin is in no doubt about what must be done. 'The greatest threat is meat consumption and the solution is meat reduction,' he said simply. For Darwin's descendant, this is no vegetarian crusade. He sees much greater scope for change among committed carnivores, by asking them to eat less and better meat. Diets high in meat can be responsible for a third more greenhouse gas emissions compared with a low-meat diet.[48]

I asked what his advice would be for someone keen to help stave off mass extinction. 'Try to give up meat once a week,' he replied. 'It's going to be good for your health, it's going to save you money, it's great for animal welfare and it's great for the planet.' No great conundrum there.

It is often alleged that factory farming is the way forward – produce more meat from confined animals fed on grain – towards reducing greenhouse gas emissions. This is to solve one problem but spawn many more. Factory farming is inherently inefficient, squanders land and water, is highly polluting in other respects, and cruel to the animals involved. The UN FAO concurs that a wholesale shift to the industrial approach to raising animals would be the wrong move to make in the fight against climate change, and says that improvements in practices rather than switching production systems is the key.[49] However, the kind of greenhouse gas reductions that are going to be necessary to avoid runaway climate change will require a cut in the amount of meat we eat.

Chris dreams of a consumer revolution in which shoppers will pay far more heed to the provenance of what they buy. They might have to spend a little more for better meat like pasture-fed, free-range or organic, but if they eat less of it, everybody wins.

There are cheering signs that such a change is already under way. 'It's amazing, meat consumption is dropping in America now!' Chris enthused. According to the US Department of Agriculture, there has been a 12 per cent fall in America's meat consumption in the five years to 2012.[50] If the figures are falling in the country that gobbles more meat than anywhere else, that must give great cause for hope, especially as shifts in behaviour in America often set trends elsewhere in the industrialised world. After all, it was the USA whose invention of factory farming sparked off the boom in cheap meat in the first place.

Perhaps even more remarkable are plans unveiled recently by the government of China's health department to reduce its citizens' meat consumption by 50 per cent. China consumes more than a quarter of the world's meat, including half of its pork. The measures encouraging more moderate meat consumption are aimed at improving public health and could also provide a significant cut in greenhouse gas emissions.[51]

In Europe, where meat consumption is among the highest in the world, halving meat and dairy consumption could reduce EU greenhouse gas emissions by up to 40 per cent.[52]

Despite the scale of the challenge, Chris has taken Charles's unfinished business to heart. He's getting ready for his next eye-catching way to get people engaged, and has America firmly in his sights. When we spoke, he was in the midst of planning a bike ride with a difference across the USA. His aim is to highlight the plight of five particular species, through a series of wacky stunts along the way.

'We've got a shrub that's actually extinct in the wild but still exists in Washington, which we're going to try and deliver to the President,' he said excitedly, before telling me about his idea to help save endangered bears. 'I'm also going to dress up in a bulletproof costume and then put a bear suit over the top, and I'm going to romp around in the back roads at dusk and see if anybody shoots me! And we're finishing off with the biggest species on the planet, having a dinner party up in a redwood tree in Yosemite . . . our grand finale.'

His treetop stunt will commemorate an epiphany experienced by US President Theodore Roosevelt,[53] who set out with the renowned Victorian Scottish-American naturalist John Muir into Yosemite for three days – a transformative trip for them both. Roosevelt and Muir subsequently set up a series of national parks across the US. Chris plans to invite direct descendants of Roosevelt and Muir to join him for dinner in the redwood tree.

'The reason for the dinner party is because it's all about food,' he said. 'If there's meat, it'll be compassionately raised, and that will be the grand finale.'

## 14

## *Homo sapiens*

Lucy awoke from another hot and humid night in the forest. She ran fingers through her matted hair and peered down from the tree where she had slept. She yawned and stretched, cast a wary eye over the dense pine and olive trees, and then clambered down from her perch in search of breakfast: fruit, nuts and perhaps a bird's egg.

She was a curious-looking creature, with long dangly arms and a pot belly. Standing just 3 ft 7 in tall, by standards yet to come she was a dwarf, but at the time she stood at the peak of mammalian evolution. She possessed a unique skill: she could walk upright on two legs. During the day, she would roam rich grassland that stretched away from the banks of a mighty river. At night she would seek the cover of the forest.

About 3 million years after she walked the Earth, Lucy's remains were found in a ravine in Hadar, northern Ethiopia. It was 1974, and an anthropologist named Professor Donald Johanson and his student Tom Gray had been looking for hominid or other animal fossils in the scorched sand, ash and silt. What they found was sensational: nearly fifty bones of what they identified as a human-like creature.

Back at camp, wild celebrations followed. The scientists stayed up all night talking and drinking in utter exuberance. As a portable stereo blasted out Beatles songs, they debated what to call their spectacular find. With the sound of The Beatles' legendary hit 'Lucy in the Sky with Diamonds' ringing out through the night, the answer was obvious: Lucy.[1]

It was one of the oldest and most complete hominid skeletons ever found, and it transformed the way we look at how we became human. The structure of Lucy's fossilised pelvis and knee bone signified bipedalism – the ability to walk as we do today. The reason experts considered the find so significant was that scientists see bipedalism as a defining feature: the biggest single difference between humans and apes. It puts Lucy firmly in the family of early humans. The ability to walk upright must have given her and those like her an evolutionary edge.

Johanson named Lucy's species *Australopithecus afarensis*, which means 'southern ape of Afar', after the Ethiopian region where she was found. Drained by the Awash River, this area is seen by some as the cradle of mankind.

The discovery of Lucy and the study of other early humans offers an insight into how we got to where we are today. It also shows how hugely the destiny of all living creatures can be affected by bigger forces in an ever-changing world.

About 3 million years ago, life's conditions were starting to change. In Africa, temperatures plummeted and the air grew drier. The dense humid forest Lucy had once known shrank, giving way to wide belts of open terrain. This had a profound effect on animals that relied on the forest, and some died out. Others adapted to the changing landscape. Ape-men proved particularly versatile, and new variations emerged all over Africa.[2]

Two million years ago, a new species appeared, perhaps the first we would recognise as human: *Homo ergaster* ('working man'). This early ancestor of modern man evolved to exploit the shrinking forest environment, developing the ability to travel on foot over vast distances in search of food. Eventually, the innate wanderlust of this species prompted it to leave Africa. Early humans reached what is now former Soviet Georgia around 1.8 million years ago. Here, they found cool, seasonal grasslands where African animals like ostriches and giraffes mingled with Eurasian species like wolves and the sabre-toothed cat *Megantereon*. They quickly spread east as far as the Indonesian island of Java.[3]

What we now think of as modern humans – *Homo sapiens* – emerged as a species as recently as 200,000 years ago – a blink of evolution's eye. Less than 100,000 years ago, they too began to leave Africa.[4] As they advanced across Europe, they met their ancestral cousins, the Neanderthals. *Homo neanderthalensis* were human too. They buried their dead, used tools, had complex social structures, employed language, and appreciated music and song.[5] Stocky, powerful hunters with no chin and a sloping forehead, they hunted dangerously large animals for food. They were also widespread, and over a period of hundreds of thousands of years became very well established across Europe and Western Asia.

Just 5,000 years after modern humans showed up, however, Neanderthals were gone. No one knows why. Perhaps they weren't as adaptable as modern humans in the face of changing climate. Perhaps they were the victims of genocide,[6] or caught diseases to which they had no immunity from their ancestral cousins. Or perhaps they were just outclassed and paid the ultimate price: extinction.

What seems likely is that they took a shine to one another: modern humans and Neanderthals had sex together, and their offspring conferred genes thought to benefit the newcomers from Africa, helping them cope better with the colder climes of Europe. Briana Pobiner, a paleoanthropologist at the Smithsonian's National Museum of Natural History, said: 'Some would say Neanderthals didn't go extinct, because everyone alive today whose ancestry is from outside of Africa (where Neanderthals never lived) carries a little bit of Neanderthal DNA in their genes.'[7]

One thing is for sure – on a planet once populated by many different types of human being, just one survived to rule the Earth: us. Our evolutionary history shows a tendency to explore and conquer. Animals large and small have disappeared in our wake, including those that we might now recognise as being of our own kind.

For much of history, humans were hunter–gatherers. It's a life-style contingent on the ecosystem. After all, any hunter who kills too many of the prey on which he or she relies for food will simply starve. Then, around 10,000 years ago, something happened that freed modern humans from the limitations of hunter-gathering: the birth of agriculture. It was perhaps the single most significant development in the history of mankind. People started growing crops and domesticating animals. It meant they were no longer constrained by the need for wide-ranging homelands or territories for hunting. They started coming together in bigger groups to live in towns and cities. They now had the liberty to do more than simply collect food. Society began to develop – and expand – at an amazing speed.[8]

The human population soared from one million people 10,000 years ago to a billion by 1800. By 1960 there were 3 billion of us. The trouble was that the population was growing at such a pace that agricultural production couldn't keep up. There were fears of widespread famine. Encouraged by successive governments, farmers became fixated on producing more at any cost. Crisis was averted by what became known as the Green Revolution: the development of new varieties of crops, which had shorter stems and were more productive.

These advances came at a price, though. The sophisticated new crops had lost some of their natural defences to pests, and were coming to depend on chemical pesticides. Artificial fertilisers began to replace grazing animals and land rotation as the chosen way to replenish soil. The mixed farming of crops and animals became a thing of the past, replaced by farms specialising in one type of crop or animal. It was an industrial approach to the countryside, pushed by industrialised nations who sold it all over the world as the modern way.

The new system was effective, in that it generated the additional food required for the burgeoning population. Despite its many drawbacks, it gave rise to a new mentality, which has now been ingrained for almost half a century, and is proving extraordinarily stubborn to shift: that production must be maximised at all costs.

The true costs of producing food in an output-led industrial way, where sheer volume trumps other concerns like nutritional quality, environmental sustainability or animal welfare, are only just being realised. It incarcerates some 50 billion animals a year in darkened sheds or feedlots, crammed and confined, while millions of acres of chemical-soaked cropland are dedicated to growing their feed.

As billions of farm animals suffer behind closed doors and wild-life retreats to the edge of extinction, one species in particular is harmed: our own. Whether it be through poorer-quality food, disease, or the fact that billions more could be fed if only cropland wasn't feeding factory farms, the truth is, cheap food costs dear.

For a long time, the environment seemed capable of absorbing the heavy knocks associated with this type of farming – after all, the planet is adaptable, resilient. It now seems that we are reaching a tipping point: the Earth's ability to take punishment, whether pollution, greenhouse-gas emissions or demand on natural resources like land, water and soil, is pushing its limit. Agriculture has a big part to play. It swallows nearly half the world's usable land, more than two-thirds of freshwater, and damages the soil so vital for nearly all that we eat. No wonder some suggest that we need a second planet to sustain us. The suggestion is we are now pushing planetary boundaries beyond the Earth's ability to cope.

The global population now stands at more than 7 billion. By the middle of the century, it is expected to rise to 9 billion. *Homo sapiens* has been spectacularly successful, but human activity is now so all-pervasive that it's becoming hard to see where we end and nature begins. Mankind has always been part of the ecosystem, forced to live in a natural environment it cannot completely control. We have always taken the brunt of nature's phenomenal force. We can forecast the weather, but we have yet to find a way to stop it raining, or to make the sun shine on a particular day. We can predict earthquakes, and design buildings that are less likely to tumble when the ground tremors, but so far we cannot prevent them from happening, any more than we can stop the wind blowing, or turn the tide.

It is hard to imagine this changing, but we continue to subjugate the natural world to what we see as our needs, however and wherever we can. In so doing, we devour our own habitat. More than half the world's ice-free land surface has been modified already by human activity.[9] 'While climate and geology have shaped ecosystems and evolution in the past,' say scientists Erle Ellis and Navin Ramankutty, there is growing evidence that 'human forces may now outweigh these across most of Earth's land surface today.'[10]

Within the last half-century, humans have changed the face of the Earth to such an extent that the traditional scientific way of classifying its main habitats (into forest, grassland, desert and tundra) looks hopelessly outdated.[11] Genuine wildland now makes up just a fraction of the Earth's land surface. With most of 'nature' engulfed within human land use, some scientists believe there needs to be a new land-classification system. Ellis and Ramankutty have suggested terms such as 'dense settlement', 'villages', 'croplands' or 'wildlands'.

The biggest single driver of this dramatic change is farming. Accounting for 47 per cent or more of useable land globally, an area the size of South America is devoted to growing crops, and an area bigger still is raising livestock.[12]

As the population rises, so the quest intensifies for more land to cultivate. Right now, we are in no danger of running out of food (distributional problems notwithstanding), but the environmental damage attached to the way we are choosing to produce it may be irreversible. Flora and fauna are falling extinct one thousand times faster than the rate viewed by scientists as the expected 'background' rate.[13] Food production is the biggest driver of this biodiversity overkill.

The last half-billion years have seen five mass extinctions: episodes of sudden dramatic loss to biodiversity. Dinosaurs developed after one of the biggest mass-extinction events some 250 million years ago, at the end of the Permian period. They disappeared, or underwent vast changes, about 66 million years ago, over a brief span of geological time.

Although the exact causes of past mass extinctions remain a mystery, volcanic eruptions and large asteroid strikes are two prime suspects. The resulting dust clouds probably blocked out sunlight for months if not years, causing plants and plant-eating creatures to die. Heat-trapping gases would also have triggered runaway global warming.

Of course, planet Earth is tough. Ecosystems bounce back eventually. After one of the most devastating extinction events of all time, things did recover, but it took a long time: some 30 million years.[14] Some scientists believe we are now on the cusp of the sixth mass extinction. It is expected to be the most devastating since the asteroid impact thought to have wiped out the dinosaurs. This time, the cause is much closer to home: us.

It appears that we have moved into our own geological era. One like none before.

Welcome to the Anthropocene.

### EXPLODING LIVESTOCK

I am lucky enough to live in a stunning part of the world. Whatever the time of year, or time of day, the views across the chalk escarpment, across lush green fields scattered with cows and sheep, take my breath away. The next village is about 4 miles away from ours, on the other side of a steep ridge. From the top of that ridge, you can see for miles. The route, much favoured by cyclists, takes you through fields of pasture and crops, past an old naval base (now converted into upmarket housing) and an environmental centre teaching everything from woodland management to campfire cooking. Disappearing into an arch of woodland, the twisting road descends again into more fields. You pass an old windmill, an early nineteenth-century corn mill now converted to a residence, commanding fantastic views over the Downs. Over the years, I've covered this route countless times, but one day it was different.

As I came down that hill into the next village, instead of the usual green vista I saw scuffed brown. Several once glorious fields had been fenced off for a housing estate. For many years, those fields were used for grazing. Foxes and rabbits could scamper through the grass, thrushes peck for worms, bees hover purposefully while butterflies danced, and cows munch away come rain or shine. Now it would just be more homes.

Don't get me wrong: those houses are attractive of their kind. And if almost everyone is drawn to southeast England, then developers are bound to seek more land. Councils are under intense pressure to nod through planning applications, and if local authorities fail to meet house-building targets, governments can and do overrule planning refusals.

I don't doubt the need for new and affordable properties, but I can't help wondering about the wisdom of concreting over pristine agricultural land for development. After all, food, and therefore farming, is not going out of fashion. Instead, it will have to go elsewhere.

That is likely to entail clearing woodland to make way for new farmland somewhere else in the country, or more likely on another continent. Once felled, that woodland is no longer taking carbon out of the atmosphere and helping combat climate change, or giving back the oxygen we breathe. The animals and birds that lived there lose their habitat. The toughest will find somewhere else to live; the rest will die. Every year, an area of forest equivalent to half the UK is cleared somewhere in the world for extra farmland.

I can see my own village being swallowed up by the nearest city – Portsmouth – as it continues to sprawl. Although the heart of the city is nearly 20 miles away, its outer reaches are now just the other side of the hill. In this way, discrete villages become conjoining towns then subsumed into cities. Farmland has to move out.

The trouble is that globally, farmland is in short supply. Agriculture – croplands, pasture or, in the case of palm, wooded plantations – already covers nearly half the planet's available land surface, almost half of which is pastures and meadows.[15]

According to the World Bank, the total area of land suitable for rain-fed crop production is around 30 million square kilometres.[16] This may seem a lot, but population growth, urbanisation and soil erosion mean an alarming rate of land loss. Almost half of the suitable land area is already under crops, and much of the rest is forest.

To me it seems obvious that losing farmland by whatever means puts greater pressure on the world's remaining forests. This holds especially true as population pressure keeps on rising. Every billion extra people in the world amount to a hundred more Londons plus thirty Los Angeles. And that's not the end of the story. Like a fried egg with its bright yellow yolk in the middle of a spreading area of white, each city requires even more land somewhere else to grow food. Where will this extra land come from?

It is at this point that policymakers begin to think the answer lies in cramming animals indoors – doesn't the strategy save space? What they forget is that animals confined indoors still need land elsewhere growing their feed. Worse still, they now need arable land to grow corn, soya and so on, rather than the much more common pasture. It's a classic case of 'Out of sight, out of mind'. Keeping animals indoors and bringing food to them does not change the reality: arable land is in short supply. Most of it is already being used. Much of the rest? Well, that's under forest . . .

As we have seen, an area of cropland equivalent to the entire land surface of the European Union (or half the United States) is growing feed crops for industrially reared animals. The combined yield could feed an extra 4 billion people. For now, it cannot, because animals locked in cages, barns or feedlots get it instead. Defenders of the system like to suggest that it's not a zero-sum game, because incarcerated animals are converting grain into meat. Sadly, there's no such thing as a free lunch. In fact, most of the food value – whether calories or protein – gets lost in the conversion process. Some 70 per cent or more of the food fed to farm animals is wasted in this way.

I remember hearing about the way in which a meat industry spokesman argued this point with a former UK government minister, saying that the food wasn't actually lost but transformed into something else. 'Well, sir,' came the answer, 'give me your wallet with a hundred pounds in it. I'll take the money out, put thirty pounds back and see if you think that's a good deal!' That sums it up. For once, a government figure seemed to get it.

The alternative to bulldozing forests for more arable land is to keep farm animals on pasture – in other words, land that is unsuitable for crops. Indeed, a quarter or more of the world's land surface is covered in grassland pastures.[17] Farm animals have also long been kept on permanent pastures, or as part of a rotational farming system where grass is interspersed with crops to build soil fertility naturally.

Some pasture, particularly in temperate lowlands as in Britain, is there by choice: we choose to graze cattle rather than grow crops. Yet much of the world's pasture or 'rangelands' is in places too steep, too dry or on too poor a soil to be much use for arable land without copious chemicals and irrigation.[18]

The steep slopes of the chalk downlands where I live are a prime example. They are largely covered in grass, as crop farming would be difficult and precarious. Other examples of grasslands in areas unsuitable for major crop farming include the drylands of Africa, the steppes of Central Asia and the highlands of Latin America. Places like these are prone to drought and desertification if the land is worked too hard. Nevertheless, they remain productive as grazing land for animals.[19]

The best way to produce healthy meat with the fewest resources is to use permanent pasture or keep animals on the grassland rotation of a mixed farm. In this latter routine, soils are rested from the relentless demands of arable cropping for a few years by turning them for a while into grazing land. By transforming grass into meat, milk and eggs, we convert something we can't eat – grass – into something we can.

Instead, by taking animals off grass and feeding them grain, we have created a rivalry between people and animals for food. That makes it harder, not easier, to feed a growing world population, but there is no sign of a change of approach. Policymakers and the farming and food industry continue to argue for more industrial meat production to meet what is predicted to be a near-doubling of demand for food by the middle of this century.

This seems totally misconceived. After all, globally, we already produce enough food calories for around 16 billion people, way more than enough even for the huge projected population rise.[20]

Unless there is a major global policy shift, the majority of additional farm animals will be raised on grain-guzzling factory farms, and pressure for additional land will be so intense that farming is likely to replace forests as well as spread further into marginal lands.

An area of extra cereal cropland the size of France and Italy combined will be needed by 2050 to keep pace. Up to a fifth of the world's remaining forests are likely to be lost over the next three decades, including an area of tropical forest equivalent to much of Argentina.[21]

Great swathes of extra croplands look set to join the chemical-soaked arable monocultures of East Anglia in England. The seas of swaying corn in the Midwest of America and soya in Brazil bid fair to extend still further. There'll be more fields of maize like the ones I saw in rural Asia – such a waste of land, to grow animal feed when it could be feeding people – while even more virgin forest will be converted to palm plantations.

The encroachment of agriculture into remaining wildlands, together with the onward march of industrial farming, will almost certainly cause irreversible damage to biodiversity, forests, soil and water. Wildlife extinctions will follow.

Derek Joubert, a conservationist and explorer with *National Geographic*, noted that fifty years ago there were nearly half a million lions left in the world, and that every time the human population rises by one billion, the population of lions falls by half.

'Today we're at 20,000 to 30,000 lions and the same is true for leopards, for cheetahs, for snow leopards,' he has written.[22]

To me, the link is obvious. An extra billion people come with 10 billion extra farm animals, together with all that means for land, water and soil. As land is carved up and pared down, so species start to teeter on the edge. What were once strong flames like campfires find themselves snuffed out like a candle.

This isn't about people versus animals. Far from it. I am not arguing for draconian population control, Chinese style (though there may be a case for more gentle ways of discouraging unfettered expansion). The real sting in the tail is the population explosion in farm animals and the way they are kept. The most harmful population pressure comes from the sheer number of farm animals, particularly in industrial systems, and their demand on global resources, not least land, water and soil. That's so often what does the real damage, for nature and for humanity. As nature retreats, she stops providing things like pollination, soil replenishment and carbon sequestration too.

Throughout human history, for better or for worse, *Homo sapiens* has outdone all-comers, from magnificent mammals like the bison that roamed the American plains in vast numbers, to birds like the passenger pigeons that once flocked in great grey rivers through the sky, and to species of fellow human like the Neanderthal. Whatever has stood in our way, and more often just in our reach, we have erased it. Now we may have met our match. The great irony is that our most fearsome competitor for food – livestock – has been put there by us.

### DIGGING DEEP, RUNNING DRY

The night before Thanksgiving, Carey Wilson was washing the dishes in the kitchen sink when the tap began to sputter and spit until nothing but air came out. The groundwater well she relied on for drinking water had run dry.

Living in California's Central Valley, she knew what to do (it happens quite a lot out there). She called a service company to lower her water well, and for a while that did the trick. A year later, however, the single mother and federal government worker found the well had run dry again. This time there was no quick fix. She ended up spending $12,000 to restore running water to her property, via a powerful pump and a new well 389 ft deep.

Wilson quickly realised that she was in competition with her neighbours for water. They too were facing supply problems and having to drill deeper. 'They were pulling the plug out from underneath us,' she told the *Guardian* newspaper. 'It was homeowner against homeowner.'[23]

Farms dug deeper still, often thousands of feet. By August 2014 the water table in Wilson's area had dropped 18 feet. The land had dropped too, twisting and crushing the PVC pipe connected to her well. 'I know the writing is on the wall,' Wilson said. 'It doesn't matter if it rains for forty days and forty nights, here the water table is never going to go up.'

Central Valley is the beating heart of California's land of milk and honey. It is a hugely productive area for agriculture, and generates about 40 per cent of the nation's fruit, nuts and vegetables, but it is so arid that it relies on a hugely expensive and complex system of artificial irrigation which is not proving sustainable. The land is now sinking.

Some parts of the valley are collapsing at the rate of 2 inches (5 cm) a month. It may not sound much, but the effects are drastic. About 1,200 square miles of land, roughly bounded by interstate 5 and state route 99, has caved in to what scientists describe as a cone of depression. As it collapses, it takes roads, bridges and farmland with it.

By 2015, California found itself in the fourth year of a prolonged dry spell that some have labelled a hundred-year drought. Great swathes of the nation's most productive soils lay parched and cracked. Farmers would crumble bone-dry clods in their fingers and look to the sky and long for rain.

As the drought stretched on, rivers and reservoirs started to run dry. In a desperate 'every man for himself' measure, some farmers started tapping deeper into groundwater reserves to keep their businesses afloat. As drilling for water intensified, so the parched land sank further.

Mark Cowin, director of California's department of water resources, explained: 'Because of increased pumping, groundwater levels are reaching record lows – up to 100 feet lower than previous records. As extensive groundwater pumping continues, the land is sinking more rapidly and this puts nearby infrastructure at greater risk of costly damage.'[24]

The situation in the area became so serious that one NASA scientist warned that California might have just a year of water left.[25]

Californian Governor Jerry Brown told a news conference: 'People should realise, we're in a new era. The idea of your nice little green grass getting lots of water every day, that's going to be a thing of the past.'[26] He was announcing the first compulsory water-use limits in the state's history. Householders faced cutbacks on watering gardens and lawns as well as on washing cars and taking showers. Water use had to be cut by a quarter.

In a concession that caused widespread anger, some large farms were exempt from the cuts.[27] 'To be sure, California's drought demands action,' wrote Stephen Wells, Executive Director of the Animal Legal Defense Fund. 'But, the governor's plan not only falls short in conserving water, it unfairly places the burden on individual consumers and non-agricultural businesses.'

The increasingly desperate scene in Central Valley highlights the huge quantities of water that industrial agriculture requires. Wells voiced the question many were asking: was it reasonable to restrict household use while allowing factory farms 'to continue their wasteful business-as-usual practices?'[28]

More than 90 per cent of California's water use is associated with agricultural products.[29] Meat and dairy alone account for nearly half of the state's so-called 'consumptive' use of water, meaning that the water extracted can't be replaced.[30]

Meat and dairy products from industrial farms have especially large water footprints due to the water-intensive feed required to raise the animals. The amount of water used in producing a kilo of beef would keep a person in daily baths for three months. A kilo of chicken takes twenty-four bathtubs of water.

Feeding animals on grass can hugely reduce the toll on rivers and underground water sources. Rearing them on factory farms where they are fed grain is over forty times more water-intensive. And there are a lot of factory farms in the Central Valley. When I was there in 2011, I saw a number of dairy farms with up to 12,000 cows in a single muddy paddock, not a blade of grass in sight. It was before the drought, but the area still looked dry.

Wells maintained that under Governor Brown's executive order, mandatory reductions in domestic water use would achieve very little. Cutting a quarter off things like watering lawns, drinking water and taking showers, which combined only constitute 4 per cent of California's water uses, would only curtail total water use by about 1 per cent: a drop in the bucket. 'We can stop showering, stop watering our lawns, and stop ordering water in restaurants, but the water used to raise and slaughter millions of cows, pigs, and chickens in California will still drain the state dry,' he argued.

Prolonged droughts are nothing new for California. The state's climate history is marked by much longer episodes, including mega-droughts lasting 100 years, and several decades long.[31] What is new is that California now supports tens of millions of people and a large and thirsty agricultural industry. The picture is mirrored in many other parts of the world where water is in dwindling supply. Already more than a billion people live in conditions of extreme water shortage.[32] By the middle of this century, between 4 and 7 billion people could be living in areas where water is scarce.[33]

Agriculture is by far the biggest user of this precious resource, taking 70 per cent of the planet's freshwater.[34] Overall, the amount we divert from rivers or pump from underground aquifers is expected to rise by nearly a fifth by 2050. Quite where all this extra water is going to come from isn't clear.

As the livestock population explodes, so too does its water use. The amount of water used for irrigating crops – much of which is devoted to animal feed – is expected to more than double worldwide by 2050.[35] Agriculture threatens to literally dry up ecosystems.[36]

### TREATING SOIL LIKE DIRT

Charles Darwin knew that the humble earthworm is one of the enduring signs of healthy soil. He was fascinated by them, observing their behaviours during experiments in his study and billiard room, as well as in more natural settings outside.[37]

He studied them at Stonehenge, the prehistoric monument in Wiltshire, England, in what became one of the first scientifically recorded excavations at the site. There he discovered that the cumulative effect of millions of worms in a field munching their way through earth and depositing it on the surface actually raises the surface of the soil.[38]

Writing in his 1897 book entitled (not too grippingly) *The Formation of Vegetable Mould Through the Action of Worms*, he observed: 'Farmers in England are well aware that objects of all kinds, left on the surface of pasture-land, after a time disappear, or, as they say, work themselves downwards.'[39]

'At Stonehenge,' he wrote, 'some of the outer Druidical stones are now prostrate, having fallen at a remote but unknown period; and these have become buried to a moderate depth in the ground . . . most of this mould [soil] must have been brought up by worms from beneath its base.'[40]

In other words, while they look small and insignificant, worms do big things. They act like archaeological JCBs. When they eat soil, it goes through their muscular tube, and comes out the other end as worm casts. It is thought that the collective action of worms in processing and pushing up soil in this way is the reason giant stones at Stonehenge have fallen and become buried.[41]

Toppling great rocks is impressive enough, but worms perform another and far more important function: they mix soil and nutrients, stirring up the essential ingredients for growing the food on which we depend. It has been estimated that earthworms completely turn over the equivalent of all the soil on the planet to a depth of 1 inch (2.5 cm) every ten years.[42] It was Darwin who discovered their crucial role in enhancing soil fertility.[43]

The disappearance of these wriggly creatures, beloved of blackbirds and thrushes the world over, is a sure sign of something badly wrong, so when I heard about a farm that had no worms, my ears pricked up. At first I thought it must be a joke, or at least an exaggeration, but as I found out on a trip to England's East Anglia region one wet summer's day, there really is a farm which, for a while, had no worms at all.

Richard Morris is a farm manager in Cambridgeshire for the National Trust of England. With more than thirty years of farming experience, he was given the job of bringing that unfortunate farm's soil back to life. He told me that for years, it had suffered a relentless siege of chemicals: 'Nitrogen, pesticides, herbicides – the bugs and the beasts that should be living in the soil, they were just getting slaughtered. And that's where we ended up. And that's the reason why we had five or six hundred acres of land with no worms.'

'No worms at all?' I asked.

'No worms,' he confirmed.

A retired soil scientist came along as a volunteer and dug 200 holes across the estate without finding a single worm. The intensive agricultural system had 'led to disaster, really, in terms of soil and soil protection in the environment, a real disaster,' Morris said. 'It's a lack of care,' he concluded: the soil had been treated like a mere 'growing medium rather than a living asset'.

As the soil deteriorated, so yields declined, a fact that mirrors the national picture.

A visit to my local garden centre reminded me that it's not only some farmers who have become obsessed with chemicals that kill creatures in the soil. Walking the massed ranks of dahlias, petunias and daffodils, all manner of things designed to enrich our gardens, I also saw the dark side of this utopia: the serried ranks of . . . killers: packets and sprays that proudly proclaimed their ability to eliminate and eradicate . . . well, a host of natural things. The list was endless: weeds, insects, caterpillars, beetles, lava, whitefly, wasps, slugs, snails, ants, termites, woodlice, all ready for immediate and indiscriminate use. I wondered how worms might fare under this domestic battery of chemicals.

Out in the countryside, where things are happening on such a massive scale, restoring soil life instead of destroying it could have a big part to play in our future. I asked Morris how he turned things around, bringing wormless soils back to life.

In a way, he told me, it was quite simple. He changed the way the soil was treated, cut out chemicals, rotated crops and matched the machinery to the job in hand. The land was worked when conditions were appropriate. He avoided trying to turn wet, heavy soil with big tractors, a process that compacts the soil. Instead of artificial fertilisers, he used nitrogen-fixing leguminous plants.

So far, the signs are encouraging. 'We've not put any nitrogen on for four years and we're getting good yields from our fourth crop,' he reported. 'What that tells me is the fertility's there. What's helped me most is the improvements in the condition of the soil, which I wasn't expecting to happen so quickly.'

He sees worms as a 'brilliant' indicator of the health of the soil. 'We find worms now in most holes we dig . . . they are coming back!' As for biodiversity on the farm, he told me: 'The improvement has been phenomenal. Absolutely phenomenal.' Butterflies have multiplied in the fields, as have bees. He is seeing more birds – in all, a remarkable change.

Morris has shown how the right farming practices can transform soil quality.

Not so far away from where Morris is farming is another striking indicator of what happens to soil if we don't look after it. When the Victorians began to drain the fens that once covered much of eastern England, a landowner named William Wells decided to sink a cast-iron post into the peat at Holme Fen in Cambridgeshire to see how much it shrank as it dried out. In 1848, the top of the post was at ground level. Now, it stands 4 metres above the ground; a real-life dipstick assessing the rate of soil loss. The area is now part of the Great Fen Project, where intensive cropland is being bought up to re-form a 3,700-hectare wetland and grazing area in one of the largest restoration projects of its kind in Europe. Cattle and sheep are being returned to the land to graze the reflooded pastures in a bid to bring back wildlife and save the soils, which have been disappearing at the rate of 2 cm a year.[44]

But the evidence is mounting to show that elsewhere soil is still in serious trouble.

According to a report by a government advisory body, the Committee on Climate Change (CCC), large areas of farmland in the United Kingdom are in danger of becoming unproductive within a generation due to declining soil health and erosion.[45] As a result, Britain is in danger of producing less food in the coming decades, just as demand is increasing. Farmers have been able to improve yields through technological advances, but there is mounting evidence that it is only a matter of time before productivity declines.

Lord Krebs, chairman of the CCC's adaptation subcommittee, has said: 'Soil is a very important resource which we have been very carefree with. At the moment we are treating our agricultural soils as though they are a mined resource – that we can deplete – rather than a stewarded resource that we have to maintain for the long-term future.'[46] Intensive agriculture is directly responsible for the problem, according to the CCC report, which says that 'deep ploughing, short-rotation periods and exposed ground' is leading to soil erosion from wind and heavy rain.[47]

The figures are stark. Since 1850, Britain has lost 84 per cent of its fertile topsoil, with erosion continuing at a rate of 1–3 cm a year. Given that soil can take hundreds of years to form,[48] these losses are not sustainable. Krebs has warned that the most fertile topsoils in the east of England – where 25 per cent of our potatoes and 30 per cent of our vegetables are grown – could be lost within a generation.[49]

Soil is the foundation of life on Earth. Without it we can't grow food, it's as simple as that. Yet, over the last half-century, industrial farming has treated it with disdain. As the environmental journalist George Monbiot put it:

'Imagine a wonderful world, a planet on which there was no threat of climate breakdown, no loss of freshwater, no antibiotic resistance, no obesity crisis, no terrorism, no war. Surely, then, we would be out of major danger? Sorry. If we don't address the issue of our deteriorating and disappearing soils, then we're finished.'[50]

So far from taking steps to protect what is left, policymakers are under intense pressure from vested interests focused on short-term gains to do nothing. A proposed European directive setting out rules to protect soil was withdrawn by the EU Commission in 2014 after Germany, France, the Netherlands, Austria and the UK formed a blocking minority against it. They argued that there was enough regulation already in this area. Farmers' groups had lobbied hard for the proposal to be scrapped.

Guy Smith, vice president of the UK's National Farmers Union (NFU), was reported as saying: 'Our long-held and firm belief has been that there is no need for additional legislation in this area – soils in the UK, and across the EU, are already protected by a range of laws and other measures.' He went on to say: 'Farmers have an inherent interest in maintaining their land in good condition and in assuring its long-term fertility and productivity.'[51]

On the face of it, this seems credible. If it were true, however, soil would not be in the desperate state it is today. The truth is that for most farmers, it's business as usual, because what remains of the British earth is still enough to keep going – for now. The question is what will be left for the next generation.

Writing in the *Guardian*, Monbiot rounded on the agricultural industry for blocking the move. 'Few sights are as gruesome as the glee with which the NFU celebrated the death last year of the European soil framework directive,' he said, describing it as the only measure with the potential to stop the growing crisis of soil erosion. 'The NFU, supported by successive British governments, fought for eight years to destroy it, then crowed like a shedful of cockerels when it won . . . Looking back on this episode, we will see it as a parable of our times.'

That same year, the UK farming press ran a story headlined: 'Only 100 harvests left in UK farm soils, scientists warn.'[52] The magazine article was waved by a concerned delegate from the floor of the prestigious Oxford Farming Conference. Agriculture Minister Liz Truss responded in all too predictable style by dodging his question, choosing instead to wax lyrical about the black fenland soils of her East Anglian constituency of South West Norfolk. It was down to Lord Krebs, a subsequent speaker, to point out how soon there might not be enough soil left in the Fens to eulogise over.

The prospect of fewer than one hundred remaining harvests is alarming enough, but time may run out even faster in other parts of the world. A recent UN report by 200 soil scientists in sixty countries concluded that the condition of most of the world's soils is only fair, poor or very poor, and is getting worse. According to the FAO, at current rates of depletion the world's topsoils could be gone within sixty years.[53]

There is an ancient Sanskrit quotation from 1500 BC which reads: 'Upon this handful of soil our survival depends. Husband it and it will grow our food, our fuel, and our shelter and surround us with beauty. Abuse it and the soil will collapse and die, taking humanity with it.'[54]

We forget this at our peril.

## MELTDOWN IN THE ANTHROPOCENE

Night-time. A piercing scream tore into the silence of the Arctic wilderness.

Matt Dyer, a 49-year-old legal attorney from Maine, had been asleep in his tent when the polar bear attacked. He opened his eyes to see the bear's forelegs looming over him, silhouetted against the light of the bright moon. He remembers crying out for help as the animal bore down on him, but his cries stopped when he felt his jaw break as the bear's teeth cut through his head and neck and the bear's mouth locked around the crown of his head.

'He was trying to get me out of my tent with his mouth, holding the tent down with his hands,' he recalls in one of many interviews about the terrifying attack.

Dyer was one of seven American hikers who set off on the wilderness adventure of a lifetime in summer 2013. They were dropped by seaplane at the edge of a breathtaking fjord in northern Canada to experience a place both pristine and magical – the sales ad called it 'a land of spirits and polar bears rarely seen by humans'.[55]

Dyer was dragged away, he explains, 'in the mouth of the bear', with his face banging against the bear's chest: 'I can remember looking out and I could see his belly, his leg and everything. He didn't take his claws to me, which is good.'

The adventurer was saved by quick-thinking companions who used a flaregun to startle the bear into dropping him and making a run for it.

Near the top of the world, just 530 miles from the Arctic Circle, the group was alone in polar-bear country, experiencing the terrifying consequences of the man-made meltdown that is driving starving polar bears to attack people.

Global warming is the wild card, the game-changer that threatens to throw a world already stretching planetary limits into chaos. Sea-level rises could see land disappear just when more is needed. It could disrupt the water cycle, just when freshwater is at a premium. And if there's still enough soil for planting, it could reduce crop yields across the globe by as much as a fifth.[56]

The world's governments gathered in Paris in December 2015 to strike an historic deal to limit global warming within the 2 degree Centigrade temperature rise deemed by scientists to be the 'safe' maximum level. Even at this level, scientists believe we could doom about a third or more of all land-based species of plants and animals to extinction.[57] A third or more! The figure bears repeating. Think about what that actually means: so many mammals, birds and plants gone for ever: a massacre of life's variety.

One thing is for sure – business as usual is not an option; not if we want to bequeath our children and grandchildren a world anything like as beautiful and plentiful as the one we inherited. Fuelled by runaway meat production, the way we produce food alone could take us to the brink. That's without the negative role of other industries, like energy and transport.

As the temperature creeps up, the world as we know it starts to change, just as it did during Lucy's day. Drastic changes are likely this century to water cycles, ecosystems and forests, which could mean whole forests disappearing and the Amazon turning to savannah or even desert. The world could be lashed by more severe storms, drought, floods and crop failures. This may sound apocalyptic, and it is; but it is only what leading climate authorities like the Intergovernmental Panel on Climate Change (IPCC) have been warning about.[58]

People are going to be deeply affected. Low-lying cities and regions could disappear underwater, including hundreds in America.[59] Bangladesh faces the threat of disappearance. Millions of 'climate migrants' are likely to be forced from their homelands by extremes of weather, crop failures, or conflicts over increasingly scarce resources.

These changes will be irreversible – and they're already happening.

Yet it doesn't have to be like this. As we'll see in the next chapter of this book, when it comes to how we produce and consume food, there are common-sense ways to change things for the better. Whether we choose those changes is down to us.

In my role as chief executive of the animal welfare charity Compassion in World Farming, my fear is that society may cling to business as usual for as long as possible. That would be human nature. After all, we – together with our growth-driven economics and political systems with brief five-year time horizons – seem all too often programmed to do what is in our own immediate interests, and perhaps those of our offspring.

The attachment to the status quo includes the way we keep farm animals. We could end the competition between farm animals and people for food, but instead, our choices mean that it intensifies. Governments talk of 'sustainable intensification', and that sounds good, but politicians are rarely, if ever, able to explain what it means. I can answer that question: it means more of the same – industrial farming – with a bit of greenwash. Meanwhile researchers look into making animals grow faster and bigger. More cows are kept indoors under the guise of 'managing' their emissions. Cages and corn-feeding continue to sweep the world as if they're a good idea.

There are reasons for this. Multi-billion-dollar industries benefit from intensification. Policymakers are stuck in a mindset that views industrial farming as some kind of bargain, producing lots at little cost. The true cost is deferred to future generations. We've been encouraged to 'live for today', partying on seemingly cheap meat subsidised by taxpayers and nature.

If *Homo sapiens* continue to produce, consume and waste food as they currently do, they will continue to be able to feed themselves for another few decades or so – but there'll be nothing left for nature.

Society could choose to keep animals ever more cruelly in a desperate attempt to keep things as they are. Or it could choose a better way, based on common sense and long-held wisdom, adapted for a modern world. I hope we choose that better way, not just for polar bears, barn owls, chickens and cows, but also for our children.

For the sake of generations to come, I hope we learn to treat animals better during the rest of the Anthropocene than we have done since it started.

Our future as a species may just depend on it.

## 15

# Living landscapes

### PASTURE FOR LIFE

I travelled several hours to rural Lincolnshire to visit the scene of a quiet revolution. As I leaned against the farm gate, I couldn't help thinking how there was nothing dramatic to look at. Just cows grazing. Yet, that was the point: they were *grazing*! After all the intensive farming I'd seen around the world in recent months, this was sweet relief.

Nothing extraordinary perhaps, but a wind of change was blowing through those fields. Here was a place where the agricultural rulebook was being turned in the right direction; where common sense was being restored to the way food is produced; where renegade farmers were fighting back against the notion that intensive farming rules and nature doesn't. And making it pay.

When I arrived at Little Bytham village I found it more steeped in railway history than in anything agricultural. The Willoughby Arms, a limestone hostelry opposite an abandoned railway station, used to be a booking office selling train tickets. Record-breaking feats by steam trains in the 1930s, first by the *Flying Scotsman* and then by the *Mallard*, are still talked about today. The last person old enough to actually witness those glory days of steam is Billy Windsor. He was five years old when the *Mallard* came full-throttle out of the nearby Stoke Tunnel, rocking scarily on its rails, straining every last rivet as it sped toward a record-breaking 126 miles per hour.

Yet it wasn't the huff and puff of railway history that I'd come to see, it was the cows. In the decades after the *Mallard*'s daring feat, farming started to change, to become more intensive. As a result, the landscape and increasing numbers of farm animals started to suffer. These 'modern' ways of farming may have felt like progress at the time, but their short-sightedness grows more and more apparent. Now, this quiet corner of the countryside is playing host to a new way of doing things that some see as the next cutting edge in agriculture.

Keen to learn more, I was out walking the fields before breakfast.

The sun struggled on a chill April morning as I wandered a scrubby raised bank. This unassuming promontory once hosted the private railway line of the late Lord Willoughby de Eresby, now remembered in the name of the local pub and my bed for the night. Either side of the bank were tussocky fields soon to be grazed by local cattle. A riotous hawthorn hedge had burst into a sea of white blossom. Ivy clung to stumps of hedgerows past. Spring was heralded by the sound of songbirds singing from a corner copse behind which the slow wash of the West Glen River ran into view. The ripples of the river led to a brick archway, a kind of watery underpass through what used to carry His Lordship's carriages.

As I stood scanning the fields, a local dog-walker with wellies and overcoat approached with a bouncy brown and white springer spaniel.

'It's great round here, en't it?' he said before passing the time of day. 'You're on the ball this morning,' he went on, looking at my notebook and camera. 'What you doin'?' I told him I was writing a book. 'Oh, great!' he replied. 'What on?'

'Living landscapes; how doing the right thing in farming brings landscapes to life,' I said, not wanting to get into the harm that factory farming does both to wildlife and ourselves so early in the morning.

'That'll be a good read!' he said with a reassuring smile, then wandered on.

After breakfast, I crossed a stone railway bridge and walked through a patchwork of crops and grassy fields divided by hedges and mature trees. Twenty minutes later, a cluster of cowsheds came into sight, straw bulging out of the sides, which was where I found John and Guy Turner busy with their early morning routine of bedding in the cattle. When John saw me coming, he bounded through the yard, to greet me with a smile and a warm handshake.

Wearing blue overalls and baseball cap, 54-year-old father of four John had plenty he wanted me to see. He and Guy are brothers and third-generation farmers on a hundred hectares of land. The farm has been in their family since the 1930s and those heady days of steam. Largely mixed crops and cattle, it also boasts permanent pastures that haven't seen the plough for decades.

In truth, I'd come about two weeks too early. Apart from the handful of cows I'd seen earlier, most were still in their winter quarters: roomy covered strawyards open to the fresh air. Late April, when the grass starts to grow properly, is when all the Turners' cows are turned out to graze. They then stay out until early November, when winter rain sets in.

Saler, Redpoll and Limousin-cross breeds of cattle, some jet-black, others reddy-ginger, stood with their calves – about eighty animals altogether. They watched me curiously as they reached out to munch on cut grass.

I couldn't help noticing their alert-looking eyes, ears pressed forward purposefully as their heads bobbed, swayed and nosed at the grass with obvious enthusiasm. They looked very different to the intensively reared cattle I'd seen in the UK, USA or South America, where so many hundreds if not thousands of mega-dairy cows looked tired and moved as if in slow motion; where the feed-lot beef cattle looked overcrowded, filthy and listless.

John Turner is co-founder of the Pasture-Fed Livestock Association (PFLA), a group of nearly a hundred farmers who are overturning one of the glaring myths in modern farming: that raising cows and other ruminant farm animals successfully means feeding them grain.

Pasture containing grasses, wildflowers and herbs is, of course, the age-old diet of cattle and sheep. Yet today, very few animals are fed on pasture alone. Many farmers now try to produce their meat as quickly as possible, by feeding things like cereals and soya, keeping them indoors for some or all of the time. So animals have vanished from our fields, and the tasty, healthy, grass-fed food they produce has become hard to find.

The Turners are bucking the trend: their cows have the pick of the farm's plantlife. I picked up handfuls of what the cows were eating – cut grass and clover from surrounding fields – and lifted it to my nose, breathing in the rich, herby smell. I could almost have eaten it myself, it smelt that good. Although John called it 'silage', the stuff looked more like straw and didn't have that pungent, acrid smell I've come to associate with the fermented grass silage of industrial farms.

John explained the difference between what he's doing and the way of the industrialists. 'Conventional farms see silage as the filler, and the food coming from [grain-based] concentrates,' he said. The Turners make much of their credentials for feeding their cattle only grass, so I pushed them on it. I looked them both in the eye and asked if they ever fed cows concentrates like corn, soya or other grains.

'Never,' they said in unison.

'Not a single grain?'

'Never,' they insisted. 'It's not a natural diet for the animal and they're not particularly efficient at converting it to meat. It can cause stress and pressure on the animal, taking them beyond their natural capacity to cope, which has an impact on their welfare. The quality of the meat and milk too is far better when they're not on concentrates.'

Which is why John and Guy market their produce as 'Pasture for Life', a certification mark only available to those who raise their animals a hundred per cent on the green leaves of pasture through-out the animal's lifetime.

They decided to set up their own 'Pasture for Life' label to distinguish themselves from what has become the much looser understanding for terms such as grass-fed: that the animal concerned should be fed primarily on grass in the field.[1] Fed *primarily* on grass from the field is a step in the right direction, of course, but not the same as *solely* on grass. Studies have shown that even small amounts of grain fed to an animal at the end of her life can have a big negative impact on the quality of the eventual food.

John pointed out how his cows eat more than grass: they browse the trees and hedges around the field, picking those minerals and other nutrients they want, self-medicating as they go. The contented lifestyle, along with a rich and varied diet, means that the cows rarely need the vet, they told me. On the odd occasion when a vet is called, it tends to be for something like a calving difficulty or an accidental injury. John jokes about how his veterinary medicine cabinet is pretty empty – no routine antibiotics or other things you might find on industrial farms: 'We just don't have any, which is good for us and good for the cattle.'

The Turners are particularly proud of how the grazing cattle move round the farm in rotation with their crops. Arranged in seven-year cycles, their rotation consists of fields being planted with wheat in the first year, barley the next, then oats for the third year. The cereal crops take a lot of the nutrients out of the soil. Instead of resorting to artificial fertiliser, the Turners leave the fields to grow grass and clover for the next four years, and their cattle graze on it. In this way, a patchwork of fields develops on the farm with a blend of crops and grass of different ages.

For them, grazing represents the recovery period for the soil. Nitrogen, the essential building block of life, is restored in the soil by clover, a common grassland member of the leguminous pea family which has nitrogen-fixing bacteria in the swellings of its roots. The cows do their bit too by scattering manure across the field, which also helps build soil fertility for future harvests.

'By having grass and grazing animals on the farm, we're putting fertility back into the soil,' John said. Grass also helps to remove unwanted weeds from the soil, so there's no need for chemical herbicides. Their rotational grazing system means that even when soils are being regenerated, the farm continues to earn an income from the animals raised on grass.

The Turners' mixed rotational farm stands out from the arable monocultures more the norm in this part of Lincolnshire. Much of the surrounding farmland is turned over to wheat and oilseed rape.

I was keen to hear what wildlife made of bringing farm animals back into the mix.

John told me: 'There's been a massive increase in the amount of wildlife: butterflies, day moths, bees . . . kites, buzzards, kestrels, barn owls . . . in order for these to thrive and stay on the farm, you've got to have the foodweb beneath them. You've got to have the small mammals, and for the small mammals to thrive, you've got to have the insects and worms and that sort of thing,'

I asked whether their more chemical-driven neighbours viewed things as a bit of a competition. John laughed.

'We watch our neighbours flying around, putting all these chemicals on,' he told me with a grin. He recounted how one neighbour – a large arable farmer using lots of chemicals – had given them some winter wheat seed and was keen to see how they managed with it.

There couldn't be much more difference in the way the two farmed. John told me how his neighbour was always busy with his chemical applications and so on: 'His sprayer is rarely in the yard, he's just out constantly with it . . .' The neighbour probably expected his yields to be dramatically higher than those achieved by the Turners, given how they put in much less effort and no chemicals.

They compared yields after harvest. 'We'd got two and a half tonne [of wheat] an acre off it,' John told me. As for the neighbour? 'He wasn't very happy . . . he'd spent all year putting all these chemicals and fertilisers on and he'd got three tonnes.'

The neighbour had clearly expected a much bigger difference.

I asked John whether chemical farming affects the soil.

'I think it has a huge impact,' he said. 'We see the contrast because there are a lot of arable people in the area, and over the last twenty years we've definitely seen a degradation in terms of the soils on surrounding farms . . . We're now seeing rills [shallow channels in the soil] forming where the soil structure has completely disappeared, and that's washing then into the streams and rivers.'

When soil washes off exposed fields, it runs into rivers and causes them to silt up.

'When you're having to dredge rivers to keep them clean, you're taking an awful lot of the life out of the stream as well,' John explained.

Yet, after all is said and done, the question many will ask is: Does it pay?

More intensive producers are spending a significant proportion of their income on inputs like grain-based feed, a big contrast to the cheaper, more stable cost attached to grass.

John's conclusion was that: 'We are totally in control of our input costs, we know what our rent is going to be, we know what the cost of the [grass] seed is going to be, we know our forage costs . . . it's counter-intuitive, but by doing less, by taking the foot off the pedal a bit, it's actually a more productive farm, and definitely more sustainable.'

A recent study showed that pasture-fed livestock farmers like the Turners are able to make as much if not more than anyone else in the country.[2]

The PFLA worked with the UK's statutory body charged with improving farm efficiency, the Agriculture and Horticultural Development Board (AHDB), to benchmark its members' performance and finance data against other producers across the industry. Although a small sample size, the results spoke for themselves.

When the report was launched at the Oxford Real Farming Conference in 2016,[3] its co-author, and senior lecturer at the Royal Agricultural University (Cirencester), Jonathan Brunyee, explained to a packed audience that, compared with farms that feed grain to their animals, the cost of feeding grass is much lower. Costs are reduced still further by the effect of keeping animals in a more natural environment. They tend to be healthier, so vets' bills are lower too.

Pasture-fed systems for sheep are finding that their profits match those of other producers within the top third of English sheep herds. The story for beef cattle is even better, and comes at a time when most beef farmers in England are losing money. 'The only farmers making money [from beef cattle] are those that are pasture-fed and selling direct' to the consumer, Brunyee reported.

The fusion of lower costs and a more natural brand is lending momentum to pasture-fed farming. 'While the average livestock farm is losing money,' Brunyee said, '"Pasture for Life" farmers are profitable . . . And that is without taking into account other benefits that could be given a value – such as the storage of carbon in grassland and providing wildlife habitat.'

Globally, pasture covers about a quarter of the planet's land surface. In Britain, nearly two-thirds of all farmland is pasture. With so much grass, doesn't Britain have the potential to become a leader in pasture-fed animal rearing?

'Without a doubt, the potential is huge,' Brunyee responded. 'The way grass-fed is growing, we could produce as many livestock [this way] with all the environmental and social benefits too.'

The pasture farmers I've spoken to are forward-thinking and see this as the practice of the future. Yet pasture-based farming is nothing new: most farm animals used to be reared this way, and in many parts of the world they still are. During my travels I've seen animals reared on glorious pastures in the USA, from ranches in the Midwest to the grasslands of Georgia. I've also seen some of the most impressive pasture-rearing of cattle on the grassy plains of the Pampas and across the Brazilian Cerrado.

I've found that raising animals on pasture as part of the mix never really went away, it simply became eclipsed by a more industrial approach. It fell out of favour, to be replaced by feeding confined animals on grain, or what I call 'factory farming'.

This switch seems to have been driven in part by the animal-feed industry, selling industrial grain crops to a new generation of factory farmers. It is almost as if the food system has been hijacked by the feed industry. Now seems as good a time as any for its rescue.

## FEEDING THE WORLD

Nature loves diversity, but will it feed the world?

That was the question I took with me on my first visit to South Africa in 2014, where I met leading figures in the food and farming debate. No longer the sole domain of richer countries, industrial farming is now sweeping developing countries too, all under the guise of food security, that bogus mantra of being 'needed to feed the world'.

I was launching my book *Farmageddon* in South Africa, and had a whole tour of media and speaking engagements arranged. I'd prepared well and thought through all the reasons why factory farming was as much a bad idea for Africa as it had been for Britain, Europe, America and elsewhere.

I admit I was nervous. I wondered what kind of reception awaited me. Would I be seen as something of a lone voice? Would people even listen? Would I face open hostility?

As it turned out, I needn't have worried. People in South Africa were just as shocked at the idea of having factory farms in their country as anywhere else I'd been in the world. As well as paying heed to animal welfare and the environmental effects, they understood that, in a country struggling with massive unemployment, replacing lots of small farmers with a few industrial farms would only make matters worse.

What I found was a surprising openness to the idea that land-based farming is better all round: for people, animals and the environment, and for the future well-being of us as a species.

Amid my whistle-stop series of meetings with government officials, religious leaders, retail bosses, farmers' representatives and the like, I also spoke to an invited audience at Johannesburg's famous Constitutional Court. On Constitutional Hill overlooking the city, South Africa's highest court sits on the 100-acre site of a century-old prison complex where the leaders of every major South African social justice movement – Mahatma Gandhi and Nelson Mandela among them – were once detained. Officially opening the Court in 1995, President Nelson Mandela said: 'The last time I appeared in court was to hear whether or not I was going to be sentenced to death. Fortunately for myself and my colleagues we were not.'

Hugely aware of the weight of historic struggles represented by the building, I rose to my feet in the grand auditorium keen to put industrial agriculture in the dock. I wasn't the only one. Beside me was Professor David Bilchitz, director of the South African Institute for Advanced Constitutional, Public, Human Rights and International Law (SAIFAC).

Bilchitz described factory farming as 'neither good for humans, animals or the environment. On the human front, South Africa needs the growth of small-scale farming, which can help improve the livelihoods of rural South Africans.' In his view: 'Factory farming is devastating for animal welfare. It treats animals like units in an industrial process . . . and has no regard for their intrinsic value.' Bilchitz also sees it as devastating for the environment, causing 'massive' pollution and huge emissions of greenhouse gases.

My day in the Constitutional Court left me in no doubt that people in South Africa were also joining the global movement, questioning the wisdom of industrial farming. I also discovered how, in South Africa as in many other countries, consumers are starting to become aware of what's happening.

Jeanne Groenewald is the founder of Elgin Free Range Chickens, a farm business outside Cape Town. She spoke passionately about the bright future she sees for free-range farming in South Africa. New mums especially, she told me, are becoming more aware of what they buy and what they're feeding their children. For her, it all started out of concern for what to feed her own family. She had grown more and more worried about the health impact of processed foods, to the point where she refused point-blank to feed her children any mass-produced chemically enhanced meat. That was when she decided to experiment with free-range chicken.

After tasting what she described as her 'plump and healthy' chickens, friends and family started placing orders: '"Where did you get these?" they would ask. They were blown away that I'd reared them myself.'

We took off in Groenewald's truck to see the farm, tucked among forested hillsides under a clear blue sky. 'Safe food starts here' said the farmgate sign. Behind it were chickens scattered everywhere, some lying on the grass enjoying the sun, others under the shade of a tree. Yet more were pecking beside long, open-sided barns where they would sleep at night.

Keen to avoid feeding her chickens routine antibiotics, she paid close attention to their rearing conditions. Her recipe for healthy chickens, she told me, is to reduce any stress in their lives by giving them plenty of space, fresh air, good food, and not pushing them too hard to grow fast.

'If you remove stress from the bird, they build their own immunity,' she said.

Elgin now produces nearly 90,000 chickens a week from several farms, selling to major retailers like Woolworths as well as direct to consumers.

I was struck by how South Africa, like Europe and the USA, is seeing a surge of interest in free-range and pasture-based farming. Woolworths, which has about 10 per cent of the grocery market in South Africa, is clearly proud of its free-range produce. I walked past their busy supermarket aisles to get to the chicken counter. There I found a big photo of an engaging farmer among outdoor chickens. It was all part of the store's marketing to draw attention to the shelves of free-range chicken, including some of Groenewald's birds.

While free-range rearing is taking off, I wondered how much scope there is – in Britain for example – for all meat chickens to be out roaming in the fields. After all, as one British poultry industry spokesman suggested, wouldn't we be knee-deep in chickens? Britain rears nearly a billion chickens for meat every year, almost all of them indoors and intensively. Very few meat chickens ever get to venture outside, even though nearly three-quarters of the entire British land surface is agricultural, and much of it pasture.

Despite the huge number of chickens produced each year in Britain, and indeed the world, the actual space they take up is deceptively small. To qualify for the 'free-range' label in the UK and Europe, chickens each have to be allocated at least a square metre of outside space. On that basis, the UK's whole stock of meat chickens could be reared free-range on much less than 1 per cent of available pasture. In fact, little more than one acre in a thousand would be needed for chickens to accommodate them all.[4]

And with far fewer laying hens, there is plenty of room outside for them too. And why keep chickens on their own anyway? Why not mix it up a bit, put them out on the grassland alongside sheep or cattle as part of the rotation? In South Africa, I discovered a farmer doing just that.

I drove 30 miles or so out of Cape Town to the Spier estate, part of the famous Cape Winelands in the shadow of the Hottentots Holland Mountain range. Here I met Angus McIntosh, a farmer who believes firmly in rearing animals on grass.

Now in his early forties, McIntosh used to work in the UK as a stockbroker, but gave it all up because he didn't want to bring up children in a 'Goldman Sachs lifestyle'. We chatted inside his tailor-made clay farmhouse with its rounded corners, smooth vanilla walls and wooden shutters. Pure white florets on frangipani trees looked stunning against the covered patio. We were sheltering from the heat of the day, drinking coffee and smearing honey from an unfeasibly large jar over delicious spelt muffins.

McIntosh is no stranger to food and farming, having grown up on a cattle ranch in Kwa-Zulu Natal, South Africa, and having in-laws, he told me, who own Nando's, the South African multinational chicken restaurant company.

After beverages and homemade bakes, we were out on his 126-hectare farm with his 3,000 or so laying hens and mixed herd of cattle. Under the orange glow of late afternoon sunlight, and with a refreshing breeze brushing my face, I walked across the pasture to where cattle were grazing. As I did, a flock of curious chickens ran toward me, pecking lightly at my shoelaces, trouser bottoms and anything else they could reach.

The cattle were a mixed herd of Limousin cross and Angus breeds reared for beef. The sandy-tan coloured cows, some with white faces, are moved to new pasture four times a day in a rotational system known as 'mob grazing' and designed to mimic the behaviour of bison herds; the herd can feed on part of the field for a few hours before being moved on.

Hens follow the cattle, pecking bugs out of cowpats as they go. They roost in moveable chicken coops that McIntosh calls 'eggmobiles', like large igloo tents on runners to make shifting them easier.

As I stood with McIntosh surveying his busy mix of cattle and chickens, he told me how his system helps restore soil fertility and stores carbon out of the atmosphere, thereby helping to combat climate change. 'The overriding principle is that we are custodians of the land and we need to ensure that at all times fertility is improving on the farm,' he said.

The Turners had told me something similar about their farm too. Why then is there such a big push by some away from this type of farming?

Perhaps the biggest reason cited by those in favour of industrial farming is the need to produce more food to feed a growing world population. Faced with the prospect of billions more mouths to feed in decades to come, they suggest, 'we have no choice' but to intensify.

I asked McIntosh what he makes of this kind of argument.

'That ludicrous canard is only believed by the media, agricultural institutions and those working for the agricultural chemical companies,' he said angrily, before going on to insist that we are already producing much more food in the world than needed now or in decades to come.

Yet, under the guise of terms like 'sustainable intensification', producing more food seems to have become an obsession with many of the world's policymakers. The latest round of 'produce more' panic seemed to have been sparked off in 2009 by the chief of the United Nations Food and Agriculture Organisation, who warned that world food production must double by 2050 to 'head off mass hunger'.[5] That warning was seized upon by those in favour of industrial farming as the perfect justification for more of the same.

In December 2013, just months before my trip to South Africa, a new report on tackling the coming food crisis was launched in Johannesburg. Published jointly by the United Nations, the World Bank and the World Resources Institute (WRI), the report warned that the world needs 70 per cent more food (in terms of calories) to feed a global population of 9.6 billion in 2050.[6] It called for crop and livestock productivity to be boosted on existing farmland, providing yet more impetus it seemed for 'sustainable intensification'.

However, on reading the report, I noticed a gentle retreat from the previously held position centred squarely on 'Produce more or we starve'. A 'menu' of ideas was put forward to help close the 'food gap' between today's need and that foreseen by mid-century. These included tackling food waste and shifting diets away from the over-consumption of resource-sapping animal products.[7]

Today, about a quarter of calories from food grown for human consumption is commonly lost, or wasted through being thrown away. The 2013 report suggested that cutting the rate of food loss and waste in half would help close this food gap. UN Under-Secretary General and United Nations Environment Programme (UNEP) Executive Director Achim Steiner described the waste of over 1.3 billion tons of food every year, worth around US$1 trillion, as causing 'significant' economic losses, while placing 'added pressure on the natural resources needed to feed the planet'.

The report also highlighted the need to reduce excessive demand for animal products, particularly by developed countries. In this way, hundreds of millions of hectares of forests could be spared from clearance for new farmland.[8]

In a clear warning against taking nature for granted, Steiner talked about the 'steep environmental price' that would be paid if the ecological foundation of food systems were undermined, including adverse impacts on land, water, biodiversity and climate change. 'To bring about the vision of a truly sustainable world, we need to transform the way we produce and consume our natural resources,' he concluded. 'The restoration of ecosystems will not only increase the amount of food produced but also improve the state of the environment upon which food production is dependent.'

Steiner's message seemed clear: mess with the environment at our peril.

Being careful with food and producing it in an ecologically sound way seems to square with this new, more nuanced message from the UN. However, I was still puzzled by quite how the world's leading authority on food, the United Nations Food and Agriculture Organisation, arrived in the first place at its original conclusion that food *production* needed to 'double' to stave off a global food crisis.

When I interrogated the FAO's own data, the total crop harvest for 2014 provided enough calories to feed 15.8 billion people.[9] In addition, scientists have worked out that 30 per cent of the current amount of meat, milk and eggs produced in the world could be produced from grazing on pasture unsuitable for cropping, plus crop residues and processing byproducts that are not suited to feeding people.[10] If we add these two together – the crop harvest and meat, milk and eggs from pasture-based grazing – the total food basket before food waste is large enough to feed more than 16 billion people, which is much more than enough food for everyone today and in the foreseeable future.

So why talk of a looming food crisis?

Well, as Steiner points out, part of the answer lies in the vast quantities of food currently lost or wasted. About a quarter of the entire food basket of the world – enough to feed an extra 3.9 billion people – is wasted by being binned or left to rot.[11] As well as huge amounts of fruit and vegetables, the global food-waste mountain includes the meat equivalent of about 12 billion farm animals a year: reared, slaughtered and binned. Effectively, an incredible one in six farm animals globally is wasted in this way.

To me, that seems like the most shocking waste of life, not to mention of land cleared of forests and precious wildlife habitats to produce the food in the first place.

The United Nations is right to stress the need to reduce food waste, and we can all play a part by simply eating what we buy. However, the biggest reason for the world being short-changed by its food basket is often overlooked: feeding more than a third of food crops globally to farm animals.[12]

Let us be clear: feeding human-edible crops – grains like corn and soya – to industrially reared animals is just as much food waste as that unwanted ham sandwich, discarded pizza or chicken leftovers thrown in the bin.

Some 35 per cent of the world's cereal harvest and most of its soya meal is fed to industrially reared animals – enough to feed around 4.8 billion people. Yet as we have seen in previous chapters, animals reared on grain give much less food back in the form of meat, milk or eggs than they consume.[13] The bottom line is that feeding crops to industrially reared animals wastes food, rather than makes it.

None of this is to suggest that everyone must eat more grain. What it does highlight is the sheer inefficiency of feeding farm animals on crops that could be feeding people; or, more properly, from *croplands* that should be growing food for people. With so much of the world's land surface covered in pasture, common sense must surely back returning animals to the land, where they can add to the global food basket, rather than reduce it.

A scientific study in 2014 identified grazing on pasture and the use of crop residues as efficient forms of feeding animals. The study found that together these could support about a third of current global livestock production. The remaining 70 per cent produced industrially was described as a 'very inefficient use of land to produce food'.[14]

While herbivores like cows and sheep are biologically attuned to living on a diet of grass, pigs and poultry are not. They are omnivorous, eating a wide range of both plant and animal food.

However, while grain in their diet may be good for them, there are ways of reducing the amount they eat, for example by allowing pigs and poultry to forage in fields, woodlands or yards where they can find food for themselves; or by integrating them as part of grazing rotations with cattle, as on McIntosh's farm, where chickens can peck bugs from cowpats, eat grass, worms, seeds and other natural things, instead of just monotonous pellets of grain.

Perhaps the best example I've seen of this was in Georgia, USA, at the farm of an extraordinary man named Will Harris. I was astonished to see his chickens, ducks and guinea fowl following sheep, which themselves followed cattle in the most magnificent rotational pasture operation. My days spent at Harris's White Oak Pastures fired my enthusiasm to see animals restored to the land in this way.

And why not restore chickens to the historic role for which they are supremely adapted – recycling food waste? Chickens can be great food-waste recyclers. An estimated 500,000 British households now keep chickens in their backyards, including celebrities like Jamie Oliver, Jeremy Clarkson, Amanda Holden and Sadie Frost.[15] As I know from my own backyard flock of hens, they love nothing more than gobbling up food scraps. In return, we get delicious eggs fresh every day. Much better than scraping leftover food into the bin.

Perhaps the supreme recycler of food waste is the pig.

For thousands of years pigs have been man's perfect partner in consuming the waste that humans produce and converting it straight into calories as pork. By far the most efficient thing to do with food waste – on food efficiency and environmental grounds – is to feed it directly to pigs. Around twenty times more carbon dioxide emissions can be saved by feeding food waste to pigs rather than sending it for anaerobic digestion (the next-best recycling option). Of course, any unwanted food destined for the commercial feeding of animals would need to be properly treated to prevent disease, but this can be done. In Japan, South Korea and Taiwan, laws encourage using food waste to feed pigs. Yet, under European laws, feeding most food waste to pigs is banned.[16]

Keeping chickens and pigs outside where they can forage and feed on food waste could be part of a stepwise approach to a food system based on common sense. Expecting the world to move in a trice from where it is now to a scenario where no human-edible grain is ever fed to a farm animal would clearly be unrealistic. However, big strides can be taken that would make all the difference in finding enough 'extra' food to feed the coming billions.

Reducing the amount of food waste in all its forms globally by half would go an enormous way toward closing the 'food gap'. If we could cut by half the amount of food wasted through being binned or left to rot, it would free up enough food for nearly 2 billion extra people. Another 2 billion people's worth of food could be freed up by halving the amount of grain fed to farm animals. Together, these actions would swell the world's food basket enough to feed an extra 4 billion people without the need for a hectare more of farmland. That is far more than enough to cover the expected human population growth by the end of the century, let alone 2050.

The question then is much less about *producing* more food, but using it wisely.

## BRINGING LANDSCAPES TO LIFE

When you close your eyes and imagine where the very best food comes from, what does it look like?

In my experience, most people imagine rolling pastures sprinkled with cattle or sheep grazing under the warmth of the sun; orchards with chickens; patchworks of fields; golden swaying crops of corn, wheat or barley; the buzzing of bees. They think of diverse landscapes, the kind of place you wouldn't mind visiting, a view to admire. That sense of what feels right turns out to be ethical as well as aesthetic – and monocultures come nowhere near meeting it.

What I've discovered through my travels for this book is that when we restore animals to the land in the right way – in well-managed, mixed rotational farms – amazing things can happen. Landscapes start coming back to life. There can be a cascade of positive benefits for farmers, consumers, the local environment, forests both near and far, and for animal welfare too.

Free-ranging animals on pasture can run and jump and stretch their legs and wings. They can scratch and graze and peck and root. They can feel fresh air and sunshine, roll in grass, bathe in dust or wallow in cooling wet mud. They can express their nature, enjoy that freedom to behave normally, something viewed as so important by the internationally recognised guidelines known as the 'Five Freedoms'.[17]

And this gift of freedom matters so much to them. I can see just how much every morning when I let our hens out at home by the way they burst out of the coop with a flurry of excitement. I could see it too in the curiosity of McIntosh's chickens, in Groenewald's sunbathing birds, and in the eyes of Turner's cows.

And is it really too much to ask? After all, animals just want the space and scope to be themselves. And allowing them to do so brings more contented animals with better immunity and less disease.

Returning animals to the farm, as I learned during my time with McIntosh, Harris and the Turners, can help soils regenerate too. The age-old nitrogen cycle comes back into play: sunlight, soil, plants and the droppings of farm animals work together to return fertility to the soil. Cowpats from naturally healthy animals (without chemical treatments) become hives of life – harbouring numerous insects, like dung beetles that thrive on taking parcels of poo underground to further enrich the soil.

Healthier soils encourage all sorts of creatures in a magical circle of life, from earthworms and oribatid mites to springtails and a whole host of tiny microscopic creatures.

Small they may be, but their contribution to our survival can be huge. They play key roles in maintaining fertility, structure, drainage and aerated soils, breaking down plant and animal tissues, releasing stored nutrients and converting them into forms that plants can use. Earthworms can multiply, perhaps the most important topsoil creatures, mixing soil and nutrients together, stirring up essential ingredients for healthy plant growth.

Restoring animals to the land in mixed, rotational systems, as Tim May discovered in earlier chapters – breathing new life into tired soils – brings benefits to crop yields and the overall sustainability of the system. It can reduce reliance on chemical pesticides and fertilisers, encourage more plants, insects and other farmland wildlife.

The landscape now grows more varied, bursting with plants and flowers, luring back indispensable pollinating insects like bumblebees, along with hoverflies, butterflies, beetles and moths. This revitalised landscape provides patches of cover, homes for voles and other small creatures that also offer a living to barn owls and other predatory birds. Seeds and insects provide food for farmland birds to thrive once again, sustaining them through the harshness of winter and feeding hungry chicks during the summer.

Grasses with their mass of deep roots and perennial growth help reduce the amount of soil and nutrients washed away by the rain, and hold more water too. Their deeper roots enable them to tap into water sources shorter-rooted plants can't reach, so that landscapes grow resistant to drought as well as to flood.

With less soil erosion and nutrient pollution come cleaner rivers less likely to silt up. Natural communities of flora and fauna have a chance to revive, like water crowfoot, starwort and water celery on chalkstreams, providing home to all manner of aquatic creatures as well as cover, shade and refuge for fish. These, together with insects like the mayfly, encourage fish like the native brown trout in a web of life graced by the scurry of the water vole.

Rearing animals on pastures rather than grain crops takes less water from rivers and aquifers for irrigation. Switching from grain-feeding, which is forty times more water-intensive than grass, helps relieve some of the relentless demand on hard-pressed water courses.

Reducing the clamour for more farmland by cutting down on grain-fed farm animals, plus easing off on resource-intensive meat, can cut the risk to remaining forests. Trees that might otherwise go the way of the chainsaw are free to carry on removing carbon from the atmosphere and returning oxygen for us to breathe.

And at the same time we gain healthier, more nutritious food. Animals fed on grass – the fruit of a timeless interaction between sun, rain and soil – provide meat lower in saturated fats and higher in health-giving nutrients like omega-3s. And wherever I go in the world, the one thing people consistently say about food from the land is that it tastes so much better, has so much more flavour.

In crossing continents, talking to the people behind our food, I've discovered that when animals are returned to the land in the right way, in well-managed mixed and rotational farms, whole landscapes spring to life.

Helping to revive a living countryside can be as easy as choosing to eat less and better meat, milk and eggs from pasture-fed, free-range or organic animals.

Through our food choices three times a day, we can support the best animal welfare and bring landscapes to life.

# 16

# Nightingale

I stood spellbound and drank in the birdsong.

'*So, so, so . . . huit, huit, huit . . .*' First one and then another, in sonic duels of clicks and rippling whistles.

From a wooden terrace high in a mature oak, I scoured the trees for a glimpse of these sweet singers, though more in hope than expectation. They were too well camouflaged, and besides, I was distracted by the sight of a group of red deer picking their delicate way across an earthy hollow, snatching at vegetation and playfully tussling as they went.

It was thrilling – and all the more so because it was so unexpected. I was on a safari that I simply hadn't seen coming; a farm visit like no other. Farms are my bread and butter. I have been to hundreds. This was something else.

In the farmer's jeep, we trundled across scrubby grassland, passing blackthorn and dog-rose bushes and trees of young oak, alder and willow. The late April day was glorious – warm sunshine, light breeze, joyful birdsong. Crazy as it sounds, it felt as if we could almost be in Africa, and not just a train hop from London, near the southeast coast of England.

Ten years ago, it all looked very different. Knepp Castle Estate, near West Grinstead, West Sussex, was the sort of farm this book is all about: thousands of acres surrendered to intensive arable cultivation, boosted by truckloads of artificial fertilisers, the fields thinly divided by tightly clipped hedges.

The owner, Charlie Burrell, had been running the estate since he was twenty-one years old. He was no stranger to the work, for both his grandfather and great-grandfather before him were presidents of the Royal Agriculture Society of England (RASE) and champion redpoll cattle breeders. He himself studied at the Royal Agricultural College, Cirencester.

By his own admission, from the moment he took over the farm in 1987 he worked the land hard in pursuit of 'maximisation', squeezing the soil to the utmost. The farm drew its income from cereal crops, as well as a 600-strong dairy herd, beef cattle, sheep – and of course, generous subsidies. For decades the going was good, but the weather and vagaries of the commodity market began to take their toll and the overdraft kept climbing.

'It was like an endless cycle of pumping more and more money into the infrastructure to continue farming in this sort of industrial way,' he told me. 'Because you're always having to buy a new combine, or put in a dairy plant, or new regulations come in on dirty water or whatever it is.' Despite all the modern equipment, the chemical inputs and subsidies, it just didn't pay. 'I suppose on average we made £150,000 a year, but we always spent at least £200,000 a year in terms of capital.'

Only generous government subsidies kept it afloat. 'It certainly became clear in the mid-Nineties that it was not going to work for ever,' he reflected.

It was around this time that he met a group of naturalists whose ideas would be transformative, both for him and for the estate. They inspired him with accounts of how big wild animals once shaped the landscape of much of Europe through grazing. Animals like bison, aurochs (wild cattle), tarpan (wild horse) and deer would graze the lowlands, creating scrubby grasslands instead of the dense, mature forests that once covered the continent. These grazing animals literally shaped the ecology, the natural habitat, bringing landscapes to life in a way since long forgotten, until now.

It was one of those clichéd light-bulb moments. The very next year, Burrell did something amazing: he switched it all off, stopped farming and let nature come back. No more ploughing and planting, hedge-trimming or harvesting. He left the land to find its own way. Burrell decided to be led by nature, rather than controlling it, an approach he calls 'process-led conservation' or 'self-willed land'. Knepp became a totally different place.

Now in his early fifties, Burrell has become renowned as the figure behind one of the biggest lowland 'rewilding' projects in Europe. It transpires that what he is doing here is unique: it is the only example in Europe of an industrialised farming system deliberately being returned to scrubland. The new business model has involved opening the estate to visitors, who can take 'wildland safaris' in open-sided vehicles and camp – or rather 'glamp' – in luxurious bell tents.

Animals on the estate – longhorn cattle, fallow, roe and red deer, Exmoor ponies and Tamworth pigs – are near to the type of breeds that would have grazed the land thousands of years ago. They are carefully managed to ensure that they help maintain the vegetation. It is a delicate process: too many animals, and the land would be grazed bare, turned into an open plain. Too few, and the estate would soon be overrun with dense growths of shrubs and trees.

I was intrigued as to what it would all look like. Frankly, I didn't expect much – maybe some overgrown fields and scrambling woods. I couldn't have got it more wrong.

Initial impressions were deceptive: the approach to Knepp is via a well-manicured deer park with acres of perfectly kept lawns. Visitors then arrive at what looks like a proper old-fashioned castle, complete with turrets and battlements. Set within a 3,500-acre estate, the 1806 property was the work of architect John Nash, best known for designing Brighton Pavilion and Buckingham Palace. I got out of the car wondering if I was wasting my time.

I was led through darkened corridors lined with paintings of occupants past to meet my host, Charlie Burrell. Only a few hours earlier he'd been on a sleeper coming back from Scotland, where he'd been meeting other rewilding enthusiasts. He looked tired but relaxed, and for a while we sat chatting in his office. On the walls hung butterfly collections in glass cases and rows of deer antlers.

His secretary brought mugs of coffee, but I sensed that Burrell didn't want to linger: he was itching to show me around. Reluctantly, I left the coffee and we set off in his 4x4. I've done many a farm tour where I've sallied forth to see cows in this field, sheep in that one, all neat and tidy. And very predictable. This was to be less of a tour than a safari: animals here are either wild or might as well be, so seeing them would be a matter of luck. Burrell is generating a decent income from the concept, with Knepp 'wildland' safaris for tourists a significant enterprise in themselves.

We passed a group of Exmoor ponies, brown with long black tails, grazing on open grass. They were part of Burrell's grand scheme, a ranching system that has involved reintroducing grazing animals to mimic the way it used to be. We drove on. I hadn't imagined the estate to be quite so big: 3 miles at its widest point and a full 4 miles long.

We reached an old cattle yard which has been converted into a centre for safari-goers. It also serves as an upmarket shower block for glampers staying in the tents, tepees and gypsy caravans. There was also a small farm shop selling 'Knepp wild range organic produce', including venison and longhorn beef. A sofa and easy chairs surrounded a makeshift coffee table fashioned from an old wooden cable-reel turned on its side.

Hanging from a wall was a chalk board heralding the coming of spring and the latest sightings: cuckoo, kingfisher, spotted flycatcher and . . . nightingale.

Penny Green from the Sussex Wildlife Trust works on the estate and told me about the wildlife she'd been monitoring here for the past decade. The Trust is trying to encourage what they call 'landscape-scale conservation', gathering groups of neighbouring landowners who own sections of the same rivers, streams and hedges and helping them work together. It's a way to overcome the limitations of focusing on small, isolated pockets of land, and so create something much bigger. In future, the Trust wants to become even more ambitious, crossing county boundaries.

She told me we were unlikely to see cuckoos, because many were still in Africa, seeing out the tail end of the British winter, but she felt spring was well on its way. They had seen turtle doves on the estate recently. Nationally, the species is in serious decline, but Knepp is now home to more pairs than in all the land owned by the National Trust. Green told me excitedly that there were also six nightingales on the estate, with more expected.

Nightingales don't look anything special: they are nondescript fawn-coloured birds about the size of a robin. But then you rarely get to see them. They like hiding deep in bushes, from where they emit the most beautiful sound.

'So, so, so . . . huit, huit, huit . . .'

Their song seems so deliberate, so pitch-perfect, so precise, that I am always mesmerised when I hear it.

I saw my first nightingale as a teenager. I remember the day as if decades had not intervened. I was in Suffolk during my August summer holidays at the RSPB's flagship nature reserve, Minsmere. It flitted past me like a blackbird, giving me a flash of its reddish-brown tail before disappearing – characteristically – into a thick bush, never to be seen again. I didn't get to hear one sing until the following spring, when I was on a visit to Northward Hill in Kent. I knew what I was listening for, because I'd familiarised myself with the sound on a vinyl record of classic birdsong given to me by my grandad. That day in mid-May, I heard it, the sound imprinted on my mind from the record: 'So, so, so . . . huit, huit, huit . . .'

Down the centuries, nightingales have inspired so many poets and writers – and no wonder. Long-distance migrants, they spend summer in the most temperate parts of Britain, mainly southeast of a line from the Humber to the Severn, and winter somewhere between the Sahara and the rainforests of West Africa.[1] Today's technology makes it possible to monitor their migration patterns. One nightingale tagged by a satellite tracker in May 2010 flew past the Pyrenees in August and was in Senegambia and then Guinea by the year's end.[2]

Britain is a nation of bird-lovers, and every year an army of volunteers helps gather vital data about their welfare and migratory patterns by looping harmless rings around their legs. It's a well regulated process that requires several years of training under the watchful eye of an experienced coach, and a licence issued by the British Trust for Ornithology (BTO).

I used to spend many an early morning catching nightingales in harmless mistnets in the hope of learning more about their lives. I was lucky enough to live near one of the few remaining hotspots for the species, Botley Wood local nature reserve in Hampshire. As part of a nationally coordinated research programme organised by the BTO, each bird would be carefully fitted with a metal leg ring with a unique number so that it could be monitored after being released. We also put coloured rings in different combinations so as to keep tabs on them without having to catch them again. The flaw in this plan was that nightingales don't like to show themselves! But it seemed a good idea at the time. I'm still licensed by the BTO to ring birds, and do so from time to time, but haven't been involved in monitoring nightingales for a few years now. However, monitoring their numbers has never been more necessary. Britain is in danger of losing nightingales altogether as a breeding bird.[3]

Ten years ago, in common with industrial farms generally, Knepp had none. Now they have a growing number, but the national trend is dismal. The species has declined by 43 per cent in the last twenty years.[4] Ornithologists had hoped that nightingales might actually benefit from climate change, being lovers of warmer skies. Some predicted that rising temperatures might tempt them further north in Britain, perhaps as far as southern Scotland. Sadly, it hasn't happened. Instead, their range is shrinking, confined to southeast England, and numbers dwindling. Their plight is thought to be linked to loss of habitat, both in Britain, where they breed, and perhaps abroad, where they winter.[5]

In Britain, deer have been blamed for overbrowsing the dense scrub that nightingales prefer for making nests.[6] What struck me about Burrell's project, 'Knepp Wildland', is that he's actually encouraging the deer by deliberately reintroducing them as part of what he describes as a natural grazing system, yet nightingales, together with a host of other wildlife, have come back.

Burrell is glad and proud: 'In our last big survey, which was two years ago, we had two per cent of the UK population [of nightingales] on Knepp. We've got a good population of lesser spotted woodpeckers. We've got a growing number of Bechstein bats. We've got a good population of green woodpeckers. We've got ants, lots and lots of ants. And we've got an incredibly good population of cuckoos.'

Much of modern conservation entails preserving or creating habitats for given species or ecological communities. For example, reedbeds maintained for bitterns are prevented from silting up or taking their natural course and turning to woodland. Wet pastures can be prevented from drying out, so as to attract breeding wading birds. It's a way of protecting species by maintaining their individual habitats. There's nothing wrong with the approach, and over the years I've spent months of my life volunteering on projects like this. What I discovered at Knepp, however, was another way.

'We're not trying to produce the right habitat for plovers or for an insect or a plant,' Burrell told me. 'Our system is really just seeing what happens if you allow a process to run. Free-willed bit of land, sort of idea.'

Burrell's plan was to stop controlling the landscape and see what happened – what took off and, crucially, what came back. He wanted to introduce animals that would be as equivalent as he could get to the ancient species that shaped the European landscape centuries ago. So where once there were the aurochs, tarpan, bison and wild boar, he chose longhorn cattle, Exmoor pony, red and fallow deer, and Tamworth pigs – 'We put in Tamworth pigs. We've put in fallow deer, we've put in Exmoor ponies, roe deer and longhorn cattle, and just recently we introduced red deer. And those are all proxies of the wild versions.'

Once there was enough wild vegetation, Burrell was keen to get grazing animals into the system. Ten years on, a complex savannah of scrub, bushes, grasslands and coppices has replaced the monocultured fields.

'I go out to mates' farms and think, crikey, it's silent, there's nothing there,' he reflected. As we stood there surveying what he has created, we could hear nightingales, warblers and drumming woodpeckers. A cuckoo joined in too, just back from Africa.

Where there was once bare earth or a carpet of wheat, now dog roses thrive, and thickets of bramble and blackthorn. Hedges once clipped back to the quick are thick and unruly now, glorious homes for all sorts of little creatures. Sallows (a type of willow) have seeded well and are kept at browsing height by munching cattle and deer.

Given the chance, grazing animals interact naturally with vegetation. 'Look here at this patch of alder,' Burrell said, pointing at a row of trees. I could see that lower branches accessible to the animals had been browsed heavily to a consistent height. He pointed out that the back of the trees had escaped the attentions of the cattle and deer and were thus taller.

'Some manage to "get away" and grow taller, creating a more diverse habitat. Deer will naturally target flowering plants, but they'll survive around the edges of scrub where they are shielded by protective thorns,' he said. Butterflies and bees relish this scrubscape: they love the flowers protected by thorny neighbours. 'If you allow the shrubby plants to get to a stage where they've got good enough root systems, then allow the grazers back, you can get it to work, unlike the bare landscapes of the highlands of Scotland for example.'

In other words, you need to let the vegetation get a good foothold before letting the grazers loose. Burrell pointed out that in days gone by, populations of wild animals would periodically be decimated or wiped out of an area altogether as a result of diseases like winter pest or anthrax. It would give plants, trees and scrub a chance to grow back in a single wave, or 'pulse', before the animal population recovered.

'What you're seeing here is the creation of open-zone wood pasture that you would have seen over much of temperate Europe, Kenya and Tanzania,' he said. It's a system that's been lost from this landscape for several hundred years. He taught me about the inbuilt self-defence mechanisms used by certain plants and trees, and the way they can work together as a type of community, thereby ensuring the survival of the species. Leave them to it, and they can look after themselves. He singled out thorn bushes as an example:

'Hawthorn has a low tannin content. As soon as it's browsed it starts to warn other plants to produce tannins and their thorns start to thicken up.' Apparently browsed bushes release pheromones that warn other plants of impending danger. They then produce tannins that make the plants less palatable to the likes of cattle and deer.

As our safari went on, we saw fallow deer with spotted russet-brown backs, flicking their little white tails like morris dancers flicking hankies. We drove past a woodland glade looking for pigs, but disappointingly we only saw pig-rootled bluebells. There was the odd flicker of cornflower blue among the woody vegetation, but most of it had been gobbled up.

'Bluebells get completely hammered by pigs. This is why you don't get bluebell woods in Europe – because they have wild boar . . . These animals hunt out bluebells wherever they are,' Burrell explained.

On a more positive note, however, pigs have encouraged the return of the very rare butterfly the purple emperor, nowadays one of the scarcest and most magnificent of Britain's butterflies, so sought after by wildlife enthusiasts that in the few locations where sightings have been recorded, it is not unusual to find several butterfly watchers, cameras poised.[7]

It had long been assumed that they will only live in mature woodland, but Knepp has shown that they can adapt to other environments, especially if there are pigs around. Like wild boar, pigs break up the ground with their powerful snouts, and this can enhance their environment. At Knepp there were plenty of signs of their rooting behaviour. Sallows had taken advantage of the broken ground to lay down vast quantities of seeds, followed by a flush of seedlings. Purple emperors from miles around had smelt all of this attractive activity and moved in. Knepp now boasts the second biggest purple emperor site in the UK.

Other species too benefit from the broken ground created by pigs, among them certain types of solitary bee.

Although the pigs themselves remained elusive on the day of my visit, it was a thrill to see some of the other wildlife Knepp has to offer. Every now and then we came across some curious green corrugated metal sheets – there were hundreds across the estate.

'Come on,' Burrell said, stopping the car to lift one up. Underneath lay two small grass snakes, green and coiled. They woke up in a flash and vanished even faster, leaving two shiny grey slow worms. Knepp has lizards too.

'We never saw lizards here before. Now we see them regularly,' Burrell said.

We passed a large triangular nestbox nailed to a tree. It was for barn owls. In its days as an industrial farm, there would have been precious few, if any, barn owls on Knepp. They simply would have had nowhere to live and breed.

I asked Burrell how he feels about the whole project now.

'For someone like me who was always interested in nature to then be able to do it on a scale that allows all these processes to happen – it's just thrilling,' he enthused.

He acknowledged that it has not always been easy, saying that he'd come under attack from some in the farming community who are sceptical about what he's doing. In a world that struggles to feed itself, some see his rewilding scheme as an indulgence. Yet, as we have seen – and as Burrell himself pointed out – there's more than enough to go round. Production is not the issue. In any case, Knepp produces significant quantities of organic meat.

'To see life coming back . . . is very special,' he concluded.

He berated the double standards of the intensive-farming lobby for only talking about the 'need' for greater food production while in the next breath designating vast tracts of land to grow crops designed to fuel biodigestor systems. These purpose-grown crops are used for 'green' energy. He does not believe the two positions stack up. In his view, the debate is much less about food production and more about looking after our life-support systems.

'None of us are going to survive without a robust ecology,' he said.

I asked if he feels as if he is really farming, or running a nature reserve. 'I don't feel I'm running either,' he replied. 'To me, it's like a grand experiment, seeing what will happen . . . Already this extensive grazing system is throwing up lots of lovely results.'

The UK is one of the most heavily farmed nations in the world: farms cover more than 70 per cent of the country's land surface.[8] That might sound appealing – many people would prefer it to housing – but when farms are being run like factories, using machinery and chemicals to eliminate anything that does not support the main product, they're just another ugly industry. They bear no relation to the benign images of farms displayed in children's books. There is simply no room for nature in such places.

That is why I believe farms should be much more than food factories. After all, if we don't look after ecosystems and wildlife on farmland, where do they go?

Knepp shows that farms run in ways that embrace rather than pulverise nature are not just playthings for those who can afford to indulge Marie Antoinette-style dreams. They can be made to work as profitable businesses too. Knepp sells around 75 tonnes of live-weight meat, all free-range, pasture-fed and organic, and worth up to £120,000 a year.

Without the expensive machinery and chemicals from the estate's industrial era, this income goes a long way. When you add rental money from various buildings, together with safaris and camping, Knepp Estate is on course to pay for itself without needing public subsidy. That says a lot about the far-sightedness of what's happening here.

Burrell has created something truly beautiful. It's a model that could be replicated elsewhere. As a lifelong farmer and naturalist, he is letting the land do what it wants. It is a very different approach to the one his father and grandfather before him chose. He is both keeper and servant, owner and observer. His enthusiasm is infectious.

As I was leaving, I thought how the benefits of a living landscape like this really speak for themselves. And just then, I heard the distant sound of another rippling chorus: '*So, so, so . . . huit, huit, huit . . .*'

# Notes

PREFACE

1   Jan J. Boersema (translated by Diane Webb), *The Survival of Easter Island: Dwindling resources and cultural resilience.* Cambridge University Press, 2015, p. 98.

2   ibid., pp. 95–7; D. Attenborough, *The Lost Gods of Easter Island.* BBC Bristol, 2000. Available to view: http://www.dailymotion. com/video/xsynkz_lost-gods-of-easter-by-david-attenborough_ shortfilms

3   Jo Anne Van Tilburg, *Easter Island: Archaeology, ecology and culture,* London: British Museum Press, 1994, pp. 59–60; Attenborough, *Lost Gods.*

4   Attenborough, *Lost Gods.*

5   Boersema, *Survival of Easter Island,* pp. 77–8.

6   Attenborough, *Lost Gods.*

7   History (Phases of island culture). http://www.history.com/topics/ easter-island

8   History (AD 300–400). http://www.history.com/topics/easter-island; J. Diamond, *Collapse: How societies choose to fail or survive,* London: Penguin, 2011, p. 87; Charles River Editors, *Easter Island: History's Greatest Mysteries,* Amazon: Great Britain, 2013; Boersema, *Survival of Easter Island,* p. ix.

9   History (AD 300–400). http://www.history.com/topics/easter-island

10  Diamond, *Collapse,* p. 88.

11  Boersema, *Survival,* p. 179.

12  Attenborough, *Lost Gods*; Charles River Editors, *Easter Island.*

13    Diamond, *Collapse*.

14    R. McLellan, L. Lyengar, B. Jeffries & N. Oerlemans (eds), *Living
      Planet Report 2014: Species and Spaces, People and Places*, WWF,
      2014. http://www.worldwildlife.org/publications/living-planet-
      report-2014; S. Bringezu, H. Schütz, W. Pengue, M. O'Brien,
      F. Garcia, R. Sims, R. W., Howarth, L. Kauppi, M. Swilling &
      J. Herrick (leading authors), *Assessing Global Land Use: Balancing
      consumption with sustainable supply*, UNEP International Resource
      Panel, 2013. http://www.unep.org/resourcepanel/Portals/24102/
      PDFs/Summary-English.pdf; J. Owen, 'Farming Claims Almost
      Half Earth's Land, News Maps Show', *National Geographic
      News*, 9 Dec 2005. http://news.nationalgeographic.com/
      news/2005/12/1209_051209_crops_map.html

15    Secretariat of the Convention on Biological Diversity (2014),
      *Global Biodiversity Outlook 4*. Montréal, 155 pages, accessed at:
      https://www.cbd.int/gbo/gbo4/publication/gbo4-en.pdf

16    T. Searchinger et al., *The Great Balancing Act*. Working Paper,
      Installment 1 of Creating a Sustainable Food Future. Washington,
      DC: World Resources Institute, 2013. Available online at: http://
      www.worldresourcesreport.org

17    H. Steinfeld et al., *Livestock's Long Shadow*, Rome: Food and
      Agriculture Organization of the United Nations, 2006, p. 45.

18    D. Attenborough, *State of the Planet: The future of life*, BBC, 2000.
      Clip available at: http://www.bbc.co.uk/programmes/p004hsk7


ELEPHANT

1     S. Katsineris, 'Save the Leuser Rainforest Ecosystem',
      *Workers' Weekly Guardian* magazine (Australia), #1657, p. 6,
      24 Sep 2014. http://www.cpa.org.au/guardian-pdf/2014/
      Guardian1657_2014-09-24_screen.pdf

2     WWF website: Sumatran elephant. http://www.worldwildlife.org/
      species/sumatran-elephant

3     *Daily Telegraph*, Can elephant tourism be ethical?, 2nd February
      2016. http://www.telegraph.co.uk/travel/safaris-and-wildlife/Can-
      elephant-tourism-be-ethical/

4     Y. Robertson, *Briefing document on road network through the Leuser
      Ecosystem*, Cambridge University, Wildlife Research Group, 1 Dec
      2002. http://www-1.unipv.it/webbio/api/leuser.htm

5   B. A. Margono, P. Potapov, S. Turubanova, F. Stolle & M. Hansen, 'Primary forest cover loss in Indonesia over 2000-2012', *Nature Climate Change* 2014, Supporting Information (open access). http://dx.doi.org/10.1038/nclimate2277

6   Katsineris, *Save the Leuser Rainforest Ecosystem.*

7   A. Gopala, O. Hadian, Sunarto, A. Sitompul, A. Williams, P. Leimgruber, S. E. Chambliss & D. Gunaryadi, *Elephas maximus ssp. sumatranus,* IUCN Red List of Threatened Species, 2011. Version 2014.3. www.iucnredlist.org

8   IUCN red list of threatened species, *Elephas maximus ssp. Sumatranus. http://www.iucnredlist.org/details/199856/0*

9   FAOSTAT, http://faostat.fao.org/

10  G. Usher, Personal communication, Medan, Sumatra, 8 Sep 2015.

11  REDDdesk, REDD Indonesia, accessed May 2015. http://theredddesk.org/countries/indonesia

12  WWF (USA) website. http://www.worldwildlife.org/pages/which-everyday-products-contain-palm-oil

13  FAOSTAT, http://faostat.fao.org/; WWF Palm Oil Buyers Scorecard 2013, WWF (Global) website, http://wwf.panda.org/what_we_do/footprint/agriculture/palm_oil/solutions/responsible_purchasing/palm_oil_buyers_scorecard_2013/

14  N. Gilbert, 'Palm-oil boom raises conservation concerns: Industry urged towards sustainable farming practices as risking demand drives deforestation', *Nature*, vol. 487, issue 7405, pp. 14–15, 4 July 2012, http://www.nature.com/news/palm-oil-boom-raises-conservation-concerns-1.10936

15  A. R. Alimon & W. M. Wan Zahari, Recent advances in the utilization of oil palm by-products as animal feed (Malaysia), 2012. http://umkeprints.umk.edu.my/1148/1/Paper%203.pdf

16  FAOSTAT, http://faostat.fao.org/

17  Nuansa Kimia Sejati (Chemical Supplier, Indonesia), Palm Fatty Acid Distillate (PFAD). http://www.nuansakimia.com/en/palm-fatty-acid-distillate-pfad.html

18  Proforest, for Defra, *Mapping and understanding the UK palm oil supply chain*, Final report to the Department for Environment, Food and Rural Affairs (EV0459), 2011 http://www.proforest.net//proforest/en/files/mapping-palm-oil-supply-chains-report

19  ibid.

20    R. Howard (Wellington), 'Fight against palm snares
      unexpected users: New Zealand farmers', Reuters, 23 Dec
      2015. http://www.reuters.com/article/us-fonterra-dairy-
      idUSKBN0U705820151224

21    G. Hutching, 'Fonterra wants farmers to cut back on palm
      kernels', Stuff.co.nz / NZFarmer.co.nz, 21 Sep 2015. http://
      www.stuff.co.nz/business/farming/agribusiness/72272820/
      Fonterra-wants-farmers-to-cut-back-on-palm-kernels

22    H. Halim, 'Minister says sorry, nixes new rule for foreign media',
      *Jakarta Post*, 28 Aug 2015. http://www.thejakartapost.com/
      news/2015/08/28/minister-says-sorry-nixes-new-rule-foreign-media.
      html

23    United Nations Economic and Social Commission for Asia and
      the Pacific, *Economic and social survey of Asia and the Pacific
      2005: Dealing with shocks*, 2005, p. 172. http://www.unescap.org/
      publications/survey/surveys/survey2005.pdf

24    O. Balch, 'Sustainable palm oil: how successful is RSPO
      Certification?', *Guardian*, 4 July 2013. http://www.theguardian.
      com/sustainable-business/sustainable-palm-oil-successful-rspo-
      certification

25    Greenpeace UK, Palm oil, last edited 5 Nov 2013. http://www
      .greenpeace.org.uk/forests/palm-oil

26    FAOSTAT, http://faostat.fao.org/

27    Roundtable on Sustainable Palm Oil (RSPO), Principles and
      Criteria for the Production of Sustainable Palm Oil, April 2013,
      http://www.rspo.org/file/PnC_RSPO_Rev1.pdf

28    Greenpeace International, Certifying Destruction: Why
      consumer companies need to go beyond the RSPO to stop forest
      destruction, Sep 2013, http://www.greenpeace.org/international/
      en/publications/Campaign-reports/Forests-Reports/Certifying-
      Destruction/

BARN OWL

1    The Barn Owl Trust, State of the UK Barn Owl Population, 2013
     (updated Sep 2014). http://www.barnowltrust.org.uk/wp-content/
     uploads/State-of-the-UK-Barn-Owl-population---2013-updated-
     links.pdf

2 'Barn owl is Britain's favourite farmland bird', *Daily Telegraph*, 30 July 2007. http://www.telegraph.co.uk/news/earth/3301816/Barn-owl-is-Britains-favourite-farmland-bird.html

3 RSPB, 44 million birds lost since 1966, last modified 19 Nov 2012. http://www.rspb.org.uk/news/details.aspx?id=329911

4 G. Paton, 'Pupils to "dissect animal hearts" in new biology A-level', *Daily Telegraph*, 27 June 2014. http://www.telegraph.co.uk/education/educationnews/10931475/Pupils-to-dissect-animal-hearts-in-new-biology-A-level.html

5 D. Ramsden, 'Save our barn owls!', *Ecologist*, 6 Feb 2014. http://www.theecologist.org/campaigning/2268926/save_our_barn_owls.html

6 Donald MacPhail, 'Autumn sowing disaster for skylarks', *Farmers Weekly*, 19 Jan 2000. http://www.fwi.co.uk/news/autumn-sowing-disaster-for-skylarks.htm

7 R. A. Robinson, BirdFacts: profiles of birds occurring in Britain & Ireland, BTO Research Report 407, 2015. BTO, Thetford. http://www.bto.org/birdfacts, accessed 9 Dec 2015. http://blx1.bto.org/birdfacts/results/bob7350.htm#trends; M. Toms, *Owls*, London: Harper Collins, 2014.

8 European Bird Census Council, Trends of common birds in Europe, 2014 update, accessed Feb 2015, http://www.ebcc.info/index.php?ID=557

9 J. R. Sauer, J. E. Hines, J. E. Fallon, K. L. Pardieck, D. J. Ziolkowski, Jr. and W. A. Link, The North American Breeding Bird Survey, Results and Analysis 1966 – 2013. 2014. Version 01.30.2015 *USGS Patuxent Wildlife Research Center*, Laurel, MD, accessed Feb 2015, http://www.mbr-pwrc.usgs.gov/bbs/

10 BirdLife International, Europe-wide monitoring schemes highlight declines in widespread farmland birds, 2013. Presented as part of the BirdLife State of the world's birds website. Available from: http://www.birdlife.org/datazone/sowb/casestudy/62, checked: 23/02/2016. Accessed Feb 2015.

11 Michael T. Murphy, *Avian population trends within the evolving agricultural landscape of the eastern and central United States* (2003), Biology Faculty Publications and Presentations. Paper 70. http://pdxscholar.library.pdx.edu/bio_fac/70

12    M. Shrubb, *Birds, Scythes and Combines: A History of Birds and Agricultural Change,* Cambridge University Press, 2003.

13    S. R. Baillie, J. H. Marchant, D. I. Leech, A. R. Renwick, S. M. Eglington, A. C. Joys, D. G. Noble, C. Barimore, G.J. Conway, I. S. Downie, K. Risely & R. A. Robinson, *Bird Trends 2011,* BTO Research Report No. 609, 2012. BTO, Thetford. http://www.bto. org/birdtrends. Accessed Feb 2015. http://blx1.bto.org/birdtrends/ species.jsp?year=2011&s=goldf; BTO, *Garden Bird Feeding Survey results,* http://www.bto.org/volunteer-surveys/gbfs/results/results-species

14    Defra National Statistics Publication, *Wild Bird Populations in the UK, 1970 to 2014,* Annual Statistical release, 29 Oct 2015 https://www.gov.uk/government/uploads/system/uploads/ attachment_data/file/372755/UK_Wild_birds_1970-2013_ final_-_revision_2.pdf

BISON

1    Elahe Izadi, 'Say hello to our first national mammal', *Washington Post,* 29 April 2016. https://www.washingtonpost.com/news/ animalia/wp/2016/04/27/how-the-bison-once-nearing-extinction-lived-to-become-americas-national-mammal/

2    National Park Service, US Department of the Interior, Visitation Statistics. http://www.nps.gov/yell/planyourvisit/visitationstats.htm

3    P. Schullery, *The Greater Yellowstone Ecosystem,* Our Living Resources, US Department of the Interior National Biological Service, US Geological Survey. http://web.archive.org/ web/20060925064249/http://biology.usgs.gov/s+t/noframe/r114 .htm

4    City-Data.com West Yellowstone, Montana. http://www.city-data .com/city/West-Yellowstone-Montana.html

5    J. N. McDonald, 'Quaternary extinctions: A prehistoric revolution', in *The Reordered North American Selection Regime and Late Quaternary Megafaunal Extinctions,* University of Arizona Press, 1984, pp. 404–39.

6    National Geographic, American Bison. http://animals. nationalgeographic.com/animals/mammals/american-bison/

7    K. Zontek, *Buffalo Nation: American Indian Efforts to Restore the Bison,* Lincoln: University of Nebraska Press, 2007, pp. 16–17.

8   D. F. Lott, *American Bison: A Natural History,* Los Angeles: University of California Press, 2003. San Diego Zoo Global *American Bison – Bison, bison.* March 2009. http://library .sandiegozoo.org/factsheets/bison/bison.htm; B. Davis & K. Davis, *Marvels of creation: Magnificent mammals*, Master Books, 2006.

9   National Bison Association – A community bound by the heritage of the American Bison *Bison FAQs.* http://www.bisoncentral.com/ faqs#faq-nid-77; R. Rettner, 'The Weight of the World: Researchers Weigh Human Population', *Live Science,* 17 June 2012. http:// www.livescience.com/36470-human-population-weight.html; Wikipedia, Human body weight. https://en.wikipedia.org/wiki/ Human_body_weight

10  Zontek, *Buffalo Nation,* p. 25.

11  ibid.

12  ibid.

13  Lott, *American Bison.* Page 180.

14  History.com *Dust bowl.* http://www.history.com/topics/dust-bowl

15  WETA – Public Television and Classical Music for Greater Washington, Local Focus: Hugh Bennette and the Perfect Storm. http://www.weta.org/tv/program/dust-bowl/perfectstorm

16  Iowa Public Television, The Great Depression Hits Farms and Cities in the 1930s. http://www.iptv.org/iowapathways/mypath. cfm?ounid=ob_000064

17  K. Masterson, The Farm Bill: From Charitable Start to Prime Budget Target. The Salt – What's on your plate. 26 Sep 2011. http://www.npr.org/sections/thesalt/2011/09/26/140802243/the- farm-bill-from-charitable-start-to-prime-budget-target

18  G. Harvey, *The Carbon Fields: How our countryside can save Britain,* Somerset: Grass Roots, 2008. Page 50.

19  S. R. Allen, As the World Changes, So Must John Deere: Feeding Fueling and Housing a Growing World. Remarks given at Executives' Club of Chicago, John Deere & Co., May 2011. https://www.deere.com/en_US/corporate/our_company/news_ and_media/speeches/2011may10_allen.page

20  USDA, Economic Research Service, Farm Income and Wealth Statistics. http://www.ers.usda.gov/data-products/farm-income- and-wealth-statistics/annual-cash-receipts-by-commodity.aspx#P65 2a26c7d8b74b3d87dcb00f153b89b3_3_16iToR0x27

21    Statista, *Distribution of global corn production in 2014, by country.*
      http://www.statista.com/statistics/254294/distribution-of-global-
      corn-production-by-country-2012/
22    USDA, Economic Research Service, *Corn – Background.* http://
      www.ers.usda.gov/topics/crops/corn/background.aspx
23    ibid.
24    John Deere & Co., Our Company – About Us. https://www.deere
      .co.uk/en_GB/our_company/about_us/about_us.page
25    P. Lymbery & I. Oakeshott, *Farmageddon: The true cost of cheap
      meat*, London: Bloomsbury, 2014; Global Agriculture, Hunger in
      Times of Plenty. http://www.globalagriculture.org/report-topics/
      hunger-in-times-of-plenty.html
26    Tristram Stuart, Food Waste Facts. http://www.tristramstuart
      .co.uk/foodwastefacts/
27    Compassion in World Farming, Down to Earth – Charter
      for a Caring Food Policy. 2014. https://www.ciwf.org.uk/
      media/5954386/down-to-earth-charter-for-a-caring-food-policy.pdf
28    J. Lundqvist, C. de Fraiture & D. Molden, *Saving Water: From
      Field to Fork – Curbing Losses and Wastage in the Food Chain*,
      SIWI Policy Brief, SIWI, 2008. http://www.siwi.org/wp-content/
      uploads/2015/09/PB_From_Filed_to_fork_2008.pdf ; Nellemann,
      C., MacDevette, M., Manders, T., Eickhout, B., Svihus, B., Prins,
      A. G., Kaltenborn, B. P. (Eds). The environmental food crisis – The
      environment's role in averting future food crises. A UNEP rapid
      response assessment. United Nations Environment Programme.
      February 2009. www.unep.org/pdf/foodcrisis_lores.pdf
29    E. S. Cassidy, P. C. West, J. S. Gerber & J. A. Foley, 'Redefining
      Agricultural Yields: from tonnes to people nourished per hectare',
      University of Minnesota, *Environmental Research Letters* 8 (2013)
      034015. 2013. http://iopscience.iop.org/article/10.1088/1748-
      9326/8/3/034015/meta
30    FAO, World Livestock 2011 Livestock in Food Security http://
      www.fao.org/docrep/014/i2373e/i2373e.pdf
31    ibid.
32    ibid.
33    R. Bailey, A. Froggatt and L. Wellesley, *2014 Livestock – Climate
      Change's Forgotten Sector: Global Public Opinion on Meat and Dairy
      Consumption*. Chatham House.

34  Beef USA – National Cattlemen's Beef Association, Beef Industry
    Statistics. http://www.beefusa.org/beefindustrystatistics.aspx
35  USDA, *Farm Income and Wealth Statistics.*
36  National Bison Association, A community bound by the heritage
    of the American Bison, *Data and Statistics.* http://www.bisoncentral
    .com/about-bison/data-and-statistics
37  American Heart Association, Meat, Poultry and Fish. http://www.heart
    .org/HEARTORG/GettingHealthy/NutritionCenter/HealthyEating/
    Meat-Poultry-and-Fish_UCM_306002_Article.jsp#.VjNSp7fhAgs
38  National Bison Association, A community.
39  IUCN Red List of Threatened Species, *Bison bison.* http://www
    .iucnredlist.org/details/2815/0
40  A. Gunther, 'Putting Bison on Feedlots: Unnatural, Unnecessary,
    Unsafe', *Huffington Post – Healthy Living,* 9 April 2010. http://
    www.huffingtonpost.com/andrew-gunther/putting-bison-on-
    feedlots_b_665636.html
41  Ted's Montana Grill, Sustainability *Bison* https://www
    .tedsmontanagrill.com/about_sustainability_plate_bison.html
42  I. Zukerman, 'Yellowstone to Kill 900 Bison During Winter Cull',
    Reuters. 16 Sep 2014. Available from: http://www.huffingtonpost
    .com/2014/09/16/yellowstone-kill-bison_n_5833016.html
43  National Park Service, US Department of the Interior, Frequently
    Asked Questions: Bison Management. http://www.nps.gov/yell/
    learn/nature/bisonmgntfaq.htm

SHRIMP

1  NOLA.com / The Times – Picayune, 'Gulf champion Nancy
   Rabalais gets her due: An editorial', 19 Sep 2011. http://www
   .nola.com/opinions/index.ssf/2011/09/gulf_champion_nancy_
   rabalais_g.html
2  US Environmental Protection Agency (EPA), Mississippi River /
   Gulf of Mexico Hypoxia Task Force. http://water.epa.gov/type/
   watersheds/named/msbasin/zone.cfm
3  The Weather Channel – Environment, Dead Zone in Gulf of
   Mexico large enough to fit Connecticut, Rhode Island combined.
   5 Aug 2015. https://weather.com/science/environment/news/2015-
   dead-zone-gulf-of-mexico

4   R. Gillett, *Global study of shrimp fisheries – Part 1 Major issues in shrimp fisheries*, FAO Fisheries and Aquaculture Department – Technical Paper #475, pp. 89 ff. 2008. http://www.fao.org/docrep/011/i0300e/i0300e00.HTM

5   J. Rudloe, & A. Rudloe, 'Shrimp: The Endless Quest for Pink Gold', *FT Press Science*, Aug 2009, p. 198.

6   A. Chernoff, 'Gulf "dead zone" suffocating fish and livelihoods', CNN, 19 Aug 2008. http://edition.cnn.com/2008/TECH/science/08/18/dead.zone/

7   NOLA.com / The Times – Picayune, 'Louisiana shrimp season threatened by US ethanol policy: Larry McKinney', 16 June 2014. http://www.nola.com/opinions/index.ssf/2014/06/louisiana_shrimp_season_threat.html

8   National Oceanic and Atmospheric Administration (NOAA), US Department of Commerce, 2015 Gulf of Mexico dead zone 'above average', 4 Aug 2015. http://www.noaanews.noaa.gov/stories2015/080415-gulf-of-mexico-dead-zone-above-average.html

9   National Oceanic and Atmospheric Association (NOAA), *The Causes of Hypoxia in the Northern Gulf of Mexico*, http://service.ncddc.noaa.gov/rdn/www/media/documents/hypoxia/hypox_finalcauses.pdf

10  The National Centers for Coastal Ocean Science (NCCOS) – News and Features, 'NOAA, partners predict an average "dead zone" for Gulf of Mexico', 17 June 2015. http://coastalscience.noaa.gov/news/coastal-pollution/noaa-partners-predict-average-dead-zone-gulf-mexico/

11  ibid.

12  United Nations Environment Programme (UNEP) – Environment for Development, 'Further Rise In Number of Marine "Dead Zones"'. http://www.unep.org/Documents.Multilingual/Default.asp?DocumentID=486&ArticleID=5393&l=en

13  C. L. Dybas, 'Dead Zone Spreading in World Oceans', *Oxford Journals – Bio Science*, vol. 55, issue 7, 2005, pp. 552–7. http://bioscience.oxfordjournals.org/content/55/7/552.full

14  ibid.

15  ibid.

16  Sky News, 18 May 2010, 'BP Chief: Oil spill impact "very modest"'. http://news.sky.com/story/780332/bp-chief-oil-spill-impact-very-modest; YouTube; 'Gulf of Mexico oil spill: BP

insists oil spill impact "very modest" ', *Daily Telegraph*,
18 May 2010. http://www.telegraph.co.uk/finance/
newsbysector/energy/oilandgas/7737805/Gulf-of-Mexico-oil-
spill-BP-insists-oil-spill-impact-very-modest.html; BBC News,
20 June 2010, BP boss Tony Hayward's gaffes. http://www.bbc
.co.uk/news/10360084

17  YouTube, BP CEO Tony Hayward: 'I'd Like My Life Back', 31
May 2010. https://www.youtube.com/watch?v=MTdKa9eWNFw;
BBC News – US & Canada, BP boss Tony Hayward's gaffes, 20
June 2010. http://www.bbc.co.uk/news/10360084

18  S. Goldenberg, 'Tony Hayward's worst nightmare? Meet Wilma
Subra, activist grandmother', *Guardian*, 20 June 2010. http://www
.theguardian.com/environment/2010/jun/20/tony-hayward-bp-oil-
spill; Business and Human Rights Resource Centre, *US Deepwater
Horizon explosion and oil spill lawsuits – Health of cleanup workers*.
https://business-humanrights.org/en/us-deepwater-horizon-
explosion-oil-spill-lawsuits-health-of-cleanup-workers

19  BP Global, 'New report shows Gulf environment returning to pre-
spill conditions', 16 March 2015. http://www.bp.com/en/global/
corporate/press/press-releases/bp-releases-report-gulf-environment
.html

20  Virginia Institute of Marine Science (VIMS), Trends, Low-oxygen
'dead zones' are increasing around the world. http://www.vims
.edu/research/topics/dead_zones/trends/index.php

21  Virginia Institute of Marine Science (VIMS), Dead Zones, Lack of
oxygen a key stressor on marine ecosystems. http://www.vims.edu/
research/topics/dead_zones/index.php

22  Dybas, 'Dead Zone Spreading'.

RED JUNGLEFOWL

1  USDA, National Agricultural Statistics Survey, *Poultry –
Production and Value 2013 Summary*, April 2014.

2  Watt Poultry USA, March 2014. http://www.wattpoultryusa-
digital.com/201403#&pageSet=0&contentItem=0

3  J. Perdue, YouTube Video: *Jim Perdue, Chairman, Perdue Farms*.
https://www.youtube.com/watch?v=2a8x_8liZWA

4  HSUS, Settlement reached in lawsuit concerning Perdue chicken
labeling, 13th October 2014. http://www.humanesociety.org/

news/press_releases/2014/10/Perdue-settlement-101314
.html?referrer=https://www.google.co.uk/

5   Wildscreen Arkive, *Red Junglefowl (Gallus gallus)* http://www
    .arkive.org/red-junglefowl/gallus-gallus/video-12.html

6   J. Del Hoyo, A. Elliott & J. Sargatal (eds), *Handbook of the Birds
    of the World. Vol. 2. New World Vultures to Guineafowl*, Barcelona:
    Lynx Edicions, 1994.

7   J. Diamond, *Collapse: How societies choose to fail or survive*,
    London: Penguin, 2005, p. 91.

8   A. Spiegel, 'Chicken More Popular Than Beef in US for First
    Time in 100 Years', Huff Post – Food for Thought. 1 Feb
    2014. http://www.huffingtonpost.com/2014/01/02/chicken-vs-
    beef_n_4525366.html

9   K. Laughlin, *The Evolution of Genetics, Breeding and Production*,
    Temperton Fellowship, Report No. 15. 2007. http://en.aviagen
    .com/assets/Sustainability/LaughlinTemperton2007.pdf

10  I. De Jong, C. Berg, A. Butterworth & I. Estevez, *Scientific report
    updating the EFSA opinions on the welfare of broilers and broiler
    breeders*, Supporting Publications, 2012: EN-295. Report for the
    European Food Safety Authority (EFSA). 16 May 2012. Available
    online: www.efsa.europa.eu/publications

11  N. Kristof, 'Abusing Chickens We Eat', *New York Times*, 3 Dec
    2014. http://www.nytimes.com/2014/12/04/opinion/nicholas-
    kristof-abusing-chickens-we-eat.html?_r=0

12  Perdue, Perdue Farms at a Glance. http://www.perduefarms.com/
    uploadedFiles/Perdue%20At%20a%20Glance2013!.pdf

13  P. Valley, 'Hugh Fearnley-Whittingstall: Crying fowl', *Independent*,
    12 Jan 2008. http://www.independent.co.uk/news/people/profiles/
    hugh-fearnleywhittingstall-crying-fowl-769860.html

14  N. Kristof, 'Abusing chickens we eat', *New York Times*, 3 December
    2014. http://www.nytimes.com/2014/12/04/opinion/nicholas-
    kristof-abusing-chickens-we-eat.html?_r=1; CIWF USA, *Chicken
    factory farmer speaks out*. YouTube, 3 December 2014. https://
    www.youtube.com/watch?v=YE9l94b3x9U

15  S. Strom, 'Perdue sharply cuts antibiotic use in chickens and jabs
    at its rivals', *New York Times*, 31 July 2015. http://www.nytimes
    .com/2015/08/01/business/perdue-and-the-race-to-end-antibiotic-
    use-in-chickens.html?_r=0

16  Perdue Farms Inc., Press Release: *Perdue announces industry-first animal care commitments.* 27 June 2016. http://www
    .perduefarms.com/News_Room/Press_Releases/details.
    asp?id=1417&title=Perdue%20Announces%20Industry-First%20
    Animal%20Care%20Commitments

17  T. E. Whittle, *A Triumph of Science*, Poultry World Publications, 2000.

18  Compassion in World Farming and World Society for the
    Protection of Animals (now known as World Animal Protection),
    *Zoonotic diseases, human health and farm animal welfare*, May
    2013. https://www.ciwf.org.uk/media/3756123/Zoonotic-diseases-
    human-health-and-farm-animal-welfare-16-page-report.pdf

19  ibid.

20  Veterinary Medicines Directorate, 2013, UK Veterinary Antibiotic
    Resistance and Sales Surveillance. https://www.gov.uk/government/
    uploads/system/uploads/attachment_data/file/440744/VARSS.pdf

21  Unilever, Farm Animal Welfare – Sourcing of cage-free eggs. https://
    www.unilever.com/sustainable-living/what-matters-to-you/farm-
    animal-welfare.html; P. Lymbery, 'Unilever USA: Solution to killing
    of male chicks', Compassion in World Farming, Sep 2014. http://
    www.ciwf.org.uk/philip-lymbery/blog/2014/09/congratulations-
    unilever-usa-pledging-solution-to-killing-of-male-chicks

22  Christine J. Nicol, *The Behavioural Biology of Chickens*. CABI,
    2015.

23  ISA company website, Eggs Earth Earnings – information accessed
    Jan 2015. http://www.isapoultry.com/~/media/Files/ISA/isa_
    brochure.pdf (accessed 9 May 2016).

WHITE STORK

1  Campaign for Real Milk, Who and What we Are. http://www
   .campaignforrealmilk.co.uk/id1.html

2  European Commission, The common agricultural policy (CAP)
   and agriculture in Europe – Frequently asked questions – Farming
   in Europe – an overview, 26 June 2013. http://europa.eu/rapid/
   press-release_MEMO-13-631_en.htm

3  M. Semczuk, 'Agricultural Exploitation in the Rural Areas of
   the Polish Carpathians', Centre for Research on Settlements and
   Spatial Planning – Journal of Spatial Planning, 2012. http://

geografie.ubbcluj.ro/ccau/jssp/arhiva_si2_2013/03JSSPSI022013
.pdf

4   Babiógorski Park Narodowy, *Mammals.* http://www.bgpn.pl/
    nature/animated-nature/mammals

5   A. Kirby, 'Europe's farms push birds to brink', BBC News, 5 Jan
    2001. http://news.bbc.co.uk/1/hi/sci/tech/1100939.stm

6   J. D. Rose, *In Defence of Life: Essays on a radical reworking of green
    wisdom,* Winchester: Earth Books, 2013, pp. 47–8.

7   ibid., p. 67.

8   Eurostat – Statistics Explained, Agricultural census in Poland, Nov
    2012. http://ec.europa.eu/eurostat/statistics-explained/index.php/
    Agricultural_census_in_Poland

9   European Commission, Directorate-General for Agriculture and
    Rural Development, Rural development in the European Union:
    statistical and economic information, 2013 report http://ec.europa
    .eu/agriculture/statistics/rural-development/2013/full-text_en.pdf

10  FAOSTAT database: Inputs.

11  Metis/WIFO/aeidl for European Commission, 2014, Investment
    Support under Rural Development Policy, FINAL REPORT,
    12 Nov 2014, Section 5.2.5.2, http://ec.europa.eu/agriculture/
    evaluation/rural-development-reports/2014/investment-support-
    rdp/fulltext_en.pdf

12  The Common Agricultural Policy after 2013 – Environment, Food
    and Rural Affairs Committee – 2 Objectives of the Common
    Agricultural Policy. http://www.publications.parliament.uk/pa/
    cm201011/cmselect/cmenvfru/671/67105.htm

13  European Commission, Economics and Financial Affairs –
    Common Agricultural Policy. http://ec.europa.eu/economy_
    finance/structural_reforms/sectoral/agriculture/index_en.htm

14  USDA – Farm Service Program, ARC / PLC Program. http://
    www.fsa.usda.gov/programs-and-services/arcplc_program/index

15  European Commission, The common agricultural policy (CAP)
    and agriculture in Europe.

16  European Commission, Directorate-General for Agriculture and
    Rural Development, Rural development in the European Union:
    statistical and economic information, 2013 report. http://ec.europa
    .eu/agriculture/statistics/rural-development/2013/full-text_en.pdf

17  ibid.

18  L. Marino & C. M. Colvin, 'Thinking Pigs: A Comparative
    Review of Cognition, Emotion, and Personality in *Sus domesticus*',
    *International Journal of Comparative Psychology,* 2015. 28.
    uclapsych_ijcp_23859. Retrieved from: http://escholarship.org/uc/
    item/8sx4s79c

19  ECDC/EFSA/EMA first joint report on the integrated analysis
    of the consumption of antimicrobial agents and occurrence of
    antimicrobial resistance in bacteria from humans and food-
    producing animals, *EFSA Journal* 2015;13(1):4006. Jan 2015.
    Table 4. http://www.efsa.europa.eu/en/efsajournal/doc/4006.pdf

20  European Commission, *The EU Explained: Agriculture,*
    Luxembourg: Publications Office of the European Union, Nov
    2014. http://europa.eu/pol/pdf/flipbook/en/agriculture_en.pdf

21  Friends of the Earth Briefing, Feeding the beast – how public
    money is propping up factory farms, April 2009. http://www.foe
    .co.uk/sites/default/files/downloads/feeding_the_beast.pdf

22  G. Harvey, *The Carbon Fields: How our countryside can save Britain,*
    Somerset: Grass Roots, 2008.

23  P. Hogan, My Weekly Update, European Commission, 17 March
    2015. https://ec.europa.eu/commission/2014-2019/hogan/blog/
    my-weekly-update-13_en

24  A. Bergschmidt & L. Schrader, Application of an animal welfare
    assessment system for policy evaluation: Does the Farm Investment
    Scheme improve animal welfare in subsidised new stables?
    Landbauforschung – vTI Agriculture and Forestry Research 2
    2009 (59), 95–104.

25  ibid.

26  Metis/WIFO/aeidl for European Commission, 2014, Investment
    Support.

27  European Commission, *The EU Explained: Agriculture.*

28  Radio Poland, Polish stork population drops 20% in ten years,
    7 April 2015. http://www.thenews.pl/1/9/Artykul/202687,Polish-
    stork-population-drops-20-in-ten-years

29  PAP – Science and Scholarship in Poland – News of Polish Science.
    Stork numbers continue to drop – we know the initial results of a
    nationwide counting, 24 April 2015. http://scienceinpoland.pap
    .pl/en/news/news,404676,stork-numbers-continue-to-drop---we-
    know-the-initial-results-of-a-nationwide-counting.html

WATER VOLE

1    Wessex Chalk Stream & Rivers Trust, 'The Chalk Streams – South
     England's Rainforests', Presentation to the CPRE Hampshire
     AGM by Tom Davis. 17 May 2012.
2    S. Cooper, *Life of a Chalkstream*, London: William Collins, 2015.
     Page 3–4 & 6.
3    Game & Wildlife Conservation Trust, Water Vole. http://www
     .gwct.org.uk/wildlife/research/mammals/water-vole/
4    Derek Gow Consultancy Ltd, Conservation. http://watervoles.
     com/wv%20-%20conservation.htm; *Cambridge News*, 'Why Ratty
     is at serious risk', 30 Sep 2013. http://www.cambridge-news.co.uk/
     Ratty-risk/story-22752519-detail/story.html; O. Dijksterhuis,
     Ecologist, The Canal and River Trust *Water voles*, BBC Two
     Springwatch Guest Blog, 30 May 2013. http://www.bbc.co.uk/
     blogs/natureuk/entries/5262c709-19ba-39f6-910f-7a15a6e6d1a9
5    Graham Roberts, personal communication, 3 May 2016.
6    Game & Wildlife Conservation Trust, Mink in Britain. https://www
     .gwct.org.uk/wildlife/research/mammals/american-mink/mink-in-britain/
7    M. Townsend, 'Mink face cull to save Ratty from wipeout',
     *Observer*, 2 March 2003. http://www.theguardian.com/uk/2003/
     mar/02/politics.greenpolitics
8    Animal Aid, Under threat – UK mink population, 1 September
     2003. http://animalaid.org.uk/h/n/NEWS/news_wildlife/ALL/
     928//
9    Graham Roberts, as above.
10   R. Body, *Farming in the Clouds*, Hounslow: Maurice Temple
     Smith, 1984. See Preface.
11   BBC News, 'Jump in water vole numbers', 19 Nov 2003. http://
     news.bbc.co.uk/1/hi/england/southern_counties/3284093.stm
12   Environment Agency and English Nature, *The State of England's
     Chalk Rivers: A report by the UK Biodiversity Action Plan Steering
     Group for Chalk Rivers*, 2004.
13   ibid.
14   G. Farnworth & P. Melchett, 'Runaway Maize – Subsidised
     soil destruction', Soil Association, June 2015. https://www
     .soilassociation.org/media/4671/runaway-maize-june-2015.pdf
15   R. C. Palmer & R. P. Smith, 'Soil structural degradation in SW
     England and its impact on surface-water runoff generation', *Soil*

*Use and Management*, vol. 29, issue 4, Dec 2013, pp. 567–75, DOI: 10.1111/sum.12068; G. Monbiot, 'How we ended up paying farmers to flood our homes', *Guardian*, 18 Feb 2014. http://www.theguardian.com/commentisfree/2014/feb/17/farmers-uk-flood-maize-soil-protection

16   Palmer & Smith, 'Soil structural degradation'.

17   Birmingham & Black Country Wildlife Trust, 'Water Voles'. http://www.bbcwildlife.org.uk/water_voles

18   Derek Gow Consultancy Ltd, The future. http://watervoles.com/ wv%20-%20future.htm

19   A. Goudie, *Encyclopedia of Global Change: environmental change and human society*, Oxford University Press, 2001. https:// books.google.co.uk/books?id=5YrqQqW11aYC&pg=PA570& lpg=PA570&dq=chalk+aquifer+more+water+than+man-made +reservoir&source=bl&ots=6uegpaMXZ4&sig=3Sw4WARM 21fMg94iVKzXNTvGIhI&hl=en&sa=X&ved=0ahUKEwi12_ DV_u_LAhVFtxQKHRdLAwgQ6AEILDAE#v=onepage&q=c halk%20aquifer%20more%20water%20than%20man-made%20 reservoir&f=false

20   Environment Agency and English Nature, *The State of England's Chalk Rivers: A report by the UK Biodiversity Action Plan Steering Group for Chalk Rivers*, 2004.

21   R. O'Neill & K. Hughes, *The State of England's Chalk Streams*, WWF UK, 2014. http://assets.wwf.org.uk/downloads/wwf_ chalkstreamreport_final_lr.pdf

22   WWF UK, WWF Report Reveals the Shocking State of England's Chalk Streams, 24 Nov 2014. http://www.wwf.org.uk/about_wwf/ press_centre/?uNewsID=7378

23   ibid.; BBC News, 'Water voles "thriving"'.

PEREGRINE

1   A. Jobson, *The First English Revolution: Simon de Montfort, Henry III and the Barons' War*, London: Bloomsbury, 2012.

2   D. A. Carpenter, *The Reign of Henry III*, London: Hambledon Press, 1996, p. 255.

3   S. E. Carroll, Ancient & Medieval Falconry: Origins & Functions in Medieval England, Richard III Society American Branch website, http://www.r3.org/richard-iii/15th-century-life/

15th-century-life-articles/ancient-medieval-falconry-origins-functions-in-medieval-england/

4    A. F. Langham, *The Island of Lundy*, Stroud, Gloucestershire: The History Press, 1994 (2011 reprint).

5    Bulls Paradise, Lundy Island. Gatehouse Gazetteer website, http://www.gatehouse-gazetteer.info/English%20sites/871.html

6    Langham, *Island of Lundy*; M. S. Ternstrom, *Lords of Lundy*, Cheltenham: M. S. Ternstrom, 2010.

7    T. Davis & T. Jones, *The Birds of Lundy*, Devon: Harpers Mill Publishing, 2007, p. 86.

8    D. Cobham with B. Pearson, *A Sparrowhawk's Lament: How British Breeding Birds of Prey Are Faring*, Oxfordshire, England: Princeton University Press, 2014.

9    Davis & Jones, *Birds of Lundy*.

10   Cobham with Pearson, *Sparrowhawk's Lament*, p. 254.

11   Royal Pigeon Racing Association website, Pigeons in War. http://www.rpra.org/pigeon-history/pigeons-in-war/

12   D. M. Fry, 'Reproductive Effects in Birds Exposed to Pesticides and Industrial Chemicals', *Environmental Health Perspectives*, vol. 103, supplement 7, Oct 1995. http://www.ncbi.nlm.nih.gov/pmc/articles/PMC1518881/pdf/envhper00367-0160.pdf

13   Davis & Jones, *Birds of Lundy*, p. 87.

14   ibid., p. 246.

15   D. Gibbons, C. Morrissey, Dr P. Mineau, 'A review of the direct and indirect effects of neonicotinoids and fipronil on vertebrate wildlife', *Environ Sci Pollut Res* (Jan 2015), vol. 22, issue 1, pp. 103–18. http://www.tfsp.info/worldwide-integrated-assessment/

16   D. Goulson, 'An overview of the environmental risks posed by neonicotinoid insecticides', *Journal of Applied Ecology* (Aug 2013), vol. 50, issue 4, pp. 977–87. https://www.sussex.ac.uk/webteam/gateway/file.php?name=goulson-2013-jae.pdf&site=411 / http://www.sussex.ac.uk/lifesci/goulsonlab/publications

17   Dr P. Mineau & C. Palmer, *The Impact of the Nation's Most Widely Used Insecticides on Birds*, American Bird Conservancy, March 2013. http://abcbirds.org/wp-content/uploads/2015/05/Neonic_FINAL.pdf

18   Michael L. Avery, David L. Fischer & Thomas M. Primus, *Assessing the Hazard to Granivorous Birds Feeding on Chemically Treated Seeds*, USDA National Wildlife Research Center – Staff

Publications, Paper 615,1997. http://digitalcommons.unl.edu/ icwdm_usdanwrc/615

19    M. Chagnon, D. Kreutzweiser, E. A. Mitchell, C.A. Morrissey, D. A. Noome, J. P. Van Der Sluijs, 'Risks of large-scale use of systemic insecticides to ecosystem functioning and services', *Environ Sci Pollut Res Int* (Jan 2015), vol. 22, issue 1, pp 119–34.

20    Hinterland *Who's Who* (Canadian Wildlife Federation/ Environment Canada) website: http://www.hww.ca/en/issues-and-topics/pesticides-and-wild-birds.html

21    Dr P. Mineau & M. Whiteside (2013), Pesticide Acute Toxicity Is a Better Correlate of U.S. Grassland Bird Declines than Agricultural Intensification. PLoS ONE 8(2): e57457. doi:10.1371/journal .pone.0057457 (See Table 1). http://journals.plos.org/plosone/ article?id=10.1371/journal.pone.0057457

22    Hinterland *Who's Who* (Canadian Wildlife Federation/ Environment Canada) website.

23    M. B. van Lexmond, J.-M. Bonmatin, D. Goulson, D. A. Noome, 'Worldwide integrated assessment on systemic pesticides – Global collapse of the entomofauna: exploring the role of systemic insecticides', *Environ Sci Pollut Res* (2015), vol. 22, pp. 1–4.

24    Official Journal of the European Union, DIRECTIVE 2009/128/ EC OF THE EUROPEAN PARLIAMENT AND OF THE COUNCIL of 21 October 2009 establishing a framework for Community action to achieve the sustainable use of pesticides.

25    Caroline Cox, 'Pesticides and birds: from DDT to today's poisons', *Journal of Pesticide Reform*, vol. 11, no. 4, Winter 1991, pp. 2–6. http://eap.mcgill.ca/MagRack/JPR/JPR_14.htm

26    N. Simon-Delso, V. Amaral-Rogers, L. O. Belzunces, J.-M. Bonmatin, M. Chagnon, C. Dawns, L. Furlan, D. W. Gibbons, C. Giorio, V. Girolami, D. Goulson, D. P. Kreutzweiser, C. H. Krupke, M. Liess, E. Long, M. McField, P. Mineau, E. A. D. Mitchell, C. A. Morrissey, D. A. Noome, L. Pisa, J. Settele, J. D., Stark, A. Tapparo, H. Van Dyck, J. Van Praagh, J. P. Van der Sluijs, P. R. Whitehorn, M. Wiemers, 'Systemic insecticides (neonicotinoids and fipronil): trends, uses, mode of action and metabolites', *Environ Sci Pollut Res* (2015), vol. 22, pp. 5–34.

27    D. Goulson, 'An overview of the environmental risks posed by neonicotinoid insecticides', *Journal of Applied Ecology* (Aug 2013), vol. 50, issue 4, pp. 977–87. https://www.sussex.ac.uk/webteam/

gateway/file.php?name=goulson-2013-jae.pdf&site=411 / http://
www.sussex.ac.uk/lifesci/goulsonlab/publications
28   ibid.
29   Pesticides Action Network (PAN) UK, Pesticides on a Plate: a
     consumer guide to pesticide issues in the food chain, 2013, www
     .pan-uk.org/attachments/050_Pesticides_on_a_Plate.pdf
30   ibid.
31   Cox, 'Pesticides and birds'.

### BUMBLEBEE

1    D. Goulson, A Sting in the Tale, London: Vintage Books, 2013.
2    'Short-haired bumblebee numbers on the rise in UK',
     Guardian, 11 Aug 2015. http://www.theguardian.com/
     environment/2015/aug/11/short-haired-bumblebee-numbers-
     on-the-rise-in-the-uk
3    Goulson, Sting in the Tale.
4    W. Jordan, 'More people worried about bees than climate
     change'. YouGov. 26 June 2014. https://today.yougov.com/
     news/2014/06/26/more-worried-bees-than-climate-change/
5    BBC News, 'What is killing Britain's honey bees', 2 Aug 2013.
     http://www.bbc.co.uk/news/science-environment-23546889
6    D. Jones, 'Europe lacks bees to pollinate its crops', Farmers Weekly,
     9 Jan 2014. http://www.fwi.co.uk/arable/europe-lacks-bees-to-
     pollinate-its-crops.htm
7    International Union for Conservation of Nature (IUCN), Bad
     news for Europe's Bumblebees, 2 April 2014. http://www.iucn
     .org/?14612/Bad-news-for-Europes-bumblebees
8    IUCN, 'Systemic pesticides pose global threat to biodiversity
     and ecosystem services', 24 June 2014. http://www.iucn.org/
     ?uNewsID=16025
9    Taskforce on Systemic Pesticides, 2015, Worldwide Integrated
     Assessment of the Impacts of Systemic Pesticides on Biodiversity
     and Ecosystems. http://www.tfsp.info/assets/WIA_2015.pdf
10   P. Barkham, 'Returning rare bumblebee to Britain is a dauntingly
     complex mission', Guardian, 5 June 2013. http://www
     .theguardian.com/environment/2013/jun/05/returning-rare-
     bumblebee-britain-complex-task

SCAPEGOATS

1   T. Knoss, Concerns Remain About Yellowstone Wolf Population.
    Yellowstonepark.com website. http://www.yellowstonepark.com/
    concerns-about-yellowstone-wolf-population/
2   YouTube, How Wolves Change Rivers, 13 Feb 2014 https://www
    .youtube.com/watch?v=ysa5OBhXz-Q
3   Yellowstonepark.com website, Wolf Reintroduction Changes
    Ecosystem. http://www.yellowstonepark.com/wolf-reintroduction-
    changes-ecosystem/
4   H. Smith Thomas, 'Western Ranchers Fight the Curse of Introduced
    Wolves', *Beef* Magazine, 10 Sep 2010. http://beefmagazine.com/
    cowcalfweekly/0910-western-ranchers-fight-wolves
5   R. Landers, 'Montana, Idaho wolf kill below previous levels',
    *Spokesman-Review*, 3 March 2015. http://www.spokesman.com/
    blogs/outdoors/2015/mar/03/montana-idaho-wolf-kill-below-
    previous-levels/
6   J. Wickens, 'Shades of Gray: America's wolf dilemma', *Ecologist*,
    11 March 2013. http://www.theecologist.org/News/news_
    analysis/1844053/shades_of_gray_americas_wolf_dilemma.html
7   R. B. Wielgus & K. A. Peebles, Effects of Wolf Mortality on
    Livestock Depredations, 2014. PLoS ONE 9(12): e113505.
    doi:10.1371/journal.pone.0113505 http://journals.plos.org/
    plosone/article?id=10.1371/journal.pone.0113505
8   E. Sorensen, 'Research finds lethal wolf control backfires on
    livestock', WSU News. 3 Dec 2014. https://news.wsu.edu/
    2014/12/03/research-finds-lethal-wolf-control-backfires-on-
    livestock/#.VIZLS5PF_6h
9   Wickens, 'Shades of Gray'.
10  ibid.
11  O. Milman, 'Wolf population reaches new high at Yellowstone
    park', *Guardian*, 3 Dec 2015. http://www.theguardian.com/
    environment/2015/dec/03/wolf-population-yellowstone-national-park
12  'Getting Territorial Over Delisting – Controversy ignites over
    move to permanently remove wolf designation', *Salem Weekly*,
    Willamettelive.com. 21 Jan 2016. http://www.willamettelive
    .com/2016/news/getting-territorial-over-delisting-controversy-
    ignites-over-move-to-permanently-remove-wolf-designation/

13   M. Geissler, 'Wild bird "may be behind bird flu outbreak"', ITV
     News. 17 Nov 2014. http://www.itv.com/news/2014-11-17/wild-
     bird-may-be-behind-birdflu-outbreak/

14   European Centre for Disease Prevention and Control, Outbreak
     of highly pathogenic avian influenza A(H5N8) in Europe, 20
     Nov 2014. Stockholm: ECDC; 2014. http://ecdc.europa.eu/en/
     publications/Publications/H5N8-influenza-Europe-rapid-risk-
     assessment-20-November-2014.pdf

15   R. Mulholland, 'Bird flu strain which can be passed to
     humans detected in Holland', *Daily Telegraph* 16 Nov 2014.
     http://www.telegraph.co.uk/news/health/flu/11234213/
     Bird-flu-strain-which-can-be-passed-to-humans-detected-
     in-Holland.html; T. Escritt, 'Dutch authorities identify
     highly contagious bird flu strain', Reuters, 17 Nov 2014.
     http://www.reuters.com/article/us-netherlands-birdflu-
     idUSKCN0J00CE20141117

16   BBC News, 'Bird flu: New EU measures after Dutch and
     UK cases', 17 Nov 2014. http://www.bbc.co.uk/news/world-
     europe-30076909

17   'Avian influenza: Avian influenza outbreak in Yorkshire: strain
     identified as H5N8', *Veterinary Record*, vol. 175, issue 20, Nov
     2014, News and Reports. 175:20 495–496 doi:10.1136/vr.g6947

18   Department for Environment, Food and Rural Affairs (Defra),
     Summary of initial epidemiological and virological investigations
     to determine the source and means of introduction of highly
     pathogenic H5N1 avian influenza virus into a turkey finishing unit
     in Suffolk, as at 14 February 2007. Defra, Feb 2007.

19   Food Standards Agency / Health Protection Agency / Meat
     Hygiene Service / Defra, Possible transmission of H5N1 avian
     influenza virus from imported Hungarian meat to the UK. 15 Feb
     2007. http://tna.europarchive.org/20111116080332/http://www
     .food.gov.uk/multimedia/pdfs/birdfluinvest.pdf

20   ibid.

21   C. Lucas, 'Bird flu's link with the crazy trade in poultry', *Financial
     Times*, 25 Feb 2007. http://www.ft.com/cms/s/0/f23b5320-c4e4-
     11db-b110-000b5df10621.html#axzz44rIpI49U

22   J. P. Graham, J. H. Leibler, L. B. Price, J. M. Otte, D. U. Pfeiffer,
     T. Tiensin & E. K. Silbergeld, 'The animal-human interface and
     infectious disease in industrial food animal production: rethinking

biosecurity and biocontainment', Public Health Report, 2008
May–Jun; 123(3): 282–99.

23 UN Scientific Task Force on Avian Influenza and Wild Birds,
Statement on H5N8 Highly Pathogenic Avian Influenza (HPAI)
in Poultry and Wild Birds, 3 Dec 2014. http://www.wetlands
.org/Portals/0/Scientific%20Task%20Force%20on%20Avian%20
Influenza%20and%20Wild%20Birds%20H5N8%20HPAI%20
December%202014%20final.pdf

24 FAO Agriculture Department, Animal Production and Health
Division, Avian Influenza Q&A, 2007. (Last accessed January
2015) http://www.fao.org/avianflu/en/qanda.html#7

25 D. Cobham with B. Pearson, *A Sparrowhawk's Lament: How
British Breeding Birds of Prey Are Faring*, Woodstock, Oxfordshire:
Princeton University Press, 2014.

26 M. Toms, *Owls: A Natural History of British and Irish Species*,
London: William Collins, 2014, p. 240.

27 Cobham with Pearson, *Sparrowhawk's Lament*, p. 19.

28 C. Simm, 'Birds choose whether to feed in gardens or the wider
countryside', *BTO News*, issue 312, Nov–Dec 2014, p. 15.

29 R. Morelle, 'BTO survey suggests goldfinches visiting more
gardens, BBC News, 7 March 2012. http://www.bbc.co.uk/news/
science-environment-17269770

30 Cobham with Pearson, *Sparrowhawk's Lament*.

31 S. E. Newson, E. A. Rexstad, S. R. Baillie, S. T. Buckland &
N. J. Aebischer, 'Population change of avian predators and grey
squirrels in England: is there evidence for an impact on avian prey
populations?', *Journal of Applied Ecology*, vol. 47, issue 2, April
2010, pp. 244–52; M. Whittingham, 'Does predator control
alter bird populations?', *Journal of Applied Ecology*. http://www
.journalofappliedecology.org/view/0/predatorsprey.html

JAGUAR

1 http://www.birdlife.org/datazone/speciesfactsheet.php?id=1547

2 Convention on Biological Diversity, Brazil Overview. https://www
.cbd.int/countries/?country=br

3 USDA, Economic Research Service, Brazil, 30 May 2012. http://
www.ers.usda.gov/topics/international-markets-trade/countries-
regions/brazil/trade.aspx

4   C. Galvani, personal communication, 23 Feb 2016.

5   WWF Global, Jaguar South America's Big Cat. http://wwf.panda
.org/about_our_earth/teacher_resources/best_place_species/
current_top_10/jaguar.cfm

6   A. Caso, C. Lopez-Gonzalez, E. Payan, E. Eizirik, T. de Oliveira,
R. Leite-Pitman, M. Kelly & C. Valderrama, *Panthera onca,*.
IUCN Red List of Threatened Species 2008: e.T15953A5327466.
http://dx.doi.org/10.2305/IUCN.UK.2008.RLTS.
T15953A5327466.en

7   E. Dinerstein, *The Kingdom of Rarities*, Washington DC: Island
Press, 2013, p. 162.

8   Jaguar Conservation Fund website, homepage: http://www.jaguar
.org.br/en/index.html

9   WWF Global, Jaguar South America's Big Cat.

10  UNEP/WCMC, Cerrado Protected Areas: Chapada Dos Veadeiros
& Emas National Parks Goias, Brazil. October 1999, updated
11-2001, June 2009, May 2011. http://observatorio.wwf.org.br/
site_media/upload/gestao/documentos/Cerrado_Protected_Areas.pdf

11  Dinerstein, *Kingdom of Rarities*, p. 153.

12  WWF Global, Brazilian Forest Law – What is happening? http://
wwf.panda.org/wwf_news/brazil_forest_code_law.cfm

13  Woods Hole Research Center, 'Untangling Brazil's controversial
new forest code', *ScienceDaily*, 24 Apr 2014. https://www
.sciencedaily.com/releases/2014/04/140424143735.htm

14  UNESCO, Cerrado Protected Areas: Chapada Dos Veadeiros &
Emas National Parks. http://whc.unesco.org/en/list/1035

15  A. Rabinowitz, *An Indomitable Beast: The remarkable journey of the
jaguar*, Washington DC: Island Press, 2014, p. 14.

16  Beckhithe Farms website, 'About us': http://www.beckhithefarms
.co.uk/about-us.html

17  FAOSTAT, trade, soybeans and cake, soybean. http://faostat.fao.org

18  Instituto Mato-grossense de Economia Agropecuaria (IMEA) (Mato
Grosso Agriculture Economic Institute), Agronegócio em Mato
Grosso (Agribusiness in Mato Grosso), Aug 2012. http://imea.com
.br/upload/pdf/arquivos/2012_09_13_Apresentacao_MT.pdf

19  Instituto Mato Grossense de Economia Agropecuaira (IMEA),
Soja, boletim 26 February 2016 http://www.imea.com.br/upload/
publicacoes/arquivos/R404_392_BS_REV_AO.pdf

20  A. Stewart, Soy Frontier at Middle Age – 2, Hertz Farm Management, Inc., 18 May 2015. https://www.hertz.ag/ag-industry/current-headlines/0702bf5305182015112700/

21  E. Barona, N. Ramankutty, G. Hyman, & O. T. Coomes, 'The role of pasture and soybean in deforestation of the Brazilian Amazon', *Environmental Research Letters* 5 (2010) 024002. http://iopscience.iop.org/1748-9326/5/2/024002/media

22  ibid., citing D. Nepstad, C. M. Stickler & O. T. Almeida, 'Globalization of the Amazon soy and beef industries: opportunities for conservation', *Conserv. Biol.* 20 1595–1603, 2006. http://iopscience.iop.org/article/10.1088/1748-9326/5/2/024002?fromSearchPage=true

23  E. Y. Arima, P. Richards, R. Walker & M. M. Caldas, 'Statistical confirmation of indirect land use change in the Brazilian Amazon', *Environmental Research Letters* 6 (2011) 024010. http://iopscience.iop.org/article/10.1088/1748-9326/6/2/024010/meta

24  Dinerstein, *Kingdom of Rarities*, pp. 152–3.

25  Soyatech, Growing Opportunities, Soybeans and Oilseeds. http://www.soyatech.com/soy_oilseed_facts.htm

26  WWF Global, The Growth of Soy, Impacts and Solutions – The Market for Soy in Europe, 2014 http://wwf.panda.org/what_we_do/footprint/agriculture/soy/soyreport/the_continuing_rise_of_soy/the_market_for_soy_in_europe/

27  Encyclopædia Britannica. Encyclopædia Britannica Online. Xavante, 2016. http://www.britannica.com/topic/Xavante

28  Brasil De Fato, Dom Pedro Casaldáliga receives tribute for the defense of Xavante Indians, 4 Feb 2013. https://translate.google.co.uk/translate?hl=en&sl=pt&u=http://www.brasildefato.com.br/node/11835&prev=search

29  S. Branford, The 'Red Bishop' of the Amazon, Latin America Inside Out Blog. 8 Jan 2013. http://lab.org.uk/the-red-bishop-of-the-amazon

30  ibid.

31  Prof. W. Pignati, personal communication, 3 March 2016.

32  Globo News, Poison played in school can not be used in aircraft, says delegate, 5 April 2013, updated 4 May 2013. https://translate.google.co.uk/translate?hl=en&sl=pt&u=http://g1.globo.com/goias/noticia/2013/05/veneno-jogado-em-escola-nao-pode-ser-usado-em-avioes-diz-delegado.html&prev=search

33 H. M. M. de Paula & L. C. de Oliveira, Dialogue with community affected by the aerial spraying of pesticides, Cadernos de Agroecologia – ISSN 2236-7934-vol 8, no 2, Nov 2013. Resumos do VIII Congresso Brasileiro de Agroecologia – Porto Allegre/RS – 25 a 28/11/13. http://www.aba-agroecologia.org.br/revistas/index .php/cad/article/viewFile/14617/9077; H. A. Dos Santos, personal communication. 25 Feb 2016; Globo News, cited in n. 32.

34 L. Alves, 'Brazil Shown to Be Largest Global Consumer of Pesticides', Rio Times, 5 May 2015. http://riotimesonline.com/ brazil-news/rio-politics/brazil-is-largest-global-consumer-of- pesticides-shows-report/#

35 L. Rojas, International Pesticide Market and Regulatory Profile. Worldwide Crop Chemicals. http://wcropchemicals.com/ pesticide_regulatory_profile/#_ftn28

36 AgroNews, Brazil uses 22 agro chemicals banned in other countries, 11 Dec 2015. http://news.agropages.com/News/ NewsDetail---16577.htm

37 B. Van Perlo, A Field Guide to the Birds of Brazil, Oxford: Oxford University Press, 2009. http://www.lynxeds.com/product/field- guide-birds-brazil

38 Brazilian Beef Exporters Association, The beef sector – Brazilian livestock. http://www.brazilianbeef.org.br/texto.asp?id=18; USDA, Economic Research Service, Brazil, 30 May 2012. http://www.ers .usda.gov/topics/international-markets-trade/countries-regions/ brazil/trade.aspx

39 A. Caso, C. Lopez-Gonzalez, E. Payan, E. Eizirik, T. de Oliveira, R. Leite-Pitman,M. Kelly, M. & C. Valderrama, Panthera onca, IUCN Red List of Threatened Species 2008: e.T15953A5327466. http://dx.doi.org/10.2305/IUCN.UK.2008.RLTS. T15953A5327466.en

40 Brazilian Beef Exporters Association, The beef sector.

41 Caso et al., Panthera onca.

42 Instituto Mato-grossense de Economia Agropecuaria (IMEA) (Mato Grosso Agriculture Economic Institute), Agronegócio em Mato Grosso (Agribusiness in Mato Grosso), Aug 2012. http:// imea.com.br/upload/pdf/arquivos/2012_09_13_Apresentacao_ MT.pdf

43 Oncafari Jaguar Project. https://oncafarijaguarproject.wordpress.com/

PENGUIN

1  D. deNapoli, *The Great Penguin Rescue*, New York: Free Press, Simon & Schuster One, 2010.

2  BBC – On this Day 1950–2005, 2000: Record-breaking penguin rescue, 5 July 2000 http://news.bbc.co.uk/onthisday/hi/dates/stories/july/5/newsid_2494000/2494745.stm

3  deNapoli, *Great Penguin Rescue*, pp. 279–80.

4  IUCN Red List of Threatened Species, *Spheniscus demersus*. http://www.iucnredlist.org/details/22697810/0

5  South Africa – Inspiring new ways, Penguins in peril – Boulders Beach penguins. http://www.southafrica.net/za/en/articles/entry/article-southafrica.net-boulders-beach-penguins

6  Simonstown.com, The African Penguin – The Boulders Colony. http://www.simonstown.com/tourism/penguins/penguins.htm

7  IUCN Red List of Threatened Species, *Spheniscus demersus*.

8  A. Jan de Koning, 'Properties of South African fish meal: a review', *South African Journal of Science* 101, Research in Action, Jan/Feb 2005. http://reference.sabinet.co.za/webx/access/electronic_journals/sajsci/sajsci_v101_n1_a13.pdf; T. Hecht & C. L. W. Jones, *Use of wild fish and other aquatic organisms as feed in aquaculture – a review of practices and implications in Africa and the Near East*, FAO Fisheries and Aquaculture Technical Paper No. 518, pp. 129–57. 2009. http://www.fao.org/docrep/012/i1140e/i1140e03.pdf

9  deNapoli, *Great Penguin Rescue*.

10  ibid.

11  Seos Project, Ocean Currents – 4. The Benguela Current Large Marine Ecosystem (BCLME). http://www.seos-project.eu/modules/oceancurrents/oceancurrents-c04-p05.html

12  J. Smith, Seafood sustainability not a sustainable reality. The Conversation – Environment + Energy. 15 March 2013. http://theconversation.com/seafood-sustainability-not-a-sustainable-reality-12813

13  T. Hecht & C. L. W. Jones, *Use of wild fish and other aquatic organisms as feed in aquaculture – a review of practices and implications in Africa and the Near East*, FAO Fisheries and

Aquaculture Technical Paper No. 518, pp. 129–57, 2009. http://
www.fao.org/docrep/012/i1140e/i1140e03.pdf

14    ibid.

15    M. Memela, 'Penguins facing extinction', *Times Live*
(South Africa), 19 Feb 2013. http://www.timeslive.co.za/
thetimes/2013/02/19/penguins-facing-extinction

16    Birdlife South Africa, *African Penguin Conservation*, accessed
Aug 2014. http://www.birdlife.org.za/conservation/seabird-
conservation/african-penguin-conservation

17    M. Cherry, 'African penguins put researchers in a flap', *Nature*,
vol. 514, issue 7522, 15 Oct 2014, News, p. 283.

18    FAOSTAT Food Balance Sheet for South Africa 2011.

19    J. Hance, Penguins face a slippery future, Mongabay, 26 Sep
2012. http://news.mongabay.com/2012/0926-hance-interview-
borboroglu.html

20    IUCN Red List of Threatened Species, *Spheniscus humboldti* http://
www.iucnredlist.org/details/22697817/0

21    Hance, Penguins face a slippery future.

22    Seafish March 2012 Annual Review of the status of the feed
grade fish stocks used to produce fishmeal and fish oil for
the UK market, http://www.seafish.org/media/Publications/
SeafishAnnualReviewFeedFishStocks_201203.pdf

23    FAO GLOBEFISH, Small pelagics, June 2012 http://www
.globefish.org/small-pelagics-june-2013.html

24    V. Christensen, S. de la Puente, J. C. Sueiro, J. Steenbeek,
P. Majluf, 'Valuing seafood: The Peruvian fisheries sector'. Marine
Policy, 44 (2014) 302-311.

25    World fishing and aquaculture, 'Anchovy worth more as food
than feed', 14th Nov 2014. http://www.worldfishing.net/news101/
industry-news/anchovy-worth-more-as-food-than-feed

26    IUCN Red List of Threatened Species, *Spheniscus mendiculus*
http://www.iucnredlist.org/details/22697825/0

27    WWF, The Galapagos. http://www.worldwildlife.org/places/the-
galapagos

28    S. A. Earle, 'The world is blue: How our fate and the ocean's are
one', *National Geographic*, Washington DC, Oct 2010.

29    FAO Fisheries and Aquaculture Department statistical database:
sections Global capture production 1950–2012.

30   Quasar Expeditions, Farming in the Galapagos. http://www
     .galapagosexpeditions.com/blog/farming-in-the-galapagos-islands/
31   J. Koebler, Farming the Galapagos Islands is miserable,
     Motherboard, 25 Feb 2014. http://motherboard.vice.com/
     blog/farming-on-the-galapagos-islands-is-miserable?trk_
     source=recommended
32   N. L. Gottdenker, T. Walsh, H. Vargas, J. Merkel, G. U. Jimenez,
     R. E. Miller, M. Dailey & P. G. Parker, 'Assessing the risks of
     introduced chickens and their pathogens to native birds in the
     Galapagos Archipelago', *Biological Conservation* 126 (2005), May
     2004, pp. 429–39. http://www.umsl.edu/~parkerp/Pattypdfs/
     gottdenker%20et%20al.%20chickens%202005.pdf
33   ibid.
34   ibid.
35   ibid.
36   http://www.nhm.ac.uk/nature-online/species-of-the-day/
     collections/our-collections/pinguinus-impennis/index.html
37   E. Kolbert, *The Sixth Extinction: An Unnatural History*, London:
     Bloomsbury, 2014.
38   Scotland's National Nature Reserve, The Story of Hermaness
     National Nature Reserve. http://www.snh.org.uk/pdfs/
     publications/nnr/The_Story_of_Hermaness_National_
     Nature_Reserve.pdf; Shetland Hermaness Circular. http://
     www.walkshetland.com/hermaness-circular.php; A. Fraser,
     Wind Extremes. http://www.landforms.eu/shetland/wind%20
     extremes.htm; Gulberwick, About Gulberwick Weather. http://
     gulberwickweather.co.uk/page2.html
39   Joint Nature Conservation Committee (JNCC), Impacts of
     Fisheries (last updated 21/07/10). http://jncc.defra.gov.uk/page-
     5407
40   F. Urquhart, 'Sandeel Fishing Linked to Scottish Seabird
     Decline', *The Scotsman*, 1 Dec 2013. http://www.scotsman.com/
     news/environment/sandeel-fishing-linked-to-scottish-seabird-
     decline-1-3216052
41   Marine Conservation Society, Fishing Methods Information.
     http://www.mcsuk.org/downloads/fisheries/Fishing_Methods.pdf
42   R. Freethy, *Auks: An Ornithologist's Guide*, Poole, Dorset: Blandford
     Press, 1987.

43   J. Del Hoyo, A. Elliott & J. Sargatal, *Handbook of the Birds of the World*, vol. 3, *Hoatzin to Auks*, Barcelona: Lynx Edicions, 1996.

44   Sustainable Fisheries Partnership, *North Sea sandeel*. December 2015. https://www.sustainablefish.org/fisheries-improvement/small-pelagics/north-sea-sandeel; Blue Planet Society, *Where have all the sandeels gone?* 24th June 2009. http://blueplanetsociety. blogspot.co.uk/2009/06/where-have-all-sandeels-gone.html

45   IUCN Red List of Threatened Species, *Fratercula arctica* http://www.iucnredlist.org/details/22694927/1

46   deNapoli, *Great Penguin Rescue.*

47   P. N. Trathan et al., 2014, *Pollution, Habitat Loss, Fishing, and Climate Change as Critical Threats to Penguins*, Conservation Biology, 2015 Feb;29(1):31-41.

48   S. A. Earle, *The world is blue: How our fate and the ocean's are one.* Washington DC: National Geographic Society, 2009. Page 264.

49   B. Worm, et al (2006) Impacts of biodiversity loss on ocean ecosystem services. Science, 314: 787.

50   S. A. Earle, 'My wish: Protect our oceans', speech given at the February 2009 Technology, Entertainment and Design (TED) conference. https://www.ted.com/talks/sylvia_earle_s_ted_prize_wish_to_protect_our_oceans/transcript?language=en

MARINE IGUANA

1    I. Tree, *The Bird Man: The Extraordinary Story of John Gould*, 1991, London: Ebury Press, 1991 (2004 new edition), p. 67; AboutDarwin.com, HMS *Beagle* Voyage. http://www.aboutdarwin .com/voyage/voyage02.html

2    AboutDarwin.com, HMS *Beagle* Voyage.

3    Tree, *Bird Man*, pp. 67–8.

4    N. Barlow (ed.), *Charles Darwin and the Voyage of the Beagle*, London: Pilot Press, 1945.

5    P. D. Stewart, *Galapagos: The islands that changed the world*, London: Random House, 2006.

6    Stewart, *Galapagos*, pp. 63–4.

7    R. D. Keynes (ed.), *Charles Darwin's Beagle Diary*, Cambridge: Cambridge University Press, 1988, p. 292.

8    A. J. Tobin & J. Dusheck, *Asking about Life*, California: Brooks/ Cole, 3rd edition, 2005.

9   H. Nicholls, *The Galapagos: A Natural History*, London: Profile Books, 2014, p. 90.
10  *Galapagos with David Attenborough,* a Colossus Production for Sky 3D. 2013.
11  ibid.
12  C. Darwin, *Complete Works of Charles Darwin*, Hastings, East Sussex: Delphi Classics, 2015.
13  Nicholls, *Galapagos.*
14  K. Donohue (ed.), *Darwin's Finches: Readings in the evolution of a scientific paradigm,* Chicago: University of Chicago Press, 2011.
15  Stewart, *Galapagos.*
16  Tree, *Bird Man.*
17  ibid., p. 73.
18  Stewart, *Galapagos*, pp. 74–7.
19  C. Darwin, *On the Origin of Species,* London: Harper Collins, 2011; Tree, *Bird Man,* p. 67.
20  WWF Global, Galapagos tortoise: The gentle giant. http://wwf.panda.org/about_our_earth/teacher_resources/best_place_species/current_top_10/galapagos_tortoise.cfm
21  J. Tourtellot (National Geographic Fellow Emeritus), 'Galapagos Tourism Backfires', *National Geographic,* 5 Jan 2015. http://voices.nationalgeographic.com/2015/01/05/galapagos-tourism-backfires/
22  Galapagos Conservancy, Tourism and Population Growth. http://www.galapagos.org/conservation/conservation/conservationchallenges/tourism-growth/
23  Directorate of the Galapagos National Park, Tourism administration: Management programs – Control of tourism operations, page updated 29 June 2009. http://www.galapagospark.org/nophprg.php?page=programas_turismo_control
24  Nicholls, *Galapagos,* London: Profile Books, 2014, paperback edition (2015), Prologue.
25  GalapagosIslands.com, The Rock: Galapagos during World War II. http://www.galapagosislands.com/blog/galapagos-islands-during-second-world-war/
26  Nicholls, *Galapagos,* pp. x–xi.
27  GNPS, GCREG, CDF and GC. 2013. Galapagos Report 2011–2012. Puerto Ayora, Galapagos, Ecuador. http://www.galapagos.org/wp-content/uploads/2013/06/6.-HUMAN-SYS-pop-migration.leon-salazar.pdf

28   Galapagos Conservancy, Tourism and Population Growth.

29   R. Carroll, 'UN withdraws Galapagos from world danger list', *Guardian*, 29 July 2010. http://www.theguardian.com/world/2010/jul/29/galapagos-withdrawn-heritage-danger-list

30   Sea Shepherd Conservation Society, Galapagos: Facts About the Islands. http://www.seashepherd.org/galapagos/facts-about-the-islands.html

31   Charles Darwin Foundation, Invasive Plants. http://www.darwinfoundation.org/en/science-research/invasive-species/invasive-plants/

32   Stewart, *Galapagos*, p. 103.

33   Nicholls, *Galapagos*, p. 136.

34   BBC News, 'Galapagos Islands taken off UNESCO danger list', 29 July 2010. http://www.bbc.co.uk/news/world-latin-america-10808720

35   Stewart, *Galapagos*, p. 113.

36   Stewart, *Galapagos*, pp. 182–3; *Living on Earth* (PRI's Environmental News Magazine), 'Finches Change' (transcript of interview with Jonathan Weiner, author of *The Beak of the Finch*, New York, NY: Vintage Books, 1994), aired week of 22 July 1994. http://loe.org/shows/segments.html?programID=94-P13-00029&segmentID=2

37   C. Brooks, Consequences of increased global meat consumption on the global environment – trade in virtual water, energy & nutrients, Stanford Woods Institute for the Environment. https://woods.stanford.edu/environmental-venture-projects/consequences-increased-global-meat-consumption-global-environment

38   H. Steinfeld, P. Gerber, T. D. Wassenaar, V. Castel, M. Rosales & C. de Haan, *Livestock's Long Shadow: environmental issues and options*, Food & Agriculture Organisation of the United Nations (FAO), Rome, 2006. ftp://ftp.fao.org/docrep/fao/010/a0701e/a0701e.pdf

39   N. Alexandratos & J. Bruinsma (Global Perspective Studies Team, FAO Agricultural Development Economics Division), *World Agriculture towards 2030/2050: the 2012 revision*, ESA Working paper no. 12-03, FAO, Rome, June 2012. http://www.fao.org/fileadmin/templates/esa/Global_perspectives/world_ag_2030_50_2012_rev.pdf

40   P. J. Gerber, H. Steinfeld, B. Henderson, A. Mottet, C. Opio, J. Dijkman, A. Falcucci & G. Tempio, *Tackling Climate Change*

*through Livestock – A global assessment of emissions and mitigation opportunities,* Food and Agriculture Organisation of the United Nations (FAO), Rome, 2013.

41   R. Bailey, A. Froggatt & L. Wellesley, *Livestock – Climate Change's Forgotten Sector,* Chatham House, 2014.

42   F. Hedenus, S. Wirsenius & D. J. Johansson, 'The importance of reduced meat and dairy consumption for meeting stringent climate change targets', *Climatic Change,* 124(1–2), 79–91. 2014; B. Bajželj, K. S. Richards, J. M. Allwood, P. Smith, J. S. Dennis, E. Curmi & C. A. Gilligan, 'Importance of food-demand management for climate mitigation,' *Nature Climate Change,* 4(10), 2014, pp. 924–9. http://www.nature.com/doifinder/10.1038/nclimate2353 B. Bajželj, T. G. Benton, M. Clark, T. Garnett, T. M. Marteau, K. S. Richards & M.Vasiljevic, *Synergies between healthy and sustainable diets,* brief for GSDR. 2015. https://sustainabledevelopment.un.org/content/documents/635987-Bajzelj-Synergies%20between%20healthy%20and%20sustainable%20diets.pdf

43   *Climate Change 2014: Impacts, adaptation, and vulnerability,* Part A: Global and sectoral aspects. Contribution of IPCC working group II to the fifth assessment report of the intergovernmental panel on climate change.

44   ibid.; E. Galatas, Wildlife Biologist: Climate Change Threatens Mountain Goats, Public News Service, 1 April 2015. http://www.publicnewsservice.org/2015-04-01/endangered-species-and-wildlife/wildlife-biologist-climate-change-threatens-mountain-goats/a45442-1 P. A. Matson, T. Dietz, W. Abdalati, A. J. Busalacchi, K. Caldeira, R. W. Corell & M. C. Lemos, *Advancing the Science of Climate Change,* The National Academy of Sciences, 2010, ch. 9, 'Ecosystems, Ecosystem Services, and Biodiversity'. http://www.nap.edu/catalog.php?record_id=12782 T. V. Padma, 'Himalayan plants seek cooler climes', *Nature,* 512(7515), 2014, p. 359.

45   C. Cookson, 'Climate change strongly linked to UK flooding', *Financial Times,* 8 Jan 2016. http://www.ft.com/cms/s/0/831d04d4-b5ee-11e5-b147-e5e5bba42e51.html#axzz45L5IANMp; WWF Global, 'Climate change impacts: Floods and droughts'. http://wwf.panda.org/about_our_earth/aboutcc/problems/weather_chaos/floods_droughts/

46   P. Smith, M. Bustamante, H. Ahammad, H. Clark, H. Dong,
     E. A. Elsiddig, H. Haberl, R. Harper, J. House, M. Jafari, O.
     Masera, C. Mbow, N. H. Ravindranath, C. W. Rice, C. Robledo
     Abad, A. Romanovskaya, F. Sperling & F. Ture, 'Forestry and
     Other Land Use (AFOLU)', in: *Climate Change 2014: Mitigation
     of Climate Change*, contribution of Working Group III to the Fifth
     Assessment Report of the Intergovernmental Panel on Climate
     Change (O. R. Edenhofer, Y. Pichs-Madruga, E. Sokona,
     S. Farahani, K. Kadner, A. Seyboth, I. Adler, S. Baum, P. Brunner,
     B. Eickemeier, J. Kriemann, S. Savolainen, C. Schlömer, C. von
     Stechow, T. Zwickel & J. C. Minx [eds]), Cambridge and New
     York: Cambridge University Press.

47   Bailey, Froggatt & Wellesley, *Livestock*.

48   P. Scarborough, P. N. Appleby, A. Mizdrak, A. D. Briggs, R. C.
     Travis, K. E. Bradbury & T. J. Key, 'Dietary greenhouse gas
     emissions of meat-eaters, fish-eaters, vegetarians and vegans in the
     UK', *Climatic Change*, 125(2), 2014, pp. 179–92.

49   Gerber et al., *Tackling Climate Change through Livestock*.

50   CME Group, *Daily Livestock Report*, vol. 9, no. 243, 20 Dec 2011.
     http://www.dailylivestockreport.com/documents/dlr%2012-20-
     2011.pdf; D., Grandoni, 'Americans are eating less meat', *The
     Wire*, 11 Jan 2012. http://www.thewire.com/national/2012/01/
     americans-are-eating-less-meat/47295/

51   O. Milman and S. Leavenworth, 'China's plan to cut meat
     consumption by 50% cheered by climate campaigners', *Guardian*,
     20 June 2016. https://www.theguardian.com/world/2016/jun/20/
     chinas-meat-consumption-climate-change

52   H. Westhoek, J. P. Lesschen, T. Rood, S. Wagner, A. De Marco,
     D. Murphy-Bokern & O. Oenema, 'Food choices, health and
     environment: effects of cutting Europe's meat and dairy intake', *Global
     Environmental Change*, vol. 26, May 2014, pp. 196–205. http://www
     .sciencedirect.com/science/article/pii/S0959378014000338

53   National Park Service, Theodore Roosevelt and Conservation.
     http://www.nps.gov/thro/learn/historyculture/theodore-roosevelt-
     and-conservation.htm

*HOMO SAPIENS*

1    D. Johanson & M. A. Edey, *Lucy: The beginnings of humankind*,
     New York: Simon and Schuster Paperbacks, 1981.

2 BBC Home, Science & Nature: Prehistoric Life, 'Food for thought – 3 million years ago'. http://www.bbc.co.uk/sn/ prehistoric_life/human/human_evolution/food_for_thought1 .shtml

3 BBC Home, Science & Nature: Prehistoric Life, 'Leaving home – 2 million years ago'. http://www.bbc.co.uk/sn/prehistoric_life/ human/human_evolution/leaving_home1.shtml

4 Smithsonian Institution, Human Evolution Evidence, *Homo sapiens*. http://humanorigins.si.edu/evidence/human-fossils/ species/homo-sapiens

5 D. Phillips, 'Neanderthals Are Still Human!', Acts & Facts. 29 (5). http://www.icr.org/article/neanderthals-are-still-human/ K. Than, 'Neanderthal: 99.5 Percent Human', *Live Science*, 15 Nov 2006. http://www.livescience.com/1122-neanderthal-99-5- percent-human.html National Geographic – Genographic Project, Neanderthals. https://genographic.nationalgeographic.com/ neanderthals-article/

6 J. Diamond, *The Third Chimpanzee: The evolution and future of the human animal*, Harper Perennial, 1993.

7 J. Gibbons, 'Why Did Neanderthals Go Extinct?', *Smithsonian Insider*, 11 Aug 2015. http://smithsonianscience.si.edu/2015/08/ why-did-neanderthals-go-extinct/

8 New World Encyclopedia, History of Agriculture. http://www .newworldencyclopedia.org/entry/History_of_agriculture

9 R. L. Hooke, J. F. Martín-Duque & J. Pedraza, 'Land transformation by humans: a review', *GSA Today*, 22(12), 2012, pp. 4–10. http://www .geosociety.org/gsatoday/archive/22/12/article/i1052-5173-22-12-4.htm

10 E. C. Ellis & N. Ramankutty, 'Putting people in the map: anthropogenic biomes of the world', *Frontiers in Ecology and the Environment*, 6(8), 2008, pp. 439–47. http://ecotope.org/people/ ellis/papers/ellis_2008.pdf

11 Worldbiomes.com http://www.worldbiomes.com/

12 T. Searchinger et al., *The Great Balancing Act*, Working Paper, Installment 1 of Creating a Sustainable Food Future. Washington, DC: World Resources Institute, 2013. Available online at http:// www.worldresourcesreport.org.; J. Owen, 'Farming claims almost half Earth's land, new maps show', *National Geographic News*, 9 Dec 2005. http://news.nationalgeographic.com/ news/2005/12/1209_051209_crops_map.html

13    B. Gavrilles, 'Species going extinct 1,000 times faster than in pre-
      human times, study finds', *UGA Today*, 17 Sep 2014. http://news.
      uga.edu/releases/article/species-extinct-1000-times-faster-than-pre-
      human-times-0914/
14    University of Bristol, 'Recovering From A Mass Extinction',
      *ScienceDaily.* 20 Jan 2008. Retrieved from: http://www
      .sciencedaily.com/releases/2008/01/080118101922.htm
15    Searchinger, et al., *Great Balancing Act.*
16    K. W. Deininger & D. Byerlee, *Rising global interest in farmland:
      can it yield sustainable and equitable benefits?*, World Bank
      Publications. 2011. http://siteresources.worldbank.org/DEC/
      Resources/Rising-Global-Interest-in-Farmland.pdf
17    Searchinger et al., *Great Balancing Act.*
18    Food and Agriculture Organisation of the United Nations, Rome,
      *The State of the World's Land and Water Resources for Food and
      Agriculture (SOLAW) – Managing Systems at Risk*, 2011.
19    ibid.
20    For crop and animal production: FAOSTAT: Production database:
      production data for crops primary, crops processed, livestock
      primary. Production data from 2012–2014 period as available on
      database. For calorific values: FAOSTAT Food supply database:
      Food balance and food supply. People fed calculated as 2250 kcal
      per person per day for one year. http://faostat3.fao.org/home/E
21    Organisation for Economic Cooperation and Development
      (OECD), *Environmental Outlook to 2050: the consequences of
      inaction. Key findings on biodiversity*, Figure 2. 2012. http://www
      .oecd.org/env/indicators-modelling-outlooks/49897175.pdf;
      R. J. Keenan, G. A. Reams, F. Achard, J. V. de Freitas, A. Grainger
      & E. Lindquist, 'Dynamics of global forest area: results from the
      FAO global forest resources assessment 2015', *Forest Ecology and
      Management*, 352, 2015, pp. 9–20.
22    K. Langin, 'Big Cats at a Tipping Point in the Wild, Jouberts
      Warn', Cat Watch, *National Geographic*, 7 Aug 2014. http://voices.
      nationalgeographic.com/2014/08/07/big-cats-at-a-tipping-point-
      in-the-wild-jouberts-warn/
23    S. Goldenberg, 'The Central Valley is sinking: drought forces
      farmers to ponder the abyss', *Guardian*, 28 Nov 2015. http://www.
      theguardian.com/us-news/2015/nov/28/california-central-valley-
      sinking-farmers-deepwater-wells

24  ibid.

25  A. Holpuch, 'Drought-stricken California only has one year of water left, Nasa scientist warns', *Guardian*, 16 March 2015. http://www.theguardian.com/us-news/2015/mar/16/california-water-drought-nasa-warning

26  Z. Guzman, 'The California drought is even worse than you think', CNBC. 16 July 2015. http://www.cnbc.com/2015/07/16/the-california-drought-is-even-worse-than-you-think.html

27  A. Nagourney, 'California Imposes First Mandatory Water Restrictions to Deal with Drought', *New York Times*, 1 April 2015. http://www.nytimes.com/2015/04/02/us/california-imposes-first-ever-water-restrictions-to-deal-with-drought.html

28  S. Wells, 'Water Wars in California: Factory Farms Draining the State Dry', Huffpost Green. 4 Aug 2015. http://www.huffingtonpost.com/stephen-wells/water-wars-in-california-factory-farms-draining-the-state-dry_b_7021414.html

29  J. Fulton, H. Cooley & P. H. Gleick, 'California's Water Footprint', Pacific Institute, Dec 2012. http://pacinst.org/publication/assessment-of-californias-water-footprint/

30  Wells, 'Water Wars in California'.

31  B. Oskin, 'California's Worst Drought Ever Is 1st Taste of Future', *Live Science*, 5 Dec 2014. http://www.livescience.com/49029-california-drought-worst-ever.html

32  United Nations Department of Economic and Social Affairs (UNDESA), International Decade for Action 'WATER FOR LIFE' 2005–2015. http://www.un.org/waterforlifedecade/scarcity.shtml

33  B. Bates, Z. W. Kundzewicz, S. Wu & J. Palutikof, *Climate change and water: Technical paper vi*, Intergovernmental Panel on Climate Change (IPCC), 2008. http://ipcc.ch/pdf/technical-papers/climate-change-water-en.pdf

34  Organisation for Economic Cooperation and Development (OECD), *Water use in agriculture*. http://www.oecd.org/agriculture/wateruseinagriculture.htm; WWF Global, *Farming: Wasteful water use*. http://wwf.panda.org/what_we_do/footprint/agriculture/impacts/water_use/

35  B. Bajželj, K. S. Richards, J. M. Allwood, P. Smith, J. S. Dennis, E. Curmi, & C. A. Gilligan, 'Importance of food-demand management for climate mitigation', *Nature Climate Change*, 4(10), 2014, pp. 924–9.

36   Global Agriculture, *Agriculture at a Crossroads: Findings and recommendations for future farming – Water.* http://www .globalagriculture.org/report-topics/water.html

37   Science Learning Hub – The University of Waikato, Charles Darwin and earthworms. http://sciencelearn.org.nz/Science-Stories/Earthworms/Charles-Darwin-and-earthworms

38   C. Darwin, *The Formation of Vegetable Mould, Through the Action of Worms, with Observations on Their Habits,* London: John Murray, 1881 (Forgotten Books edition www.forgottenbooks.org), p.144.

39   ibid., p. 150.

40   ibid., pp. 157–8.

41   NFU online, Soil Framework Directive withdrawn. Last edited: 22 May 2014. http://www.nfuonline.com/archived-content/more-news/soil-framework-directive-withdrawn/ ; BBC Inside Out West, 'Darwin's earthworms', Feb 2009. http://www.bbc.co.uk/ insideout/content/articles/2009/02/20/west_earthworms_darwin_ s15_w7_video_feature.shtml

42   Encyclopaedia Britannica online, Soil Organism. http://www .britannica.com/science/soil-organism

43   Darwin, *Formation of Vegetable Mould.*

44   Great Fen Project website: *Frequently asked questions.* http://www .greatfen.org.uk/about/faqs; Discovering Britain, Viewpoint: The shrinking fens. https://www.discoveringbritain.org/content/ discoveringbritain/viewpoint%20pdfs/Holme%20Fen%20view-point.pdf; N. Higham, *BBC Springwatch: Wetland recovery.* BBC News, 23rd May 2007. http://news.bbc.co.uk/1/hi/sci/ tech/6685321.stm

45   Global Agriculture, 'Soil erosion a major threat to Britain's food supply, warns report', 8 July 2015. http://www.globalagriculture. org/whats-new/news/news/en/30894.html; T. Bawden, 'Soil erosion a major threat to Britain's food supply, says Government advisory group', *Independent,* 29 June 2015. http://www.independent.co.uk/ news/uk/home-news/soil-erosion-a-major-threat-to-britains-food-supply-says-government-advisory-group-10353870.html

46   ibid.

47   Committee on Climate Change June 2015, 'Progress in preparing for climate change 2015': Report to Parliament, https://www. theccc.org.uk/wp-content/uploads/2015/06/6.736_CCC_ASC_ Adaptation-Progress-Report_2015_FINAL_WEB_250615_RFS.pdf

48   Syngenta, Why is soil so important? https://www.syngenta.com/
     global/corporate/SiteCollectionImages/Content/news-center/
     full/2014/why-is-soil-so-important-syngenta-infographic.pdf
49   Committee on Climate Change June 2015, Progress.
50   G. Monbiot, 'We're treating soil like dirt. It's a fatal mistake, as our
     lives depend on it', *Guardian*, 25 March 2015. http://www
     .theguardian.com/commentisfree/2015/mar/25/treating-soil-like-
     dirt-fatal-mistake-human-life
51   *NFU News*, 'Withdrawal of Soil Framework Directive welcomed',
     22 May 2015. http://www.nfuonline.com/news/press-centre/
     withdrawal-of-soil-framework-directive-welcomed/
52   P. Case, 'Only 100 harvests left in UK farm soils, scientists warn',
     *Farmers Weekly*, 21 Oct 2014. http://www.fwi.co.uk/news/only-
     100-harvests-left-in-uk-farm-soils-scientists-warn.htm
53   C. Arsenault, 'Only 60 years of farming left if soil degradation
     continues', *Scientific American*, 5 Dec 2014. http://www
     .scientificamerican.com/article/only-60-years-of-farming-left-if-
     soil-degradation-continues/
54   United Nations Convention to Combat Desertification
     (UNCCD), *Proverbs on land and soil.* http://www.unccd.int/en/
     programmes/Event-and-campaigns/WDCD/Pages/Proverbs-on-
     land-and-soil-.aspx
55   S. Shankman, 'Meltdown: Terror at the top of the world',
     *InsideClimate News*, Nov 2014.
56   D. Leclère, P. Havlík, S. Fuss, E. Schmid, A. Mosnier, B. Walsh
     & M. Obersteiner, 'Climate change induced transformations of
     agricultural systems: insights from a global model', *Environmental
     Research Letters*, 9(12), 2014, 124018.
57   C. D. Thomas, A. Cameron, R. E. Green, M. Bakkenes, L. J.
     Beaumont, Y. C. Collingham, F. N. E. Barend, M., Ferreira
     de Siqueira, A. Grainger, L. Hannah, L. Hughes, B. Huntley,
     A. S. van Jaarsveld, G. F. Midgley, L. Miles, M. A. Ortega-
     Huerta, A. Townsend Peterson, O. L. Phillips & S. E. Williams,
     'Extinction risk from climate change', *Nature*, 427(6970), 2004,
     pp. 145–8.
58   IPCC Summary for policymakers, in: *Climate Change 2014:
     Impacts, Adaptation, and Vulnerability*, Part A: Global and
     Sectoral Aspects. Contribution of Working Group II to the
     Fifth Assessment Report of the Intergovernmental Panel on

Climate Change [C. B. Field, V. R. Barros, D. J. Dokken, K. J. Mach, M. D. Mastrandrea, T. E. Bilir, M. Chatterjee, K. L. Ebi, Y. O. Estrada, R. C. Genova, B. Girma, E. S. Kissel, A. N. Levy, S. MacCracken, P. R. Mastrandrea & L.L. White (eds)], Cambridge, United Kingdom and New York, NY, USA: Cambridge University Press, 2014, pp. 1–32. http://www.ipcc.ch/pdf/assessment-report/ar5/wg2/ar5_wgII_spm_en.pdf

59   M. Le Page, 'US cities to sink under rising seas', *New Scientist*, vol. 228, issue 3043, 17 Oct 2015, p. 8; M. Le Page, 'Even drastic emissions cuts can't save New Orleans and Miami'. *New Scientist*, 14 Oct 2015. https://www.newscientist.com/article/mg22830433-900-even-drastic-emissions-cuts-cant-save-new-orleans-and-miami/; B. H. Strauss, S. Kulp & A. Levermann, 'Carbon choices determine US cities committed to futures below sea level', *PNAS* early edition, vol. 112, no. 44, 2015. www.pnas.org/cgi/doi/10.1073/pnas.1511186112

LIVING LANDSCAPES

1    John Meadley, 'Is there such a thing as "better" when it comes to meat?', 2015. http://www.eating-better.org/blog/83/Is-there-such-a-thing-as-better-when-it-comes-to-meat.html

2    *Pasture for Life: It can be done*, Pasture-Fed Livestock Association booklet, Jan 2016. http://www.pastureforlife.org/media/2016/01/pfl-it-can-be-done-jan2016.pdf

3    ibid.

4    Around 930 million meat chickens (broilers) were reared in the UK in 2012. If kept free-range according to EU rules at 10,000 birds per hectare, they would need 93,000 hectares, which is 930 square kilometres. As broiler chickens are generally slaughtered at six weeks old, but free-range live a few days longer, for the total alive at any one time, divide by six: 155 million, needing if kept free-range, 155 square kilometres. The UK has 119,000 square kilometres of agricultural grassland. The amount of UK pasture that would be needed to rear all the nation's chickens free-range would be 0.13 per cent, or just over one hectare in a thousand.

5   World Food Programme, 'World must double food production by 2050: FAO Chief', 26 Jan 2009. https://www.wfp.org/content/world-must-double-food-production-2050-fao-chief

6   United Nations News Centre, 'World must sustainably produce 70 per cent more food by mid-century – UN report', 3 Dec 2013. http://www.un.org/apps/news/story.asp?NewsID=46647#.Vx9_slYrLX5

7   United Nations Environment Programme News Centre, New Report Offers Menu of Solutions to Close the Global Food Gap', 3 Dec 2013. http://www.unep.org/newscentre/Default.aspx?DocumentID=2756&ArticleID=9716&l=en

8   ibid.

9   For crop and animal production: FAOSTAT: Production database: production data for crops primary, crops processed, livestock primary. Production data from 2012–2014 period as available on database. For calorific values: FAOSTAT Food supply database: Food balance and food supply. People fed calculated as 2,250 kcal per person per day for one year. http://faostat3.fao.org/home/E

10  B. Bajželj, J. M. Allwood, P. Smith, J. S. Dennis, E. Curmi & C. A. Gilligan, 'Importance of food-demand management for climate mitigation', *Nature Climate Change*, 2014, 4:924–9. http://www.nature.com/nclimate/journal/v4/n10/full/nclimate2353.html

11  B. Lipinski, C. Hanson, J. Lomax, L. Kitinoja, R. Waite & T. Searchinger, *Reducing Food Loss and Waste*, Working Paper, Installment 2 of Creating a Sustainable Food Future, Washington, DC: World Resources Institute. June 2013. http://www.wri.org/sites/default/files/reducing_food_loss_and_waste.pdf

12  E. S. Cassidy, P. C. West, J. S. Gerber & J. A. Foley, 'Redefining Agricultural Yields: From Tonnes to People Nourished Per Hectare', *Environmental Research Letters*, vol. 8, issue 1, 1 Aug 2013.

13  J. Lundqvist, C. de Fraiture & D. Molden, *Saving Water: From Field to Fork – Curbing Losses and Wastage in the Food Chain*, SIWI Policy Brief, SIWI, Nov 2008. http://www.siwi.org/publications/saving-water-from-field-to-fork-curbing-losses-and-wastage-in-the-food-chain/ / www.siwi.org/documents/Resources/Policy_Briefs/PB_From_Field_to_Fork_2008.pdf; C. Nellemann, M. MacDevette,

T. Manders, B. Eickhout, B. Svihus, A. G. Prins & B. P. Kaltenborn, *The Environmental Food Crisis – The Environment's Role in Averting Future Food Crises*, A UNEP rapid response assessment, Feb 2009. United Nations Environment Programme, GRID-Arendal, www .unep.org/pdf/foodcrisis_lores.pdf; E. S. Cassidy, P. C. West, J. S. Gerber & J. A. Foley, 'Redefining Agricultural Yields: From Tonnes to People Nourished Per Hectare', *Environmental Research Letters*, vol. 8, issue 1, 1 Aug 2013.

14   Bajželj et al., 'Importance of food-demand management'.

15   A. Hough, 'Chicken owning fad lauded by Jamie Oliver "hurting birds"', *Daily Telegraph*, 19 Nov 2002. http://www.telegraph.co.uk/ foodanddrink/foodanddrinknews/9687529/Chicken-owning-fad- lauded-by-Jamie-Oliver-hurting-birds.html

16   The Pig Idea, The Solution. http://thepigidea.org/the-solution.html

17   Farm Animal Welfare Council, 2009, 'Five Freedoms'. http:// webarchive.nationalarchives.gov.uk/20121007104210/http:/www .fawc.org.uk/freedoms.htm

NIGHTINGALE

1   C. Wernham, *The Migration Atlas: Movements of the Birds of Britain and Ireland*, British Trust for Ornithology BTO), 2002; D. W. Snow & C.M. Perrins, *The Birds of the Western Palearctic*, Concise Edition, Oxford: Oxford University Press, 1998, pp. 1146–7.

2   BTO, Tracking Nightingales to Africa. http://www.bto.org/science/ migration/tracking-studies/nightingale-tracking

3   BTO, BTO Nightingale Survey 2012. http://www.bto.org/ volunteer-surveys/nightingale-survey

4   RSPB, The state of the UK's birds 2014. https://www.rspb.org.uk/ Images/state-of-the-uks-birds_tcm9-383971.pdf

5   BTO, Nightingale. http://www.bto.org/about-birds/bird-of- month/nightingale

6   BTO, BTO Nightingale Survey 2012; BTO, Deer are bad news for birds, Nov 2011. http://www.bto.org/news-events/press-releases/ deer-are-bad-news-birds

7   Steven Cheshire's British Butterflies, British Butterflies: Species: Species Account – the Purple Emperor. http://www.britishbutterflies. co.uk/species-info.asp?vernacular=Purple%20Emperor

8   The World Bank, Data, Agricultural land (% of land area) http:// data.worldbank.org/indicator/AG.LND.AGRI.ZS

# Index

# A Note on the Author

Philip Lymbery is chief executive of leading international farm animal welfare organisation, Compassion in World Farming (Compassion), and Visiting Professor at the University of Winchester.

His book, *Farmageddon: The True Cost of Cheap Meat*, was chosen as one of *The Times* Writers' Books of the Year in 2014, and was cited by the *Mail on Sunday* as a compelling 'game-changer'.

He played leading roles in many major animal welfare reforms, including Europe-wide bans on veal crates for calves and barren battery cages for laying hens.

Described as one of the food industry's most influential people, he has spearheaded Compassion's engagement work with over 700 food companies worldwide, leading to real improvements in the lives of over three quarters of a billion farm animals every year.